The Definitive Guide to db4o

Jim Paterson, Stefan Edlich,
Henrik Hörning, and Reidar Hörning

Apress®

The Definitive Guide to db4o

Copyright © 2006 by Jim Paterson, Stefan Edlich, Henrik Hörning, Reidar Hörning

ISBN-13: 978-1-59059-656-2

ISBN-10: 1-59059-656-0

Printed and bound in the United States of America 9 8 7 6 5 4 3 2 1

Lead Editor: Jason Gilmore
Technical Reviewer: Brian Breneman
Editorial Board: Steve Anglin, Ewan Buckingham, Gary Cornell, Jason Gilmore, Jonathan Gennick,
    Jonathan Hassell, James Huddleston, Chris Mills, Matthew Moodie, Dominic Shakeshaft, Jim Sumser,
    Keir Thomas, Matt Wade
Project Manager: Kylie Johnston
Copy Edit Manager: Nicole LeClerc
Copy Editor: Liz Welch
Assistant Production Director: Kari Brooks-Copony
Production Editor: Ellie Fountain
Compositor: Susan Glinert Stevens
Proofreader: Linda Seifert
Indexer: Valerie Perry
Artist: Kinetic Publishing Services, LLC
Cover Designer: Kurt Krames
Manufacturing Director: Tom Debolski

Distributed to the book trade worldwide by Springer-Verlag New York, Inc., 233 Spring Street, 6th Floor, New York, NY 10013. Phone 1-800-SPRINGER, fax 201-348-4505, e-mail orders-ny@springer-sbm.com, or visit http://www.springeronline.com.

For information on translations, please contact Apress directly at 2560 Ninth Street, Suite 219, Berkeley, CA 94710. Phone 510-549-5930, fax 510-549-5939, e-mail info@apress.com, or visit http://www.apress.com.

The source code for this book is available to readers at http://www.apress.com in the Source Code section.

Contents at a Glance

PART I ■■■ Introduction and Concepts

PART II ■■■ Working with db4o

PART III ▪▪▪ db4o in the Real World

Contents

PART I ▪▪▪ Introduction and Concepts

PART II ■■■ Working with db4o

PART III ■■■ db4o in the Real World

■CHAPTER 13 From RDBMS to OODBMS

About the Authors

 **DR. JIM PATERSON** is a lecturer in computing at Glasgow Caledonian University. He specializes in object-oriented software and web development, and has a particular interest in the use of new software tools, including db4o, in a teaching context. He received a doctorate in physics from Glasgow University in 1988, and has since worked as a software engineer and as an educator, in addition to holding research positions with IBM and the universities of Cambridge and Strathclyde.

 **PROF. DR. STEFAN EDLICH** works for TFH-Berlin. His research areas are software engineering, object databases, and frameworks. Formerly he worked for several OO companies and for BEA Systems as a trainer and consultant. He is the author of several books covering J2EE, open source technologies, and the Apache projects.

 **HENRIK HÖRNING** holds a diploma in computer science from the University of Applied Sciences Brandenburg. He was temporarily assigned as a lecturer in adult IT education, and later accepted a temporary part-time university teaching position. Since 2002 he has worked for one of the top ten German IT companies as an independent consultant. In 2004 he also joined forces with three other experts in the mobile business. As CTO of Biting Bit, he specializes in J2EE engineering and the development of mobile applications.

Besides the German book *Jakarta Commons*, he has published international papers on mobile technology.

 **REIDAR HÖRNING** is an experienced software engineer and coauthor of the German book *Jakarta Commons* as well as several international papers on mobile technology. After his military career in the Signal Corps, he launched his own company, which specializes in mobile application development. He also works as a J2EE architect and developer for German Pension Insurance.

Reidar lives in Berlin with his lovely wife and two children.

About the Technical Reviewer

BRIAN BRENEMAN is an independent software designer and developer who is recognized for his ability to deliver innovative applications and solve difficult problems. Brian specializes in data-driven applications and has developed and deployed solutions for state government agencies, Fortune 500 companies, and medium-sized businesses. In addition to custom software, Brian has worked on a number of vertical-market products and has domain expertise in a wide variety of industries.

Brian lives in Cincinnati, Ohio, with his wife Marianne and two exuberant Golden Retrievers. In his free time he manages Koka Coffehouse (his other business) and runs triathlon.

Acknowledgments

This book could not have been written without the support of professionals, friends, and the community. First of all we must thank the db4o developers who took an interest in this project and took the time to answer our questions: Carl Rosenberger, Patrick Römer, Eric Falsken, Larysa Visengeriyeva, Albert Kwan, and Rodrigo Barreto de Oliveira.

Then of course we would like to thank Brian Breneman and Jason Gilmore for their helpful and detailed review. Many thanks also to everyone at Apress who was involved in the production and marketing of this book and who helped keep the project on track, including Kylie Johnston, Julie Miller, Liz Welch, and Ellie Fountain. Further acknowledgments are due to Christof Wittig (db4objects, Inc.), Roberto Zicari (OODBMS.org), and finally Jörg Schlapinski and Simone Busoli for their contributions to Chapter 15 and Chapter 12, respectively.

Introduction

Sometimes we make things more difficult for ourselves than they really need to be. Programmers are no exception to this. For example, those of us of an object-oriented persuasion devote time and expertise to creating a model of a problem domain in terms of objects. We produce solutions that model real-world objects and that are highly extensible and reusable. And then we decide that we need those objects to stick around after the program stops, so we go ahead and create another, totally different model, just so that we can use a database. Our carefully designed objects are then chopped and squeezed to fit this new data model.

In fact, most developers would argue that object persistence is a fundamental problem that has yet to be adequately solved. While there are frameworks that hide some of the details of the mismatch between object and data models from the programmer, none of them convincingly make what should be a simple job really simple. We held the same opinion, until we found out about db4o. db4o—the database for objects—simply stores native objects. "Native" means that these are the objects that your C# or Java program creates, stored exactly as they are. There's no need to create a database schema, no need to map objects to tables, no need to do anything really, except store objects. Problem solved!

So, if it's that simple, why write a book about it? Well, db4o's simplicity is really more a case of avoiding unnecessary complication: as you explore it you'll find that it is actually a sophisticated, powerful tool. Features like Native Queries, which let you write database queries in the programming language itself, rather than an embedded "foreign" query language, are clever, useful, and truly innovative. One of the main reasons for writing this book was to provide a detailed guide to what db4o is capable of and how to go about using it.

The other reason is the need to put db4o into the correct perspective. For some situations and applications, db4o does indeed solve the persistence problem. For others, it is not the best choice. It's important to know which is which, and above all, to think about your choice. The more understanding you have of the data models, the more likely you are to make a choice that will gain you a competitive advantage. If you ask most developers what they think of when you mention persistence, the answer is usually "relational databases"; maybe MySQL or Oracle, or perhaps one of the lightweight SQL databases that are becoming popular for embedding into applications. Push the point a bit further, and you'll hear about object/relational mappers and container-managed persistence, but still with a relational database behind the scenes. This perception of databases is shared by developers in industry and students in universities—and those students take what they have learned out into the real world with them.

In our view, the single best argument for using a relational database is that you can build different applications on top of the same database. Moreover, all these different applications can use different object models or schemas. This is vital for databases that might, for example, need to be used for extensive data mining. In contrast, db4o allows the application and the database to have exactly the same model of the world. Other applications would have to know this specific object schema in order to make sense of the database. However, if the data belongs exclusively to an application, this is not a problem. Accordingly, db4o can dramatically reduce the overhead in development time and performance compared to a relational database.

Who This Book Is For

This book is mainly intended for C# and Java programmers who are writing applications that need to store and retrieve objects. It should be useful for programmers of all skill levels, as db4o is incredibly simple to begin using, but it also has sophisticated features and configurations that will appeal to the more experienced programmer. Further, equal time is devoted to each of these popular languages: it's not a C# book or a Java book. The vast majority of code examples are given in both languages, so the reader who has a preference for one over the other can easily find the relevant code. The reader who will benefit most from this book is one who knows how to program in his chosen environment, but needs to know enough about db4o to start to use it in that environment. The book doesn't try to teach C# or Java, or to go into detail about all the possible platforms that these languages and db4o support. It sticks to the main objective, which is to comprehensively describe and demonstrate the db4o API and how to make the most of it. For example, a db4o query returns a list of objects. You can do many things with that list: for example, you could simply print it out, or you could bind its contents to be displayed in one of the many different kinds of user interface controls that are available. The task of this book in this case is to show how to get the right list of objects from the database in the first place.

Of course, the majority of programmers who might be interested in db4o are probably already working with databases. They may not be specialized database administrators or developers, but they will in all likelihood have a working knowledge of SQL and be experienced working with it in their programs, and they will want to know how db4o compares with the usual databases from development, performance, technological, and business perspectives. The book addresses these issues in detail.

How This Book Is Structured

The book is structured in three distinct sections. The first part gives an overview of db4o and explains the concepts of object-oriented development and data models. Part II is "hands-on" and demonstrates the db4o's features and the techniques for using them. Finally, Part III looks at how db4o fits into the real world alongside SQL and relational databases. There are 15 chapters, and three appendixes.

Part I

Chapter 1 introduces db4o and some of the topics that are covered in more detail later on.

Chapter 2 provides an overview of the concepts of object-oriented systems.

Chapter 3 describes the evolution of data models from the 1960s to the present day, and compares the relational and object data models

Chapter 4 goes into more detail about the object data model, and how db4o implements it.

Part II

Chapter 5 gives a quick guide to getting started with installing and using db4o.

Chapter 6 introduces the simple and advanced query mechanisms that it supports, including the innovative Native Queries.

Chapter 7 describes how to work with complex structured objects using db4o.

Chapter 8 describes db4o's client/server operating modes.

Chapter 9 explains the way that db4o transactions work and how to deal with concurrent database clients.

Chapter 10 gives a comprehensive overview of db4o's configuration and tuning options.

Chapter 11 describes how data can be replicated between db4o databases, and also between db4o and relational databases.

Chapter 12 rounds off the hands-on section with a selection of advanced topics, including encryption and the use of db4o in web application environments.

Part III

Chapter 13 gives a side-by-side comparison of how to accomplish tasks with SQL and with db4o.

Chapter 14 compares the performance of db4o with that of other solutions, and describes the types of application that will gain benefits from using db4o.

Chapter 15 considers the business issues involved in selecting a db4o-based solution.

Appendix A offers a guide to db4o's graphical database browser, the ObjectManager.

Appendix B provides a quick reference guide to common db4o operations, split into separate sections for C# and Java programmers.

Appendix C provides some suggestions for further reading.

Downloading the Code

The full code for the examples found in Part II of the book is available for download from the book's page on the Apress website (www.apress.com). There are separate C# and Java code folders for each chapter.

Contacting the Authors

Jim Paterson can be contacted via www.paterson.co.uk. Stefan Edlich can be contacted via www.edlich.de, and Henrik Hörning and Reidar Hörning can be contacted via www.bitingbit.com.

PART I

■■■

Introduction and Concepts

Most people who write software for a living have at least some familiarity with databases. Many of them are also familiar with object-oriented programming, and have probably needed to use a database to provide persistence for software objects. db4o is an object database, which means that unlike the more common relational databases, it looks at data the same way that programs do. In Chapter 1 we provide a brief overview of db4o and the features that set it apart from other databases, while Chapter 2 gives an overview of the concepts of object orientation. In Chapter 3 we look at how databases have evolved, and compare the way relational databases model data to the way object databases do it. The last chapter of this opening part looks in detail at the object data model, and in particular at db4o's implementation of it.

CHAPTER 1

■■■

Introduction to db4o

Db4o has a simple job to do. It is a database that is specifically designed to provide *persistence* for object-oriented programs. Object persistence is the capability to save the objects in a system so that they exist even after the application that created them has stopped running. In today's computing environment, this is a pretty important feature. After all, if you are running a banking system, you don't want the objects that represent your customers' accounts to be transient— in other words, to only exist in the system's memory. If the power goes off, then you've got the problem of explaining to your customers that the system can't remember how much money they have.

There are various methodologies for making objects persistent by storing them permanently to a durable storage device. For example, *serialization* turns an object into a stream of data that can be written to and read back from a file. However, while serialization is easily implemented, it is pretty limited in the way you access the information you have stored. For instance, you can't search within the data you have stored—you need to retrieve all the information in the file at once. Serialization has some other limitations, too. It runs into problems when the class definitions change, so it does not work well with an evolving object model. Also, it does not easily support remote access to data over a network.

It is usually much better to use a database for persistence. Databases provide the ability to run queries to find specific data, and provide features like transactions and rollback for reliable persistence.

To most people, the term *database* generally refers to a relational database management system (RDBMS). Relational databases have been around since the 1970s, and are associated with big players in the software industry such as Oracle and IBM. However, object-oriented developers have become painfully familiar with the problem of persisting objects in relational databases, because object-oriented applications and relational databases use fundamentally different ways of modeling data. Object orientation models and encapsulates the entities in a domain and the relationships between them, while relational databases aim to make data independent of the applications that use them, thereby minimizing duplication of data and providing flexibility in accessing that data.

As a result, saving the state of a single object may involve splitting the values of its attributes between two or more relational tables. The difference between the object and relational views of data is often known as the *impedance mismatch*. It's a bit like taking a square peg, chopping it up, and fitting the little pieces into a bunch of round holes. Digital technology consultant Esther Dyson put it another way:

3

> *Using tables to store objects is like driving your car home and then disassembling it to put it in the garage. It can be assembled again in the morning, but one eventually asks whether this is the most efficient way to park a car.*

To use a relational database to store your objects, you need to create a database table with columns matching the fields of each class that you want to persist. Also, your application needs to talk a language that the database understands. For example, JDBC and ADO.NET both provide the capability to embed SQL statements in code and to execute them in the database. So, a customer object might consist of attributes representing a customer's first name, last name, and address. These details would be stored using a SQL INSERT statement in a record in the Customers table. To restore a specific customer object, you execute a SQL SELECT to retrieve the first name, last name, and address and thereby construct a new customer object with these attribute values.

Life is not always so simple, though. In even the simplest system, objects are often structured; that is, they contain references to other objects or collections of objects. Therefore, you need to design your database so that the structure of your objects is stored accurately, ultimately producing an object-relational mapping between the object model and the data model. The mapping needs to specify what attributes are stored where, and what relationships between the tables are required to allow the data to be retrieved so that the original objects can be reconstructed. Some common object relationships are not particularly simple to map to relational tables. Inheritance, for example, is not supported in the relational model. Sometimes, the need to be able to fit to a manageable object relational mapping can have an undesirable influence on the way in which a domain model is designed.

Some observers believe that the impedance mismatch is not just a technical issue. Agile Data Modeling guru Scott Ambler, for example, talks about the cultural impedance mismatch, the politics between the object community and the data community. Database developers often believe that application designers should build their object models to match the data models, for example. As in any form of politics, the standpoint that people take is often not based closely on facts. A good understanding of both object and data models is essential to making the right decisions.

Transparent Persistence

If you are using SQL explicitly in your code, for example through JDBC, you need to manage the persistence process pretty closely. If your system needs to store data, you must write SQL INSERT statements to do it, and you should make sure that the object attributes are added correctly to the string that contains the statement. If you want to get objects back from the database, you need to write a SQL INSERT statement to get the data, probably including joins to bring in data from more than one table, and you must write code to take the results and use them to reconstruct your objects. There are plenty of opportunities for errors here, and because the SQL statements are just strings as far as the compiler is concerned, you won't find most of the errors until runtime.

Transparent persistence seems a much more attractive approach. This is the ability to directly manipulate data stored in a database using an object programming language rather than using embedded SQL. It allows you to query for and work with objects directly, cutting out most of these problems at a stroke. To accomplish this, you can use an object-relational mapping layer with your database such as Hibernate, EJB Container-Managed Persistence, and various implementations of the Java Data Objects (JDO) specification.

This approach sounds plausible—you declare in your code that an object is to be persistent, and you can then use the object and update it without having to explicitly store it again. The mapper generates the SQL as required to communicate with the database, but the developer does not see this happen. The code becomes much simpler, more maintainable, and less prone to error.

However, transparent persistence isn't without its problems. First, using a mapper does not eliminate the need to specify your object relational mappings—these need to be specified somewhere, in an XML file or as annotations in the code. The impedance mismatch is still there; it is just hidden behind the mapping layer. Just because you are implementing the translation between objects and database tables in a different way, the nature of the translation doesn't become any simpler. Second, performance can be an issue, as the overhead of generating the required SQL behind the scenes can really slow matters down.

Object Databases

This book is about db4o (www.db4o.com). db4o is a database of an entirely different ilk from what you're probably accustomed to using, as it is a pure native object database. Object databases store objects directly without having to change their characteristics or chop them up to fit into tables in the relational data model. Figure 1-1 shows the difference.

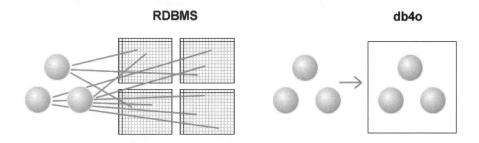

Figure 1-1. *db4o stores objects as objects, not in tables.*

With an object database, the database schema matches the domain model very closely. With a native object database the match is better than this—the database schema *is* the domain model: objects are stored exactly as they are created in the application. From the developer's point of view, storing objects in an object database is quite similar to storing them in a file using serialization. The difference is that the object database provides the database features that serialization does not offer.

Object databases are not new. Object database management systems (ODBMS) have been available commercially since the early 1990s, but have not had a great deal of impact outside niche markets. The data definition and query language standards for these systems, defined by the Object Data Management Group (ODMG), have never achieved the widespread acceptance that the relational database standards (well, sort-of standards) such as SQL have. Also, crucially, they were non-native—objects were stored as objects, but they weren't the same as the original objects. You still had to create a database schema and a binding to translate your applications objects into database objects.

So what makes db4o different? Its key features are performance, compactness, zero administration, simplicity, and the unique ability to store native Java or .NET objects, providing cross-platform portability. Objects are stored exactly as they are—there is no need for a data definition language. Zero administration is a rather atypical characteristic for most DBMSs. Typical database administration tasks like installing and configuring the database server software, creating and optimizing tables, and creating views and stored procedures are simply not necessary with db4o. Adding a single small archive file (JAR or DLL) to your classpath gives access to the db4o API, which has all the classes you need to store and retrieve objects. db4o is incredibly simple to use, and its small footprint means that it opens up the use of object databases to a whole range of embedded applications.

db4o Basics

Okay, so we said db4o is simple. So exactly how simple is it to store an object? Look at the C# and Java code fragments in Listing 1-1, which do the job of storing an object cust representing a customer. You just open a file (which will be created if it does not already exist) and instantiate an ObjectContainer—this is a db4o API class that encapsulates the database. To store an object, you call the Set method of the ObjectContainer, specifying the object you want to store. The two class definitions for this example are also listed (a Customer has an Address). Note that there is nothing special about these classes: db4o stores "plain" objects—ones that have no need to know about, or be altered to work with, persistence mechanisms. In Java these are often called Plain Old Java Objects (POJOs).

Listing 1-1. *Storing Using db4o*

```
// C#
Address addr = new Address("1 First Street", "San Jose");
Customer cust = new Customer("Michael",addr,"4089999999");
try{
    // open database file - database represented by ObjectContainer
    ObjectContainer db = Db4o.OpenFile("customers.yap");

    // store customer
    db.Set(cust);        //cust is an object of type Customer
}
finally{
    // close database
    db.Close();
}
```

```
// C# CLASS DEFINITIONS
class Customer{

    string _name;
    Address _address;
    string _phoneNumber;

    public Customer(string name, Address address, string phoneNumber)
    {
        _name = name;
        _address= address;
        _phoneNumber = phoneNumber;
    }

    public Address Address
    {
        get
        {
            return _address;
        }
    }
}

class Address{

    string _street;
    string _city;

    public Address(string street, string city)
    {
        _street = street;
        _city = city;
    }
}


// JAVA
Address addr = new Address("1 First Street", "San Jose");
Customer cust = new Customer("Michael",addr,"4089999999");
try{
    // open database file - database represented by ObjectContainer
    File file = new File("customers.yap");
    String fullPath = file.getAbsolutePath();
    ObjectContainer db = Db4o.openFile(fullPath);

    // store customer
    db.set(cust);          //cust is an object of type Customer
}
```

```
finally{
    // close database
    db.close();
}

// JAVA CLASS DEFINITIONS
class Customer{

    String _name;
    Address _address;
    String _phoneNumber;

    public Customer(String name, Address address, String phoneNumber)
    {
        _name = name;
        _address = address;
        _phoneNumber = phoneNumber;
    }

    public Address getAddress() {
        return _address;
    }
}

class Address{

    String _street;
    String _city;

    public Address(String street, String city)
    {
        _street = street;
        _city = city;
    }
}
```

That's all there is to it. There is no need to set up any database tables or define any mappings before running this code. db4o just takes objects and stores them. By the way, if the object you store is a structured object, the associated objects will also be stored, with no additional code. The Customer object has a reference to another object representing the address, and so this Address object will also be stored as an object in the database.

Restoring the object is just as simple. Listing 1-2 finds a specified Customer object in the database and retrieves it (with its Address object). The results are returned as an ObjectSet, which is another db4o API class.

Listing 1-2. *Retrieving Objects with db4o*

```csharp
// C#
try{
    Customer cust = null;
    // open the database
    ObjectContainer db = Db4o.OpenFile(fullPath);
    // query by example - create example team object
    Customer example = new Customer("Michael");

    // retrieve object(s) which match the example
    // should retrieve Customer and associated objects
    ObjectSet set = db.Get(example);
    cust = set.Next() as Customer;

    // do something with this Customer, e.g. get address
    Address address = cust.Address;
}
finally{
    db.Close();
}
```

```java
// JAVA
try{
    Customer cust = null;
    // open the database
    File file = new File("customers.yap");
    String fullPath = file.getAbsolutePath();
    ObjectContainer db = Db4o.openFile(fullPath);

    // query by example - create example team object
    Customer example = new Customer("Carl");

    // retrieve object(s) which match the example
    // should retrieve Customer and associated objects
    ObjectSet set = db.get(example);
    cust = (Customer)set.next();

    // do something with this Customer, e.g. get address
    Address address = cust.getAddress();
}
finally{
    db.close();
}
```

Queries in db4o

Querying is a key capability of any database. The example presented in Listing 1-2 demonstrated a particularly simple kind of query—it just retrieved an object with a specified value for one field. The method used is called query-by-example (QBE). This is the basic query mechanism offered by db4o. QBE is fine for retrieving objects with one or more specific attributes, but it doesn't help when you need to ask more complicated questions of your database, such as:

- Retrieving all the accounts with a balance greater than $1,000

- Retrieving all the transactions for a particular customer within the last month

Queries like these require a more flexible query mechanism. db4o supports two advanced query mechanisms.

Native Queries

From db4o version 5.0, *Native Queries* is the preferred query mechanism for complex queries. A native query is written entirely in the language of the application—for example, in a C# application, the query is expressed purely in C#.

Native queries have some important advantages over commonly used object query languages, such as JDOQL and Hibernate's HQL, and db4o's own earlier SODA query API, described in the next section. These are all to some extent string based: queries include strings that are passed to the persistence engine for interpretation. In the previous example, the name of the field that is to be constrained (`balance`) is defined in a string parameter. The compiler cannot check that this is a valid attribute of the `Account` class.

Listing 1-3 shows the code for a query that returns all the `Account` objects in a database with the `balance` attribute having a value greater than 1000. Native queries make use of delegates in .NET 2.0 and generics in Java 5.0, but earlier versions are also supported, as shown in the listing.

Listing 1-3. *A Native Query*

```
// C# .NET 2.0
IList <Account> accounts = database.query <Account>(
    delegate(Account account) {
    return account. Balance > 1000.0;
    }
});

// C# .NET 1.1
IList <Account> accounts = database.query(new BalanceQuery());
public class BalanceQuery : Predicate
{
    public boolean match(Account account) {
    return account. Balance > 1000.0;
    }
});
```

```csharp
// C# CLASS DEFINITION
class Account{

    double _balance;

    public double Balance
    {
        get
        {
            return _balance;
        }
    }
}
```

```java
// JAVA 5.0
List <Account> accounts = database.query <Account> (
    new Predicate <Account> () {
        public boolean match(Account account){
        return account.getBalance() > 1000.0;
    }
});
```

```java
// JAVA 1.2 — 1.4
List accounts = database.query (
    new Predicate () {
        public boolean match(Account account){
        return account.getBalance() > 1000.0;
    }
});
```

```java
// JAVA CLASS DEFINITION
class Account{

    double _balance;

    public double getBalance()
    {
        return _balance;
    }
}
```

Since the queries are expressed as native (C# or Java) method calls, the compiler will pick up any errors—if balance is not a valid attribute of Account, then the code will not compile. Native queries are considered to be type safe.

A further benefit of native queries is that since they are written entirely in the application's programming language, they can benefit from the tools provided by modern IDEs, including refactoring and code completions.

Simple Object Data Access (SODA)

The SODA API provides classes to perform complex queries on an object database, and has been supported by db4o for some time. SODA queries contain strings, and are therefore not type safe. The use of native queries is now recommended over SODA for most applications. Internally, db4o converts native queries to SODA for execution. The SODA API will continue to be supported by db4o.

An instance of the Query API class represents a node in a query criteria graph to which constraints can be applied. A node can represent a class, multiple classes, or a class attribute. Listing 1-4 shows the code for same query as Listing 1-3.

Listing 1-4. *A SODA Query*

```
// C#
Query q = db.Query();
q.Constrain(typeOf(Account));
q.Descend("_balance").Constrain(1000.0).Greater();
ObjectSet result = q.Execute();
```

```
// JAVA
Query q = db.query();
q.constrain(Account.class);
q.descend("balance").constrain(1000.0).greater();
ObjectSet result = q.execute();
```

You can find full details of how to use db4o queries in Chapters 6 and 7 of this book.

The ObjectManager

Although db4o is designed to be used within applications, via the API, it is often useful to be able to look inside a database file. You might want to check that your application is storing the correct data when you are developing, or you might want to take a look at the state of a running system.

The db4o ObjectManager (see Figure 1-2) provides a quick graphical way to get inside a database. You can explore a full list of the objects in the database and the relationships between them, or you can use the interface to build complex queries for specific objects. A full guide to using the ObjectManager is given in Appendix A.

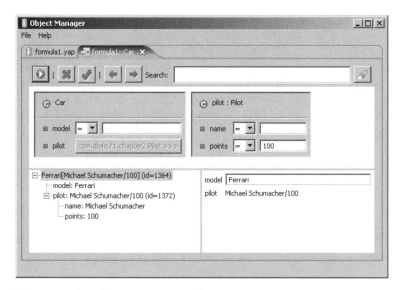

Figure 1-2. *The ObjectManager interface*

db4o Application Areas

db4o is being used by a rapidly expanding customer base in a wide range of applications. At the time of this writing, db4o has been downloaded more than 250,000 times. Users and customers of db4o currently come from almost 170 countries, ranging from multinationals like Boeing, Hertz, and Bosch to small, start-up companies (see the sidebar "db4o in Action").

db4o is most likely to be used in applications where there is no legacy data, which is to say no existing data architectures to integrate. This is primarily the case with applications that run on clients or on middleware. There are no technical reasons why it can't be used in the enterprise data center, but it is more difficult to introduce a new, agile solution into the world of legacy RDBMSs and DBAs who are highly trained in their use, and of course legacy data and multiple applications that need to access the same data are far more prevalent in enterprise systems.

While db4o can provide a persistence solution for any application developed using Java or .NET, there are particular areas where it is a good fit. These tend to have one or more of the following characteristics.

Complexity

An object database is particularly well suited to handling complex and evolving object structures, which can become a maintenance nightmare with a relational database. db4o is designed to handle schema evolution easily, and requires no database administration. It has been chosen for large-scale developments in biomedical industries, finance, transportation, and utilities.

Mobility

db4o is designed to be embedded in clients or other software components completely invisible to the end user. No installation is required—just the deployment of a single library file about 400KB in size. The database is part of the application, so if the application is running, the database is running.

The compactness and cross-platform capability make db4o well suited to applications in PDAs, smartphones, and so on. Compared to other embeddable SQL database engines like IBM's Cloudscape, db4o has the pure object database advantages of simplicity and maintainability.

Connectivity

db4o is ideal for use as an embedded standalone database in compact clients in devices like smartphones, but these days it is increasingly rare to have truly standalone clients. After all, the first C of the CDC configuration for J2ME stands for *Connected*. Mobile middleware, which connects enterprise mobile devices to the back-end applications running on corporate servers, is a major growth area.

db4o therefore not only provides an embedded mode, but also a client/server-mode ready to move into the enterprise or server-side software. In all cases, db4o is multithreaded.

db4o is not always the right solution. If you need to use data that is shared by several applications, then the data will be distinct from your application. A relational database is the obvious solution, since it allows data to be queried flexibly. If the data belongs to your application, then db4o may well make sense. It's really important when you're choosing a persistence solution that you understand the merits of the various options. We hope that by the time you've read this book that you'll know whether db4o is the right option for your application.

The Open Source Advantage

db4o is currently the only open source cross-platform object database. Like a number of other successful open source products, MySQL for example, it is offered by db4objects Inc. under two different kinds of license: the GNU General Public License (GPL) and a commercial license.

The GPL specifies that the software can be distributed to and modified by anyone, but that if a modified version is distributed, the source must be distributed too. The full source code for db4o is included when you download the product. The GPL license is ideal if you plan to use db4o in house or you plan to develop and distribute your own derivative work as free software under the GPL as well.

The advantages of GPL are obvious. It is widely recognized that open source code quality can match or exceed the quality of commercial applications. Open source applications allow anyone to look at the source code. Developers can read the source code to learn how it works, to make modifications, or to look for mistakes. These independent reviewers can report the defects they find and even suggest appropriate fixes. db4objects Inc. is building an active community of partners, customers, and academics who can contribute to the process.

One of the key restrictions of GPL software is that you need to distribute your derived applications under the GPL too. If you want to use db4o in a commercial, or non-GPL, application, or you want to get a higher level of technical support from the company, then you can get a commercial license. Contact db4objects Inc. to learn more.

The dual-licensing model allows db4o to closely meet the needs of a wide range of developers. All users, commercial or not, benefit from its wide adoption: better-tested software, as well as better suggestions (with users actually looking into the code). db4o has experienced phenomenal growth in popularity since it was released in this form in 2004.

Structure of This Book

There are three main parts to this book, which are intended for readers with a variety of levels of experience with object orientation and databases.

Part I will be useful to you if you are unfamiliar with object data models and the differences between them and the relational model. After an introduction to some basic concepts of object orientation, it goes on to describe the development of data models since the 1960s and how the object model used by db4o fits into this picture. The key differences between relational and object models are illustrated. This is followed by an introduction to some of the basic concepts of object databases.

Part II takes you through many examples of how to use db4o and takes advantage of its features, including:

- How to store objects

- How to query the database

- How to work with complex objects

- How to use db4o as a client/server database

- How to use transactions

- How to do configuration and replication

Part III is crucial if you are currently using relational databases and are considering switching to db4o. It deals with migration strategies, technical considerations, including performance and scalability, and the business case for db4o.

A guide to using the graphical ObjectManager is given in Appendix A, while Appendix B provides a "quick reference" guide.

Languages and Versions

db4o is a multiplatform solution: it supports .NET, including the Compact Framework, Java, and Mono. This means that it can be used with any language that can be compiled to .NET Common Language Runtime (CLR) as well as Java. The majority of code examples in this book, particularly in the "hands-on" chapters found in Part II, are provided in both C# and Java. The listings in the two languages are sometimes very similar. However, unless code is absolutely identical in both languages, separate listings are given. For other .NET languages, such as Visual Basic (VB.NET), the db4o API calls are identical to those listed for C#.

db4o also moves fast. Writing this book has been a case of aiming at a moving target. Some significant features, including Native Queries, were released while we were working on it. The code examples have been written to work with the most recent version of db4o available to us, version 5.2.

CHAPTER 2

■■■

Object-Oriented Concepts

Over the last ten years or so, the object-oriented development paradigm has gone mainstream. In fact, today's object-oriented programming languages have matured to the point where they represent the dominant programming paradigm in a wide range of application areas. Java has evolved from its early focus on web browser–based applets to the point where it is a highly scalable platform for systems from mobile devices to large enterprise applications. Microsoft has embraced the concept of a software platform supporting object-oriented applications with its .NET Framework and its associated languages, of which C# is arguably the most important.

There are good reasons for the growth of these languages. Object-oriented languages offer key benefits—code reuse, the ability to model real-world environments, and understandability. In this chapter we outline the basic concepts of the object-oriented paradigm and discuss how they are applied in a programming language. This is not, however, intended to be a complete tutorial on how to write programs in C# or Java (the two languages supported by db4o)—if you need that, we've recommended some useful titles at the end of the book.

Objects

The object-oriented paradigm changes the way developers represent entities in their applications. In a traditional procedural program, an entity is a piece of data to be processed. If there is an entity representing an employee, then you represent that employee as a data element. The program consists of separately defined procedures, which act on that data element. The design process for a traditional application involves logical data modeling, data flow models, and so on—it is very much focused on the data.

In an object-oriented program, an entity is represented as an object that represents the state of the employee in terms of properties. For example, some of these properties might include the employee's name, age, and current location. Additionally, this state might include means for representing the employee's behavior, determining all the things that an employee can do. This approach is focused on the responsibilities and interactions of the objects. In this sense, the entities in an object-oriented program behave more like the real-world counterparts than those in a procedural one.

Encapsulation and Information Hiding

The only way that another part of the program can interact with an employee object is to invoke some part of its behavior. For example, to make an employee change the "current location" property, you need to invoke a behavior called something like "move to a new location". You don't need to know how the object will actually perform that move; you just tell it where to go. Furthermore, you don't have direct access to the "current location" property. Packaging properties within the protection of behavior is called *encapsulation*.

An object has a public interface that other objects use to communicate with it. Because of encapsulation, the details of how state is stored or how behavior is implemented can be hidden from other objects. This means that the object's private details can be changed without affecting other objects that depend on it. Hiding design or implementation details from other objects is called *information hiding*.

Responsibilities and Collaboration

So why is this a good thing? Well, encapsulation allows objects to have *responsibilities*, which in turn allows objects to *collaborate* with each other. A single object is not particularly useful on its own. However, an object-oriented program typically consists of a number of software objects that can interact with each other, just as real-world objects can interact.

If you think about it, many real-world systems work like this. In a company, each employee has a job to do, which defines responsibilities, and people collaborate to achieve the company's aims. A manager can ask an assistant to send a fax, for example, and doesn't have to know how to use the fax machine. That task is part of the assistant's responsibilities, not the manager's (good thing, too, since fax machines are a bit too complicated for most managers).

Messages

Collaborating objects need to interact with each other. They do this by sending messages. For example, the manager uses a "send a fax" message to the assistant to invoke the appropriate behavior.

Sometimes the receiving object needs more information. The assistant will have to know who to send the fax to. This information is passed as a *parameter* of the message. In fact, a message consists of three parts:

- The object to which the message is being sent

- The name of the method to perform

- Any parameters needed by the method

Sometimes a message needs a reply. The manager may want to know whether or not the fax was sent successfully. Objects can respond to messages by providing a *return value*, which is itself an object that encapsulates the result.

Classes

An application may need to use many objects of the same kind that share common characteristics. A *class* is a template from which you create objects based on the blueprint it specifies. For instance, an Employee class is a blueprint from which many Employee objects are created. An Employee object represents an *instance* of the Employee class, and its state can be different from that of other Employees. One Employee might have the name Carl and live in Munich, while another might have the name Carlos and live in San Francisco. Therefore, the following is true:

- A *class* is a blueprint that defines the variables and methods common to all objects of that class.

- An *object* is a specific instance of a class.

  Until an instance of the class is created, no actual objects exist to be used within a program.

■Note In C# and Java, class names are usually capitalized, like `Employee` in the previous paragraph.

Class Diagrams

A class is often represented diagrammatically by a box split into separate sections that contain the class name, the properties, and the behavior, or *methods*, as shown in Figure 2-1. This notation is used in class diagrams, one of the diagram types of the Unified Modeling Language (UML) used to model and design object-oriented systems.

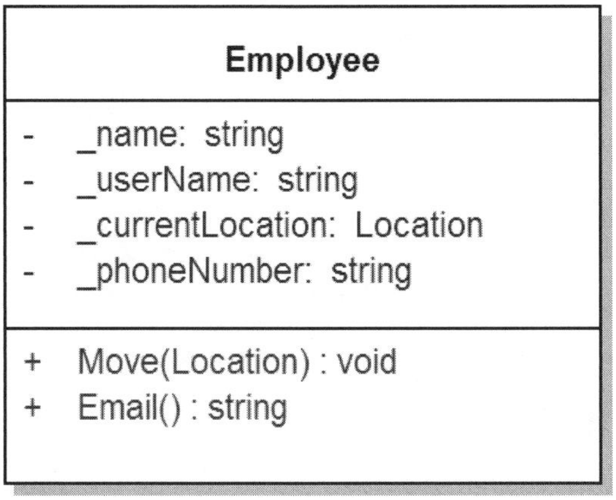

```
┌─────────────────────────────────────┐
│              Employee                │
├─────────────────────────────────────┤
│  -   _name:  string                  │
│  -   _userName:  string              │
│  -   _currentLocation:  Location     │
│  -   _phoneNumber:  string           │
├─────────────────────────────────────┤
│  +   Move(Location) : void           │
│  +   Email() : string                │
└─────────────────────────────────────┘
```

Figure 2-1. *A class represented in a class diagram*

There are a few items to note in Figure 2-1:

- The *qualifiers* (the – or + sign beside the name of each property or method) mean private (-) or public (+). In the figure, the properties are private and the methods are public. You will only be able to change the location of an `Employee` by invoking the `Move` method.

- Each property or method has a *reference type*. This is the type of information that is contained in a property, or the type of information returned by a method. The `Move` method in this figure has a return type `void`, which means it does not return any information. The `Age` method returns an integer value.

- Reference types can be other classes in the system. In the figure, the `_currentLocation` property is of type `Location`, which would be another class encapsulating all the details of a location.

Creating a Class

Classes are the building blocks of an object-oriented program. You create a program by writing the code to create classes in the language of your choice. While the details vary somewhat between C# and Java, the basic parts of the class are the same. The example in Listing 2-1 is written in C#.

Listing 2-1. *The Employee Class in C#*

```
public class Employee
{
    string _name;
    string _userName;
    Location _currentLocation;
    string _phoneNumber;

    public Employee(string name, string userName, Location location,
    string phoneNumber)
    {
        name = name;
        username = _username;
        currentLocation = location;
        phoneNumber = phoneNumber;
    }

    public void Move(Location newLocation)
    {
        currentLocation = newLocation;
    }

    public string Email()
    {
        return _username + "@db4objects.com";
    }
}
```

The equivalent code in Java is very similar.

Listing 2-1 shows some of the main features you will find in pretty much every class:

- **Instance variables**: These variables represent the properties of an object created using this class as a template (the convention used in this book is that instance variable names start with an underscore).

- **Constructor**: This is a special method with the same name as the class, which can be used to set the initial values for instance variables. Some classes have multiple constructors, allowing objects to be initialized in different ways.

- **Methods**: In Listing 2-1, the `Move` method simply changes the `_currentLocation` property to refer to another `Location` object, while the `Email` method returns the employee's email address by combining his username with the company domain name. The method name, the return type, and the list of parameters and their types are together known as the *signature* of the method.

Creating an Object

You create, or instantiate, a new object in C# or Java by using the `new` keyword. For example:

```
Employee p = new Employee("Michael", "michael", loc, "1234");
```

Note that the values in parentheses are the initial values to be assigned to the object properties. The list of values must match the list of parameters in a constructor.

You now have an *object reference*, p, which points to an `Employee` object. The *reference type* of p is `Employee`.

■**Note** The creation of other objects can be one of the responsibilities of a class. The previous line of code would be found in a class whose responsibilities include creating `Employee` objects.

`loc` is a reference to a `Location` object, which has already been created; for example:

```
Location loc = new Location("San Jose");
```

Sending Messages to Objects

You send a message to an object by invoking, or calling, one of its methods. Messages are sent from one object to another.

For example, an employee works overtime one weekend and there is a need to record the hours worked in the company's time sheet. There is no need for the `Employee` object to know how the information is recorded: that is the responsibility of another object—an instance of a class called `TimeSheet`. The `Employee` object simply sends a message to the `TimeSheet` object to ask it to record that that employee worked a certain number of hours.

The `TimeSheet` class's behavior for recording hours worked might be implemented in a method with the following signature:

```
public void AddEntry(string name, int hours)
{
    // do something
}
```

The Employee class could then have a method like this, which sends an "add entry" message to the TimeSheet:

```
public void RecordOvertime(TimeSheet theTimeSheet, int hours)
{
    theTimeSheet.AddEntry(_name, hours);
}
```

Of course, another object would have to send a message to the Employee object to make this happen! The object that does so might be a control object, as described in the next section.

Class Types

An object-oriented system is constructed from classes that have responsibilities and that collaborate with each other. Some classes model entities in the system, which may be abstractions of real-world entities. Other classes play different roles in the system. The most common types of class are:

- **Entity classes**: These model the entities, or data, in the system.

- **Boundary classes**: These essentially provide the interface between the system and the outside world, usually the user interface. The interface might, for example, consist of GUI components or web pages.

- **Control classes**: These handle the flow of control in the system, typically taking input from the user interface and using entity classes to perform the "business logic," and in turn providing the interface with a response to display to the user.

For example, an interface form might allow the user to input information about an employee and click a button to process the information. Clicking the button would pass the information to a control object, which would then instantiate an Employee object and do something with this object, perhaps record overtime or store the object in a database. The control object would then pass the result of the processing back to a user interface component.

Dividing responsibilities among different types of classes provides a separation of concerns, so that entity classes, for example, do not need to know anything about the user interface. This approach makes the system more understandable, and promotes reuse of code. The same entity classes could be reused in other systems with completely different interfaces.

Inheritance

You often need to use types of objects that are similar to each other in some ways and different in others. In other words, they have some properties and behavior in common. For example, an Employee object and a Customer object both represent people, and would have a lot in common, such as name, date of birth, and age. However, they would probably have some differences.

The things they have in common are basically the properties and behavior of a person. Each of the different types of the Person class implements different features. In object-oriented programming, *inheritance* allows us to express common features in a single class, and create specialized versions to represent the variations.

Figure 2-2 depicts how this works. The Person class is known as the *superclass*. The Employee and Customer classes *extend* this to add specific properties and behavior. These are known as *subclasses*. Note that some of the features of the Employee class you saw earlier are in the Person class in this version.

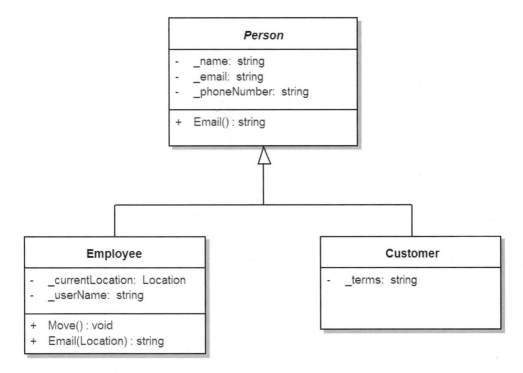

Figure 2-2. *An example of inheritance*

The Employee and Customer classes do not need to have name, dateOfBirth, and so on, as these are automatically inherited from Person. Because Employee is a type of Person, and Person has a name property, then an Employee object has a name property.

Note that the Employee class in Figure 2-2 has an Email method, while Customer does not. This shows that subclasses can *override* the features they inherit. A Customer object returns its email address in the way defined in Person, which could be simply to return the value of _email, while an Employee does it in a different way, based on the _userName attribute.

Note Sometimes there's a need for even more specialized classes. For instance, there could be particular kinds of Employee, such as Manager or Temp, which would be subclasses of Employee. With inheritance, a *class hierarchy* can be created that can have as many levels as you need.

You create a subclass in C# by specifying the name of the superclass in the class declaration at the top of the class, like this (in Java you use the extends keyword instead of the colon):

```
public class Employee : Person
```

The benefits of inheritance are that you can create new subclasses to represent different types of Person without creating a new class from scratch, so you are reusing the same code. Also, if you want to change the default way for objects to work out their age, for example, you only need to change one class, Person, as all the subclasses will inherit the new method (unless they override it, of course).

Reusing code through inheritance also lets you adapt code that has been created by someone else and adapt it for your specific purpose. The language Application Programming Interfaces (APIs) for Java and .NET, for example, contain many useful classes that you can extend for your own purposes.

Polymorphism

Literally meaning "many forms," polymorphism works closely together with inheritance. In the earlier example, Employee and Customer objects both have a method called Age. You could have some code like this:

```
Employee emp = new Employee("Michael","michael",loc,"1234");
Console.WriteLine("Email address is " + emp.Email());
```

or you could have:

```
Customer cust = new Customer("Anne","anne@gmail.com","cash","9876543210");
Console.WriteLine("Email address is " + cust.Email());
```

But both of these objects have a method called Email, so we could rewrite these lines as:

```
Person pers1 = new Employee("Michael","michael",loc,"1234");
Console.WriteLine("Email address is " + pers1.Email());
Person pers2 = new Customer("Anne","anne@gmail.com","cash","9876543210");
Console.WriteLine("Email address is " + pers2.Email());
```

This time the reference type of both objects is Person. The actual, or runtime, types of the objects are still Employee and Customer, respectively. The rule is that the runtime type of an object can be either the reference type or any of its subclasses.

You can call the Email method of both these objects using the name of a Person reference because the Person class defines an Email method. However, the object pers1 will use the Employee version of the Email method.

This illustrates that the only thing you need to know when sending a message to an object is that the object will understand that message. Any object that is an instance of Person or any of its subclasses will understand a message asking to calculate its age. The way it does that calculation will depend on exactly what type of object it is.

This can be incredibly powerful in many situations. For example, you can have an array or collection of objects that may be of different types, but where those types are subclasses of a single base class. You can iterate through the whole array, sending the same message to each object in turn, and each object will respond in its own way.

Abstract Classes

You would probably want all the people in your system to be of specific types—everybody needs to be either an employee or a customer. It is unlikely that you want to have someone who is just a person. If this isn't obvious, think about another example—apples, oranges, and bananas are all specific kinds of fruit. You can have an apple or an orange, but you are not likely to have a thing that you can hold in your hand that is just "a fruit." Fruit and person are abstract concepts that represent what the more specific types have in common.

You can make sure that your Person class only represents the concept, and that you cannot actually create a Person object, by declaring it to be *abstract*:

```
public abstract class Person
```

This means that any attempt to compile code that creates a Person instance will result in an error. For example, you can't do this:

```
Person pers = new Person ("Anne","anne@gmail.com","cash","9876543210");
```

Interfaces

In our example of polymorphism you saw that before you send a message to an object you have to know what behavior it is capable of—in other words, what public interface it presents. Any instance of a subclass of Person has a public interface that includes a method called Age. By using the superclass (Person) as the reference type, you can call the same method on objects that share the same interface, even if the way they implement that interface is different.

You can take this further by using a reference type containing only a list of the public methods that are available. An *interface* type contains no code to actually implement the methods. The implementations of the methods are provided in a class, which is said to *implement the interface*. An interface in C# is presented in Listing 2-2.

Listing 2-2. *IPerson Interface in C#*

```
public interface IPerson
{
        string Email();
}
```

Look at the Email method. It doesn't contain any code at all. So how do you use this? Well, you could declare our Employee class like this and make sure it has an appropriate Email method:

```
public class Employee : IPerson
```

In Java you use the implements keyword instead of the colon. You can create an object like this:

```
IPerson pers = new Employee("Michael","michael",loc,"1234");
Console.WriteLine("Email address is " + pers.Email());
```

The reference type of pers is IPerson, so it must have an Email method, as Employee implements the IPerson interface. An interface is basically a *contract*—any class that implements an interface agrees to implement all the methods listed in the interface. You can think of an interface as a description of what an object is *capable of doing*.

Using interfaces as reference types fully separates the public interface presented by an object from the actual implementation of the methods. This is a commonly used and recommended approach.

Note The way C# and Java apply inheritance means that a class can only belong to a single hierarchy. It cannot inherit its features from two or more different superclasses. These languages do not directly support multiple inheritance. In practice this is rarely a problem. However, sometimes you want to create an object that combines capabilities that do not fit into a single hierarchy. Interfaces fit this situation very well. For example, a T-shirt and an apple are dissimilar items, which you probably don't want to include in the same hierarchy. However, a supermarket might sell both, which means they have something in common—you can buy them. You could make them both implement an interface called Buyable in addition to belonging to Clothes and Food hierarchies, respectively.

Interfaces and Abstract Classes

It is common to use interfaces and abstract classes together at the root of a hierarchy, as shown in Figure 2-3.

- The IPerson interface is used as a reference type.

- The Person abstract class provides a basic implementation of the interface methods, and can be extended to provide specific behavior. This can reduce the effort required to create a new class that implements the interface.

This approach is widely used, and can be seen, for example, in the API classes used for collections of data in Java.

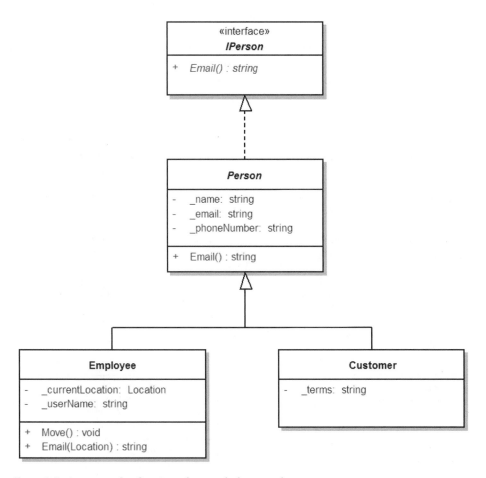

Figure 2-3. *An example of an interface and abstract class*

Object Relationships

Objects do not generally exist alone. A system needs its objects to collaborate to do something useful, and this means that there are relationships between the objects in the system.

This book is about databases, so we are interested in what happens when objects are stored permanently, or made persistent, in a database. It is usually important that object relationships be preserved. Objects retrieved from the database need to have the same relationships with each other as they did before they were stored; otherwise, important information has been lost.

The main types of relationship are:

- The **is-a** relationship

- The **has-a** relationship

- The **uses-a** relationship

is-a

One type of object is a more specific version of a general type. The *is-a* relationship is modeled with inheritance, as you have already seen. It is important that the object stored in a database retain the ability to access properties that it has through inheritance.

has-a

This means that one type of object contains another or is composed of another—for example, a car *has-an* engine, a manager *has* employees. The *has-a* relationship is modeled with *aggregation* or *composition*.

- **Aggregation**: Aggregation means an instance of one class may consist of or include instances of another class.

- **Composition**: Composition is similar to aggregation, but there's a stronger relationship in that the included object cannot exist on its own.

Figure 2-4 shows an example of an aggregation relationship between Manager and Employee. The diamond indicates the container end of the relationship. Note that multiplicities are indicated in the diagram—one Manager is associated with many (*) Employees.

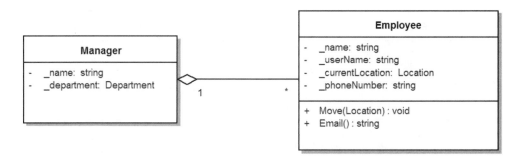

Figure 2-4. *Aggregation*

This kind of relationship is usually implemented as an instance variable in the including class, for example in the implementation of the Manager class:

```
public class Manager
{
    private IList _employees;
    // remaining code omitted
}
```

The instance variable may be single-valued, or multivalued as in the example, where Manager holds a reference to a list (IList is the C# interface for a list of objects) of Employees. The _employees variable is not shown in the class diagram as its existence is implicit in the aggregation relationship.

It is important that these relationships be maintained after storage in a database—you want to make sure that a Manager still has the right Employees.

uses-a

This type of association is generally weaker, and is often a transient association where one object uses another during some activity. In an earlier example in this chapter, a Person uses a TimeSheet to record overtime. The Employee doesn't maintain a reference to a TimeSheet other than while that process is happening. Transient relationships such as this do not need to be maintained in a database.

Design Patterns

Classes, objects, relationships, and interactions are the building blocks of object-oriented systems. Of course, there are many different ways of putting the blocks together, and some ways work better than others. With experience you start to notice that the same situations arise again and again in your design scenarios, and that you can apply the same solution each time.

Design patterns are recurring solutions to software design problems you find again and again in real-world application development. These patterns distill and document the experience of many people. A pattern describes a problem and a solution in the form of a group of classes and interactions. The relationships between the classes in a pattern are essentially the ones described earlier, but these can be combined in way that may not be obvious when you first consider a problem.

Note The Gang of Four (GoF) patterns are generally considered the foundation for all other patterns. The "Gang" is Erich Gamma, Richard Helm, Ralph Johnson, and John Vlissides, and their patterns were recorded in *Design Patterns: Elements of Reusable Object-Oriented Software* (Addison-Wesley Professional, 1995). The patterns are categorized in three groups: Creational, Structural, and Behavioral.

An ideal example of a design pattern is the Composite pattern, illustrated in Figure 2-5. The Composite pattern lets you compose objects into tree structures to represent part-whole hierarchies. Figure 2-5 shows a class hierarchy—there is an Employee class and subclasses representing different kinds of Employee. For example, a Manager *is-an* Employee. However a Manager also has a different relationship with Employees—a Manager *has* Employees, as shown by the aggregation relationship in the figure.

So what kind of Employees can a Manager have? Well, thanks to polymorphism, they can be instances of any subclass of Employee, so they can include other Managers. This makes sense— a senior line manager might have several more junior line managers on the team. The Worker class represents a simple soul (probably a programmer) who is not trusted to have any Employees of any kind to manage.

Storing a part-whole hierarchy like this in a database requires that the fairly complex relationships defined by the pattern be preserved.

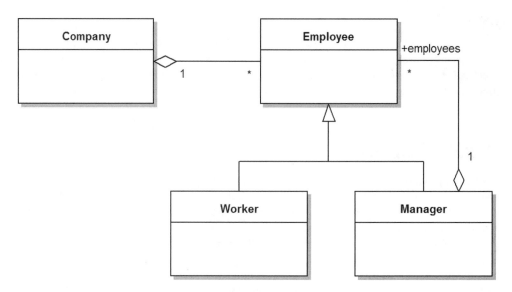

Figure 2-5. *An example of the Composite pattern*

This pattern would be implemented in code like this:

```
public class Employee
{
    // remaining code omitted
}

public class Manager : Employee
{
    private IList _employees;
    // remaining code omitted
}

public class Worker : Employee
{
    // remaining code omitted
}
```

This pattern has many applications, and can be seen, for example, in the API classes used for graphical user interface components. The composite pattern is just one example of a design pattern. If you want to see more design patterns, then the GoF book is a good place to start.

The points to note here are that relationships between objects are crucial in an object-oriented system, that these relationships can become quite complex, and that maintaining them is a crucial requirement for a persistence solution.

In the next chapters you will see how different data models cope with the challenge of storing objects and their relationships.

CHAPTER 3

■■■

Comparing the Object and Relational Data Models

When people talk about databases, they almost always mean relational databases. This wasn't always the case, though, as databases existed before the relational data model was developed. Now, the case for considering alternatives has become stronger with the increasing dominance of object-oriented languages in a widening range of application areas, and with the emergence of native object databases such as db4o. It's vital to understand the benefits and limitations of today's data models, particularly in the context of object-oriented systems.

This chapter describes the evolution of data models, including the relational and the object-based "post-relational" models, and compares their characteristics, both good and bad. It discusses the strategies needed to make the relational model work with object-oriented systems. It then describes how object databases reflect the features expected in relational databases. The next chapter will examine the object data model in detail, and explain how this model is applied in db4o.

Data Models

Before the first DBMS was developed, programs accessed data from flat files. These did not allow representation of logical data relationships or enforcement of data integrity. Data modeling has developed over successive generations since the 1960s to provide applications with more powerful data storage features. In this chapter we will look at the differences between data models, concentrating on the relational model and the object model.

Generally speaking, data models have evolved in three generations. The early generation data models tend to refuse to completely go away, however. After all, companies often have made significant investments in databases, or have critical data dependent on them. Even some first-generation products are still in use and are still supported by their vendors.

Yet so far, the most commercially successful databases have certainly been those using the relational model, which is considered to be the second generation. Relational databases are definitely not about to disappear, and their dominance in the marketplace has made it very difficult for a new generation of databases to gain a foothold.

However, the application language world has changed. With the continuing evolution of Java and Microsoft's commitment to .NET, the developer's choice in many application areas is no longer between object-oriented and non-object-oriented; it is now a choice of which object-oriented platform (Java or .NET). The mismatch between the relational data model and the object-oriented application model puts new object databases like db4o in a strong position to offer a real alternative.

First Generation

The emergence of computer systems in the 1960s led to the development of the hierarchical and network data models, which are usually referred to as the first-generation data models. These models are described in this section.

Hierarchical Data Model

Most computer users are very familiar with a hierarchical way of storing information. The file system used by most personal computer operating systems is an example of a hierarchy, and accordingly this is known as the *hierarchical data model*. It represents directories and files as a system of trees. Typically a file system has the following characteristics:

- It allows one-to-one or one-to-many relationships between entities—a directory or folder may contain one file, or it may contain many files (or it may contain no files).

- An entity at a "many" end of a relationship can be related to only one entity at the "one" end—in other words, a file can only be in one directory.

This storage model is often described as *navigational*. This means that to find one particular item, you have to navigate your way down through the hierarchy using predefined relationships until you reach it. This can be very efficient if the searches you want to do follow these relationships closely. However, it can be very inefficient if you want to query your data in an ad hoc way—for instance looking at data from a user's point of view in ways that the database designer could not anticipate. If the information you want to find in a file system is contained in several files in different directories, then the process of gathering it can be very laborious.

Figure 3-1 shows an example of hierarchical data. Each customer can have many orders, and each order can contain many items. Each item belongs to a particular order, and only to that order.

Hierarchical databases, which were the first generation of databases, store their data pretty much like this. The best-known hierarchical database is IBM's Information Management System (IMS), which has been around since the 1960s and is still supported by IBM.

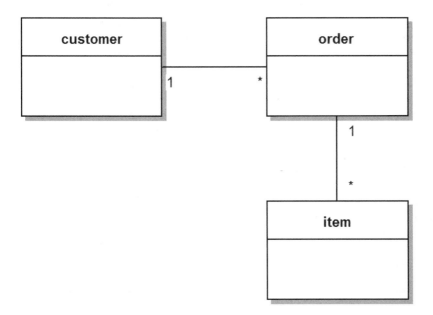

Figure 3-1. *Hierarchical data example*

Network Data Model

The network data model standard was developed in the late 1960s by the Committee on Data Systems Languages (CODASYL), the same organization that developed Cobol. It added one important feature for data modeling. Multiple parentage means that a single entity can be at the "many" ends of multiple relationships. This is a bit harder to imagine in terms of a file system: it would mean that a file could be in more than one directory at the same time.

In many scenarios, the network model allowed data to be modeled more realistically. In the example in Figure 3-1, it probably doesn't make sense to have every item as a separate entity that belongs to a specific order. What if there are several orders for the same type of item? A better way of modeling this data is shown in Figure 3.2. Now, the order is made up of orderlines, each of which could refer to an item and the required quantity of that item. Each item can appear in many different orderlines. orderline is at the "many" end of its relationships to item and order, which is allowed by the network model.

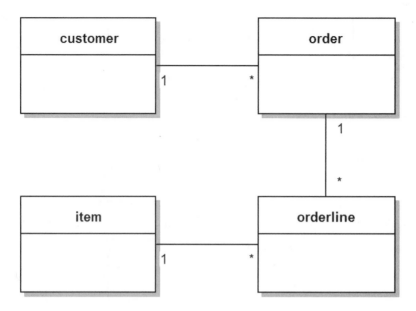

Figure 3-2. *Network data example*

The network model gave an extra degree of flexibility in data modeling, but it was still a navigational model. The network defines a set of relationships, and you have to follow them. Relationships are directional. For example, the relationship between customer and order in Figure 3-2 might have been defined to allow you to find the item for a particular orderline. If you needed to find all the orderlines that contain a particular item, you may have to change the data model itself to allow this new query to be performed.

The CODASYL query language had statements that allowed the user to jump from one data element to the next, through a graph of pointers among these elements. These queries were quite difficult to write, even for very simple queries. Listing 3-1 shows an example of a CODASYL query.

Listing 3-1. *CODASYL Query to Find How Much Wine Carl Has Ordered*

```
NAME := "Carl"
FIND CUSTOMERS RECORD USING CALC-KEY
LOOP: repeat forever
    FIND NEXT ORDERS RECORD IN CURRENT CUSTORD SET
    if FAIL then break LOOP
    FIND OWNER OF CURRENT ITEMORD SET
    GET ITEMS; ITYPE
    if ITEMS.ITYPE = "Wine" then do
        FIND CURRENT OF ORDERS RECORD
        GET ORDERS; QUANTITY
        print QUANTITY
        break LOOP
    end
end LOOP
```

As we have seen, the first-generation models were not suited to ad hoc queries, where you don't necessarily know how the data will need to be retrieved before you create the database. A criticism that is often made of object databases is that they are little more than a rehash of the old network databases. It is true that the object data model is also essentially navigational, and is also not well suited to ad hoc queries. However, as you will see, it is substantially different in other ways, and offers its own advantages, primarily the fact that it is a good match to the object model used in modern application design.

Second Generation: The Relational Model

The relational model has undoubtedly been the most widely used and commercially successful way to date of modeling data. Its characteristics are very different from the earlier models. To begin, data entities are represented by simple tabular structures, known as relations. Entity relationships and data integrity are defined by primary keys and foreign keys. The design of a relational database is based on the idea of normalization, the process of removing redundant data from your tables in order to improve storage efficiency, data integrity, and scalability.

■**Note** The relational model was proposed in 1970 by Edgar Codd to represent the natural structure of data without the database user needing to know about the machine representation. It promoted the idea of end-user programming and interactive querying of a database. This was a big step forward in the usability of databases.

Data Access in the Relational Model

Data access uses a high-level nonprocedural language (SQL). This makes relational databases great for ad hoc querying. If the data you require is in the database, you will almost certainly be able to write a SQL query that retrieves it, though it may involve joining many tables to get the data. The query in Listing 3-1 becomes much more natural and understandable in SQL, as shown in Listing 3-2.

Listing 3-2. *SQL Query to Find How Much Wine Carl Has Ordered*

```
select QUANTITY
    from ORDERS
    where NAME='Carl' and ITEMTYPE='Wine'
```

SQL has evolved as a standard that is supported by most commercial database products, although those products usually add their own proprietary extensions to the language. The way queries are constructed is based on the branch of mathematics known as set theory, although you don't need to know the details of set theory to write SQL. To some people, the basis on formal mathematical principles is a major advantage of the relational model, although it is not entirely obvious why this should be of such great benefit. There are no particular foundations in mathematical theory for object-oriented programming languages, yet they are successful because they provide tools to get the job done well.

Relational queries are not navigational. You don't have to follow predefined paths. You can write a SQL query to select data from any table in a database. If you want to get data from more than one type of entity, you can write your queries to join tables. Usually, you join tables that have foreign key relationships or at least common field names, so that associated data from different tables can be assembled. There is no direction implied in a join, so there is no concept of navigating from one table to another.

Using the Relational Model with Procedural Programs

Relational databases are a great fit for procedural programs. You use entity relationship modeling to design your database schema, and then write procedural code that gets some data, does something with it, and stores the data. The application is heavily dependent on the database design. You can connect to that database from an application written in any language for which you can get a suitable database driver. The same database can be the target for many different applications.

An application will not be written in SQL itself. That's because SQL is a declarative language, not a programming language. It is not computationally complete, so you can't write a full program with it. Its job is to express queries and perform some manipulation of the data in the database. As a result, SQL is either used at an interactive prompt or, more commonly, appears as strings embedded within another language. Of course, many relational database systems have the ability to use stored procedures, which are program modules that exist within the DBMS. Even though these are within the DBMS, they still need to combine SQL with another language, such as Oracle's PL/SQL.

The use of embedded SQL strings in application code external to the database can present a problem to the programmer. The compiler simply interprets these as strings—if it's a valid string then it's okay as far as the compiler is concerned. It might be complete nonsense as far as the database is concerned: it may refer to tables or columns that don't exist, for example. You have to wait until runtime to find that out, and debugging can be difficult.

Using the Relational Model with Object-Oriented Programs

As you learned in Chapter 2, object-oriented systems try to model the problem domain in terms of objects. The entities in the system are described in the class diagram, rather than in the *entity relationship diagram*, or ERD, of the traditional system. Suddenly, the database is not the driver for the application—instead, its primary function is to provide a service to the application, namely the capability to persist objects.

This shift is significant because of the differences between the object model and the relational data model. A class diagram and an ERD may look superficially similar, but you can find many examples of relationships in the former that are hard to model in the latter. For example, inheritance is not directly supported in the relational model.

■**Note** There are some significant variations between RDBMSs in their features, including their support for object orientation. The PostgreSQL RDBMS now features table inheritance, which supports polymorphism in queries. This is not, however, a standard RDBMS capability.

One result of this is often seen when object-oriented systems are created within a "data culture." The object model is reined in so that the class diagram matches a database designer's lovingly crafted ERD. This rarely produces a good object model.

The problem of embedded SQL strings also applies to object-oriented programs, perhaps more so as tools that support safe and easy refactoring cannot understand or modify them.

Third Generation: "Post-Relational" Models

The third-generation models, first proposed in the 1980s, are a response to the problems that often arise when marrying an object-oriented system to a relational database. They are sometimes described as "post-relational," although it is more realistic to consider them as coexisting with the relational model and providing additional options for developers. Unlike the second generation, where the relational model was pretty much universally adopted, with some proprietary variations, the object-oriented third generation has evolved in two distinct directions, which are described in this section.

The Object Data Model

The object data model is pretty much the same as the object-oriented paradigm described in Chapter 2, except that the objects are persistent. That is, they continue to exist after the program run finishes.

An object in an object database is analogous to an object in application memory. In most object databases, there are language bindings that allow you to use the persistent objects in applications. A Java application requires a Java language binding, and so on. The database schema itself is created using an object definition language, which defines the object classes that can be stored, and their relationships.

On the other hand, a native object database like db4o stores objects exactly as they are created in the application. Native object databases don't need an object definition language—the database schema is identical to the object domain model of the application. They are, therefore, closely tied to the applications that use them.

ORIGINS OF THE OBJECT DATABASE

The object database emerged from the "manifesto" written by Malcolm Atkinson and others in 1989, which specified a list of requirements that should be met by an object database, including some object-oriented features and some database-like features. The Object Database Management Group (ODMG) tried to establish standards for object databases, including ODL, an object definition language, and OQL, an object query language. These standards have been adopted to some extent, but have never achieved universal acceptance.

The final version of the ODMG standard, ODMG 3.0, was released in 2001, and ODMG disbanded after that. The ODMG Java language binding was the basis for Java Data Objects (JDO), an API for transparent persistence. JDO is not a database or data model: it is a persistence API that can be used with a variety of data stores, including relational databases.

db4o doesn't use the ODMG standards because it doesn't need to. Since it is a native database, it doesn't need an object definition language, and the native query capabilities it offers are more advanced than OQL. Similarly, although it is quite possible for a native object database to offer a JDO-compliant API for Java developers, db4o doesn't do this. The db4o API is simpler and more intuitive, and unlike JDO, supports .NET as well as Java.

The object data model is navigational—object access follows well-defined relationships as specified in the design model. It is not just the network model revisited, though. The key benefits come from the close match to application languages and the elimination of the impedance mismatch—fewer lines of code are needed for data access, and database configuration is reduced or eliminated. The result is greater developer productivity. Performance can also be greatly enhanced for queries that follow the defined relationships.

The Object-Relational Model

At roughly the same time that the object data model was being proposed, the problem of storing objects in databases was being approached from a different angle. The object-relational model extends the capabilities of the relational model to allow objects to be stored in the columns of a relational database. An object relational DBMS is sometimes referred to as a *hybrid* DBMS.

■**Note** The hybrid DBMS approach was proposed by Michael Stonebraker in 1990, and has been implemented in some commercial RDBMSs, including Oracle. The motivation was a desire for databases that could store more complex entities and rules but that retained all the strengths of the second-generation databases.

The object-relational data model is an extension of the relational model, with the following features:

- A field may contain an object with attributes and operations.

- Complex objects can be stored in relational tables

For example, Oracle supports the ability to declare a new data type that is basically a class, and to set this new type as the data type for a table column.

The object-relational data approach is pretty much the opposite of what object databases, particularly native ones, are trying to achieve. Instead of giving persistence capability to an object-oriented system, it provides object-oriented capabilities within the database. This approach is certainly not suitable for the embedded applications for which db4o excels as you need a full-blown RDBMS to make use of it.

The use of terms like "third generation" and "post-relational" has not been particularly accurate—they implied that these types of databases would replace relational databases, the way that the second generation effectively supplanted the first. The third generation has not taken the place of relational databases, but instead exists in parallel to widen the options open to developers to use appropriate solutions for their own applications. db4o, with its small footprint and zero administration capability, further opens up the choices within the third generation to a new range of applications.

Fitting Objects into a Relational Database

If the design of an object-oriented system is application driven rather than data driven, then the database needs to provide a way to persist the objects in the system. If the database is relational, there needs to be a mapping of objects to database tables. This requirement is there regardless of the mechanism used to allow the application to communicate with the database (either hard-coded SQL within the application or a mapping layer such as Hibernate).

This can sometimes be a straightforward matter of mapping individual classes to separate database tables. However, if the class structure is more complex, then the mapping must be carefully considered to allow data to be represented and accessed as efficiently as possible. Looking at object-relational mapping strategies is a good way to understand the practical differences between the object and relational models. Let's take a look at some of the common object relationships that you might find in a class diagram, as described in Chapter 2. Remember that the data model that you would use in each case for an object database would be very similar, or identical in the case of a native object database, to the class diagram.

Aggregation

In an aggregation relationship, as shown in Figure 3-3, the owner object holds a reference to its owned objects, which are either single objects or collections. An owned relationship like this is implemented in the relational model using a foreign key column in the table on the many side of the relationship, as shown in Figure 3-4. You need to include foreign key columns in your data model that are not required in the object model.

■**Note** Relational databases rely on primary keys to ensure that each row in a table is unique. Any unique field or combination of fields can be used as the primary key. In the object model, each object is unique already, and no key field is needed. In an object database, each object has a unique UID assigned to it automatically. This does mean that you can create objects that have identical field values but that are different objects—it is up to the application logic to enforce unique values if this is required.

Association is modeled in exactly the same way in the relational model, which does not distinguish between ownership and simple reference.

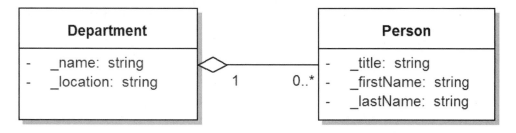

Figure 3-3. *Aggregation object model*

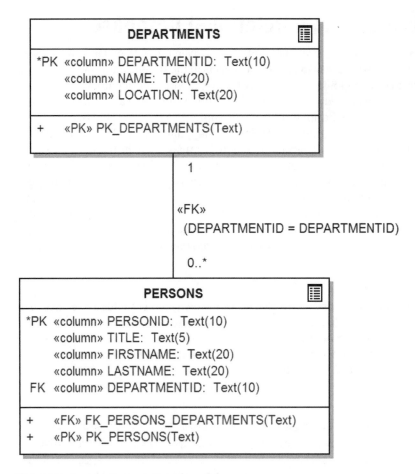

Figure 3-4. *Aggregation relational model*

■**Note** Associations between objects are implemented by *object references*. The reference type is the class name of the associated object. A common beginner's mistake is to try to associate objects by giving them text or numeric fields with matching names, just like foreign keys in a relational database—very tempting if you have been brought up in the relational way, but not a good idea.

Inheritance

The relational model as used by most RDBMSs has no concept equivalent to inheritance. As a result, the mapping can become quite involved. There are several possible strategies, and there is no single best way to do it. The optimum strategy depends on the precise nature of the inheritance tree. To illustrate, we will map the tree shown in Figure 3-5, which has a simple two-layer hierarchy (things can become much more complicated for deeper hierarchies).

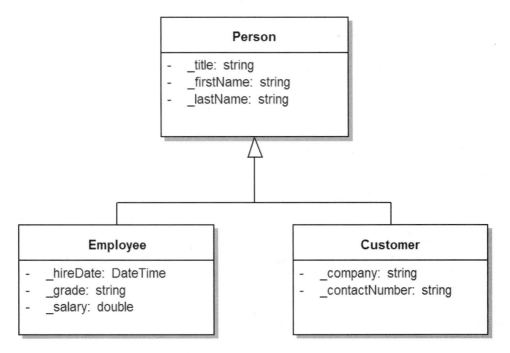

Figure 3-5. *A simple class inheritance tree*

This can be mapped to a relational database in three ways, illustrated by the following examples.

Vertical Mapping: One Table per Class

There is separate table for each class, including any abstract classes, as shown in Figure 3-6. Subclass tables are related by foreign keys to the superclass tables. You need an additional key field (`PersonID`) to create relationships. Creating an `Employee` object in the application involves joining `Person` and `Employee` tables in the database. This approach can result in complex queries in cases with deeper levels of inheritance than this example shows.

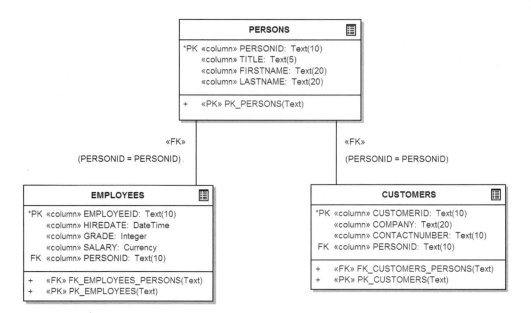

Figure 3-6. *Data model using vertical mapping*

Horizontal Mapping: One Table per Concrete Class

In this approach, each concrete class is mapped to a different table, and each table contains columns for all the attributes of its class, including inherited ones, as shown in Figure 3-7. This is the simplest to work with in your application, as every object you create will map onto one row of one table. It is not very resilient to schema changes, however. Changes in design of the class at the root of the inheritance tree require changes in *all* tables.

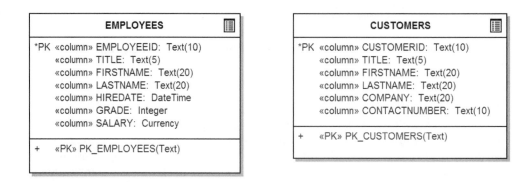

Figure 3-7. *Data model using horizontal mapping*

Filtered Mapping: One Table per Tree

This ducks the issue of dealing with subclasses by lumping the whole tree together in a single table that has all the attributes of all the classes in the tree, as shown in Figure 3.8. A filter column (PERSONTYPE) is included to distinguish between subclasses. This approach manages to violate principles of both object and relational modeling at the same time!

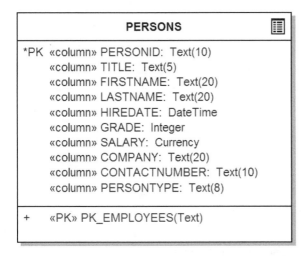

Figure 3-8. *Data model using filtered mapping*

Many-Many Relationships

The class diagram in Figure 3-9 shows a many-many relationship between the Person and Project classes. A Person can be assigned to more than one Project, while a single Project has many Persons assigned to it.

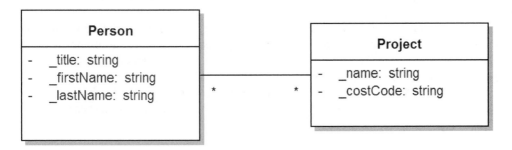

Figure 3-9. *A many-many relationship*

This is a common relationship, quite feasible in the object model, but it can't be represented directly by the relational model. This is a well-known problem: the workaround has been used since long before the object model appeared. In a relational database a join table is required to represent this relationship, introducing more key fields, as shown in Figure 3-10.

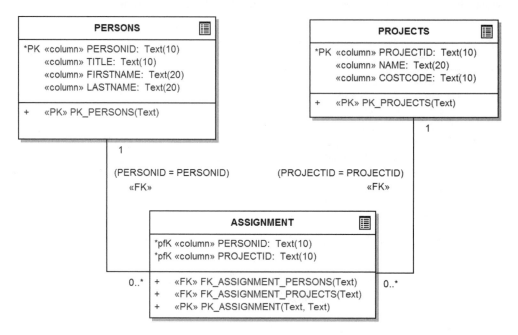

Figure 3-10. *Data model for many-many relationship*

Complex Relationships

Clearly, the relational model is different enough from the object model to make life complicated when you are trying to map anything but the simplest type of object relationship. Even in the simplest cases, you need to add key fields to make relationships work.

In Chapter 2, you saw that object relationships can become more complicated, and that many useful ones have been captured as design patterns. For example, the composite pattern example that we saw in Chapter 2 combines aggregation and inheritance to represent whole-part hierarchies, as illustrated in Figure 3-11.

Sorry, we're going to leave the mapping of this scenario as an exercise for the reader—have fun with this! Remember, in the object data model these relationships stay just as they are.

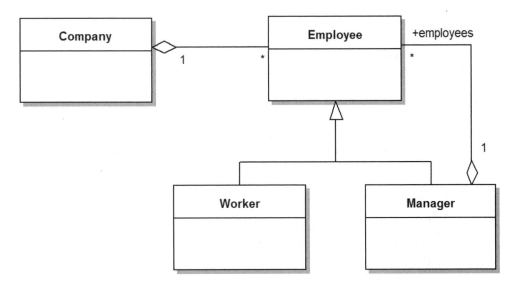

Figure 3-11. *Composite pattern example class diagram*

Referential Integrity and All That

Many people who are considering using db4o have a lot of experience with relational databases. Their first questions are often about whether an object database can provide the features they take for granted. In Chapter 13 we will look in detail at the issues of moving from RDBMS to db4o, but for now let's look at some common database features, and see how they relate to the object model.

Queries

Querying using SQL is a fundamental capability of a relational database. Atkinson's original manifesto for object databases (see the earlier sidebar, "Origins of the Object Database") stated that a query facility was a mandatory feature of an object database, and the ODMG standards defined a high-level query language, OQL. The nature of the data model dictates that object database queries be expressed somewhat differently from SQL queries, making use of object references rather than joins. db4o supports a new approach to querying, the type-safe native query, which is described in Chapter 6.

Referential Integrity

Referential integrity ensures, for example, that you couldn't create an order in the database for a customer who does not exist in the database.

In the relational model, referential integrity is enforced by foreign key relationships. In this example, the ORDERS table would have a foreign key that referred to the primary key of the CUSTOMERS table. Before a new order is added to an ORDERS table, the foreign key field is checked to make sure there is a matching value in the CUSTOMERS table.

In the object model, integrity is controlled by the application. Object references created in the application are maintained in the database. In the example, if the application is written so that all new Order instances are created as fields of Customer objects, then it is not possible to have an orphaned Order object. The database logic matches the application logic.

The way the previously discussed features work is strongly dependent on the data model. The following features are also required for a database to be considered to have ACID (Atomicity, Concurrency, Isolation and Durability) properties. As far as the user or developer is concerned, the way these are used depends not on what data model the database is using, but on the particular database product.

Transactions

Atomicity states that database modifications must follow an "all or nothing" rule. Each transaction is said to be "atomic." If one part of the transaction fails, the entire transaction fails. db4o's support for transactions is described in Chapter 9.

Isolation

Isolation requires that multiple transactions running at the same time should not affect each other's execution. For example, if one user runs a transaction against a database at the same time that another user runs a different transaction, both transactions should operate on the database in an isolated manner. db4o supports concurrent transactions in client/server mode, either as an embedded server or a network server. Client/server mode is described in Chapter 8.

Summary

In this chapter we looked at the evolution of data models and compared the object and relational data models. We looked at some of the difficulties involved in fitting object-oriented systems and relational databases together, and we looked at how some well-known database features are implemented in an object database. In the next chapter, we take a closer look at the object data model and how db4o stores its data.

CHAPTER 4

■■■

OODBMS Basics

The object data model is the basis for *Object-Oriented Database Management Systems* (OODBMSs) in the same way that the relational model is the basis for RDBMSs. As you have seen, these data models are substantially different, so working with an OODBMS can take a bit of getting used to for people who are familiar with relational databases. This chapter describes the main concepts of OODBMSs and how they have emerged from the object data model.

Object databases have traditionally been based on the standard proposed by the Object Data Management Group (ODMG), as discussed in Chapter 3. db4o is not an ODMG-based product, so we point out where this makes a difference, and what the benefits for db4o users are.

Object Identity

Object and relational databases take fundamentally different approaches to the idea of *identity*. Identity determines how entities are distinguished from one another. In an RDBMS, entities are uniquely identified by primary keys, and relationships are represented by matching primary key-foreign key data. The relationships are used in queries as required to join tables. Identity depends on the *values* in the key fields.

In contrast, an OODBMS stores a unique object identifier (OID) within each object. The OID identifies that object uniquely, and is also used to indicate other objects to which it is related. The OID is usually a number, and is not visible to the user or database programmer.

Figure 4-1 depicts two objects stored in a db4o database, viewed using the ObjectManager, the db4o graphical database browser. In this chapter the ObjectManager is used to illustrate the contents of example db4o databases—in the second part of this book you will learn the techniques you need to create and work with db4o databases. The ObjectManager is fully described in Appendix A.

Both objects are instances of a class Person, and have been assigned the OIDs 306 and 1877, respectively. These OIDs have been assigned by the database—the program that created the objects did not set the OIDs. Further, the meaning or method used to assign OIDs is specific to a particular DBMS. In db4o the OID is a physical pointer to the database file.

Crucially, the OID is not related to any of the properties of an object, or to the class of object. This has two implications:

- Two objects can be distinct even if the values of all their properties are identical. This works just like in-memory objects: you can easily create two objects with identical properties. With db4o you do not define keys to ensure uniqueness: it is up to the application to manage this.

- An object remains the same object even when its state takes on completely new values.

Figure 4-2 shows the contents of the database after all the properties of the second object have been changed. It is still the same object, as the OID is still 1877.

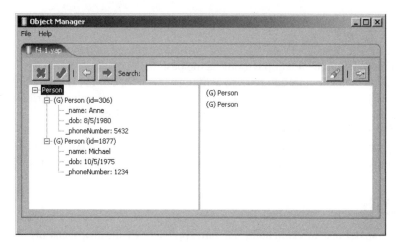

Figure 4-1. *A db4o database with two objects, viewed in the ObjectManager*

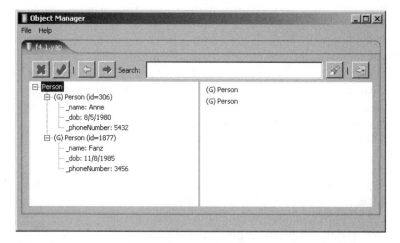

Figure 4-2. *The same db4o database with all the properties of one object changed*

Figure 4-3 depicts two objects with identical values for all attributes. The objects are distinguished in the database by the OIDs.

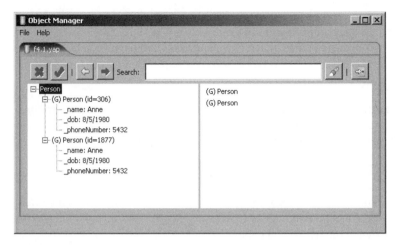

Figure 4-3. *Two objects with identical properties*

It may seem that the lack of key fields is a problem for object databases. You can't easily make the database check for duplicate values when you try to store data. It is possible to create and store a new object that duplicates an object that already exists in the database. The new object will be stored with a new OID, so the database is quite happy about this, as you can see in Figure 4-3.

In fact, you are putting the responsibility for allowing or disallowing duplicate values onto the application. If your application says that it is okay for any two objects to coexist in the system, then the database should be able to store them. The database simply persists whatever objects you allow your application to create. In the simple example here, if you want to make sure that you don't have two Person objects with the same _name value, you need to check when you create a new Person that there is not already a Person object with that _name attribute in memory or in the database.

A relational database, which is more decoupled from the applications that use it, can't necessarily rely on those applications being well behaved in this respect.

Equivalence and Equality

The fact that an object's identity is distinct from its values means that there are different concepts of equivalence and equality typically used in object database terminology:

- **Equivalent**: If two object references point to objects that have the same OID, they are equivalent. For example, you could run two queries on the database in Figure 4-2, one to find the Person with _name = "Anne" and the second to find the Person with _phoneNumber = "5432". With db4o, the database keeps track of references in memory to objects that have been stored or retrieved since the database connection was opened, and allows you to find the OID for the corresponding object in the database. The query described here would result in two references to the object with OID 306, and so these would be equivalent. The object could be manipulated or updated through either reference.

- **Equal**: If two objects have the same state values, they are equal. The two objects in the database in Figure 4-3 are equal. If you run a query to find all the Person objects, then you would have two object references that are not equivalent but that refer to equal objects.

Objects and Literals

Objects that can change their state values are described as being *mutable*. Another component of the object data model is the *literal*, which represents a value or set of values that cannot be changed. A literal is described as being immutable. Literals do not have OIDs.

Extent

The collection of objects in the database belonging to a particular class is known as the *extent* of the class. In Figure 4-1 the extent of the Person class is the group of two objects shown in the "Person" branch of the tree in the right-hand pane.

The Database Schema

You've now seen the contents of a very simple object database that stores objects of a particular class (Person). To do this, a database schema has been defined to support storage of this data. The schema is the structure of a database system. This section describes the aspects of the objects that are included in the schema, as well as those aspects that are not included.

Properties and Relationships

In a relational database, the schema defines the tables, the fields in each table, and the relationships between tables. In an object database, the schema must define the classes, the properties of each class, and the possible object relationships.

A database schema is usually defined with a formal data definition language (DDL). Relational databases use a DDL that includes, for example, CREATE TABLE statements to define table structures. The equivalent in the object database world is ODL, the object definition language that is part of the ODMG standard. For instance, the example database schema could be defined using ODL like this:

```
class Person
{
    attribute string name;
    attribute string dob;
    attribute string phoneNumber;
}
```

Note that although this class definition looks a bit like a class definition in C# or Java, it is not actually part of any application programming language. It simply defines the database schema. To access the database from an application, you need to make use of an appropriate *language binding*, which maps database classes to the appropriate C# or Java language classes and allows operations and queries to be invoked. The application would need its own class definition for Person.

db4o takes a much more direct approach to schema definition. It simply takes the object that has been created in the C# or Java application and stores it exactly as it is—this is native object storage. You don't have to define the schema separately.

In this chapter we will look at how the features of an object database schema are implemented in both ways: for the sake of generality the ODL approach is shown, and this is compared with specific db4o database examples. In some cases, db4o allows you do things you can't do with ODL, and vice versa.

Methods

As you learned in Chapter 2, objects encapsulate properties and behavior. For a given class, the behavior that is possible for all objects, expressed as methods of the class, will be the same— it is the properties that vary between objects. There is little point in attempting to store methods, as they should be available when the object is retrieved from the database into memory. The runtime object is constructed by combining the information stored in the database, which is the state and identity of the object, with the runtime class definition.

ODL includes the capability to include method signatures in the database schema, but the implementation code is not an element of ODL. db4o does not store methods.

Class Variables

Similarly, a class variable, sometimes known as a static field, is a property whose value is shared by *all* instances of the class. Class variables do not need to be stored in the database, as an instance that is retrieved will assume the current values in the application of any class variables.

Object Relationships

Chapter 2 described the ways in which objects in an object-oriented system can be related to each other, through association, aggregation, or inheritance. It is important that a database maintain the correct relationships between the objects it stores, and Chapter 3 discussed how the relational model copes, sometimes with difficulty, with this task. The object data model is basically the same as the object model, so these relationships are maintained in a much more straightforward way. In this section you will see how these relationships are actually persisted in an object database.

Storing OIDs to Represent Relationships

Relationships between objects in memory are maintained by object references. Once the objects have been stored in an object database, the object references are no longer available, so the objects maintain their relationships by storing the OIDs of any related objects.

Figure 4-4 shows some example objects to be stored. They are illustrated in the form of an object graph, which is a structure of nodes that represent objects and directed edges that represent object references. There are three Person objects and two Address objects. Figure 4-5 shows a db4o database containing these five objects. The extent of the Person class is three objects, while the extent of the Address class is the other two objects. The Person objects stored here have an additional attribute, which is of type Address. This attribute refers to another object stored in the database, rather than to a literal like the other attributes.

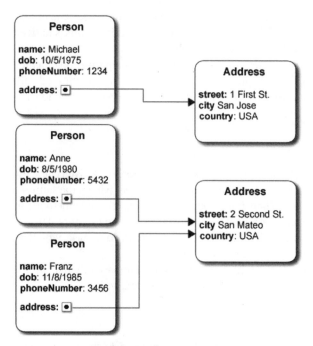

Figure 4-4. *An object graph showing related objects*

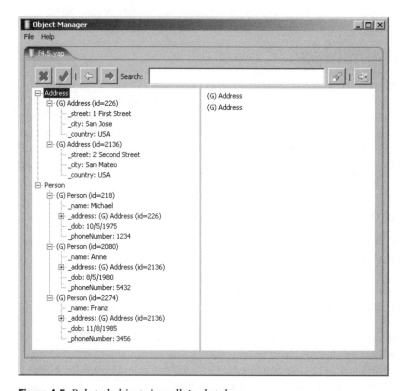

Figure 4-5. *Related objects in a db4o database*

Note that for each Person object, an OID for the Address attribute is stored, and that the OID corresponds to one of the Address objects also stored in the database. It is possible for the same Address to be shared by more than one person—the Person objects with OIDs 2080 and 2274 both store the OID 2136, so they are both related to the same Address object.

Inverse Relationships

If you were to look at an Address object, how would you know who lived there? In fact, you can't, because the Address objects do not store the OIDs of any Person objects. On the other hand, it is straightforward to find out the address for a particular Person by using the stored OID. The only relationships that can be used for querying or traversing the database are the ones that have been predefined by storing the appropriate OIDs. In other words, as you saw in Chapter 3, the object model and object databases are navigational. You need to make sure that the database schema will support any traversal of the database that your application will need to do.

If you need to traverse the relationship in both directions, then you need to make sure that OIDs are stored in both Person and Address objects, as shown in Figure 4-6. In this version of the database, each Person stores the OID of one Address, and each Address stores the OID of one Person.

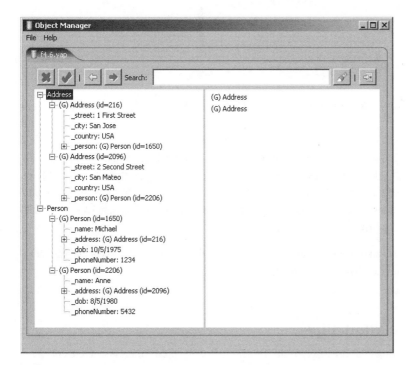

Figure 4-6. *Related objects with inverse relationships*

The object graph for this scenario is shown in Figure 4-7. This illustrates the inverse relationship between Person and Address objects. This is now a one-to-one relationship—only one Person can live at each Address. One-to-many relationships will be introduced later in the chapter.

If you look at this object graph, you can see that you can traverse it from a Person to an Address. Once you get there, you can traverse back again to the Person. This is a *circular reference*—you could traverse your way around in circles all day without reaching an end point. Circular references are common in object-oriented systems.

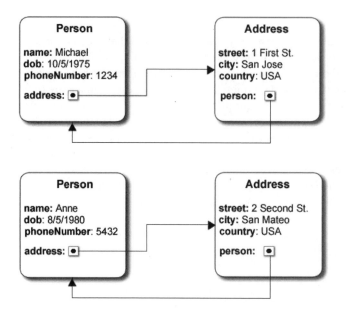

Figure 4-7. *The object graph for objects with an inverse relationship*

■**Note** Which objects do you need to store? When you store an object in an object database you store all the attributes of the object. If those attributes are themselves objects, then those are stored too. In effect, you store the object *and* all other objects that can be reached from it in the object graph by following object references. In this example, it doesn't matter whether you select to store a Person or the related Address: both objects will be stored in any case.

Similarly, when you retrieve an object from the database, the default behavior is that objects that can be reached from it through relationships in the stored objects will also be retrieved.

Defining the Relationships

You can use ODL to define relationships within the schema of an ODMG database. ODL defines inverse relationships to enforce relationship integrity. Listing 4-1 shows ODL definitions of Person and Address classes.

Listing 4-1. *Definitions of Person and Address Classes in ODL*

```
class Person
{
    attribute string name;
    attribute string dob;
    attribute string phoneNumber;
    relationship Address address
        inverse Address :: person;
}
class Address
{
    attribute string street;
    attribute string city;
    attribute string country;
    relationship Person person
        inverse Person :: address;
}
```

This means that a Person object has a relationship to an Address object, and this relationship is labeled "address". The inverse of this is the relationship labeled "person" for the Address object. (You can take the same sentence and swap the words around to understand the meaning of the relationship definition in Address).

This approach to defining relationships is different from the way they would appear in the C# or Java code, where each class would simply have an attribute that is an object reference, as shown in Listing 4-2, which shows excerpts from equivalent class definitions in C# (the Java version is virtually identical).

Listing 4-2. *Definitions of Person and Address Classes in C#*

```
public class Person
{

    string _name;
    Address _address;
    string _dob;
    string _phoneNumber;

    // remaining code omitted
}

public class Address
 {
    string _street;
    string _city;
    string _country;
    Person _person;
```

```
    // remaining code omitted
}
```

As was the case for a single class, the language binding would handle the mapping between the database classes and application language classes.

On the other hand, the language class definitions together are sufficient to define the schema for a db4o database, and there is no need for a separate database schema definition.

Note that in the C# or Java code there is no requirement to define an inverse relationship. It would be valid to leave the _person attribute out of the definition of the Address class, and indeed this was done for the objects shown in Figure 4-5. The decision on whether to include the inverse is dictated by the navigability you require in the database.

In this example, it is straightforward to find the address for a specific person: you simply retrieve the Person object and access the Address attribute. If you want to find the Person at a specific Address, you need to approach the problem differently if there is no inverse relationship defined. Rather than retrieving the Address directly, you can retrieve Person objects using the specified Address as a search criterion. The navigability influences the way you need to design your queries, and possibly the performance of those queries.

Integrity

As you have seen, ODL requires inverse relationships to be defined to help ensure relationship integrity, analogous to the facility to create foreign keys in a relational database. Relationship integrity might dictate that you could not have a Person without an Address.

db4o simply uses the class definitions provided by the application. In this case it is the responsibility of the application to ensure integrity in the relationships stored in the database. The database will simply store what it is given. This is not to say that the database does not have relationship integrity: it means that the responsibility for enforcing it lies with the application designer rather than a database designer. In the database in Figure 4-6, the requirement for every Person to have an Address, which is clearly met in the data shown, was enforced by requiring a reference to an Address object in the constructor for Person, as shown in Listing 4-3.

Listing 4-3. *Constructor for the Person Class in C#*

```
public Person(String name, Address address, String dob, String phoneNumber)
{
    _name = name;
    _address = address;
    _dob = dob;
    _phoneNumber = phoneNumber;
}
```

The database would have been quite happy to store a Person without an Address if the application was written in such a way as to create one.

If an inverse relationship is defined, as in the example of the database in Figure 4-6, it is again the responsibility of the application to ensure that the relationship makes sense. Look carefully at the data in Figure 4-8—there is something not quite right about the OIDs. The Person with OID 1650 holds the OID 1670 for its Address reference. However, if you look at the Address with OID 1670, it holds the OID 2164 for its Person reference, so the inverse relationship is not valid. The database stored the data that it was given, so the application was at fault here.

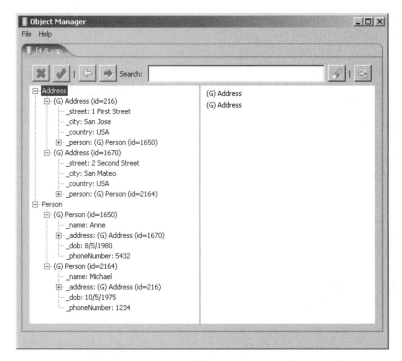

Figure 4-8. *Invalid inverse relationships*

Depth of Equality

Earlier in this chapter we mentioned the difference between equivalence and equality for objects in a database. Objects that have the same state values are said to be equal. Now you have seen that objects in a database can be related to other objects, so it is necessary to think a bit more carefully about how objects can be equal. This leads to two definitions:

- **Shallow equality**: Same state values (e.g., two Person objects have the same values).

- **Deep equality**: Same state values and related objects also contain the same state values (e.g., two Person objects have the same values and all their related Address objects have the same state values).

Common Types of Object Relationships

Chapters 2 and 3 described common object relationships and the ways in which they are represented in relational databases. In this section, the representation of one-to-many and many-to-many association or aggregation and inheritance in object databases is described.

One-to-Many Relationships

It is very common to need to store an object that is related to a collection of objects. For example, a Manager might have many Employees. In ODL this would be defined by a *set* relationship in the class at the "one" end. Listing 4-4 shows an ODL definition of Manager and Employee classes that model such a scenario.

Listing 4-4. *Definitions of Manager and Employee Classes in ODL*

```
class Manager
{
    attribute string name;
    attribute string department;
    relationship set<Employee> employees
        inverse Employee :: manager;
}
class Employee
{
    attribute string name;
    attribute string dob;
    attribute string phoneNumber;
    relationship Manager manager
        inverse Manager :: employees;
}
```

With db4o, the application class definitions form the database schema, which may or may not include the inverse relationship, as shown in Listing 4-5.

Listing 4-5. *Definition of the Manager Class in C#*

```
public class Manager
{
    private ArrayList _employees;
    // remaining code omitted
}
```

Figure 4-9 shows the contents of a db4o database containing a Manager and two related Employee objects. The object graph for these is shown in Figure 4-10. The _employees attribute exists as an ArrayList (as you can see from the package name this is an instance of the ArrayList class in the java.util package, so this database actually contains Java objects), which contains object references to individual Employee objects.

The ArrayList is therefore stored as an object in its own right in the db4o database, with an OID (3132 in Figure 4-9). The ArrayList in the database stores the OIDs of the relevant Employee objects (3333 and 3425). The Manager stores the OID of the ArrayList rather than those of the Employees. There is no inverse relationship defined in this example.

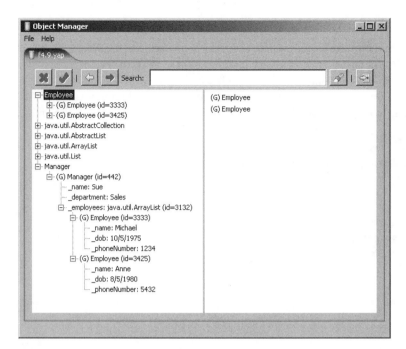

Figure 4-9. *One-to-many relationship*

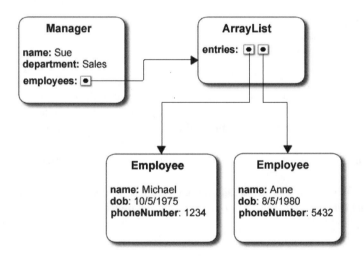

Figure 4-10. *Object graph for the one-to-many relationship example*

Many-to-Many Relationships

A many-to-many relationship would be required in a situation where an Employee can be assigned to several different Projects, while each Project team consists of several Employees. This type of relationship, which is only possible in a relational database if a separate join table is used, is more straightforward in an object database. Each object simply stores a set of OIDs for the related objects. In ODL, you simply define set relationships in each class, as shown in Listing 4-6.

Listing 4-6. *Definitions of Project and Employee Classes in ODL*

```
class Project
{
    attribute string name;
    attribute string costCode;
    relationship set<Employee> employees
        inverse Employee :: projects;
}

class Employee
{
    attribute string name;
    attribute string dob;
    attribute string phoneNumber;
    relationship set<Project> projects
        inverse Project :: employees;
}
```

With db4o, the application class definitions again form the database schema. In this case the inverse relationship may be useful, but it is still not strictly necessary, and the decision on its inclusion will be dictated by the required navigability. For example, if you are only likely to need to find the Employees for a given Project, and never the Projects for a given Employee, then there is no need for an Employee object to store OIDs of related Project objects. There is still a many-to-many relationship, as several Projects can store the OID of the same Employee among their set of OIDs.

The relationships are again defined by attributes that are references to collection objects. As before, the collection objects are stored in db4o as objects with their own OIDs, as shown in Listing 4-7.

Listing 4-7. *Definitions of Project and Employee classes in C#*

```
public class Project
{
    private ArrayList _employees;
    // remaining code omitted
}

public class Employee
```

```
{
    private ArrayList _projects;
    // remaining code omitted
}
```

Figure 4-11 shows the object graph for an example of a many-to-many relationship with inverse relationships, while Figure 4-12 shows the contents of a db4o database with these objects stored. There are two Employees, both of whom are assigned to the same two Projects. Each Employee object stores the OID of an ArrayList, which in turn stores the OIDs of the two Projects. Similarly, each Project stores the OID of an ArrayList, which stores the OIDs of these two Employees. There are thus four separate ArrayList objects.

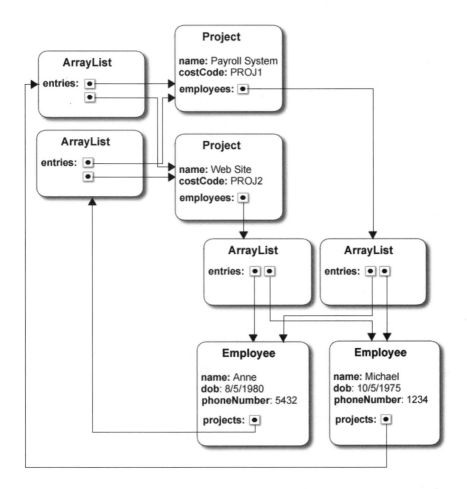

Figure 4-11. *An object graph illustrating a many-to-many relationship with inverses*

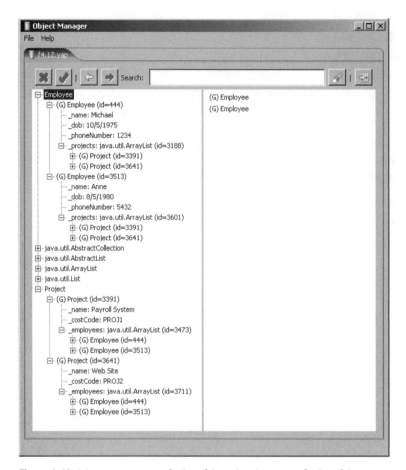

Figure 4-12. *Many-to-many relationship using inverse relationships*

As was the case for simple inverse relationships, it is the responsibility of the application to ensure that the relationships are correctly maintained.

Note that the object graph contains circular references. In fact, you can traverse relationships starting from any object on this graph to reach any object, including the one you started with. The implication of this is that you only need to select one object to store in the database, and the entire object graph will be stored!

Figure 4-13 shows the contents of a database that is similar, except that the class definition for Employee does not contain a collection of Projects. The Employee objects do not therefore store any OIDs of Projects. The information stored here is exactly the same as in Figure 4-12: it is just the navigability that is more restricted.

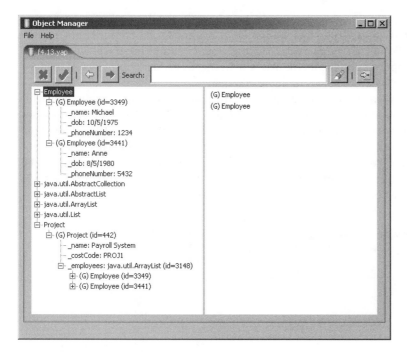

Figure 4-13. *Many-to-many relationship without inverse relationships*

Inheritance

Inheritance is a key concept of the object-oriented paradigm. As you saw in Chapter 3, inheritance is difficult for a relational database to handle because the concept doesn't exist in the relational model. However, because the object data model is so closely related to the object-oriented model, object databases must support inheritance.

In ODL you can specify in a class declaration that it implement an interface or extend a superclass. In Listing 4-8, the Employee class implements an interface Person, while the Manager class extends Employee. Therefore, in this example Manager is a specialized kind of Employee.

Listing 4-8. *Definitions of Employee and Manager Classes with Inheritances in ODL*

```
class Employee : Person
{
    attribute string name;
    attribute string dob;
    attribute string phoneNumber;
}

class Manager extends Employee
{
    attribute string department;
}
```

With db4o, the application class definitions again form the database schema. These must follow the application language rules for inheritance. In Java and C#, inheritance from multiple superclasses is not allowed, although a class can implement multiple interfaces. ODL, on the other hand, does support multiple inheritance, which it needs to do as it provides a language binding for C++, which likewise allows multiple inheritance.

Figure 4-14 shows a database containing objects from an inheritance hierarchy, which has Employee as a superclass, and two subclasses Manager and Worker. Note the extent of the classes, as indicated by the branches of object tree displayed in the ObjectManager. The extent of the Employee class contains three objects: an Employee, a Manager, and a Worker. This reflects the substitutability of the objects. Any action that can be performed with an Employee can also be performed with a Manager or Worker. The extent of each of the Manager and Worker classes is restricted to the single object of that specific type which exists in the database.

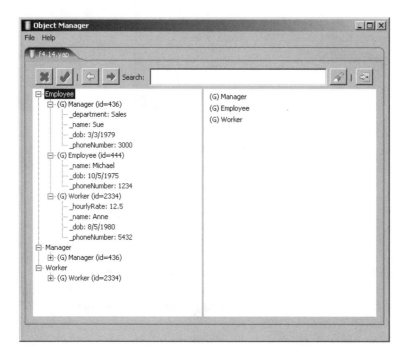

Figure 4-14. *An inheritance hierarchy represented in the ObjectManager*

When an object is an instance of a class that lies deeper in an inheritance hierarchy, then each level in the hierarchy has an extent within the database. Look at the examples (Figures 4-9 and 4-12) that include an ArrayList in the database. The database has an extent for each of the classes (AbstractCollection, AbstractList) in the hierarchy.

Indexing

The performance of relational database queries can often be improved by asking the database to create an index containing a limited amount of the information in each record in a particular table. Each index is usually stored in a suitable data structure such as a B-tree, which supports fast searching.

Object databases can use indexing in pretty much the same way—the idea of an index is not specific to the relational model. db4o allows you specify a field or fields of a class that the database should index. Indexing will de described in more detail in Chapter 12.

Queries

The ability to retrieve data using queries is a fundamental database capability. The success of relational databases is based on the availability of a query language, SQL, which is largely standard, relatively easy to use and well suited to ad hoc queries. Object databases need to provide an equivalent capability.

As you saw in Chapter 1, a basic query capability can be provided in the form of "query-by-example." This is simple—you just create an example object, perhaps with the search field value specified and the others unspecified, and ask the database to give you all matching objects. This approach is sometimes all you need, and is supported by db4o, but it doesn't come close to matching the power of SQL. Something a bit more sophisticated is needed. In this section we look at the ODMG query language, OQL, and briefly compare this with the native query capability of db4o. Queries in db4o will be examined in much more detail in Chapter 6.

What Do You Get from a Query?

A SQL query on a relational database gives you a row cursor on an essentially tabular record set. This is convenient if you want to view the results as a table, or if you want to step through them one record at a time. It's not so good if you want to get some objects that your application can use. To get to that point, you need to step through the record set and use the values in each row to construct an object instance. If your objects are structured, you may have to run more than one query to get the data you need to assemble them. For example, to find a specific Manager object with the associated Employee objects, you would need to run two SQL queries: one to find the Manager, the other to find the Employees.

An object database query works differently. A query is able to return to your application an object reference, which can be either a single object reference or a list, depending on how many objects matched the query parameters. The query may return that object fully formed—in other words, you get the object and all associated objects. In this situation, the query result consists of the specified object and all other objects that can be reached by traversing relationships in the object graph. For example, for the object graph in Figure 4-10, a query that retrieves the Manager object will also retrieve the ArrayList and the Employee objects. The way queries work reflects the close match between the data model and the application object model, which is not the case with a relational database.

This can save a lot of coding effort and minimize potential for coding errors. However, it should be handled with care when your object model contains very deep object structures or circular references. For example, if you look at the object graph in Figure 4-11 it is clear that retrieving any one object will cause all the objects in the object graph to be retrieved (remember that we said that storing one object causes all the others to be stored—the same thing applies for retrieval). This would be okay for the small number of objects shown in the figure, but would be undesirable in a more realistic situation—you want to get one Manager and her small team, but you end up loading the whole company into your application memory.

There are two ways to resolve this problem in db4o. First, you can design your model so that the problem doesn't arise (which may limit your ability to query the data the way you want). Second, you can control the *activation depth*, so that there is a limit on how many object references will be followed when retrieving or activating objects.

■**Note** An *active* object is one for which a corresponding object has been instantiated in memory. The database maintains the connection between live object references and active objects in the database. An object that has been stored in or retrieved from the database is active for the duration of the current transaction (a brief description of transactions can be found later in this chapter). It is quite possible to create more than one reference to a single stored object, as described in the discussion of equivalence earlier in this chapter. Object activation in db4o will be described in detail in Chapters 7 and 10.

To summarize this, a SQL query gives you a tabular record set that can be manipulated or displayed in a variety of ways by a variety of tools, while an object query can give you objects ready to use, but that are only meaningful to an application that understands those objects.

OQL

The ODMG standard for databases includes an Object Query Language (OQL), which was an attempt to emulate the widespread acceptance of SQL, and tries to provide similar capabilities. Like SQL, OQL is a declarative language. Declarative programming involves the creation of a set of conditions that describe a solution, but leaves the interpretation of the specific steps needed to arrive at that solution up to an interpreter. This contrasts with the imperative programming of C# or Java, which requires the programmer to provide a list of instructions to execute in a specified order.

For example, to retrieve all Employees who live in San Jose, for a scenario like Figure 4-7, the query looks like this:

```
SELECT e FROM Employee e WHERE e.address.city = "San Jose"
```

Although this looks at first glance like SQL, there are a couple of key differences. First, as described earlier, the result e is an object. Second, the content of the WHERE clause specifies a field to be matched using dot notation that represents navigation through object references to find the city field of the Address object associated with the Employee.

OQL can be used to give data that resembles tables of values, by specifying fields in the query, for example:

```
SELECT e.name, e.address.street FROM Employee e
WHERE e.address.city = "San Jose"
```

Some ODMG databases have provided graphical ad hoc query tools using OQL. The db4o graphical tool, the ObjectManager, queries navigationally.

SQL has the keywords INSERT and UPDATE—OQL does not have equivalents for these. Unlike SQL it only works for retrieving data. You need to store objects by calling appropriate methods in the database's language binding.

Probably the most important role played by OQL now is as a basis for persistence code that is independent of the nature of the actual data store. Object-relational mapping frameworks such as Hibernate, Castor, and Java Data Objects (JDO) use OQL or similar query languages to retrieve data as objects, usually from relational databases (with a lot of work being done in the background, of course).

Native Queries

The Native Queries feature in db4o is, as you saw in Chapter 1, a mechanism for type-safe queries that are entirely written in the application's programming language, with no declarative code leading to the embedding of strings with the program. With native queries, the query mechanism is integrated into the programming language. All the database actions (storing, retrieving, updating) are done in a consistent way with native method calls. Like other object database queries, native queries return objects ready to use in your application.

Currently, db4o is the only database to offer native query support. However, the idea of separating the query language from the data store is attractive—you write your application, and then you can plug in a different kind of database by changing only one line of code. JDO offers this capability—there are JDO implementations for many databases, including relational and object databases. Native queries offer the potential to extend this capability to provide type-safe querying of any kind of database and also of in-memory objects. This integration of querying and language offers great potential for the future.

Chapter 6 of this book covers db4o queries, and the Native Queries mechanism in particular, in detail.

Transactions and Concurrency

A database transaction is a unit of interaction that is treated in a coherent and reliable way independent of other transactions. Transactions must be either entirely completed or they must be aborted. The ability to handle transactions allows the user to ensure that the integrity of the database is maintained.

A single transaction might require several operations, each reading and/or writing information in the database. When this happens, it is usually important to be sure that the database is not left with only some of the operations carried out. For example, when doing a money transfer, if the money was debited from one account, it is important that it also be credited to the depositing account. Also, transactions should not interfere with each other. Transactions are particularly important when many users are accessing a database concurrently.

A simple transaction works like this:

1. Begin the transaction.

2. Execute several operations (although any updates to the database aren't actually committed permanently to the database yet).

3. Commit the transaction (updates are committed if the transaction is successful).

If one of the operations fails, the database may roll back. Rolling back returns the database to the state before the start of the transaction, as if none of the operations had taken place.

Transactions are not a function of the data model, so an object database can support transactions in much the same way as any other database. Just like any other DBMS, db4o provides a transaction mechanism and handles concurrent users. These issues will be dealt with in more detail in Chapters 8 and 9.

Summary

In this final chapter of Part I we looked at the basics and terminology of object databases. In doing so we contrasted db4o with databases that follow the ODMG standard, showing that db4o adheres much more closely to the object model familiar to .NET and Java programmers. We saw that object identity is a fundamental OODBMS concept that underpins the way that relationships between entities are represented, and we learned how object databases deal with key database capabilities such as querying and concurrency.

Part II builds on the concepts that have been introduced so far, and takes a detailed "hands-on" approach to the use of db4o, from installing and getting started all the way through to taking advantage of its advanced features.

PART II

Working with db4o

In Part I you were introduced to object orientation with a focus on its role in object-oriented databases. In Part II we formally introduce db4o, showing you how to perform queries and transactions, handle complex objects, use the client/server mode, configure replication, use db4o reflection, extend db4o using pluggable interfaces, and a lot more.

CHAPTER 5

■■■

Quick Start

The aim of this chapter is to show you how to get up and running very quickly with db4o, and to introduce some of the basic techniques you need to use it. You should be able to install db4o, and in just a few minutes create a simple standalone application that stores and retrieves some objects. The techniques described in this chapter illustrate the standard database operations: create, read, update, and delete. Once you know how to do these operations, you will want to go on to explore the other features that db4o offers.

C# or Java?

Before you can start using db4o, you need to decide what version to use. Your decision depends on the language and platform you want to use for your application. db4o provides native persistence for .NET and Java objects, so you can use several languages, such as C#, Java, and all .NET managed languages, including VB.NET, ASP.NET, Boo, and Managed C++. There are three distinct versions of db4o available: one for .NET, one for Java, and one for Mono (the Mono project offers cross-platform support for .NET and C#). In this book, we will focus on both C# and Java. db4o supports both of these languages in a very similar manner, which is perhaps not surprising as the languages themselves have many similarities. In fact, the similarities are so broad that you can even download a converter that will translate one language to the other. You can find one of the most popular such converters at http://msdn.microsoft.com/vstudio/downloads/tools/jlca, which is available as a plug-in for Microsoft Visual Studio and converts Java to C# quite reliably.

db4o was originally developed when C# hadn't yet been released, so it has a strong Java heritage. However, interest in C# and the .NET environment has grown rapidly, and so db4objects now puts a lot of effort into keeping the two versions as close and feature-equivalent as possible.

In the examples found throughout Part II of this book we try to do the same. C# and Java code listings are provided, except in cases where the code is absolutely identical in the two languages. In some cases the difference is simply the case notation supported by the db4o methods: *PascalCase* in C# and *camelCase* in Java. For example, the method that is named OpenFile in C# is named openFile in the Java version. These notations follow the common practices used by programmers in the respective languages.

■**Caution** .NET versions prior to 5.0 do not support PascalCase notation for db4o method names. db4objects recommends that new .NET users adopt PascalCase, while existing users may choose to retain camelCase.

The main language differences that arise in the examples are:

- `import`/`using` to include libraries

- `namespace`/`package` to qualify the name of the class

- Inheritance syntax

- PascalCase/camelCase notation differences

- C# properties/Java getters and setters

- C# delegates (see Chapter 6)

- Differences in collections API classes (see Chapter 7)

- Event handling

Of course, if you don't want or need to know about the differences, you can simply look at the examples in your own langauge.

Installing db4o

In this section you'll learn how to install db4o and tailor the configuration for both C# and Java, and for different IDEs. The installation is very simple and requires only that you run an installer or unzip or double-click an archive, depending on which version you are using.

You can find a link to the db4o Product Test Drive on the db4objects.com home page, `www.db4objects.com`. Clicking this link allows you to download the current release of db4o. You can choose the appropriate version for your development platform. Note that the Java version will run on any Java-enabled platform, including Windows and Linux. The .NET version is for Windows only, and is available in separate forms that support .NET 1.1 and .NET 2.0, respectively. Separate Mono versions are provided for Windows and Linux.

Let's have a look at the db4o folders:

- A `doc` folder that contains the API documentation as HTML or a Microsoft Compressed HTML Help (CHM) file, and also a useful interactive tutorial that allows you to run live examples in an applet. The tutorial, which is also provided as a PDF file, contains a wealth of examples that complement those in this book.

- The `dll` (.NET) or `lib` (Java) folder, which includes the db4o DLLs or JARs. Different libraries are provided to work with different platform versions, for example, .NET Framework or Compact Framework, or Java 1.4 or 5.0.

- The `src` folder, which includes the full db4o source code along with some tools that you might find useful.

If you go to the Download Center on the db4objects website, you can also download the ObjectManager graphical object database browser, which you have already seen in Chapter 4. A guide to getting started with the ObjectManager is given later in this chapter. To get to the Download Center, you need to follow the Free Resources link and register—this is well worth doing, as you will find further useful material there, including community forums and a knowledge base.

■**Note** All examples in this book are based on version 5.2 of db4o, which was the most recent version at the time of writing.

Installing db4o for C#

Using C# in conjunction with db4o requires that the appropriate .NET Framework be installed. Installing Microsoft Visual Studio should automatically install the .NET Framework and Compact Framework (version 1.1 with VS 2003, version 2.0 with VS 2005). Note that the examples in this book will also run in the free Visual C# 2005 Express Edition.

Alternatively, you can use the popular and free #develop IDE, which can be downloaded from www.icsharpcode.net/OpenSource/SD. In this case, you need to install the .NET Framework 1.1 or later, which can be downloaded from www.microsoft.com, before installing the IDE.

If you are using Mono, you must install the Mono libraries, and you will probably want to use the MonoDevelop IDE.

The .NET/Windows distribution of db4o provides an .msi archive. This can be installed by either double-clicking the archive or using the command prompt to extract to a location you specify, as shown here:

```
C:\DOWNLOAD\db4oNET>msiexec /a "C:\DOWNLOAD\db4oNET\db4o-5.2-net.msi" /qn ➥
TARGETDIR="C:\DOWNLOAD\INSTALL"
```

If you double-click on the .msi icon to start the installation, then you are also able to set the installation directory folder for db4o.

The Mono distribution for Windows gives you a .zip archive, which you simply extract to a location of your choice. Mono for Linux distributions are available as RPMs or as a .tar.gz archive, which you should extract to your chosen installation directory.

Using db4o in a C# Project

To start using db4o, you simply include a reference to db4o.dll in your project. The .NET distribution contains two DLL files with the same name, one in a folder called net inside the dll folder, the other in a folder called compact. The former is the library for use with the standard .NET Framework, while the latter is the Compact Framework library.

The screenshots in this section show a reference being added in #develop, but the steps required are very similar in the other .NET IDEs. If you know how to add a reference in a project in your IDE, then you know how to include db4o.

To add the reference in #develop, right-click on the References node in your project and select the Add Reference menu item (see Figure 5-1). You will then see the Add Reference dialog box, which allows you to add the db4o.dll to the project (see Figure 5-2).

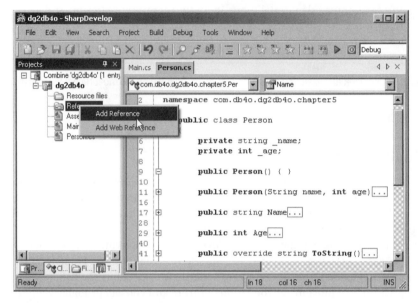

Figure 5-1. *Adding a reference to your C# project in #develop*

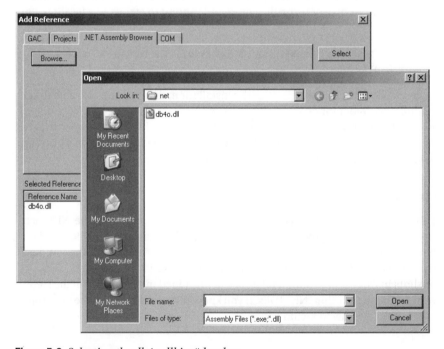

Figure 5-2. *Selecting the db4o.dll in #develop*

Installing db4o for Java

You need to make sure you have Java Runtime Environment installed. We recommend that you use Java 5.0 if possible. Many of the examples in this book use language features, such as generics and the enhanced for loop, which were introduced in Java 5.0. However, db4o provides good support for Java versions from 1.2 on.

The cross-platform Java distribution of db4o gives you a .zip archive, which you simply extract to a location of your choice.

Using db4o in a Java Project

To begin using db4o, you simply include add the appropriate JAR file to your classpath, or add it as a library to a project in an IDE. You can use db4o with any Java IDE. The procedure described that follows shows this for Eclipse, but the steps required are very similar in the other Java IDEs. If you are using NetBeans or IDEA, for example, you will know how to add libraries in your own IDE.

If you are using Eclipse, you'll have to complete the following steps, as shown in Figure 5-3:

1. Open the project Properties dialog box by right-clicking on your project in the Package Explorer pane and selecting Properties.

2. Select Java Build Path on the left and click the Libraries tab.

3. Finally, add the JAR by clicking the Add External JARs button and browsing to find the db4o JAR in the directory where you installed it.

Be careful to select the right JAR file for the version of Java you are using. For example, db4o-5.2-java5.jar supports Java 5.0.

As soon as the classpath is set to your JAR location, you are ready to create your first db4o database—by simply storing an object.

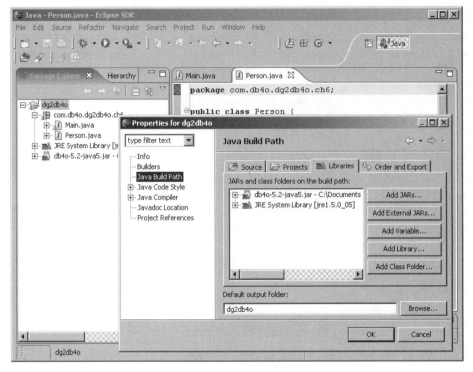

Figure 5-3. *Adding the db4o JAR to a Java project in Eclipse*

Running db4o

If you are coming to db4o with previous experience of typical RDBMSs like MySQL or Oracle, your first thoughts at this point are probably something like:

- How do I create the database?

- How do I start the database?

A database management system usually runs as a daemon or service and provides tools to allow the administrator to define and maintain database schemata, and to manage users, roles, and views. Applications usually interact with the database in a client/server model.

With db4o, the simple answer to both questions is: *you don't*. To understand the reasons for this, think about the most common use case for this kind of database. db4objects Inc. mostly targets the embedded database market, which means that db4o will typically be bundled as a library with your application code. It is often installed on standalone clients, which may have no constant connection to any server. db4o is not unique in working in this mode: there are several other relational databases, including H2 and Hypersonic (HSQLDB), which are mostly used in the same way. The difference is, of course, that db4o is an object database.

db4o can, like H2 and HSQLDB, also be used in a client/server mode, so it can in fact be started as a server. We will explain how to use db4o in the client/server mode in Chapter 8. For now, we will stick to using it in standalone mode. You can learn a great deal about db4o by using it in this mode, and this is probably the most common way in which it is used in applications at present.

Creating the Database

A db4o database is contained in a single file. If you are running db4o in the standalone mode, then you don't create a database in advance. Instead, with a single line of code, you obtain a handle to a database; this handle is then used to perform operations. The handle is actually an object reference of the db4o API type `ObjectContainer`. You get the handle by calling a static method `OpenFile` of the `Db4o` class, specifying the path to the file as a parameter. If the specified file doesn't exist, then it is created for you as a new database; otherwise, a handle to an existing database is returned. Often, for brevity, we talk about this procedure as "opening an `ObjectContainer`," which is a nicely descriptive, if not completely accurate, phrase.

Thereafter, you can benefit from one of the key advantages of native object databases as you simply store your object with no additional effort. The database and its schema are created "on the fly" for you. The database schema is simply your class definition. The great benefit of this approach is that you don't need to worry about creating tables and working out object-relational mappings. Instead, you can start storing your objects immediately.

This is fine in standalone applications. The disadvantage if you are running in client/server mode is that multiple clients using this database will usually need to have the class definitions in their classpaths. This is in turn the advantage of relational databases, where you can write different applications with different object models, which map onto the relational data model of the database.

Starting the Database

In standalone mode you don't actually need to start the database—you simply open the database file. However, there are some implications you should keep in mind when working in standalone mode:

- Since you didn't start the database, you don't need to stop it, although you do need to release the handle by closing the `ObjectContainer`.

- You don't need to connect to the database. You simply store your objects. This means that no username or password is required. Passwords may be required in client/server mode, as discussed in Chapter 8.

- New database files are created using your filesytem permissions. In standalone mode, it is likely that only you are using the database file. However, multiple clients can potentially use a database file. In this case, you have to ensure that the group permissions are set correctly for write or read-only access; db4o also directly supports the option to open an `ObjectContainer` for read-only access (see Chapter 10).

In client/server mode, db4o usage is much more conventional, and you need to consider issues like starting and stopping a server and user authentication. However, the basic database operations are identical regardless of the database mode. In the remainder of this chapter, you will see how those operations are done, while the following two chapters go further and deal with advanced queries and handling complex objects—these techniques are also independent of the operating mode.

db4o Basics

In this section you will learn to create a very simple application capable of storing, restoring, modifying, and deleting objects in a database. Later you will be able to inspect this database using the ObjectManager.

Storing Objects

Before we can do anything useful with db4o, we need to define a class. We can use the very simple Person class, shown in Listing 5-1 in C# and Java. The Person class has two attributes: a constructor and a ToString method.

Listing 5-1. *The Person Class in C# and Java*

```
// C#
using System;
namespace com.db4o.dg2db4o.chapter5
{
    public class Person
    {
        private string _name;
        private int _age;

        public Person() { }

         get{ return name; }

        public Person(String name, int age)
        {
            _name = name;
            _age = age;
        }

        public string Name
        {
            get
            {
                return _name;
            }
            set{
            {
                _name = value; }
            }
        }
    }
```

```
        public int Age
        {
            get {
            {
                return _age; }
            }
            set {
            {
                _age = value };
            }
        }

        public override string ToString()
        {
            return "[" + Name + ";" + Age + "]";
        }
    }
}


package com.db4o.dg2db4o.chapter5;

public class Person
{
    private String _name;
    private int _age;

    public Person(){}

    public Person(String name, int age)
    {
        _name = name;
        _age = age;
    }

    public int getAge()
    {
        return _age;
    }

    public void setAge(int value)
    {
        _age = value;
    }
```

```
    public String getName()
    {
        return _name;
    }

    public void setName(String value)
    {
        _name = value;
    }

    public String toString()
    {
        return "[" + _name + ";"+ _age + "]";
    }
}
```

Note that the Person class, in either language, contains no db4o code. Other persistence solutions often require the inheritance of another class, the implementation of another interface, or a class file enhancement, making the development process rather tedious and tied tightly to a specific vendor's solution.

To access a database, you need to open an ObjectContainer using the following code. The string parameter in the method call is the full path to the database file that you want to create or access.

```
// C#
ObjectContainer db = Db4o.OpenFile("C:/myDb.yap");


ObjectContainer db = Db4o.OpenFile("C:/myDb.yap");
```

The static method openFile is called directly on the class Db4o. The return value of this call is the ObjectContainer reference, named db in this example, which is your handle to the database.

As you can see from this example, db4o stores the data in a file using a name and location of your choosing. This file can grow up to 256GB and will contain any data objects you choose to store. If this still isn't enough space, you can set up more database files and put different classes in different files. This gives you virtually unlimited storage space.

If the database file you named does not exist, it will be created for you. If the database file already exists, it will be reopened for your access. For testing purposes, you might want to place the database in a known state before running your tests—for example, within a suite of unit tests. A very simple way to do this is to delete the database before running the test, which can be done by calling the method File.Delete("C:/myDb.yap") in C# or new File ("C:/myDb.yap").delete() in Java.

Now let's create and store an object:

```
// C#
Person p = new Person("Gandhi",42);
db.Set(p);
```

```
// JAVA
Person p = new Person("Gandhi", 79);
db.set(p);
```

That's it. Nothing more. This object is assigned an internal object ID (OID), the value of which is not important for now, and is stored in the file you named. If you open the file in a text editor, you may be able to see fragments of the object's representation in the database.

Closing the Database

It is important to make sure you close the `ObjectContainer` by calling `db.Close()`. This ends the transaction that began when you opened the `ObjectContainer`. It causes all database operations to be written to the database and closes the database properly. A common problem arises when an exception occurs and the database file is not properly closed. This can leave the database in a locked state, which leads to a "database locked" exception upon reopening the database file. In this case, you will also lose any data stored since the beginning of the transaction.

To avoid this kind of problem, you should take care that all your operations are enclosed in a `try`/`catch` block, with a call to `Close` in a corresponding `finally` block.

■**Note** The data you store with a call to `Set` is not actually written to the database immediately: it is stored at end of the transaction. db4o provides further features for committing and rolling back transactions—these are described in Chapter 9.

Retrieving Objects

The ability to selectively retrieve data by querying is a key feature of any database. The basic query mechanism provided by db4o is known as query-by-example (QBE). Let's see how to use it to retrieve the object that has just been stored.

Using QBE, you create an example, or template, object of the class you want to look up. You then set the values of the attribute (or attributes) you want to use as search criteria—all other attributes are left with null values, or zero values in the case of numerical primitives. To execute the query, you call the Get method of the ObjectContainer, specifying the template object as the method parameter. The query returns a collection that holds all the objects that match the attribute pattern you provided.

To make things a little bit more realistic, we will first add another object to the database:

```
// C#
db.Set(new Person("Lincoln",46));  // Later we correct Lincoln's age to 56...
```

```
db.set(new Person("Lincoln",46));
```

The following code sets up a template Person object. Let's assume we want to find Mahatma Gandhi's age. To achieve this, we fill the template object with the appropriate Name attribute and pass it to the Get method:

```
// C#
Person p = new Person(); // Java
p.Name = "Gandhi";
ObjectSet res = db.Get(p);
while(res.HasNext())
    Console.WriteLine(res.Next()); // followed by Commit and Close
```

```
Person p = new Person();
p.setName("Gandhi");
ObjectSet result = (ObjectSet) db.get(p);
while (result.hasNext()) {
    System.out.println((Person) result.next()); // followed by commit and close
```

This shows that the Get call returns a reference to an ObjectSet. ObjectSet is a db4o API class that behaves like a classical Iterator/(I)Enumeration. Using the HasNext and Next methods, you can obtain all the objects in the database that have matched your template object. The output will now be

```
[Gandhi;79]
```

Note that the ToString method of the Person class specifies exactly what is output for each object returned by the query. Incidentally, you should make sure you never call Next twice before calling HasNext, or you will bypass some data.

To achieve a better code readability, we can define a ListResult method that simply prints out all the objects contained in the ObjectSet:

```
// C#
private void ListResult(ObjectSet result)
{
    while(result.HasNext())
        Console.WriteLine(result.Next());
}
```

```
public static void listResult(ObjectSet result)
{
    while (result.hasNext())
        System.out.println(result.next());
}
```

With this definition, the query example is simplified to:

```
// C#
Person p = new Person();
p.Name = "Gandhi";
ObjectSet res = db.Get(p);
ListResult(res);
```

```
Person p = new Person();
p.setName("Gandhi");
ObjectSet result = (ObjectSet) db.get(p);
listResult(res);
```

If you need to retrieve all objects of a specific class, you can provide null values for the template object by using the default constructor, or by setting the default values explicitly:

```
// C# & JAVA
Person p1 = new Person(null,0);  // or
Person p2 = new Person();
```

Furthermore if you run a query specifying a null object as the template object, you will get a collection of all objects in the database.

■**Note** Since db4o version 4.6, the ObjectSet interface implements several superinterfaces such as IList, ICollection, and IEnumerable in C#, and java.util.Collection, java.lang.Iterable, java.util.Iterator, and java.util.List in Java. This implies that you have a wide range of methods available to handle your results. For example, if your database contains the two persons Gandhi and Lincoln, you can use the ObjectSet returned to apply, for example, the Java List method subList(1,2) to retrieve a subset of the list. Furthermore, sorting is quite simple using the Sort methods provided by C# and Java collections.

You have now seen a simple example of querying. db4o supports two additional query mechanisms that provide the capability to perform much more sophisticated queries. These will be discussed in Chapter 6.

Updating Objects

To update an object you simply retrieve it, make the required changes, and call Set again to store the modified object.

In the following example we modify Abraham Lincoln's age:

```
// C#
ObjectSet result = (ObjectSet) db.Get(new Person("Lincoln", 0));
Person lincoln = (Person) result.Next();
lincoln.Age = 56;
db.Set(lincoln);
```

```
ObjectSet result = (ObjectSet) db.get(new Person("Lincoln", 0));
Person lincoln = (Person) result.next();
lincoln.setAge(56);
db.set(lincoln);
```

If you were to now query again, you would find Lincoln's age to be set to 56 in the database.

Actually, the process is a bit subtler than this example suggests. The result of the query is that a Person object is created in memory, and db4o uses IDs to maintain a connection between the in-memory object and the equivalent object stored in the database. It does this by caching the db4o OID as a weak reference. This connection is maintained only until the database is closed.

To update an object in the database, you need to have a fresh reference in memory that is connected to the database object (see the Caution that follows). This can be obtained by querying as already described. Alternatively, creating a new object and calling Set has a similar effect—the in-memory object is connected to a new database object. This means that you can, if you wish, store a new object and update it immediately afterward.

To do the update, you call Set for the modified object, and db4o will automatically find and update this object in the database as the Java/C# and db4o IDs match.

▪**Caution** Make sure that you have stored or retrieved the object within the same transaction (i.e., since the ObjectContainer was last opened) before your update. If not, db4o will assume that this is a new object, not one that has been stored previously. The result will be to clone Abraham Lincoln in the database with different ages (and different OIDs), which is probably prohibited by the U.S. Constitution! db4o does not provide primary keys to prevent duplicate Lincolns being stored.

Deleting Objects

As you have seen, updating an object and saving an object are similar in that they use the same ObjectContainer method. While deleting an object requires a different method, the basic idea is similar. You simply retrieve the object and call the Delete method of the ObjectContainer. As was the case for updating, the database has to know what object you want to delete, so the object to be deleted either has to be set (which doesn't make much sense in this case), or more likely retrieved within the same transaction.

Let's assume we want to delete the first Person object from the database:

```
// C#
ObjectSet result = (ObjectSet) db.Get(new Person());
Person p = (Person) result.Next();
db.Delete(p);
```

```
ObjectSet result = (ObjectSet) db.get(new Person());
Person p = (Person) result.next();
db.delete(p);
```

If you then query the database for all Person objects and list the results, you find only one object, either Lincoln or Gandhi, depending on exactly how they were stored. Alternatively, you can easily query for a specific object, for example by specifying that you want the object with the name Gandhi, and then delete that target object.

Startup Options

Before you start working with the ObjectContainer, you have a wide range of options for configuring the database and the container itself to suit your application. db4o's configuration features will be described in detail in Chapter 10. To get a flavor of this, here are a few useful items you might consider configuring now:

- A call to Db4o.main prints the version of db4o you are currently running (e.g., db4o 5.2.004) to the console. This can also be done by outputting the value of Db4o.version().

- Customers who have licensed db4o might need to pass an email address in order to use the database: Db4o.LicensedTo("ray@charles.com").

- A call Db4o.configure().MessageLevel(int level) provides a simple db4o logging. It supports the four logging levels shown in Table 5-1.

Table 5-1. *db4o Logging Levels*

db4o Logging Levels	Description
0	No messages
1	Open and close messages
2	Messages for new, update, and delete
3	Messages for activate and deactivate

If you save an object with message level 2 or 3 configured, you will see output like this, which shows the db4o database object ID:

```
396 new com.db4o.dg2db4o.chapter5 Person
```

A Complete Example

The next example contains everything we have covered in this chapter in one simple console application. Note that the majority of examples in the book are console applications, as this is the simplest way to try out and learn about db4o's API and capabilities.

In this example, two Person objects are stored; then they both are retrieved from the database and the age of one Person is updated. Finally, that Person is deleted from the database.

```csharp
//C#
using System;
using System.IO;
using com.db4o;

namespace com.db4o.dg2db4o.chapter5;
{
    public class CompleteExample
    {
        public static void Main(string[] args)
        {
            File.Delete("C:/complete.yap"); // reset database
            Db4o.Configure().MessageLevel(0); // 0=silent, 3=loud
            ObjectContainer db = Db4o.OpenFile("C:/complete.yap");
            try {
            {
                db.Set(new Person("Gandhi", 79));
                db.Set(new Person("Lincoln", 56));
                ObjectSet result = (ObjectSet) db.Get(new Person());
                ListResult(result); // get all

                Person p = new Person();
                p.Name = "Gandhi";
                ObjectSet result2 = (ObjectSet) db.Get(p);
                Person p2 = (Person) result2.Next();
                p2.Age = 90; // Increase Gandhi's age again
                result2.Reset(); // reset the ObjectSet cursor
                ListResult(result2);

                db.Delete(p2); // Remove the Gandhi dataset
                ObjectSet result3 = (ObjectSet) db.Get(new Person());
                ListResult(result3); // get all
                Console.ReadLine();
            }
```

```
            finally {
            {
                db.Close();
            }
        }

        private static void ListResult(ObjectSet res){
        {
            while(res.HasNext())
            {
                Console.WriteLine(res.Next());
            }
            Console.WriteLine ("---------------");
        }
    }
}


package com.db4o.dg2db4o.chapter5;

import java.io.File;
import com.db4o.Db4o;
import com.db4o.ObjectContainer;
import com.db4o.ObjectSet;

public class CompleteExample
{
    public static void main(String[] args)
    {
        new File("C:/complete.yap").delete();  // reset the database
        Db4o.configure().messageLevel(0); // 0=silent, 3=loud
        ObjectContainer db = Db4o.openFile("C:/complete.yap");
        try
        {
            db.set(new Person("Gandhi", 79));
            db.set(new Person("Lincoln", 56));
            ObjectSet result = (ObjectSet) db.get(new Person());
            listResult(result); // get all

            Person p = new Person();
            p.setName("Gandhi");
            ObjectSet result2 = (ObjectSet) db.get(p);
            Person p2 = (Person) result2.next();
            p2.setAge(90); // Increase Gandhi's age
            result2.reset();
            listResult(result2);
```

```
            db.delete(p2); // Remove the Gandhi object
            ObjectSet result3 = (ObjectSet) db.get(new Person());
            listResult(result3); // get all
        }
        finally
        {
            db.close();
        }
    }

    public static void listResult(ObjectSet result)
    {
        while (result.hasNext())
        {
            System.out.println(result.next());
        }
        System.out.println("---------------");
    }
}
```

The output should look like this:

```
[Lincoln;56]
[Gandhi;79]
---------------
[Gandhi;90]
---------------
[Lincoln;56]
---------------
```

Getting Started with the ObjectManager

Many database users prefer to use a graphical database administration tool such as MySQL Administrator or TOAD (www.toadsoft.com) rather than relying on the command line. db4o also provides a graphical tool for browsing, running queries, and editing primitive types, known simply as the ObjectManager. This section gives a brief overview of using the ObjectManager, while a fuller guide can be found in Appendix A.

The db4o administration tool is a little different from most, because managing tables strongly differs from managing objects. Most developers are used to browsing tables, but browsing huge object tree structures is a new experience for most of us.

The ObjectManager is a Java application, but through the magic of something that db4objects calls the *generic reflector*, it can also browse databases containing .NET objects. ObjectManager is available for download from the Download Center area of the db4objects website. The download consists of a zip archive, which contains a folder called `lib`, as shown in Figure 5-4, which in turn contains the libraries that make up the application. For use in Windows environments, there is also a simple `.bat` script that starts a class from the `objectmanager.jar`. On Linux you have to make sure that the bin directory of your JDK is in your path, and then run the application with the command `java -jar objectmanager.jar`.

Figure 5-4. *The ObjectManager directory after you extract the zip file contents*

■Note Currently there is no Windows `.exe` version of the ObjectManager. If you really wish to avoid Java, then you should have a look at `http://db4oboobrowser.sourceforge.net` for a demo or `http://sourceforge.net/projects/db4oboobrowser` for a download. This alternative db4o database browser is written in a scripting language that can be used on top of the .NET CLI.

Once you have started the ObjectManager, you can open a database using one of the following methods:

- Select File ➤ Open and choose your `.yap` file. Take care here: if you named your database using a different ending (e.g., `mydata.db`), then you need to change the file type in the file selection box.

- If you choose Open Encrypted instead, you can open an encrypted file.

- You can open a connection to a db4o database that is running in client/server mode. In this case, you need to enter authentication and host/port information. In Chapter 8 you will see how to run a db4o server.

Figure 5-5 shows the ObjectManager browsing a database created with the code in this chapter. On the left side you see all the objects in the database, just one in this case. If you have a bigger database with deep objects, you can open the object tree. If you select an entry, you will see information about that object on the right side. You can also edit the values of primitive attributes. For example, you can directly change Lincoln's age in the database.

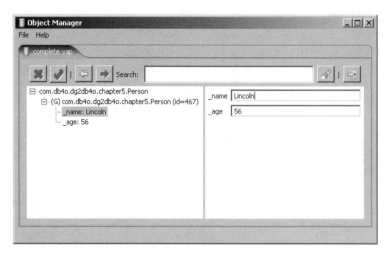

Figure 5-5. *ObjectManager showing our small example database*

Note that the objects show their database OID, which in most cases you don't need to care about. Every object is listed as a top-level object, and also as a part of the tree if it is referenced by another object.

The object in Figure 5-5 has the symbol (G) next to it, which signifies that this object was read by the generic reflector. This means that the ObjectManager doesn't have access to the original class definition. You can help the ObjectManager in displaying the object more naturally (e.g., showing the real objects IDs) by providing the original C# or Java classes. The File ➤ Preferences menu option allows you to enter either the directory or the library (.dll or .jar) files that contain the classes.

Using the ObjectManager to Query Your Objects

It can be difficult to find specific objects in a large object tree, so the ObjectManager allows you to filter the objects with queries. You can start a query using one of the following methods:

- Double-click on a top-level class in the tree view on the left side. Choosing a class deeper in the tree will do nothing.

- Click the New Query button on the very top right side.

- Choose Query from the File menu.

Each action opens a new tab that allows you to enter the query and view the results. Figure 5-6 shows an example of a query tab filtering a larger database with complex objects. You define the query by filling out fields of your class, using the symbols shown in Table 5-2 for the comparisons.

Table 5-2. *db4o ObjectManager Query Constraints*

Constraint	Description
=	Identity
id	The internal db4o object ID
>	Greater than
<	Smaller than
~	Like

To start the query just click the Run button on the upper-left side of the manager (the white arrow in the green circle). The tree view on the left shows the filtered results your query constraints have selected.

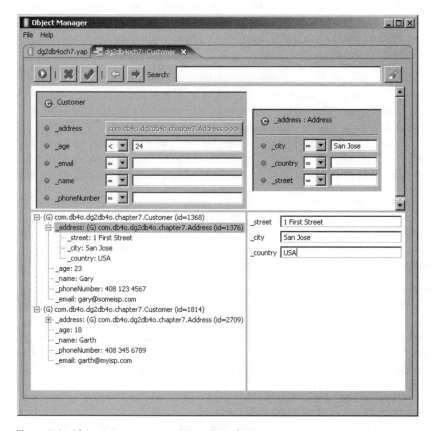

Figure 5-6. *ObjectManager running a complex query*

Troubleshooting

db4o is a relatively simple program, and there are not too many configurations that can go wrong or produce errors in your application. Nevertheless, there are some common mistakes you can make that can generally be avoided quite easily. Some of the problems you are most likely to encounter are listed here. Note that some of these issues will become clearer to you as you read the later chapters in Part II of this book.

- **db4o.jar is not in your classpath / dll not found**: This error can easily be detected when you are developing in your IDE because the compiler will simply not know the class Db4o and will in turn display error messages. A little more difficult would be the case when you don't use an IDE but where you are deploying your database solution (using db4o). In a standalone environment you would receive "class not found" messages when calling db4o methods. In an application server environment, such as Tomcat, you need to make sure that the DLL or JAR is put in the directory that the server uses for libraries.

- **The class is not in your classpath**: The objects in a database generally don't make sense to an application unless the real class (e.g., Person) appears in the classpath. The exception is the case when the generic reflector is used—as you have seen, ObjectManager can use this if it doesn't have the class files.

- **The database file is locked**: This is a common problem during development. Imagine the case where your program has a bug, and throws an unhandled exception while an ObjectContainer is open (this *will* happen to you). You correct the bug and run your program again. You get a database file locked exception. Why? It is simply because you have an old process running that has locked the database. So if you switch to the debugging mode, you can usually spot that there are old processes or threads running. Simply kill them, and restart your program in a fresh environment and the problem will disappear.

- **Changes to your class schema**: This is of course a difficult topic and will be discussed along with other advanced features in Chapter 12. Some cases of schema changes are handled quite simply, however. For example, if you add fields or remove fields, db4o ensures that you have to do nothing and can continue to work. Chapter 12 shows you how to refactor your database in more complex ways.

- **Double objects entered**: This error is very common if you are not careful. If you get an object from the database and then close the transaction, you lose the reference to the actual stored object. If you then open a new transaction on the same database file and save the in-memory object again, then you get two identical objects of the same kind. It is also possible to get similar problems in a networked environment. This means that you sometimes have to be aware of the object identity (look for getID), which is discussed in Chapters 7 and 10.

- **Objects in my object are are retrieved with null: object attributes**: A deep object is one where some attributes are themselves objects. It is possible to have a situation where you correctly retrieve your top-level object, but the object attributes are not retrieved. Chapters 7 and 10 describe the levels that determine how deep objects are stored, retrieved, and updated.

Summary

In this chapter you have learned that working with an embedded database like db4o is very different compared to working with a typical RDBMS. You don't need to create a database schema by hand, and you don't start the database. Instead, you can simply include the db4o library in your classpath, open an `ObjectContainer`, and start saving your objects, with just a few lines of code.

You have stored, retrieved, updated, and deleted objects, so you now understand the basic operations in db4o. The following chapters will guide you through the more complex topics such as advanced queries, transactions, client/server mode, and much more.

CHAPTER 6

■ ■ ■

Querying Objects

A database is only useful if you can successfully and easily retrieve data from it. Therefore, query capabilities are fundamental to any database's success. The way you define queries is very much determined by the data model. Relational databases are closely associated with their query language, SQL. Just think how many RDBMSs have "SQL" in their names—MySQL and PostgreSQL, for example. You might imagine that db4o queries are different, as its data model is different from that of a "SQL database."

In Chapter 5 you learned how to use the simple query-by-example (QBE) method to retrieve objects from a db4o database. You often need to retrieve data by selecting the items that match one or more simple criteria. For example, you might need to find the employee with a particular employee number, or find all customers called Schwarzenegger who live in California. For this type of query, which is very common, QBE is simple and effective. However, its limitations become quickly apparent as soon as you as you need to search for something like "all employees with a salary greater than $40,000," because QBE can't do anything more complex than selecting exact matches.

This would be a serious limitation if QBE were the only query mechanism provided by db4o. Fortunately, it isn't. In this chapter we will examine QBE in some additional detail, but the main focus is on the two powerful query methods that db4o provides for more advanced queries: *Simple Object Data Access* and *Native Queries*.

Simple Object Data Access (SODA) is an established query API that has been part of db4o in all but the earliest versions. It is based on the notion of a query graph. A query graph lets you specify the type of objects you want to find, and then use method calls to "descend" to and apply constraints to fields. You can build query graphs that can apply multiple constraints to express complex queries. SODA queries are fast. Writing queries using method calls can take a bit of getting used to, especially for people who are accustomed to thinking in terms of a query language like SQL, but the close correspondence between the object model and queries means that it can become a natural way to work for many developers.

A more recent, and very exciting, development is the Native Queries (NQ) feature. db4o introduced NQ support in version 5.0. A native query is a query expressed entirely in the application programming language. Native queries offer several important advantages, which are described in this chapter. The NQ mechanism is related to SODA in that db4o will optimize a native query if possible by converting it internally to a SODA query for fast execution.

db4objects, Inc., the company behind db4o, is now putting much of its effort into making NQs faster and more advanced, and they see NQ as the primary query mechanism for db4o. However, db4o will continue to support all three query mechanisms, as ultimately the decision should be left to you as to which best fits your needs. In some situations you might need fast access; in some situations you might feel comfortable with expressing queries in your own programming language. It's your choice.

Before we move on to the details, let's first get an overview of the three mechanisms (see Table 6-1).

Table 6-1. *Comparison of the db4o Query Mechanisms*

Language	Query Expression	Characteristics
QBE	Template objects	Fast, and ideal for learning. Simple but still very useful. Ideal for queries that don't need to use logical operators.
SODA	Query graphs	Build a query graph by navigating references in classes and imposing constraints. Fast, but concept can be hard to get used to.
NQ	C# or Java method	Express query in a C# or Java method by writing any code you like that returns a Boolean. db4o applies your method to all objects stored and the list of matching object instances is returned for you. The speed of execution depends on the optimization level you have chosen.

Note that these mechanisms are only capable of retrieving data. Unlike SQL, where INSERT, UPDATE, and DELETE statements are part of the query language, the Set and Delete methods of the db4o ObjectContainer, described in Chapter 5, are, despite their simplicity, able to handle any case of storing, updating, or deleting objects in a db4o database. These do not need any further elaboration in this chapter.

If you're already comfortable with QBE, consider skipping the next section and jump right into the later sections covering Native Queries and SODA.

■**Note** What does a query give you? SQL is designed to give you data presented in an essentially tabular form. In some types of application this is a good thing, but in an object-oriented system, you're usually inter- ested in retrieving data as objects. This is why when you use a relational database and a SQL interface to it in such a system, you need to devote considerable programming effort to going through tabular data row by row and constructing an object from the values of the columns in each row. Object-based query mechanisms, such as db4o's options, just give you the objects, with no messing around.

Query by Example (QBE)

To use the QBE methodology, you create a template object, which is an instance of the class you want to search for. If you assign values to one or more attributes in your template, then db4o looks for objects in the database with matching attributes. The matching objects are returned by the query in a collection, which is an instance of the db4o API type ObjectSet.

Any attributes that are not assigned values, and hence are null or zero depending on the attribute type, are always matched. The implication of this is that if you do not assign any attribute values, then all objects of the specified class will match, so the query will return all objects in the extent of that class. You assign attributes as required to *constrain* attributes, making the query more specific.

■Note Behind the scenes, QBE uses reflection to get all fields in your class. Then, a query expression is built where all fields with a nondefault value are aggregated using AND expressions.

Simple Example

Here is the simplest possible QBE example, which shows again the steps described in Chapter 5: first you'll open the ObjectContainer, store some data using calls to Set, query the database, display the results, and then finally close the ObjectContainer. The objects in the databases are instances of the Person class defined in Chapter 5. The line of code that deletes the database file is there for testing only, to reset the database to a known (empty) condition before running the example. You wouldn't do that before opening a working database!

Let's begin with the C# version:

```csharp
// C#
public static void Main(string[] args)
{
    File.Delete("mydatabase.yap");
    ObjectContainer db = Db4o.OpenFile("mydatabase.yap");
    try
    {
        db.Set(new Person("John", 42));
        db.Set(new Person("Ben", 82));
        Person template = new Person();
        ObjectSet res = db.Get(template);
        // or simply ObjectSet res = db.Get(new Person());
        ListResult(res);
    }
    finally{
        db.Close();
    }
}

private void ListResult(ObjectSet res)
{
    while(res.HasNext())
        System.out.println(res.Next());
}
```

The Java version follows:

```java
// JAVA
public static void main(String[] args)
{
    new File("mydatabase.yap").delete();
    ObjectContainer db = Db4o.openFile("mydatabase.yap");
    try
    {
        db.set(new Person("John", 42));
        db.set(new Person("Ben", 82));
        Person template = new Person();
        ObjectSet res = db.get(template);
        // or simply ObjectSet res = db.get(new Person());
        listResult(res);
    }
    finally{
        db.close();
    }
}

private void listResult(ObjectSet res)
{
    while(res.hasNext())
        System.out.println(res.next());
}
```

We used an empty Person template so the result is that all Person objects are returned:

```
[John;42]
[Ben;82]
```

We know the template is empty because the default constructor in the Person class (see Listing 5-1 in Chapter 5) does not initialize any attributes. You may need to be careful when doing this to make sure that your default constructors really do not set any attributes.

■**Note** In the remaining examples, we will only show the code used to perform the actual query and to list the results. It will be assumed that the data is in the database, and that the ObjectContainer has been opened and will be closed afterward.

Constraining Fields

Of course, you can constrain as many fields as you like to get the objects that match. Thus if you execute this query you expect to find all the Person objects with the name "Ben" in the _name field:

```java
ObjectSet res = db.Get(new Person("Ben"));
```

Actually, this will not quite work with the class definition given in Chapter 5, as it did not include a constructor that takes only the name. There are two solutions to this. One possibility is to add a suitable constructor to the Person class. The other is to build up the template by setting fields separately, for example:

```
// C#
Person template = new Person();
template.Name = "Ben"
ObjectSet res = db.Get(template);
```

```
// JAVA
Person template = new Person();
template.setName("Ben");
ObjectSet res = db.get(template);
```

You can make the query more specific by setting additional fields, for example:

```
// C#
Person template = new Person();
template.Name = "Ben"
template.Age = 42;
ObjectSet res = db.Get(template);
```

```
// JAVA
Person template = new Person();
template.setName("Ben");
template.setAge(42);
ObjectSet res = db.get(template);
```

This is a bit too specific! The query will return no results as, although there is a "Ben" in the database, he isn't 42 years old.

More Ways of Matching

If a class has a constructor that sets all the possible fields, then it can be used for your templates to show clearly what is being matched and what isn't, for example:

```
// C# & JAVA
Person template = new Person(null, 82);    // match age only
Person template = new Person("Ben", 0);    // match name only
Person template = new Person(null, 0);     // ensure an empty template
```

There is another way of calling QBEs with an empty template. You can simply pass the class definition as a template, to achieve the same result:

```
ObjectSet res = db.Get(typeof(Person)); // C#
```

```
ObjectSet res = db.get(Person.class);    // JAVA
```

Finally, you can get all the objects of all types in the database using a null template:

```
ObjectSet res = db.Get(null);    // C#

ObjectSet res = db.get(null);    // JAVA
```

That's pretty much all there is to using QBE with simple objects. In Chapter 7 you will see that it can also useful for working with more complex structured objects.

Limitations and Caveats

QBE has some limitations, the main one of which is the lack of advanced query capability discussed in the introduction to this chapter. This is where the other db4o query methods come into play.

QBE is generally remarkably simple to use, but there are a couple of areas where you need to be careful:

- You can't use the values that are defined to mean "empty" as constraints. Fields specified as null, 0, or "" (empty string) are treated as unconstrained, which could be a problem in some cases. For example, what if you actually *want* to find Person objects with _age equal to 0? You can't when using QBE.

- You might run into problems if your classes initialize fields when they are declared. For example, what if the Person class initializes the attribute string _name = "Joe"? In that case, a query that uses the default constructor to create an "empty" template will only return "Joe" objects. To get a truly empty template, you would have to explicitly set the _name attribute to null.

These issues do not arise with the other db4o query methods.

Native Queries

Although SODA is the foundation for Native Queries in db4o, and has been around in the product for longer, we discuss Native Queries first. This is because you will probably prefer to use NQ over SODA, and in fact you may never need to write SODA queries at all. Of course, the choice is yours, and therefore complete details regarding SODA's capabilities are provided later in this chapter.

Query Languages

Most approaches to querying databases involve a declarative query language, of which SQL is the classic example. In fact, this approach is so commonplace that the idea of using query languages has largely survived into the era of object-oriented programming. Many developers use SQL statements embedded in their code, for example when querying a relational database via JDBC in a Java program, or as a property of an ADO.NET SqlDataAdapter. Even if an object-relational mapper is used to conceal the SQL behind an object-based API, queries are usually expressed using some kind of query language, such as JDOQL or Hibernate's HQL. Even in the world of object databases, the ODMG standard specified an Object Query Language (OQL).

All of these approaches have something in common in that each one is a language in its own right. Queries expressed in one of these languages must be integrated into an application. If the application is written in a programming language like C# or Java, the query usually appears as a string. Usually this string appears as a parameter for a method call. For instance, consider the following HQL query definition:

```
Query q = session.createQuery(
    "select emp.name from Employee as emp where emp.salary > 40000");
```

So when do you find out that your `Employee` class doesn't actually have a `salary` field? Not when you compile the program, because as far as the compiler's concerned, that query is a string. So as long as it's in quotes and contains characters, it's okay. In fact, you find out at runtime.

And what happens when you do some refactoring, and change the `salary` field in `Employee` to `annualSalary`? Your IDE will probably do a good job of changing the name of the field in most places in your program, but it won't refactor that query—it's just a string, remember. Again, the problem is only found when someone actually tries to run that query.

Other query languages have different syntax and are used within the program in different ways, but there are still strings in there somewhere. Even SODA, which is not a query language as such, uses strings to identify what attribute you want to descend to. Native queries resolve this dilemma for you by deferring the task of query expression to the application's language.

The Programming Language As the Query Language

The Native Queries feature is based on the idea that the best language to express a query is the same language that the application is written in. If you're writing a program in C#, write the query in C#. If you're writing in Java, write the query in Java. You don't have to learn another language, and your IDE can give you the help you are used to. You can write the query simply as an expression that has a Boolean value, for example:

```
// C#
emp.Salary > 40000

// JAVA
emp.getSalary() > 40000
```

The query returns all objects for which the result of the expression is `true`. Because the query expression is written in C# or Java, the compiler will give you error messages if the name or type of any class or field is invalid, so that you are safe from runtime errors caused by this kind of issue. Because of this, native queries are sometimes referred to as safe queries.

Like many things that make life simple, a lot of clever tricks are done behind the scenes to make a native query work. The obvious problem with the approach is that it looks as if you will need to instantiate every `Employee` object in the database and run the query expression against it. This would certainly not make for fast queries.

db4o's Native Queries implementation, based on the work of William Cook at the University of Texas at Austin,[1] avoids this problem. The basic idea is that the code of the query expression is analyzed and optimized by translating it to the underlying persistence system's query language or API. In db4o, that means it is translated to a SODA query for execution.

---

1. Safe Query Objects: Statically Typed Objects as Remotely Executable Queries, by William R. Cook and Siddhartha Rai, *Proc. of the International Conference on Software Engineering* (ICSE), 2005; Native Queries for Persistent Objects, A Design White Paper, by William R. Cook and Carl Rosenberger, *Dr. Dobb's Journal* (DDJ), February 2006.

This is actually a very attractive feature of Native Queries—the query expression is independent of the actual persistence mechanism. db4o provides the first implementation of Native Queries, but as other implementations become available, the same query code may be used with db4o, with relational databases, or even with in-memory collections.

■**Note** The idea of integrating queries into the programming language is creating a lot of interest. Microsoft, for example, is working on its LINQ (Language Integrated Queries) project, and its database query version, DLINQ. db4o is ahead of the game here as NQ is already in the released product. It is likely that db4o will also support LINQ when it is released.

Using Native Queries

A native query is created by writing a method that takes an instance of the class you are querying as a parameter, and returns a Boolean expression. The result of the query is a list that contains all the objects of that class in the database for which the expression evaluates to true. Remember that db4o does not usually actually instantiate all the possible objects to evaluate the expression, but you write the query as if it does. The following examples use the Person class defined in Chapter 5.

The syntax varies depending on which language and which version of the language you are using. db4o NQ supports, and takes advantage of, the most recent language features, but also provides backward compatibility. The first simple example will be shown for C# .NET 2.0 and 1.1, and for Java 5.0, 1.2-1.4 and 1.1, to show the differences. Subsequent examples are shown for the current language versions only, but you should have enough information to work out the required syntax for earlier versions.

The data we will use to test the queries is as follows:

```
Person p1 = new Person("Gandhi", 79);
Person p2 = new Person("Lincoln", 56);
Person p3 = new Person("Teresa", 87);
Person p4 = new Person("Mandela", 86);
```

These four objects need to be stored using calls to Set before executing the query examples.

.NET NQ Example

The C# and Java implementations of db4o native queries are quite different because of the difference between delegates in C# and inner classes in Java. The result is a slightly cleaner syntax in C# 2.0 than in Java.

Delegates in C# allow you to treat methods as first-class objects. A delegate acts like an interface with a single method. An anonymous delegate is like an anonymous inner class that implements an interface by simply implementing an unnamed method. An inner class in Java, even if it is itself unnamed, must name any methods that it implements. Delegates are widely used in .NET for event handling, callbacks, and so on. The ability to use anonymous methods as delegates is a new C# 2.0 feature.

The query expression is written in an anonymous delegate method inline with the code where the query is executed. C# 2.0 generics are also supported. The query to find "all Person objects with Age greater than 60" looks like this (db is an Object Container reference):

```
// C# 2.0
IList<Person> persons = db.Query<Person>(delegate(Person person)
{
    return person.Age > 60;
});
```

In C# 1.1 the anonymous method construct is not supported. Queries can be written as classes that extend the db4o Predicate API class. The query class has a Boolean method called match that contains the query expression.

```
// C# 1.1
// Predicate class definition
public class PersonAgeGreaterThanSixty : Predicate
{
    public Boolean Match(Person person)
    {
        return person.Age > 60;
    }
}

// Code to run query
IList persons = db.Query(new PersonAgeGreaterThanSixty());
```

In this C# 1.1 example, the Predicate is defined in a separate class from that in which the query is run.

In either case the query returns a list of Person objects. You can then iterate through the list and output the contents, like this:

```
// C#
foreach(Person person in persons)
    Console.WriteLine(person);
```

The output of the query in either version is:

```
[Teresa;87]
[Mandela;86]
[Ghandi;79]
```

Java NQ Example

The Java version of db4o also has a Predicate class, but here you can write the query class as an anonymous inner class, which keeps the query definition inline with the code where the query is executed. It's not quite as elegant as the C# 2.0 version as you have to write the match method explicitly. Our earlier example now looks like this:

```
// JAVA 5.0
List<Person> persons = db.query(new Predicate<Person>()
{
    public boolean match(Person person)
    {
        return person.getAge() > 60;
    }
});
```

The only difference in Java versions from 1.2 to 1.4 is that generics are not supported:

```
// JAVA 1.2-1.4
List persons = db.query(new Predicate()
{
    public boolean match(Person person)
    {
        return person.getAge() > 60;
    }
});
```

If you need to use a "prehistoric" version of Java, earlier than 1.2, you can't use an anonymous inner class, and you need to define the query class separately:

```
// JAVA 1.1
// Predicate class definition
public static class PersonAgeGreaterThanSixty extends Predicate
{
    public boolean match(Person person)
    {
        return person.getAge() > 60;
    }
}
```

```
// Code to run query
ObjectSet persons = db.query(new PersonAgeGreaterThanSixty());
```

In each case the query returns a collection of Person objects. You could then iterate through the collection and output the contents, as in this Java 5.0 example, where the collection implements the List interface and supports the enhanced for loop:

```
// JAVA 5.0
for(Person person : persons)
    System.out.println(person);
```

The output is:

```
[Teresa;87]
[Mandela;86]
[Ghandi;79]
```

■**Tip** The really important part of a native query is the *query expression itself*, not the code you need to construct around it. The expression is what decides which objects you get from the database.

More Complex Queries

In the previous example, the query expression contained only a simple comparison operator. More complex criteria can easily be constructed using the operators provided by the native language. In the following examples, the query expression is highlighted, to emphasize that it is the only part of the query that changes—the query construct is the same in each case.

■**Tip** If you want to get *all* the objects of a particular class, the query expression is simply return true. This works, but it's simpler to use QBE.

Range Criteria

For example, you can use a range of values as your criteria. This example finds "all Person objects with Age *outside* the range 60 to 80":

```
// C# 2.0
IList<Person> persons persons = db.Query<Person>(delegate(Person person)
{
    return person.Age < 60 || person.Age > 80;
});
```

```
// JAVA 5.0
List<Person> persons = db.query(new Predicate<Person>()
{
    public boolean match(Person person)
    {
        return person.getAge() < 60 || person.getAge() > 80;
    }
});
```

Remember that the OR logical operator || here is not a C#-like or Java-like construct—it *is* the C# or Java operator. The output is:

```
[Lincoln;56]
[Teresa;86]
[Mandela;86]
```

Compound Criteria

Another example shows criteria using more than one field, and finds "all Person objects with Age greater than 80 and Name equal to *'Mandela'*":

```
// C# 2.0
IList<Person> persons persons = db.Query<Person>(delegate(Person person)
{
    return person.Age > 80 && person.Name == "Mandela";
});
```

```
// JAVA 5.0
List<Person> persons = db.query(new Predicate<Person>()
{
    public boolean match(Person person)
    {
        return person.getAge() > 80 && person.getName() == "Mandela";
    }
});
```

The output from this query is:

```
[Mandela;86]
```

Sorting

The ability to sort data was added to Native Queries in version 5.2, taking advantage of the native support for comparing and sorting provided by C# and Java. To sort the results of a native query, you add a Comparison (C#) or Comparator (Java) object as an additional parameter to the Query method. You can define whatever sorting criteria you like in the Comparison/Comparator, giving a great deal of flexibility in the way your data is sorted.

Let's look at an example of a query that finds all Person objects and returns them in a List sorted in order of Name. Here's the C# 2.0 version, with the additional query parameter highlighted:

```
// C#
// Comparison
Comparison<Person> personCmp = new Comparison<Person>(
    delegate(Person p1, Person p2)
{
    return p2.Name.CompareTo(p1.Name);
});

// Query
IList<Person> persons = db.Query<Person>(delegate(Person person)
{
    return true;
},personCmp);
```

The syntax for the Comparison is very similar to that for the query: the comparison criterion is specified within an anonymous delegate. In Java, the Comparator is defined as an anonymous inner class with a method called compare, again using similar syntax to the query. Here's the Java 5.0 version, also with the additional query parameter highlighted:

```
// JAVA
// Comparator
Comparator<Person> personCmp = new Comparator<Person>()
{
    public int compare(Person p1, Person p2)
    {
        return p1.getName().compareTo(p2.getName());
    }
};
```

```
// Query
List<Person> result = db.query(new Predicate<Person>()
{
    public boolean match(Person person)
    {
        return true;
    }
},personCmp);
```

If you are using a version of db4o earlier than 5.2, this capability is not available, and you need work around this by copying the results to an array and then sorting that array.

Optimization

When possible, db4o will optimize native queries, which involves analyzing what it needs to do and translating it into a SODA query. db4o knows how to optimize many of the query expressions you are likely to use, and extending the range of situations where optimization works is an active development area for db4o's developers.

You can, however, put any code you like inside the query method, and it is not possible for db4o to cover every possibility. If it can't optimize a query, then it falls back to instantiating every object of the specified class and running the query expression against each one. The implication of this is that

- If a query is optimized, then none of the code in the query method is ever executed.

- If the query is not optimized, all of the code in the query method is executed for every object of the relevant type in the database.

So how do you know if a particular query is optimized? There are a number of ways of checking. You could measure the performance of your query—if it's slow, then it is probably not optimized. You could run your code in a debugger and watch the flow of execution—if the query method is actually executed, then the query is not optimized.

A particularly interesting way of checking optimization is to use an *event handler* (in .NET terminology) or *listener* (in Java terminology). These allow you to get notification when a particular event or type of event happens. Event handlers and listeners are commonly used to respond to events such as button clicks in GUI applications.

The code to set this up is quite different in C# and Java due to the different event models, so we'll look at them separately.

■**Caution** The methods illustrated in this section will not work with versions of db4o earlier than 5.2. Similar functionality is available in versions 5.0–5.1, but the details of how to use it differ from those shown here.

C# Version

You can define an event handler class, called PersonQueryExecutionHandler here, which has a method called NotifyQueryExecuted. This method is triggered when a native query is executed, and a `QueryExecutionEventArgs` object is passed to it as a parameter by db4o. The `QueryExecutionEventArgs` object contains information about the execution, including an `ExecutionKind` property that indicates whether the query was optimized (`DynamicallyOptimized`) or not (`Unoptimized`). The `NotifyQueryExecuted` method shown here simply prints out the `ExecutionKind`.

To set up the event handler you can create an instance of `PersonQueryExecutionHandler` and add its `NotifyQueryExecuted` method as a delegate to handle db4o's `QueryExecution` event. This needs to be done before execution of the queries you are testing.

```csharp
// C#
// Event handler class definition
class PersonQueryExecutionHandler
{
    public void NotifyQueryExecuted(object o, QueryExecutionEventArgs e)
    {
        Console.WriteLine(e.ExecutionKind);
    }
}


// Code to add event handler
PersonQueryExecutionHandler handler = new PersonQueryExecutionHandler();
((YapStream)db).GetNativeQueryHandler().QueryExecution +=
    new QueryExecutionHandler(handler.NotifyQueryExecuted);
```

Java Version

A `Db4oQueryExecutionListener` object is a listener with a method `notifyQueryExecuted` that can be set to be called when a native query is executed. An `NQOptimizationInfo` object is automatically passed by db4o as a parameter to this method, with a message indicating whether that query was optimized (`DYNOPTIMIZED`) or not (`UNOPTIMIZED`). You can write code in this method to do whatever you like—in the example that follows we just print out the message.

To set up a listener, you simply include the following code before your queries (you also need to use or import the `com.db4o.inside.query` namespace):

```java
// JAVA
// Listener is implemented as an anonymous inner class
((YapStream)db).getNativeQueryHandler().addListener(
        new Db4oQueryExecutionListener() {
    public void notifyQueryExecuted(NQOptimizationInfo info)
    {
        System.out.println(info.message());
    }
});
```

Results

The output, with the event handler or listener enabled, from the first simple query, shows that this query is optimized (this output is from the C# version):

```
DynamicallyOptimized
[Gandhi;79]
[Teresa;86]
[Mandela;86]
```

In fact, all the queries listed in this chapter should be optimized.

You might be tempted to check whether the query method is being executed simply by putting an output statement inside it. This is not a good idea, though, as the result is not reliable. The behavior we observed was that in C#, the presence of the output statement itself prevented db4o from optimizing—the query method was not translated into a SODA query. In the Java version, the query *was* optimized and the output statement was ignored. This was tested by modifying the simple query example, adding an output statement immediately before the return statement:

```
Console.WriteLine("in query method");   // C#
```

```
System.out.println("in query method");   // JAVA
```

The output from C# shows that the query was now not optimized, and that the query method was executed for all four objects in the database:

```
Unoptimized
in query method
in query method
in query method
in query method
[Gandhi;79]
[Teresa;86]
[Mandela;86]
```

The nature of native queries means that there are many possible expressions that can be written within the query method. The range of expressions that db4o knows how to optimize is likely to grow as new versions are released. However, if you have a problem with the performance of a native query, you may need to experiment to check that the query is being optimized as you think it should be.

■**Caution** In Java, NQ optimization requires that the libraries `bloat.jar` and `db4o-5.0-nqopt.jar` (or equivalent) be in the classpath. If they are not, queries will not be optimized. You will NOT get any warning of this! BLOAT is a Java byte code optimizer that was developed at Purdue University and is used by db4o. With the .NET version of db4o, all optimization functionality is currently included in the standard db4o DLL.

Using Query Templates

As you have seen, a native query is basically a query expression (the interesting bit) wrapped in some "boilerplate" code (that is, code that is the same, or nearly the same, for every query). Most modern IDEs have a template feature that can insert the boilerplate code for you. As examples, let's see how to set up a *snippet* for C# 2.0 in Microsoft Visual Studio 2005 and a *template* for Java 5.0 in Eclipse 3.1.

Visual Studio

A code snippet in Visual Studio is created as an XML file. Create a new file with the XML code listed here, and save it as nq.snippet.

```xml
<?xml version="1.0" encoding="utf-8" ?>
<CodeSnippets xmlns="http://schemas.microsoft.com/VisualStudio/2005/CodeSnippet">
    <CodeSnippet Format="1.0.0">
        <Header>
            <Title>
                Native Query
            </Title>
            <Description>
                db4o native query
            </Description>
            <Shortcut>
                nq
            </Shortcut>
        </Header>
        <Snippet>
            <Declarations>
                <Literal>
                    <ID>extent</ID>
                    <ToolTip>Replace with class name</ToolTip>
                    <Default>"Class name"</Default>
                </Literal>
            </Declarations>
            <Code Language="CSharp">
                <![CDATA[
                IList<$extent$> list = db.Query<$extent$>(
                    delegate($extent$ candidate)
                {
                    return true;
                });
                ]]>
            </Code>
        </Snippet>
    </CodeSnippet>
</CodeSnippets>
```

Choose the Tools ➤ Code Snippets Manager menu option. In the Code Snippets Manager dialog box, click the Import button to open the Import Code Snippet dialog box. Browse to your nq.snippet file, select Visual C# as the location for your snippet, and click Finish. You should then be able to scroll to find your new snippet in the Code Snippets Manager, as shown in Figure 6-1. The screenshots in this section were taken using Visual C# Express, but the process using the full Studio version is similar.

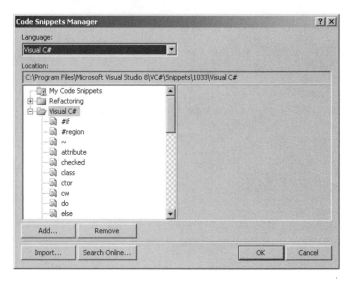

Figure 6-1. *Code Snippets Manager in Visual Studio*

The shortcut for the snippet is nq (this was defined in the <Shortcut> element of the XML file). To insert a native query in your code, place the cursor at the required insertion point and type nq, then press the Tab key twice. The snippet is placed in your code, as shown in Figure 6-2, and you can easily replace the text "Class Name" with the name of your query class, for example, Person. When you do this for the first occurrence, it is automatically done for the others. You can now replace the query expression return true with your own expression. Note that some errors will be underlined until the replacements are done.

```
25    IList<"Class name"> list = db.Query<"Class name">(
26        delegate ("Class name" candidate)
27    {
28        return true;
29    });
30
```

Figure 6-2. *Native query code snippet*

Eclipse

Choose the Window ➤ Preferences menu option, and in the Preferences dialog box choose the Java ➤ Editor ➤ Templates node, and click the New button. In the New Template dialog box, type nq in the Name box and make sure that java is selected in the Context box on the right. The dialog boxes are shown in Figure 6-3.

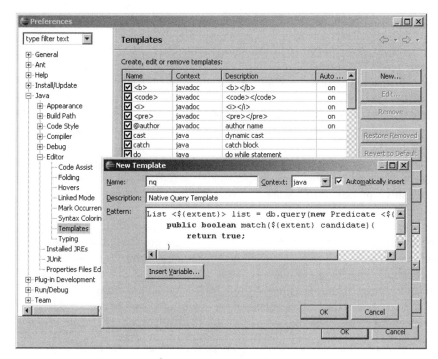

Figure 6-3. *Creating a new template in Eclipse*

Enter the following text in the Pattern box:

```
List <${extent}> list = db.query(new Predicate <${extent}> () {
    public boolean match(${extent} candidate){
        return true;
    }
});
```

To insert a native query in your code, place the cursor at the required insertion point and type nq, then press Ctrl-spacebar. The query template is placed in your code, as shown in Figure 6-4, and you can easily replace the text extent with the name of your query class, for example, Person. At this point, you can replace the query expression return true with your own expression. Note that some errors will be underlined until the replacements are done.

```
24
25  List<extent> list = db.query(new Predicate<extent>() {
26      public boolean match(extent candidate) {
27          return true;
28      }
29  });
30
```

Figure 6-4. *Native query code template*

SODA

The preceding sections have given you an introduction to the relationship between the db4o query mechanisms, QBE, NQ, and SODA. Simple Object Data Access was the first advanced query language in db4o, and was originated as a public and open project by Carl Rosenberger on the home of many open source projects, SourceForge. If you're interested, you can find the project pages at `http://sodaquery.sourceforge.net` and `http://sourceforge.net/projects/sodaquery`. You don't actually need to download anything from there, though, as SODA is fully integrated into db4o.

The basic idea of SODA was to build a *query graph*, which can be used to express the query. The resulting query is thus fast because these graphs can be parsed or traversed easily. SODA is the foundation of native queries, as NQs will be translated (optimized or unoptimized) into a SODA graph.

However, SODA has its disadvantages. A query is expressed as a set of method calls that explicitly define the graph. It's not too hard to get used to, but it's not immediately natural if you're used to the idea of query languages. Many programmers will prefer the standard programming language constructs used with new native queries. A further important disadvantage is the fact that attribute names are strings, meaning that SODA queries are not type-safe.

db4objects anticipates that many developers will enjoy writing queries natively as described in the previous section. However, SODA has been left in the db4o API for some very good reasons:

- Some developers might want the ultimate query performance, or they might like the syntax. If so, they can code SODA directly instead of letting the NQ mechanisms convert NQs to SODA.

- SODA is essentially language independent, whereas native queries use different constructs in C# and Java.

- It needs to be there to support native queries, or any other mechanism in the future that translates other query languages into SODA to take advantage of its performance.

SODA Query Graphs

A SODA query graph is basically a graph data structure, where nodes represent classes or fields of classes, and edges represent relationships that can be traversed to reach nodes. You can attach constraints to any node. A constraint is used by db4o to decide whether each candidate object in the database should be included in the result based on the value of that node in the object.

Figure 6-5 shows a diagrammatic representation of a simple query graph. Nodes are represented by circles and edges by arrows. In this example, the first node reached from the entry point has the constraint `Class` : `Person` attached to it. This means that candidate objects will only be included in the results if they are instances of `Person`. The entry point usually denotes what class of object we want to get from the query.

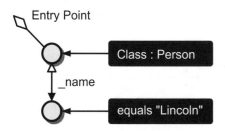

Figure 6-5. *SODA query graph representation*

The second node in the query graph is reached by following an edge with the label _name. This is known as *descending* to another node. The label indicates that this node represents the field _name. The constraint equals "Lincoln" is attached to the node. This means that candidate objects will only be included if their _name field has a value equal to "Lincoln". So, this query finds "all Person objects with _name equal to Lincoln".

Representations like Figure 6-5 can be helpful in planning and understanding queries. Now we need to see how to code this kind of query.

SODA Keywords

Before we look at some code examples, let's have a look at the SODA keywords that are used to construct query graphs. First, we need the keywords to set up the query object (see Table 6-2).

Table 6-2. *SODA Query Keywords*

Keyword (C#)	Keyword (Java)	Explanation
Query	query	This is the interface of the query object
Constrain	constrain	Add a constraint to a node.
Descend	descend	Move from one node to another.
OrderAscending	orderAscending	Add a new criterion to the query object: order the result ascending according to the actual node.
OrderDescending	orderDescending	Add a new criterion to the query object: order the result descending according to the actual node.
Execute	execute	When execute is performed on the query object, the query is started and returns an ObjectSet containing the results.

The keywords shown in Table 6-2 are actually method names, so method naming conventions apply.

A further set of keywords define the constraints to be applied (Table 6-3). These provide a much richer set of constraint types than the simple equality allowed by QBE. Again, these are actually method calls.

Table 6-3. *SODA Constraint Keywords*

Keyword (C#)	Keyword (Java)	Explanation
And	and	Links two constraints together with the logical AND.
Or	or	Links two constraints together with the logical OR.
Equal	equal	Compares the actual field to equality that is equivalent to ==.
Greater	greater	Compares the actual field using the > comparator.
Smaller	smaller	Compares the actual field using the < comparator.
Identity	identity	The actual field will be checked if it is identical to the object supplied.
Like	like	The first characters of the field will be compared.
Contains	contains	Use this to check if the supplied object is contained in the given one.
GetObject	getObject	Returns the object that was used to create the actual constraint.

Using SODA

Let's start by coding a simple query that will return all the Person objects in the database. This is equivalent to the first node in Figure 6-5. The data we will use to test the queries is similar to that used in the "Native Queries" section:

```
Person p1 = new Person("Gandhi", 79);
Person p2 = new Person("Lincoln", 56);
Person p3 = new Person("Teresa", 86);
Person p4 = new Person("Mandela", 86);
```

As before, db is our ObjectContainer reference, and we use the same ListResult method as we did in the "Query By Example (QBE)" section. Here is the code for this query. Note that you need to use or import the namespace/package com.db4o.query.

```
// C#
Query query = db.Query();
query.Constrain(typeof(Person));
ObjectSet res = query.Execute();
ListResult(res);
```

```
// JAVA
Query query = db.query();
query.constrain(Person.class);
ObjectSet res = query.execute();
listResult(res);
```

Let's look at what is going on here. We obtain the query object by calling `Query` on the `ObjectContainer`. Then we constrain the query by calling `Constrain` on the query object, passing the class we want to search as its parameter. We could have instead passed `new Person()`. Now we have set up the query and we are able to execute it, leading to the expected result:

```
[Mandela;86]
[Teresa;86]
[Lincoln;56]
[Gandhi;79]
```

This was pretty easy, wasn't it? Now let's get a little bit more advanced. What did we do to perform more complex QBE queries? We searched for matching fields. That's what the next example does—this is now the full query represented in Figure 6-5.

```
// C#
Query query = db.Query();
query.Constrain(typeof(Person));
query.Descend("_name").Constrain("Lincoln"); // search a name
ObjectSet result = query.Execute();
```

```
// JAVA
Query query = db.query();
query.constrain(Person.class);
query.descend("_name").constrain("Lincoln"); // search a name
ObjectSet result = query.execute();
```

You can see that we use the keyword `Descend` to move down from the class to the field _name. In terms of the overall query, you first had a candidate that was of the type `Person`. Then you further constrained the candidate `Person` objects by adding a new constraint with the candidate _name field specified as a string. If you execute the query you get the expected result:

```
[Lincoln;56]
```

■Caution The name of the field to descend to is specified as a string. What happens if you make a mistake and specify a field that doesn't exist in the candidate class? Suppose you type `query.Descend("_placeOfBirth").Constrain("Hardin County")`. The compiler can't check whether the field name is valid, as it's just a string. In fact, you don't even get a runtime error—you just get no matching objects. If you make a slight error in specifying the field name, the problem can be hard to spot. The Native Queries feature, on the other hand, provides compile-time checking.

Using Constraints

The following examples show how to apply various kinds of constraints using the keywords.

"Not" Example

The following query constrains the candidate age to be anything other than 56:

```
// C#
Query query = db.Query();
query.Constrain(typeof(Person));
query.Descend("_age").Constrain(56).Not(); // not 56
ObjectSet result = query.Execute();
```

```
// JAVA
Query query=db.query();
query.constrain(Person.class);
query.descend("_age").constrain(56).not(); // not 56
ObjectSet res=query.execute();
```

The result contains the three people who are not 56 years old:

```
[Mandela;86]
[Teresa;86]
[Gandhi;79]
```

Compound Constraints

To set up an example with an And compound condition, we need to set up two constraints. This is done in the third line by defining a Constraint object named firstConstr. This object constrains the value of the age to 86. In the fourth line we set up the second constraint, which is linked with And to the first constraint and applied to the query object.

```
// C#
Query query = db.Query();
query.Constrain(typeof(Person));
Constraint firstConstr = query.Descend("_age").Constrain(86); // first constraint
query.Descend("_name").Constrain("Mandela").And(firstConstr); // second, using And
ObjectSet result = query.Execute();
```

```
// JAVA
Query query = db.query();
query.constrain(Person.class);
Constraint firstConstr = query.descend("_age").constrain(86); // first constraint
query.descend("_name").constrain("Mandela").and(firstConstr); // second, using and
ObjectSet result = query.execute();
```

This returns the object that meets both criteria, as you would expect:

```
[Mandela;86]
```

This query graph could be represented as shown in Figure 6-6.

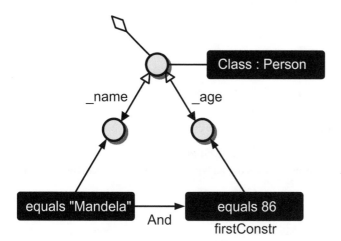

Figure 6-6. *Query graph with compound constraints*

Alternatively, you can define an Or query like this:

```
// C#
Query query = db.Query();
query.Constrain(typeof(Person));
Constraint firstConstr = query.Descend("_age").Constrain(86); // first constraint
query.Descend("_name").Constrain("Lincoln").Or(firstConstr); // second using And
ObjectSet result = query.Execute();
```

```
// JAVA
Query query = db.query();
query.constrain(Person.class);
Constraint firstConstr = query.descend("_age").constrain(86); // first constraint
query.descend("_name").constrain("Lincoln").or(firstConstr); // second using and
ObjectSet result = query.execute();
```

This returns the people aged 86 and also the person named "Lincoln".

```
[Mandela;86]
[Teresa;86]
[Lincoln;56]
```

An Alternative "And" Example

Our And example can also be written in a slightly simpler form:

```csharp
// C#
Query query = db.Query();
query.Constrain(typeof(Person));
query.Descend("_age").Constrain(86);
query.Descend("_name").Constrain("Mandela");
ObjectSet result = query.Execute();
```

```java
// JAVA
Query query = db.query();
query.constrain(Person.class);
query.descend("_age").constrain(86);
query.descend("_name").constrain("Mandela");
ObjectSet result=query.execute();
```

In this case, you are effectively ascending from one child node to the parent node and descending to another child node. This simplifies the And query, but you can't do the Or query this way.

"Greater" and "Smaller" Example

Here is a further example, using the Greater comparison:

```csharp
// C#
Query query = db.Query();
query.Constrain(typeof(Person));
query.Descend("_age").Constrain(80).Greater();
ObjectSet result = query.Execute();
```

```java
// JAVA
Query query=db.query();
query.constrain(Person.class);
query.descend("_age").constrain(80).greater();
ObjectSet result=query.execute();
```

And the result is:

```
[Mandela;86]
[Teresa;86]
```

If you invert this example using Smaller instead, you will get:

```
[Lincoln;56]
[Gandhi;79]
```

This query graph for the Greater example could be represented as shown in Figure 6-7.

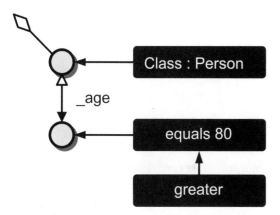

Figure 6-7. *Query graph with Greater constraint*

Range Example

The And/Or and comparison operators can also be combined and applied to a single field to query for results within a range. This example gives "all Person objects with _age between 60 and 80".

```
// C#
Query query = db.Query();
query.Constrain(Person.class);
Constraint firstConstr = query.Descend("_age").Constrain(60).Greater();
query.descend("_age").Constrain(80).Smaller().And(firstConstr);
ObjectSet result = query.Execute();
```

```
// JAVA
Query query=db.query();
query.constrain(Person.class);
Constraint firstConstr = query.descend("_age").constrain(60).greater();
query.descend("_age").constrain(80).smaller().and(firstConstr);
ObjectSet result=query
```

This gives the single operators result:

[Gandhi;79]

Advanced SODA Syntax

We have now looked at the simple keywords, but there is one further nontrivial keyword to deal with. Also in this section you will see how to search for default values, and how to sort the result.

"Like" Example

The Like keyword is a little different from the syntax we know from SQL, but is fairly straight-forward. Look at the following code:

```
// C#
string tmp = "12345";
Console.WriteLine(tmp.StartsWith("12")); // prints true
```

```
// JAVA
String tmp = "12345";
System.out.println(tmp.startsWith("12")); // prints true
```

These code fragments show an obvious example of a Like comparison: check whether a string starts with the given characters. The check is case insensitive, which means that StartsWith("ab") would match "ABCD". These methods can be understood as if they add an implicit * at the end of your pattern. Here is an example of the use of Like in a query:

```
// C#
Query query = db.Query();
query.Constrain(typeof(Person));
query.Descend("_name").Constrain("Ma").Like(); // also works with "ma"
ObjectSet result = query.Execute();
```

```
// JAVA
Query query=db.query();
query.constrain(Person.class);
query.descend("_name").constrain("Ma").like(); // also works with "ma"
ObjectSet result= query.execute();
```

And the result is:

```
[Mandela;86]
```

So what would be the correct patterns to search for "Mandela"? If you try out these patterns you will get the SODA search results shown in Table 6-4.

Table 6-4. *Patterns for the SODA Like Comparison*

Pattern	Result	Explanation
Mandela	True	The patterns match exactly, which is obvious.
Mandela	True	The search is case insensitive.
Ma	True	The characters given do match from the start.
Ma*	False	The characters don't match as this Like doesn't know "*".
M	True	The character given matches from the start.

Table 6-4. *Patterns for the SODA Like Comparison*

Pattern	Result	Explanation
m	True	The character matches from the start. The case doesn't matter.
M%	False	This is SQL syntax and cannot be used in db4o.

Query for Null Values

You can of course search for null or zero values, such as 0, 0.0, or null, which you can't do with QBE. If you execute the following query with the data we have been using, you will get no result:

```
// C#
Query query=db.Query();
query.Constrain(typeof(Person));
query.Descend("age").Constrain(0); // field has been set
ObjectSet result=query.Execute();
```

```
// JAVA
Query query=db.query();
query.constrain(Person.class);
query.descend("age").constrain(0); // field has been set
ObjectSet result=query.execute();
```

However, if you store an object in the database as shown here, this query will return that object, as the _age field is not set and defaults to 0 because it is an integer field.

```
Person p = new Person();
p.Name = "Fred";    // C#
p.setName("Fred");  // JAVA
```

If the _age was not a primitive integer but rather the object type Integer, then the search query.descend("age").Constrain(new Integer(0)) would give you the "Fred" object here, and all objects where the _age is not set.

■**Caution** If you have unset fields in your database, your query will give you false results! Thus, if you are searching for newborn babies with the age 0 and you forgot to set the age for adult persons, you will get these adult persons in your query as well. Sometimes this problem can become a huge obstacle. In this case you should think about introducing the *Null Object* design pattern, which provides an object as a surrogate for the lack of an object of a given type. For a description of this pattern see, for example, www.cs.oberlin.edu/~jwalker/nullObjPattern/.

Sorting the Results

Sorting results in ascending or descending order is done by adding the appropriate keyword after descending to a node, as shown in the following code. You can only sort on one field in any one query.

```
// C#
Query query = db.Query();
query.Constrain(typeof(Person));
query.Descend("_name").OrderAscending(); // the list should start with the lowest
ObjectSet result = query.Execute();
```

```
// JAVA
Query query=db.query();
query.constrain(Person.class);
query.descend("_name").orderAscending(); // the list should start with the lowest
ObjectSet result=query.execute();
```

This gives the following result:

```
[Gandhi;79]
[Lincoln;56]
[Mandela;86]
[Teresa;86]
```

As you saw earlier in this chapter, a sorting mechanism has been added only very recently to Native Queries. This was one case where SODA had the lead over Native Queries, but now NQ has caught up and even moved ahead with true object-oriented sorting.

Summary

In this chapter you saw the three query mechanisms provided by db4o, and you should now be able to choose which will work best for your application. Most people will probably use QBE quite often, for its simplicity in basic queries, and choose either Native Queries or SODA for more complex situations. db4objects, Inc., believes that people will favor the type-safe Native Queries, and are emphasizing that method in their future developments.

The examples in this chapter were all based on querying for a single class. The next chapter goes on to show you how to store, query, update, and delete complex structured objects in db4o. In particular, it shows how the three query mechanisms are used for more complex objects.

■ ■ ■

CHAPTER 7

Working with Objects

The objects that we worked with in the previous chapter were fairly simplistic. However, many of the objects found in a real system are likely to be *structured objects*, which are objects composed of other objects. A structured object can be as simple as an object that has an attribute that is a reference to another object. Things can get more complicated when there are one-to-many and many-to-many relationships within the structure, and even more so when there are relationships involving inheritance trees and polymorphism.

In Part I of this book you saw examples of the main types of relationships, and the ways in which these relationships can be represented in databases. Now it's time to take a look in more detail about how you can work with all sorts of objects, simple and otherwise, in db4o. The key fact to remember is that db4o stores objects as they are, and gives you the best possible match between your objects and the way they are stored in the database. The payoff increases as your structures become more complicated. If you have a complex object hierarchy, then you could end up spending most of your development time in mapping these objects to tables if you use a relational database, but with db4o you may be able simply to store a single object at the root of the hierarchy.

db4o lets you work with persistent objects almost as if they are in-memory objects—this is transparent persistence. They aren't actually in-memory objects, though, and you need to know how to make sure that the right objects get stored, and the right objects are available when you need them, which is what this chapter is all about. Interestingly, we find that thinking about how objects are going to be stored can suggest ways in which our object models can be made more elegant and effective. Thinking too deeply about how your objects can be stored in a relational database is likely to have the opposite effect . . .

Meet the Objects

The objects that will be used in this chapter are instances of the classes shown in the UML class diagram in Figure 7-1. These are, of course, much simplified compared to a real system, but they show a representative range of structures and relationships. Note that the diagram displays a minimal set of methods, with property or getter and setter methods not included. Also, attributes whose existence is implied by class associations are not shown explicitly.

The main structure is an inheritance tree with the abstract class Person, which implements the IPerson interface, at the root. All classes in the hierarchy therefore implement the IPerson interface. Classes in the tree differ in the attributes they have in addition to those defined in Person (for example, an Employee's date of birth and employee number are stored) and also in behavior (you can send an email to any Person, but the method used to send an email to an Employee is different from that used to send to a Customer).

The section of the tree with Employee at its root is an example of a composite hierarchy, since a Manager has a collection of Employees, some of whom can in turn be Managers. The remaining classes, which are not part of the inheritance tree, introduce associations of various multiplicities, including one-to-one (Customer-Address) and many-to-many (Employee-Project).

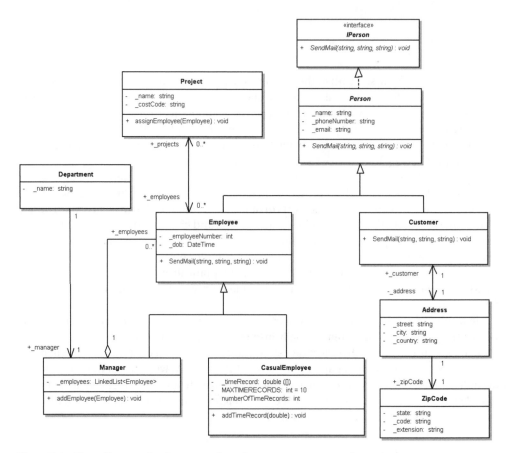

Figure 7-1. *Class diagram for the example code*

We will look at some examples of the ways in which objects from this class diagram are stored and retrieved with db4o. Each example will focus on an area of the class diagram to illustrate how to deal with a specific structure. Full code for the examples in C# and Java can be downloaded from the Apress website. Examples of db4o queries that work with older versions of C# and Java are shown in Chapter 6, and you can use them to adapt the examples in this chapter if you need to do so.

All examples will make use of classes that are part of the Person tree, so the code for the interface and the abstract Person class is shown in Listings 7-1 and 7-2. Note that the Java versions are named slightly differently, reflecting typical Java naming. In Java, the interface is called Person and the abstract class is called AbstractPerson. Code for other classes will be shown alongside the examples in which they are used.

Listing 7-1. *The IPerson Interface and Person Abstract Class in C#*

```
// C#
namespace com.db4o.dg2db4o.chapter7
{
    interface IPerson
    {
        string Name{get; set;}
        string PhoneNumber{get;set;}
        string Email{get;set;}
        void SendMail(string fromAddress, string subject, string content);
    }
}
```

```
// C#
namespace com.db4o.dg2db4o.chapter7
{
    abstract class Person : IPerson
    {
        string _name;
        string _phoneNumber;
        string _email;

        public Person(string name, string phoneNumber, string email)
        {
            _name = name;
            _phoneNumber = phoneNumber;
            _email = email;
        }

        public abstract void SendMail(string fromAddress, string subject, string
            content);

        public string Name
        {
            get
            {
                return _name;
            }
            set
            {
                _name = value;
            }
        }
```

```
        public string PhoneNumber
        {
            get
            {
                return _phoneNumber;
            }
            set
            {
                _phoneNumber = value;
            }
        }

        public string Email
        {
            get
            {
                return _email;
            }
            set
            {
                _email = value;
            }
        }
    }
}
```

Listing 7-2. *The Person Interface and AbstractPerson Class in Java*

```
// JAVA
package com.db4o.dg2db4o.chapter7;

public interface Person
{
    String getName();
    void setName(String name);
    String getPhoneNumber();
    void setPhoneNumber(String phoneNumber);
    String getEmail();
    void setEmail(String email);
    void sendMail(String fromAddress, String subject, String content);
}
```

```java
// JAVA
package com.db4o.dg2db4o.chapter7;

public abstract class AbstractPerson implements Person
{
    String _name;
    String _phoneNumber;
    String _email;

    public AbstractPerson(String name, String phoneNumber, String email)
    {
        _name = name;
        _phoneNumber = phoneNumber;
        _email = email;
    }

    public abstract void sendMail(String fromAddress, String subject, String
        content);

    public String getName()
    {
        return _name;
    }

    public void setName(String value)
    {
        _name = value;
    }

    public String getPhoneNumber()
    {
        return _phoneNumber;
    }

    public void setPhoneNumber(String value)
    {
        _phoneNumber = value;
    }

    public String getEmail()
    {
        return _email;
    }

    public void setEmail(String value)
    {
        _email = value;
    }
}
```

Simple Structured Objects

A Customer object is a simple structured object. It has an attribute that is a reference to a single Address object, so you can think of a Customer as being composed of itself and its Address. Listings 7-3 and 7-4 show the code for these classes.

Listing 7-3. *The Customer and Address Classes in C#*

```csharp
// C#
namespace com.db4o.dg2db4o.chapter7
{
    class Customer : Person
    {
        Address _address;

        public Customer(string name, string phoneNumber, string email, Address
            address) : base(name,phoneNumber,email)
        {
            _address = address;
        }

        public override void SendMail(string fromAddress, string subject, string
            content)
        {
            string toAddress = base.Email;
            string sentContent = content + "COMPANY DISCLAIMER...";
            System.Net.Mail.SmtpClient mailer = new System.Net.Mail.SmtpClient();
            mailer.Send(fromAddress, toAddress, subject, content);
        }

        public Address Address
        {
            get
            {
                return _address;
            }
            set
            {
                _address = value;
            }
        }

        public override string ToString()
        {
            return base.Name + " (Customer)";
        }
    }
}
```

```csharp
// C#
namespace com.db4o.dg2db4o.chapter7
{
    class Address
    {
        string _street;
        string _city;
        string _country;
        ZipCode _zipCode;

        public Address(string street, string city, string country)
        {
            _street = street;
            _city = city;
            _country = country;
        }

        public string Street
        {
            get
            {
                return _street;
            }
            set
            {
                _street = value;
            }
        }

        public string City
        {
            get
            {
                return _city;
            }
            set
            {
                _city = value;
            }
        }

        public string Country
        {
            get
            {
                return _country;
            }
```

```
            set
            {
                _country = value;
            }
        }

        public ZipCode ZipCode
        {
            get
            {
                return _zipCode;
            }
            set
            {
                _zipCode = value;
            }
        }

        public override string ToString()
        {
            return _street + ", " + _city + ", " + _country + " (Address)";
        }
    }
}
```

Listing 7-4. *The Customer and Address Classes in Java*

```
// JAVA
package com.db4o.dg2db4o.chapter7;

public class Customer extends AbstractPerson
{
    Address _address;

    public Customer(String name, String phoneNumber, String email, Address
        address)
    {
        super(name,phoneNumber,email);
        _address = address;
    }

    public void sendMail(String fromAddress, String subject, String content)
    {
        String toAddress = super.getEmail();
        String sentContent = content + "COMPANY DISCLAIMER...";
        Emailer mailer = new Emailer(); // class included in downloadable code
        mailer.sendMail(fromAddress, toAddress, subject, content);
    }
```

```java
    public Address getAddress()
    {
        return _address;
    }
    public void setAddress(Address value)
    {
        _address = value;
    }


    public String toString()
    {
        return super.getName() + " (Customer)";
    }
}


// JAVA
package com.db4o.dg2db4o.chapter7;

public class Address
{
    String _street;
    String _city;
    String _country;
    ZipCode _zipCode;

    public Address(String street, String city, String country)
    {
        _street = street;
        _city = city;
        _country = country;
    }

    public String getStreet()
    {
        return _street;
    }
    public void setStreet(String value)
    {
        _street = value;
    }

    public String getCity()
    {
        return _city;
    }
```

```
    public void setCity(String value)
    {
        _city = value;
    }

    public String getCountry()
    {
        return _country;
    }

    public void setCountry(String value)
    {
        _country = value;
    }

    public ZipCode getZipCode()
    {
        return _zipCode;
    }

    public void setZipCode(ZipCode value)
    {
        _zipCode = value;
    }

    public String toString()
    {
        return _street + ", " + _city + ", " + _country + " (Address)";
    }
}
```

Storing and Retrieving Simple Structured Objects

Let's store a Customer object and its Address. The code given for the examples in this chapter assumes that an ObjectContainer has been opened, and will be closed once the example code has executed.

Storing a structured object is very simple: you just need to store the top-level object, and any associated objects will also be stored. Note that as you saw in Chapter 6, parts of many of the code examples are identical in C# and Java—this is indicated in the listings.

```
// C# & JAVA
Address a1 = new Address("1 First Street", "San Jose", "USA");
Customer cu1 = new Customer("Gary", "408 123 4567", "gary@example.net", a1);

// C#
db.Set(cu1);
```

```
// JAVA
db.set(cu1);
```

In fact, when you store one object, by default the database will also store the objects that can be reached by navigating the in-memory object graph starting from that object.

■Tip Remember you can use the ObjectManager to check what has been stored in your database.

You could also store the Address object explicitly, although it is not necessary to do so. The following code will have exactly the same effect as the first version:

```
// C#
db.Set(a1);
db.Set(cu1);
```

```
// JAVA
db.set(a1);
db.set(cu1);
```

■Caution This is true if the associated objects are stored within the same transaction, which is to say before the ObjectContainer is closed. If the Address object is stored explicitly in one transaction, and the Customer object is stored within another, then the database cannot automatically associate the stored Address with the Address belonging to the Customer. As a result, an additional Address object, with the same field values but with a different OID, will be stored. The correct way to deal with this would be to retrieve the previously stored Address and associate that explicitly with the Customer before storing the Customer.

Finally, note that if you store the Address object only, then no Customer object will be stored, as an Address contains no references to other objects.

Queries

In this chapter we look at queries involving structured objects. The full range of db4o query mechanisms was covered in Chapter 6, so the examples here will not show all the ways of doing each query. Each example will be illustrated using QBE and/or Native Queries as appropriate. Since Native Queries is now the primary query method for db4o, SODA query examples will not be shown for all cases, but you should be able to use Chapter 6 to help you translate the Native Query examples to SODA if you need to do so.

Retrieving a structured object is just as simple as storing it. Again, you just need to retrieve the top-level object, and associated objects will by default be retrieved along with it.

Query for a Customer

You retrieve and display the Customer object using QBE as shown in the following listing. Note that it is assumed in the query listings that the database is opened before the query is executed, and closed afterward. The calls to OpenFile and Close are not shown explicitly.

```
// C#
Customer customerExample = new Customer("Gary", null, null, null);
ObjectSet results = db.Get(customerExample);
while (results.HasNext())
{
    Customer customer = (Customer)results.Next();
    Console.WriteLine(customer);
    Console.WriteLine(customer.Address);
}
```

```
// JAVA
Customer customerExample = new Customer(
    "Gary", null, null, new Address(null,null,null));
ObjectSet results = db.get(customerExample);
while (results.hasNext()) {
    Customer customer = (Customer)results.next();
    System.out.println(customer);
    System.out.println(customer.getAddress());
 }
```

In a real application you would take the Customer object you retrieved and do something with it. In these examples we just list the objects to show what has been retrieved, using the information provided by the ToString method for each object. The output looks like this:

```
Gary (Customer)
1 First Street, San Jose, USA (Address)
```

Note that this single query has returned both objects. The same thing can be done with a native query:

```
// C#
// execute query
IList<Customer> customers = db.Query<Customer>(delegate(Customer cust)
{
    return cust.Name.Equals("Gary");
});

// list results
foreach (Customer customer in customers)
{
    Console.WriteLine(customer);
    Console.WriteLine(customer.Address);
}
```

```java
// JAVA
// execute query
List customers = db.query(new Predicate<Customer>()
{
    public boolean match(Customer cust) {
        return cust.getName().equals("Gary");
    }
 });

// list results
for (Customer customer : customers )
{
    System.out.println(customer);
    System.out.println(customer.getAddress());
}
```

The output from this is exactly the same as for the QBE version. Again, querying for the Customer object returns the Address object too.

Query for an Address

Of course, you can also query specifically for the Address object:

```csharp
// C#
IList<Address> addresses = db.Query<Address>(delegate(Address add)
{
    return add.Street.Equals("1 First Street");
});
```

```java
// JAVA
List<Address> addresses = db.query(new Predicate<Address>()
{
    public boolean match(Address add)
    {
        return add.getStreet().equals("1 First Street");
    }
});
```

The code for displaying the results of a query will always be pretty similar to that shown for the previous Customer queries, so from now on this will not be shown in full for each example. The output for this query looks like this:

```
1 First Street, San Jose, USA (Address)
```

The Address object does not have a reference to a Customer, so you can only list the Address object itself when querying for an Address.

Query for a Customer by Address

You can also query for an object using the attributes of associated objects as criteria. For example, the following native query finds the Customer for a specific Address:

```
// C#
IList<Customer> customers = db.Query<Customer>(delegate(Customer cust)
{
    return cust.Address.Street.Equals("1 First Street");
});
```

```
// JAVA
List<Customer> customers = db.query(new Predicate<Customer>()
{
    public boolean match(Customer cust)
    {
        return cust.getAddress().getStreet().equals("1 First Street");
    }
});
```

What about doing the opposite—finding the Address for a specific Customer? Well, you actually already did this in the first example. By finding a Customer, you immediately have access to its associated Address object.

It is worth having a look at the SODA version of this query to show how the query graph works for a structured object. To query for a Customer using the _street field of the Address object, you need to descend two levels into the query.

```
// C#
Query query = db.Query();
query.Constrain(typeof(Customer));
query.Descend("_address").Descend("_street").Constrain("1 First Street");
ObjectSet results = query.Execute();
```

```
// JAVA
Query query = db.query();
query.constrain(Customer.class);
query.descend("_address").descend("_street").constrain("1 First Street");
ObjectSet results = query.execute();
```

The query graph is illustrated in Figure 7-2. Reading this graph shows that a candidate needs to be of type Customer and have a member named _address that in turn has a member named _street that is equal to the given string to be accepted for the result. The middle node corresponds to Address objects.

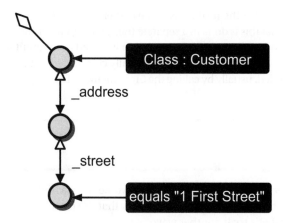

Figure 7-2. *SODA query graph for query for Customer by Address example*

Updating and Deleting Simple Structured Objects

As you saw in Chapter 5, updating an object in a db4o database is simple. You retrieve the object you want to update, modify it as you wish, and call the Set method again to update the stored object to include your modifications.

Updating a structured object is done in pretty much the same way. You can also update any associated object at the same time. For example, you can retrieve a Customer object, and update it and its Address object with one call to Set. The following code retrieves our Customer (using a native query, although you could also do this with QBE) and modifies the Street property of its Address. Note that the parameter of the Set method is a Customer, but the modified object is the Address.

```csharp
// C#
IList<Customer> customers = db.Query<Customer>(delegate(Customer cust)
{
    return cust.Name.Equals("Gary");
});
Customer cu = customers[0];    // get first returned Customer - should only be one
cu.Address.Street = "2 Second Street";
db.Set(cu);
```

```java
// JAVA
List<Customer> customers = db.query(new Predicate<Customer>()
{
    public boolean match(Customer cust)
    {
        return cust.getName().equals("Gary");
    }
});
Customer cu = customers.get(0); // get first returned Customer - should only be one
cu.getAddress().setStreet("2 Second Street");
db.set(cu);
```

You can now query for the Customer and list the results, as in the earlier section "Query for a Customer." It is important to make sure that this is done in a separate transaction (after closing the database and opening it again); otherwise it is not a true test of what is stored permanently in the database. Changes made by calling the Set method are not actually committed to the database until the current transaction is ended, usually by calling the Close method. The output is as follows:

```
Gary (Customer)
1 First Street, San Jose, USA (Address)
```

Wait a minute, the address has not been updated! Why has this not worked? It was definitely modified by the code, and the Customer object was stored, but it is clear that the modification has not been committed to the database. Let's try it another way:

```
// C#
cu.Address.Street = "2 Second Street";
db.Set(cu.Address);
```

```
// JAVA
cu.getAddress().setStreet("2 Second Street");
db.Set(cu.getAddress());
```

This time the Address object is stored explicitly. Querying for the Customer now gives the following output:

```
Gary (Customer)
2 Second Street, San Jose, USA (Address)
```

The Address has now been updated correctly. So it looks as though you can't store associated objects alongside a top-level object. Well, you can, but you won't always want to. The Customer object is simple, with only one associated object. Some structured objects are a lot more complicated, and might have many associated objects, each of which might in turn have many more. Updating a single primitive property of a single top-level object could lead to a very large number of objects being updated needlessly, with an unnecessary performance hit.

db4o gives you the choice. If you want to update associated objects, you can. By default, only the object explicitly passed to the Set method is updated. The way this is controlled is through the concept of *update depth*. This controls how deep an object graph will be traversed on update. The default update depth for all objects is 1, meaning that only primitive and string members will be updated.

You can change the behavior by setting CascadeOnUpdate for the Customer class, which is done with the following code before the ObjectContainer is opened:

```
// C#
Db4o.Configure().ObjectClass(typeof(Customer)).CascadeOnUpdate(true);
```

```
// JAVA
Db4o.configure().objectClass(Customer.class).cascadeOnUpdate(true);
```

CascadeOnUpdate is one of a range of configuration options for db4o, which are covered in detail in Chapter 10. With this option set, the Customer and Address objects are updated correctly by storing just the Customer object explicitly.

■**Tip** It is possible to have more fine-grained control of updates by setting the update depth for a specific class to a specific setting (see Chapter 10).

---

db4o gives you a lot of flexibility in updating structured objects. You can decide which object to retrieve and how much of its object graph to update. In general, it is wise to plan your update strategy using these principles:

- Plan your query so that as far as possible you retrieve only the objects you need to update.

- Control the update depth so that you only update objects that you have modified.

Deleting Simple Structured Objects

Deleting a structured object is something that needs to be done with caution. What do you actually want to delete? If you delete a Customer, do you want the Address object to remain in the database? There is no right or wrong answer to this—it really depends on the specific circumstances.

Like updating, db4o lets you make the choice. The following code deletes our Customer object:

```
// C#
IList<Customer> customers = db.Query<Customer>(delegate(Customer cust)
{
    return cust.Name.Equals("Gary");
});
Customer cu = customers[0];  // get first returned Customer - should only be one
db.Delete(cu);
```

```
// JAVA
List<Customer> customers = db.query(new Predicate<Customer>()
{
    public boolean match(Customer cust)
    {
        return cust.getName().equals("Gary");
    }
});
Customer cu = customers.get(0);  // get first returned Customer - should only be one
db.delete(cu);
```

Querying for the Address object shows that it is still in the database, even though the Customer has been deleted.

Forcing a cascading delete, where associated objects are deleted along with the top-level object, is similar to the cascading update you have already seem. You set the CascadeOnDelete configuration option for the Customer class before the ObjectContainer is opened.

```
// C#
Db4o.Configure().ObjectClass(typeof(Customer)).CascadeOnDelete(true);
```

```
// JAVA
Db4o.configure().objectClass(Customer.class).cascadeOnDelete(true);
```

Take care, as cascading deletes can be dangerous. What if the Address object is referenced by another Customer object in the database? The class diagram in Figure 7-1 implies that there is a one-to-one relationship, but nothing in the code for the classes listed prevents more than one Customer from having the same Address.

The result of a cascading delete in this case is that you could have a Customer remaining in the database with a null Address. Currently db4o does not check whether objects to be deleted are referenced anywhere else, so think carefully before enabling cascading deletes.

Incidentally, it is also possible to leave a Customer in the database with a null Address without a cascading delete. You can simply query for the Address object and delete it explicitly.

In most situations, working with objects in a db4o database is very similar to working with the objects in memory, as the object references and relationships work in exactly the same way. Object deletion is one situation where there is a very significant difference. In-memory objects in a managed environment like .NET or Java are only destroyed by the garbage collector when there are no references to them. Database objects, on the other hand, can be deleted arbitrarily. db4o does not provide referential integrity to control this within the database, so the programmer must ensure that the application deals with integrity issues resulting from deletion.

Object Activation

The first query demonstrated in this chapter retrieved a Customer object, as well as the associated Address object. After executing the query, both objects exist in memory and are ready to use. These objects are said to be *activated*. The query activated all the objects that could be reached by traversing the object graph.

It is not always desirable to activate all possible objects, as in some situations this could result in a very large object graph being loaded into memory. Just as you control updates with update depth, you can control activation with activation depth. There are various ways of implementing activation depth—we will look at one example here and return to fill in the details later in the chapter.

Activation depth can be configured as a global parameter. The minimum value is 1, which means that for each top-level object returned by a query, the object itself, and any primitive or string fields, can be accessed. Any fields that are object references will exist as nulls, and the referenced objects will not be loaded into memory. The default value of the activation depth is 5.

To illustrate this, this example sets the global activation depth to 1 and queries for a Customer as before. To see exactly what is in memory, we set a breakpoint and look at the Locals window in the IDE (Visual Studio in this case—a similar view can be found in Eclipse and other Java IDEs), as shown in Figure 7-3.

```
// C#
IList<Customer> customers = db.Query<Customer>(delegate(Customer cust)
{
    return cust.Name.Equals("Gary");
});
Customer cu = customers[0];
// Breakpoint on next line
```

```
// JAVA
List<Customer> customers = db.query(new Predicate<Customer>()
{
    public boolean match(Customer cust)
    {
        return cust.getName().equals("Gary");
    }
});
Customer cu = customers.get(0);
// Breakpoint on next line
```

cu	{Gary (Customer)}
base	{Gary (Customer)}
_address	{, , (Address)}
Address	{, , (Address)}
_city	null
_country	null
_street	null
City	null
Country	null
Street	null

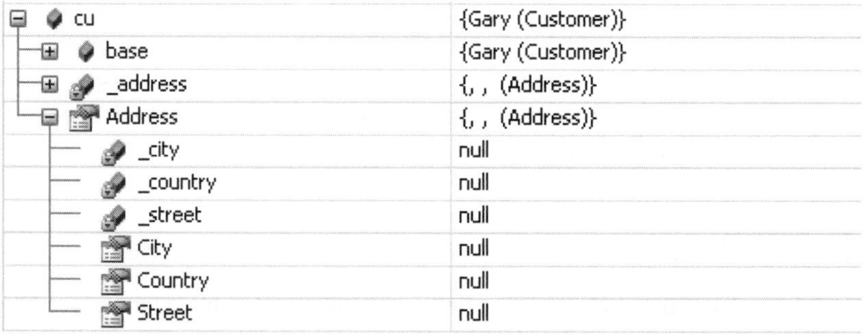

Figure 7-3. *Customer object (cu) in memory after query*

The Address has clearly not exactly been activated. That doesn't mean you can't get it if you need it. The following line activates the Address object:

```
// C#
db.Activate(cu.Address, 1);
```

```
// JAVA
db.activate(cu.getAddress(), 1);
```

The specified object is activated to the depth specified by the second parameter. The Locals window after execution of this line is shown in Figure 7-4. The Address associated with the Customer object cu is now ready to use.

⊟ ● cu	{Gary (Customer)}
├ ⊞ ● base	{Gary (Customer)}
├ ⊞ 🔗 _address	{1 First Street, San Jose, USA (Address)}
└ ⊟ 🔖 Address	{1 First Street, San Jose, USA (Address)}
├ 🔗 _city	"San Jose"
├ 🔗 _country	"USA"
├ 🔗 _street	"1 First Street"
├ 🔖 City	"San Jose"
├ 🔖 Country	"USA"
└ 🔖 Street	"1 First Street"

Figure 7-4. *Customer object (cu) in memory after activation of Address*

If an object is active and you no longer need it, you can deactivate it. Deactivating sets all member objects to null and all primitive fields to their default values. The following code deactivates the Address object that was activated previously:

```
// C#
db.Deactivate(cu.Address, 1);
```

```
// JAVA
db.deactivate(cu.getAddress(), 1);
```

The second parameter does a similar job to its equivalent in a call to Activate: it specifies the depth to which the deactivation is to cascade.

Object Hierarchies

If you look at Figure 7-1 you'll see that Address has a field _zipCode that has been ignored so far. This field is itself an object, an instance of the class ZipCode, shown in Listings 7-5 and 7-6. Hence Customer is at the top of a hierarchical structure: Customer *has-an* Address that *has-a* ZipCode. With db4o it is very straightforward to work with structures like this.

Listing 7-5. *The ZipCode Class in C#*

```
// C#
namespace com.db4o.dg2db4o.chapter7
{
    class ZipCode
    {
        string _state;
        string _code;
        string _extension;

        public ZipCode(string state, string code, string extension)
        {
            _state = state;
```

```csharp
            _code = code;
            _extension = extension;
        }

        public string State
        {
            get
            {
                return _state;
            }
            set
            {
                _state = value;
            }
        }

        public string Code
        {
            get
            {
                return _code;
            }
            set
            {
                _code = value;
            }
        }

        public string Extension
        {
            get
            {
                return _extension;
            }
            set
            {
                _extension = value;
            }
        }

        public override string ToString()
        {
            return _state + _code + "-" + _extension + " (ZipCode)";
        }
    }
}
```

Listing 7-6. *The ZipCode Class in Java*

```java
// JAVA
package com.db4o.dg2db4o.chapter7;

public class ZipCode
{
    private String _state;
    private String _code;
    private String _extension;

    public ZipCode(String state, String code, String extension)
    {
        _state = state;
        _code= code;
        _extension = extension;
    }

    public String getState()
    {
        return _state;
    }

    public void setState(String value)
    {
        this._state = value;
    }

    public String getCode()
    {
        return _code;
    }

    public void setCode(String value)
    {
        this._code = value;
    }

    public String getExtension()
    {
        return _extension;
    }

    public void setExtension(String value)
    {
        this._extension = value;
    }
```

```
    public String toString()
    {
        return _state + _code + "-" + _extension + " (ZipCode)";
    }
}
```

Storing a hierarchical structured object is just like storing a simple structured object: again you just need to store the top-level object, and any associated objects will also be stored.

```
// C#
ZipCode z1 = new ZipCode("CA", "95200", "1234");
ZipCode z2 = new ZipCode("CA", "95200", "5678");
Address a1 = new Address("1 First Street", "San Jose", "USA");
a1.ZipCode = z1;
a2.ZipCode = z2;
Customer cu1 = new Customer("Gary", "408 123 4567", "gary@example.net", a1);
Customer cu2 = new Customer("Mary", "408 101 1001", "mary@example.com", a2);

db.Set(cu1);
db.Set(cu2);
```

```
// JAVA
ZipCode z1 = new ZipCode("CA", "95200", "1234");
ZipCode z2 = new ZipCode("CA", "95200", "5678");
Address a1 = new Address("1 First Street", "San Jose", "USA");
a1.setZipCode(z1);
a2.setZipCode(z2);
Customer cu1 = new Customer("Gary", "408 123 4567", "gary@example.net", a1);
Customer cu2 = new Customer("Mary", "408 101 1001", "mary@example.com", a2);

db.set(cu1);
db.set(cu2);
```

Deep Queries

A deep query is one whose criteria involve objects deep in the hierarchy. For example, let's try to find all Customers who live at an Address that has a ZipCode with _extension "5678". With QBE, this is simply a case of constructing a suitable example object:

```
// C#
ZipCode zipExample = new ZipCode(null, null, "1234");
Address addressExample = new Address(null,null,null);
addressExample.ZipCode = zipExample;
Customer customerExample = new Customer(null, null, null, addressExample);
ObjectSet results = db.Get(customerExample);
```

```
while (results.HasNext())
{
    Customer customer = (Customer)results.Next();
    Console.WriteLine(customer);
    Console.WriteLine(customer.Address);
    Console.WriteLine(customer.Address.ZipCode);
}
```

```
// JAVA
ZipCode zipExample = new ZipCode(null, null, "1234");
Address addressExample = new Address(null,null,null);
addressExample.setZipCode(zipExample);
Customer customerExample = new Customer(null, null, null, addressExample);
ObjectSet results = db.get(customerExample);
while (results.hasNext())
{
    Customer customer = (Customer)results.next();
    System.out.println(customer);
    System.out.println(customer.getAddress());
    System.out.println(customer.getAddress().getZipCode());
}
```

This query should return one Customer object and give the following output:

```
Mary (Customer)
2 Second Street, San Jose, USA (Address)
CA95200-5678 (ZipCode)
```

The equivalent native query simply has to navigate one more object reference than the simple structured object example you saw earlier in this chapter:

```
// C#
IList<Customer> customers = db.Query<Customer>(delegate(Customer cust)
{
    return cust.Address.ZipCode.Extension.Equals("5678");
});
```

```
// JAVA
List<Customer> customers = db.query(new Predicate<Customer>()
{
    public boolean match(Customer cust)
    {
        return cust.getAddress().getZipCode().getExtension().equals("5678");
    }
});
```

Similarly, the equivalent SODA query needs to descend one more level in the query graph:

```csharp
// C#
Query query = db.Query();
query.Constrain(typeof(Customer));
Query zipQuery = query.Descend("_address").Descend("_zipCode");
zipQuery.Descend("_extension").Constrain("5678");
ObjectSet results = query.Execute();
```

```java
// JAVA
Query query = db.query();
query.constrain(Customer.class);
Query zipQuery = query.descend("_address").descend("_zipCode");
zipQuery.descend("_extension").constrain("5678");
ObjectSet results = query.execute();
```

Object hierarchies can be arbitrarily deep, of course. Later in this chapter you'll see an example of working with much deeper objects than this.

Objects with Inverse Associations

The relationship between instances of the Customer and Address classes shown in Listings 7-3 and 7-4 is a simple, unidirectional one. You can navigate from a Customer to an Address, but not vice versa. If you look at the class diagram in Figure 7-1, this is not quite what is specified—the association is shown as bidirectional. This means that you should be able to navigate from an Address to its associated Customer. This requires that both objects contain references to each other. The Address class needs a new attribute, as shown in Listings 7-7 and 7-8.

Listing 7-7. *Modification to the C# Address Class for an Inverse Association with Customer*

```csharp
// C#
class Address
{
    string _street;
    string _city;
    string _country;
    Customer _customer;
...

    public Customer Customer
    {
        get
        {
            return _customer;
        }
```

```
        set
        {
            _customer = value;
        }
    }
...
}
```

Listing 7-8. *Modification to the Java Address Class for an Inverse Association with Customer*

```java
// JAVA
public class Address {

    String _street;
    String _city;
    String _country;
    Customer _customer;

...

    public Customer getCustomer()
    {
        return _customer;
    }
    public void setCustomer(Customer value)
    {
        _customer = value;
    }
...
}
```

With inverse associations, it's important to ensure referential integrity. This is the responsibility of the classes themselves. The constructor of the Customer class can be modified as shown in Listings 7-9 and 7-10 to ensure that the inverse association is maintained correctly. The constructor requires a reference to an Address object, and it sets the Customer property of that Address to refer to this, the Customer object itself. Note that these modified classes enforce a strict one-to-one relationship.

Listing 7-9. *Modification to the C# Customer Class to Maintain Correct Inverse Association with Address*

```csharp
// C#
class Customer : Person
{
    Address _address;
```

```
    public Customer(string name, string phoneNumber, string email, Address
        address) : base(name,phoneNumber,email)
    {
        _address = address;
        address.Customer = this;
    }
...
    public Address Address
    {
        get
        {
            return _address;
        }
        set
        {
             _address = value;
            value.Customer = this;
        }
    }
...
}
```

Listing 7-10. *Modfication to the Java Customer Class to Maintain Correct Inverse Association with Address*

```java
// JAVA
public class Customer extends AbstractPerson
{
    Address _address;

    public Customer(String name, String phoneNumber, String email, Address
        address)
    {
        super(name,phoneNumber,email);
        _address = address;
        address.setCustomer(this);
    }

    public Address getAddress()
    {
        return _address;
    }
```

```
    public void setAddress(Address value)
    {
        _address = value;
        value.setCustomer(this);
    }
...
}
```

With these new class definitions, it doesn't matter which object is stored. The following code explicitly stores the Address object, and the Customer object is also stored since the Address now contains a reference to it:

```
// C# & JAVA
Address a1 = new Address("1 First Street", "San Jose", "USA");
Customer cu1 = new Customer("Gary", "408 123 4567", "gary@example.net.com", a1);
```

```
// C#
db.Set(a1);
```

```
// JAVA
db.set(a1);
```

These queries will give the same results as they did before. The only difference is that querying for an Address will also return the Customer, assuming that the activation depth is greater than 1.

Inheritance

One of the key advantages of the close match between an object data model and an object-oriented domain model is the seamlessness with which inheritance trees are handled. As Part I of this book shows, this is in sharp contrast to the way inheritance is handled in a relational database. Dealing with interfaces, superclasses, and subclasses in db4o is almost so straightforward that you don't need to think about it. If you understand how these things work in your programming language, then you pretty much understand how they work in db4o.

To demonstrate this, we need to look a bit further down the inheritance tree than we have done. The interface and abstract class at the top of the tree have been listed earlier, and so has the Customer class. Let's look at the Employee, Manager, and CasualEmployee classes. The Employee class is shown in Listings 7-11 and 7-12—we'll make more use of the others in following sections, so we'll leave a full listing of these until later. For now, all you need to know is that they are subclasses of Employee, and that Manager has a constructor that takes exactly the same list of parameters as Employee.

Listing 7-11. *The Employee Class in C#*

```csharp
// C#
namespace com.db4o.dg2db4o.chapter7
{
    class Employee : Person
    {
        int _employeeNumber;
        string _dob;

        public Employee(string name, string phoneNumber, string email, int
            employeeNumber, string dob) : base(name,phoneNumber,email)
        {
            _employeeNumber = employeeNumber;
            _dob = dob;
        }

        public override void SendMail(string fromAddress, string subject, string
            content)
        {
            string toAddress = base.Email + "@example.com";
            System.Net.Mail.SmtpClient mailer = new System.Net.Mail.SmtpClient();
            mailer.Send(fromAddress, toAddress, subject, content);
        }

        public int EmployeeNumber
        {
            get
            {
                return _employeeNumber;
            }
            set
            {
                _employeeNumber = value;
            }
        }

        public string Dob
        {
            get
            {
                return _dob;
            }
            set
            {
                _dob = value;
            }
        }
```

```
        public override string ToString()
        {
            return base.Name + " (Employee)";
        }
    }
}
```

Listing 7-12. *The Employee Class in Java*

// JAVA
```
package com.db4o.dg2db4o.chapter7;

public class Employee extends AbstractPerson
{
    int _employeeNumber;
    String _dob;

    public Employee(String name, String phoneNumber, String email, int
        employeeNumber, String dob)
    {
        super(name,phoneNumber,email);
        _employeeNumber = employeeNumber;
        _dob = dob;
    }

    public void sendMail(String fromAddress, String subject, String content) {
        String toAddress = super.getEmail() + "@example.com";
        Emailer mailer = new Emailer();   // class included in downloadable code
        mailer.sendMail(fromAddress, toAddress, subject, content);
    }

    public int getEmployeeNumber()
    {
        return _employeeNumber;
    }

    public void setEmployeeNumber(int value)
    {
        _employeeNumber = value;
    }

    public String getDob()
    {
        return _dob;
    }
```

```
    public void setDoB(String value)
    {
        _dob = value;
    }

    public String toString() {
        return super.getName() + " (Employee)";
    }
}
```

Now let's store a selection of Persons in the database. You don't need to do anything special when storing an instance of a subclass. You just store the object as it is—in fact, the examples in the previous section stored instances of the Customer subclass quite happily. None of the four objects in the listing that follows have any relationships: a Manager *is-a* type of Employee, but is not related to any specific Employee object. All four objects must therefore be stored explicitly.

```
// C# & JAVA
Employee e1 = new Employee("Michael", "1234", "michael", 101, "10/5/1975");
Manager m1 = new Manager("Sue", "9876", "sue", 102, "3/8/1982");
CasualEmployee c1 = new CasualEmployee("Tim", "5544", "tim", 103, "7/6/1986");
Customer cu1 = new Customer("Gary", "408 123 4567", "gary@example.net", new
    Address("1 First Street", "San Jose", "USA"));
```

```
// C#
db.Set(e1);
db.Set(m1);
db.Set(c1);
db.Set(cu1);
```

```
// JAVA
db.set(e1);
db.set(m1);
db.set(c1);
db.set(cu1);
```

You've seen plenty of queries for Customer objects, so let's try querying for Manager objects. QBE is used in this example, which queries for all Manager objects in the database. Note that in listing the objects returned in the following examples we are not doing anything specific to the class of object returned, so we can use some nice generic code (which could be refactored to a method) to list the ObjectSet.

```
// C#
Manager managerExample = new Manager(null, null, null, 0, null);
ObjectSet results = db.Get(managerExample);
```

```
// JAVA
Manager managerExample = new Manager(null, null, null, 0, null);
ObjectSet results = db.get(managerExample);
```

The output is:

```
Sue (Manager)
```

This seems straightforward. Let's try querying for Employee objects:

```
// C#
Employee employeeExample = new Employee(null, null, null, 0, null);
ObjectSet results = db.Get(employeeExample);
```

```
// JAVA
Employee employeeExample = new Employee(null, null, null, 0, null);
ObjectSet results = db.get(employeeExample);
```

The output is:

```
Tim (CasualEmployee)
Sue (Manager)
Michael (Employee)
```

This time we got the Employee object and also the Manager and CasualEmployee. With a little knowledge of polymorphism, this is what you'd expect. This query returns the full extent of the Employee class in the database, which contains all objects of that class and all its subclasses. The Customer object, as you'd expect, is not part of this extent.

Excellent—now let's try to get all these objects in one query. We should be able to do this by querying for Person objects. This is easy with a native query, but presents a slight problem with QBE—how do you create a prototype object when the class is abstract, and you can't actually create an instance? Fortunately, there is another way of specifying the class when we just want all the objects of that class:

```
// C#
ObjectSet results = db.Get(typeof(Person));
```

```
// JAVA
ObjectSet results = db.get(AbstractPerson.class);
```

The output from this query is, as expected:

```
Gary (Customer)
Tim (CasualEmployee)
Sue (Manager)
Michael (Employee)
```

We can query by the name of the interface too, and the output is exactly the same:

```
// C#
ObjectSet results = db.Get(typeof(IPerson));
```

```
// JAVA
ObjectSet results = db.get(Person.class);
```

So, the rules of inheritance in db4o follow those of C# and Java very closely. Once you have instantiated an object, you can store it regardless of where in any inheritance tree it belongs. The objects that are matched by a query follow the normal rules of polymorphism.

Objects with Multivalued Attributes: Arrays

The Customer and Address classes are simple in that their associations are single-valued. We need to be able to deal with objects whose structures include references to multivalued objects. For example, a Manager will be associated with a number of Employees, not just one Employee. Both C# and Java have two mechanisms for multivalued objects: *arrays* and *collections*. We will look at arrays first and then move on to collections in the next section.

Arrays give us a list of items of similar data types. An array is an object that contains multiple primitive data items or references to object data items. In C#, an array is derived from the System.Array class, while in Java, every array belongs to a class that is reflected as a Class object that is shared by all arrays that have the same element type and number of dimensions.

Arrays in C# and Java are not true first-class objects, although they have many of the characteristics of first-class objects: you can have a variable that is an array; you can construct an array at runtime; you can pass an array as a parameter to a method; and so on. Unlike any other objects, though, when you declare a new array, its type is declared as the type of the items that it contains.

In practice, the main thing to remember when using arrays in a db4o database is that you can't use an array as a prototype object in a query as you can with any true first-class object.

Let's look at some examples of working with arrays in db4o. In Figure 7-1, the CasualEmployee class has an attribute _timeRecord that is an array of numeric values, each of which represents a number of hours worked on a particular shift. This is shown as an attribute rather than an object relationship since the contained items are simple numeric values rather than nontrivial objects. The code for CasualEmployee is shown in Listings 7-13 and 7-14.

Listing 7-13. *The CasualEmployee Class in C#*

```
// C#
namespace com.db4o.dg2db4o.chapter7
{
    class CasualEmployee : Employee
    {
        double[] _timeRecord;
        const int MAXTIMERECORDS = 10;
        int numberOfTimeRecords;
```

```
        public CasualEmployee(string name, string phoneNumber, string email, int
            employeeNumber, string dob) :
            base(name, phoneNumber, email, employeeNumber, dob)
        {

            _timeRecord = new double[MAXTIMERECORDS];
            numberOfTimeRecords = 0;

        }

        public double[] TimeRecord
        {
            get
            {
                return _timeRecord;
            }
            set
            {
                _timeRecord = value;
            }
        }

        public void addTimeRecord(double newRecord)
        {
            if (numberOfTimeRecords < MAXTIMERECORDS)
            {
                _timeRecord[numberOfTimeRecords] = newRecord;
                numberOfTimeRecords++;
            }
        }

        public override string ToString()
        {
            return base.Name + " (CasualEmployee)";
        }
    }
}
```

Listing 7-14. *The CasualEmployee Class in Java*

```
// JAVA
package com.db4o.dg2db4o.chapter7;

public class CasualEmployee extends Employee
{
    double[] _timeRecord;
    final int MAXTIMERECORDS = 10;
    int numberOfTimeRecords;
```

```java
public CasualEmployee(String name, String phoneNumber, String email, int
    employeeNumber, String dob)
{
    super(name, phoneNumber, email, employeeNumber, dob);
    _timeRecord = new double[MAXTIMERECORDS];
        numberOfTimeRecords = 0;
}

public double[] getTimeRecord()
{
    return _timeRecord;
}

public void setTimeRecord(double[] timeRecord)
{
    _timeRecord = timeRecord;
}

public void addTimeRecord(double newRecord)
{
    if (numberOfTimeRecords < MAXTIMERECORDS)
    {
        _timeRecord[numberOfTimeRecords] = newRecord;
        numberOfTimeRecords++;
    }
}

public String toString()
{
    return super.getName() + " (CasualEmployee)";
}
}
```

As usual, storing the object is extremely simple—it just requires a call to Set. Retrieving the objects is more interesting. It is fairly obvious that if you retrieve a CasualEmployee by some other criteria, such as the _name attribute, then the array will be retrieved also (less obvious is that this is true even if the activation depth is set to 1). The following examples show how to use the contents of the _timeRecord array as query criteria.

Query by Values in the Array

We can use a value stored in an array as a query criterion. Here, the query will give us every CasualEmployee that has that value in its _timeRecord. First, let's create some example objects.

```
// C# & JAVA
CasualEmployee c1 = new CasualEmployee("Tim", "5544", "tim", 101, "7/6/1986");
CasualEmployee c2 = new CasualEmployee("Eva", "4433", "eva", 102, "11/3/1984");
c1.addTimeRecord(2.5);
c1.addTimeRecord(4.0);
c1.addTimeRecord(1.5);
c1.addTimeRecord(2.0);
c2.addTimeRecord(3.5);
c2.addTimeRecord(4.0);
c2.addTimeRecord(5.0);
```

```
// C#
db.Set(c1);
db.Set(c2);
```

```
// JAVA
db.set(c1);
db.set(c2);
```

Tim has worked four shifts, for a total of 10 hours. Eva has worked three shifts, for a total of 12.5 hours. Let's try to find all CasualEmployees who have worked at least one shift of exactly 4 hours (this should return both Tim and Eva). To do this with QBE, you create a prototype object with a _timeRecord array that contains only the value you want to search for.

```
// C#
CasualEmployee casEmpExample = new CasualEmployee(null, null, null, 0, null);
casEmpExample.TimeRecord = new double[]{4.0};
ObjectSet results = db.Get(casEmpExample);
```

```
// JAVA
CasualEmployee casEmpExample = new CasualEmployee(null, null, null, 0, null);
casEmpExample.setTimeRecord(new double[]{4.0});
ObjectSet results = db.get(casEmpExample);
```

Listing the results produces:

```
Eva (CasualEmployee)
Tim (CasualEmployee)
```

You can specify more than one array item to be matched. The following variation finds all CasualEmployees who have worked shifts of 2.5 hours and 4 hours:

```
// C#
CasualEmployee casEmpExample = new CasualEmployee(null, null, null, 0, null);
casEmpExample.TimeRecord = new double[]{2.5, 4.0};
results = db.Get(casEmpExample);
```

```
// JAVA
CasualEmployee casEmpExample = new CasualEmployee(null, null, null, 0, null);
casEmpExample.setTimeRecord(new double[]{2.5, 4.0});
ObjectSet results = db.get(casEmpExample);
```

Listing the results gives, as you would expect:

```
Tim (CasualEmployee)
```

Note that you can't query for the array directly—the following returns no results:

```
// C#
results = db.Get(new double[] { 2.5, 4.0 });
```

```
// JAVA
results = db.get(new double[] { 2.5, 4.0 });
```

You can use a native query to do the same thing. This example finds all CasualEmployees who have worked shifts of 2.5 hours and 4 hours. The query return expression evaluates to true for all objects that match the criteria—in other words, for which the array contains both values.

```
// C#
IList<CasualEmployee>casEmps = db.Query<CasualEmployee>(
    delegate(CasualEmployee casEmp)
{
    return Array.IndexOf(casEmp.TimeRecord, 2.5) > -1 &&
        Array.IndexOf(casEmp.TimeRecord, 4.0) > -1;
});
```

This uses the IndexOf static method of the Array class to find the index in the array of each specific value, which will be negative if the value is not present. The same query is slightly less convenient in Java, where the binary search method provided by the Arrays class is used. The binary search algorithm requires that the array be sorted (possibly using Arrays.sort) before this will work properly.

```
// JAVA
List<CasualEmployee> casEmps = db.query(new Predicate<CasualEmployee>() {
    public boolean match(CasualEmployee casEmp)
    {
        return Arrays.binarySearch(casEmp.getTimeRecord(),2.5) >= 0 &&
            Arrays.binarySearch(casEmp.getTimeRecord(),4.0) >= 0;
    }
});
```

To achieve the same result using SODA, you apply a constraint on the _timeRecord field for each value to be checked:

```
// C#
Query query = db.Query();
query.Constrain(typeof(CasualEmployee));
Query valuequery = query.Descend("_timeRecord");
valuequery.Constrain(2.5);
valuequery.Constrain(4.0);
ObjectSet results = query.Execute();
```

```
// JAVA
Query query = db.query();
query.constrain(CasualEmployee.class);
Query valuequery = query.descend("_timeRecord");
valuequery.constrain(2.5);
valuequery.constrain(4.0);
ObjectSet results = query.execute();
```

The query graph for this is shown in Figure 7-5.

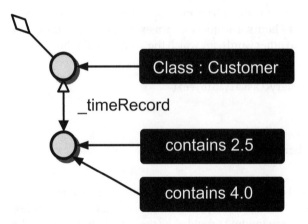

Figure 7-5. *SODA query graph for the array query*

More Complex Queries

You can construct a query using other aspects of the array as criteria by putting suitable code in the match method of a native query. The following example matches all CasualEmployees who have worked for a total of more than 10 hours (it returns only Eva, who has worked 12.5 hours).

```
// C#
IList<CasualEmployee> casEmps = db.Query<CasualEmployee>(
    delegate(CasualEmployee casEmp)
{
    double totalTime = 0.0;
    int numberOfRecords = 0;
    while ((casEmp.TimeRecord[numberOfRecords] != 0) &&
        (numberOfRecords < casEmp.TimeRecord.Length))
```

```
    {
        totalTime += casEmp.TimeRecord[numberOfRecords];
        numberOfRecords++;
    }
    return totalTime > 10.0;
});
```

```
// JAVA
List<CasualEmployee> casEmps = db.query(new Predicate<CasualEmployee>()
{
    public boolean match(CasualEmployee casEmp)
    {
        double totalTime = 0.0;
        int numberOfRecords = 0;
        while ((casEmp.getTimeRecord()[numberOfRecords] != 0) &&
            (numberOfRecords < casEmp.getTimeRecord().length))
        {
            totalTime += casEmp.getTimeRecord()[numberOfRecords];
            numberOfRecords++;
        }
        return totalTime > 10.0;
    }
});
```

This works, although the processing required for each match probably makes this query slow for large data sets. It might be preferable in practice to achieve the same effect by designing the domain class to store totalTime as a separate attribute that can be indexed (see Chapter 12).

Updating and Deleting

Updating the contents of an array is straightforward. You need to retrieve the object that contains the array, update the required array items, and call Set to store the object again. For a numeric array, it is not necessary to set CascadeOnUpdate for this to work.

This example adds a new time record entry and changes the value of another for a specified CasualEmployee. Note that for this array of numeric values, adding a new item simply involves replacing the first zero value with a new value.

```
// C#
CasualEmployee casEmpExample = new CasualEmployee("Tim", null, null, 0, null);
ObjectSet results = db.Get(casEmpExample);
CasualEmployee casEmp = (CasualEmployee)results.Next();
casEmp.addTimeRecord(6.0);
casEmp.TimeRecord[0] = 7.0;
db.Set(casEmp);
```

```
// JAVA
CasualEmployee casEmpExample = new CasualEmployee("Tim", null, null, 0, null);
ObjectSet results = db.get(casEmpExample);
CasualEmployee ce = (CasualEmployee)results.next();
ce.addTimeRecord(6.0);
ce.getTimeRecord()[0] = 7.0;
db.set(ce);
```

If you retrieve this object in a separate transaction, then listing the contents of the array in the retrieved object show that the array has been updated.

7.0 4.0 1.5 2.0 6.0 0.0 0.0 0.0 0.0 0.0

There is nothing special about deleting in this example. Deleting array items is done by updating them to zero values. If you delete the CasualEmployee object, then the array is also deleted.

Objects with Multivalued Attributes: Collections

Both .NET and Java provide collections frameworks, which are unified architectures for organizing and handling collections of data. These provide interfaces to and implementations of a range of data structures. The collections classes include dynamic data structures that can grow to accommodate new data, and provision of a wide range of methods for adding, removing, finding, and manipulating the data they contain. Arrays are useful for simple data sets, such as the numeric arrays in the previous section, and for some specialized applications, but in general, collections provide more flexibility and ease of coding.

Unlike arrays, instances of collections classes are clearly first-class objects, and can be used in exactly the same ways as any other objects. An ArrayList object, in either language, is an instance of a class called ArrayList.

To illustrate how to use collections in db4o, we will look at the Project and Employee classes in Figure 7-1. A Project has a number of Employees associated with it, and these are stored in an ArrayList. The relationship is shown in the class diagram as a many-to-many relationship—normally a Project will include several Employees, while it is possible for more than one Project to include a particular Employee. This doesn't make a lot of difference to the way we work with the objects, and in the examples in this section each Employee is associated with one Project only.

The Project class is shown in Listings 7-15 and 7-16. The Employee class was listed earlier (Listings 7-9 and 7-10).

Listing 7-15. *The Project Class in C#*

```
// C#
Using System.Collections;

namespace com.db4o.dg2db4o.chapter7
{
```

```csharp
class Project
{
    string _name;
    string _costCode;
    IList _employees;

    public Project(string name, string costCode)
    {
        _name = name;
        _costCode = costCode;
        _employees = new ArrayList();


    }

    public Project(string name, string costCode, IList employees)
    {
        _name = name;
        _costCode = costCode;
        _employees = employees;
    }

    public void AssignEmployee(Employee newEmployee)
    {
        _employees.Add(newEmployee);
    }

    public string Name
    {
        get
        {
            return _name;
        }
        set
        {
            _name = value;
        }
    }

    public string CostCode
    {
        get
        {
            return _costCode;
        }
```

```
                set
                {
                    _costCode = value;
                }
            }

            public IList Employees
            {
                get
                {
                    return _employees;
                }
            }

            public override string ToString()
            {
                return _name + " (Project)";
            }
        }
    }
```

Listing 7-16. *The Project Class in Java*

```java
// JAVA
package com.db4o.dg2db4o.chapter7;

import java.util.List;
import java.util.ArrayList;

public class Project
{
    String _name;
    String _costCode;
    List<Employee> _employees;

    public Project(String name, String costCode)
    {
        _name = name;
        _costCode = costCode;
        _employees = new ArrayList<Employee>();
    }

    public Project(String name, String costCode, List<Employee> employees)
    {
        _name = name;
        _costCode = costCode;
        _employees = employees;
    }
```

```
    public void assignEmployee(Employee newEmployee)
    {
        _employees.add(newEmployee);
    }

    public String getName()
    {
        return _name;
    }

    public void setName(String value)
    {
        _name = value;
    }

    public String getCostCode()
    {
        return _costCode;
    }

    public void setCostCode(String value)
    {
        _costCode = value;
    }

    public List<Employee> employees()
    {
        return _employees;
    }

    public String toString()
    {
        return _name + " (Project)";
    }
}
```

Storing Objects

The code to create and store some sample objects is listed. Note that we are using polymorphism here, as some of the Employee objects are instances of the CasualEmployee subclass. These are treated in exactly the same way as the Employee objects.

Storing the Project objects also stores the associated Employee objects, so the two Set calls are sufficient to store all the objects. You could store the Employee objects with additional Set calls, which makes no difference as long as it is within the same transaction.

```
// C# & JAVA
Employee e1 = new Employee("Michael", "1234", "michael", 101, "10/5/1975");
Employee e2 = new Employee("Anne", "5432", "anne", 102, "8/5/1980");
CasualEmployee c1 = new CasualEmployee("Tim", "5544", "tim", 103, "7/6/1986");
CasualEmployee c2 = new CasualEmployee("Eva", "4433", "eva", 104, "11/3/1984");
Project p1 = new Project("Finance System", "P01");
Project p2 = new Project("Web Site", "P02");
```

```
// C#
p1.AssignEmployee(e1);
p1.AssignEmployee(c1);
p2.AssignEmployee(c2);
db.Set(p1);
db.Set(p2);
```

```
// JAVA
p1.assignEmployee(e1);
p1.assignEmployee(c1);
p2.assignEmployee(c2);
db.set(p1);
db.set(p2);
```

Query for an Object

When you retrieve a structured object, then by default you also get associated objects. This includes objects that are contained in a collection, so when you retrieve a Project, you should also retrieve the Employees, if the activation depth allows it. Here is a simple QBE example. The output displays the Project and its Employees.

```
// C#
Project projectExample = new Project(null, "P01");
ObjectSet results = db.Get(projectExample);
while (results.HasNext())
{
    Project proj = (Project)results.Next();
    Console.WriteLine(proj);
    foreach (Employee empl in proj.Employees)
    {
        Console.WriteLine(empl);
    }
}
```

```
// JAVA
Project projectExample = new Project(null, "P01");
ObjectsSet results = db.get(projectExample);
```

```
while (results.hasNext())
{
    Project proj = (Project)results.next();
    System.out.println(proj);
    for(Employee empl : proj.Employees)
    {
        System.out.println (empl);
    }
}
```

The output is:

```
Finance System (Project)
Michael (Employee)
Tim (CasualEmployee)
```

Query by Objects in the Collection

Finding a particular project immediately gives you all the Employees for that project. What if you want to find the Project (or Projects) that a particular Employee is assigned to? In this case you need to use the attributes of Employee in a query for Projects. This example uses QBE to find the Project that the Employee named "Anne" is working on. The Project prototype is created by first creating an Employee prototype with the required name, and then creating a Project prototype with an ArrayList that contains the Employee prototype. This is quite similar to the way array items are matched: this prototype will match any Project with an ArrayList containing an Employee object, in any position, that matches the Employee prototype.

// C#
```
Employee emp = new Employee("Anne", null, null, 0, null);
IList empList = new ArrayList();
empList.Add(emp);
Project projectExample = new Project(null,null,empList);
ObjectSet results = db.Get(projectExample);
```

// JAVA
```
Employee emp = new Employee("Anne", null, null, 0, null);
List<Employee> empList = new ArrayList<Employee>();
empList.add(emp);
Project projectExample = new Project(null,null,empList);
ObjectSet results = db.get(projectExample);
```

Anne is only assigned to one project, so the output if we list the results is:

```
Web Site (Project)
```

Since the ArrayList is a first-class object, you can query directly for it. This could be useful if you only wanted access to the list of Employees on the same project as your prototype but not any other attribute of the Project.

```csharp
// C#
Employee emp = new Employee("Anne", null, null, 0, null);
IList empList = new ArrayList();
empList.Add(emp);
ObjectSet results = db.Get(empList);
```

```java
// JAVA
Employee emp = new Employee("Anne", null, null, 0, null);
List<Employee> empList = new ArrayList<Employee>();
empList.add(emp);
ObjectSet results = db.get(empList);
```

This can be done as a native query also. The operation of this query is quite straightforward: for each candidate Project, iterate through the list of Employees and return true if one is found with a name that matches the target, and return false if the whole list has been traversed without a match. The actual criterion for the Employees is very simple in this query, but more advanced criteria are clearly possible within this structure.

```csharp
// C#
IList<Project> projects = db.Query<Project>(delegate(Project proj)
{
    foreach (Employee empl in proj.Employees)
    {
        if (empl.Name.Equals("Michael"))
        {
            return true;
        }
    }
    return false;
});
```

```java
// JAVA
List<Project> projects = db.query(new Predicate<Project>()
{
    public boolean match(Project proj)
    {
        for(Employee empl : proj.employees())
        {
            if (empl.getName().equals("Michael"))
            {
                return true;
            }
        }
```

```
        return false;
    }
});
```

As a SODA query, this becomes:

```csharp
// C#
Query query = db.Query();
query.Constrain(typeof(Project));
Query empQuery = query.Descend("_employees");
empQuery.Constrain(typeof(Employee));
Query nameQuery = empQuery.Descend("_name");
nameQuery.Constrain("Michael");
ObjectSet results = query.Execute();
```

```java
// JAVA
Query query = db.query();
query.constrain(Project.class);
Query empQuery = query.descend("_employees");
empQuery.constrain(Employee.class);
Query nameQuery = empQuery.descend("_name");
nameQuery.constrain("Michael");
ObjectSet results = query.execute()
```

The query graph for this is shown in Figure 7-6—compare this with the array query in Figure 7-5.

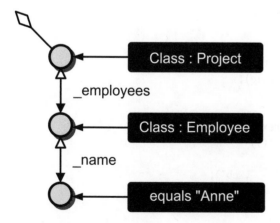

Figure 7-6. *SODA query graph for collection query*

Note You may have noticed that the C# Project class did not use a generic collection. If you use the List<T> class from the .NET 2.0 System.Collections.Generic namespace instead of the System.Collections.ArrayList, then only the Native Query method works correctly. Java 5.0 generic collections, as used in the Java Project class, are supported by all query methods.

Updating and Deleting

Updating the contents of a collection is similar to updating arrays. You need to retrieve the object that contains the collection, update the required items, and call Set to store the object again. Unlike the array example, it is now necessary to set CascadeOnUpdate for this to work.

This example does an update for all the Employees on a specified Project. It finds the Project, and changes the email address of all Employees on that project to reflect the Project name.

```
// C#
Project projectExample = new Project(null, "P02");
ObjectSet results = db.Get(projectExample);
while (results.HasNext())
{
    Project proj = (Project)results.Next();
    foreach (Employee empl in proj.Employees)
    {
        empl.Email = empl.Email + ".web";
    }
    db.Set(proj);
}
```

```
// JAVA
Project projectExample = new Project(null, "P02");
ObjectSet results = db.get(projectExample);
while (results.hasNext())
{
    Project proj = (Project)results.next();
    for(Employee empl : proj.employees())
    {
        empl.setEmail(empl.getEmail() + ".web");
    }
    db.set(proj);
}
```

The output from a suitable query, with output statements that also list the email address for each Employee, is:

Web Site (Project)
Anne (Employee): anne.web
Eva (CasualEmployee): eva.web

When deleting objects you find exactly the same issues as you saw for simple structured objects, with a slight twist. If you delete a `Project` without setting `CascadeOnDelete` for the `Project` class, then the `ArrayList` remains in the database. The `Employees` in the list are probably still valid objects as you would hope that `Employees` do not disappear if their project is canned (maybe this is being a bit optimistic!). However, the `ArrayList` itself has no particular meaning.

On the other hand, if you set `CascadeOnDelete`, then the `ArrayList` and all its `Employees` are also deleted. One option is not to set `CascadeOnDelete`, and to explicitly delete the `ArrayList` and then the `Project`.

```
// C#
db.Delete(proj.Employees);
db.Delete(proj);
```

```
// JAVA
db.delete(proj.employees());
db.delete(proj);
```

DB4O COLLECTIONS

We have used the standard C# and Java collections classes in these examples. db4o provides its own set of "database-aware" collections classes, including `Db4oList` and `Db4oHashMap`. These implement the interface `Db4oCollection`. For example, you can create a database-aware list as follows:

```
List.myList = objectContainer.Ext().Collections().NewLinkedList();  // C#
```

```
List.myList = objectContainer.ext().collections().newLinkedList();  // JAVA
```

Collections is a method of the db4o `ExtObjectContainer`, and returns a factory class that can create database-aware collections. The purpose of the `ExtObjectContainer` is explained in Chapters 9 and 10. A database-aware collection implements the usual collection interfaces, and adds two methods:

- `ActivationDepth`: Allows you to configure an activation depth specifically for objects in the collection

- `DeleteRemoved`: Allows you to specify that objects that are removed from the collection will also be removed from the database

Database-aware collections can help to manage collections of data more easily than the standard collections classes. However, using them does result in your business objects being dependent on db4o, which may be undesirable if you want them to be database-independent.

Object Activation and Circular References

You saw earlier in this chapter that it is important to control object activation when querying to make sure that you do not activate objects that you don't actually need access to. Failing to control activation can sometimes result in a large object graph being loaded into memory in its entirety. This can give you surprises particularly when there are circular references in the object model.

To illustrate this, the Employee and Project classes can be modified so that they have an inverse many-to-many relationship. This means that the Employee class now has a list of Projects to which the employee is assigned, while the Project class still has its list of Employees assigned to it. Referential integrity is ensured as when an Employee is added to a Project, the Project calls the appropriate method in Employee so that it is added to the Employee's list of Projects. The modified parts of the classes are shown in Listings 7-17 and 7-18.

Listing 7-17. *Modifications to the Employee and Project Classes in C# to Create an Inverse Many-to-Many Relationship*

```C#
// C#
using System.Collections;

namespace com.db4o.dg2db4o.chapter7
{
    class Employee : Person
    {
        int _employeeNumber;
        DateTime _dob;
        IList _projects;

        public Employee(string name, string phoneNumber, string email, int
            employeeNumber, string dob) : base(name,phoneNumber,email)
        {
            _employeeNumber = employeeNumber;
            if(dob!=null) _dob = DateTime.Parse(dob);
            _projects = new ArrayList();
        }

...


        public void AssignToProject(Project project)
        {
            _projects.Add(project);
            if (!project.Employees.Contains(this))
                project.assignEmployee(this);
        }

...
```

```
        public IList Projects
        {
            get
            {
                return _projects;
            }
        }

...
    }
}

using System.Collections;

namespace com.db4o.dg2db4o.chapter7
{
    class Project
    {
        string _name;
        string _costCode;
        IList _employees;

...

        public void assignEmployee(Employee newEmployee)
        {
            _employees.Add(newEmployee);
          if(!newEmployee.Projects.Contains(this))
              newEmployee.assignToProject(this);
        }

...
    }
}
```

Listing 7-18. *Modifications to the Employee and Project Classes in Java to Create an Inverse Many-to-Many Relationship*

// JAVA
```
package com.db4o.dg2db4o.chapter7;

import java.util.List;
import java.util.ArrayList;
```

```java
public class Employee extends AbstractPerson
{
    int _employeeNumber;
    Date _dob;
    List<Project> _projects;

    public Employee(String name, String phoneNumber, String email, int
        employeeNumber, String dob)
    {
        super(name,phoneNumber,email);
        _employeeNumber = employeeNumber;
        SimpleDateFormat formatter = new SimpleDateFormat("M/d/yyyy");
        try
        {
            Date newDate = formatter.parse(dob);
        } catch (Exception exc) {Date newDate = null;}
        _projects = new ArrayList<Project>();
    }
...
    public void assignToProject(Project project)
    {
        _projects.add(project);
        if (!project.employees().contains(this))
            project.assignEmployee(this);
    }

    public List<Project> projects() {
        return _projects;
    }

...
}

package com.db4o.dg2db4o.chapter7;

import java.util.List;
import java.util.ArrayList;

public class Project
{
    String _name;
    String _costCode;
    List<Employee> _employees;

...
```

```
    public void assignEmployee(Employee newEmployee)
    {
        _employees.add(newEmployee);
        if(!newEmployee.projects().contains(this))
            newEmployee.assignToProject(this);
    }
...
}
```

One helpful consequence of this modification is that you can perform the query to find all Projects for a specified Employee by directly querying for the Employee, rather than querying for Projects using the name of the Employee as the criterion. That query is therefore simplified.

A less helpful consequence is that you might get more Employees from your query than you bargained for. The following example shows how this can happen, and how to avoid it. First, we need some objects. This time, some Employees are assigned to more than one Project—Michael is assigned to the finance system and the CRM system, for example.

```
// C# & JAVA
Employee e1 = new Employee("Michael", "1234", "michael", 101, "10/5/1975");
Employee e2 = new Employee("Anne", "5432", "anne", 102, "8/5/1980");
CasualEmployee c1 = new CasualEmployee("Tim", "5544", "tim", 103, "7/6/1986");
CasualEmployee c2 = new CasualEmployee("Eva", "4433", "eva", 104, "11/3/1984");
Project p1 = new Project("Finance System", "P01");
Project p2 = new Project("Web Site", "P02");
Project p3 = new Project("CRM System", "P03");
```

```
// C#
p1.AssignEmployee(e1);
p1.AssignEmployee(e2);
p1.AssignEmployee(c1);
p2.AssignEmployee(c1);
p2.AssignEmployee(c2);
p3.AssignEmployee(e1);
p3.AssignEmployee(c2);
db.Set(p1);
db.Set(p2);
db.Set(p3);
```

```
// JAVA
p1.assignEmployee(e1);
p1.assignEmployee(e2);
p1.assignEmployee(c1);
p2.assignEmployee(c1);
p2.assignEmployee(c2);
p3.assignEmployee(e1);
p3.assignEmployee(c2);
db.set(p1);
db.set(p2);
db.set(p3);
```

Now let's query for a specific `Employee` object, with a simple QBE, and see what we get.

```csharp
// C#
Employee employeeExample = new Employee("Michael", null, null, 0, null);
ObjectSet results = db.Get(employeeExample);
Employee emp = (Employee)results.Next();
```

```java
// JAVA
Employee employeeExample = new Employee("Michael", null, null, 0, null);
ObjectSet results = db.get(employeeExample);
Employee emp = (Employee)results.next();
```

As we did earlier, a breakpoint can be set to allow the in-memory objects to be explored in the Locals window, as shown in Figure 7-7.

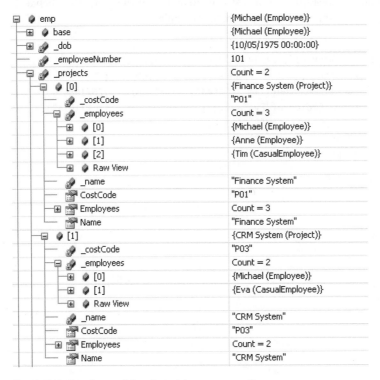

Figure 7-7. *Employee object (emp) in memory after query*

The query returns a single `Employee` object, which is what we wanted. However, drilling down the tree that represents the object graph allows you to look at the `Project` objects that also have been activated, and from there, to find the `Employee` objects activated through each `Project`. You can see from Figure 7-7 that all four `Employee` objects (Michael, Anne, Tim, and Eva) have been activated. This is not too drastic for a database with four `Employees`, but if the database is larger, then you can end up activating many more objects than you actually need, which may well affect application performance.

Controlling activation allows only the objects that are actually needed to be loaded. For example, you might want simply to find the names of all the Projects that Michael is assigned to. In this case you could set the global activation depth to 1 and explicitly activate the Projects once the single Employee object had been returned.

```
// C#
db.Activate(emp.Projects, 1);
```

```
// JAVA
db.activate(emp.getProjects(), 1);
```

The Locals window this time around is shown in Figure 7-8.

emp	{Michael (Employee)}
base	{Michael (Employee)}
_dob	{10/05/1975 00:00:00}
_employeeNumber	101
_projects	Count = 2
[0]	{Finance System (Project)}
_costCode	"P01"
_employees	Count = 0
_name	"Finance System"
CostCode	"P01"
Employees	Count = 0
Name	"Finance System"
[1]	{CRM System (Project)}
_costCode	"P03"
_employees	Count = 0
_name	"CRM System"
CostCode	"P03"
Employees	Count = 0
Name	"CRM System"

Figure 7-8. *Employee object (emp) in memory after query*

Enough objects have been activated to allow the required information, the name of the Projects, to be accessed. The Employees list for each Project is not activated, so only one Employee, the specific one that was wanted, is active.

Object Activation and Deep Object Graphs

Loading more objects than necessary into memory is one problem that can be solved with activation depth. The other side of the problem is the situation where an object graph is not activated to a sufficient depth to reach the information that is required. A deep object graph is one where the first-level object has references to objects, which in turn have references to further objects, and so on. Very complex objects can be created with many associated objects with many levels of references.

Storing deep object graphs with db4o is straightforward. As usual, storing the first-level object causes all the associated objects to be stored. Ensuring that the required information is accessible when such an object is retrieved can require a bit more care.

A Very Simple Deep Graph

The example we will look at here uses a very quick way to make a deep graph. You can see in Figure 7-1 that a Manager is associated with many Employees. Let's implement the collection of Employees as a linked list. With this structure, Manager has an attribute that is a reference to linked list object. This object just contains an item, which is an Employee object, and a reference to the next node in the list. Each node is itself a linked list object. To reach the last node in the list you have to traverse the whole list, following object references from node to node, so a list with eight nodes, for example, is in effect a deep, albeit very narrow, graph with eight levels.

We could use the LinkedList classes provided by .NET and Java, but for this example, we'll use a homemade one, shown in Listings 7-19 and 7-20. This LinkedList is much simpler than the "official" implementations, albeit not nearly as robust or useful in a real program. The simplicity helps us to see what is going on more clearly.

Listing 7-19. *A Simple LinkedList Class in C#*

```csharp
// C#
namespace com.db4o.dg2db4o.chapter7
{
    class LinkedList
    {
        private Employee _item;
        private LinkedList _next;

        public LinkedList()
        {
            _item = null;
            _next = null;
        }

        public LinkedList(Employee item)
        {
            _item = item;
            _next = null;
        }

        public Employee Item
        {
            get
            {
                return _item;
            }
            set
            {
                _item = value;
            }
        }
    }
```

```java
    public LinkedList Next
    {
        get
        {
            return _next;
        }
        set
        {
            _next = value;
        }
    }

    public void append(LinkedList node)
    {
        if (_next == null)
        {
            _next = node;
        }
        else
        {
            _next.append(node);
        }
    }
  }
}
}
```

Listing 7-20. *A Simple LinkedList Class in Java*

```java
// JAVA
package com.db4o.dg2db4o.chapter7;

public class LinkedList
{
    private Object _item;
    private LinkedList _next;

    public LinkedList()
    {
        _item = null;
        _next = null;
    }

    public LinkedList(Object item)
    {
        _item = item;
        _next = null;
    }
```

```csharp
    public Object getItem()
    {
        return _item;
    }

    public void setItem(Object item)
    {
        _item = item;
    }

    public LinkedList getNext()
    {
        return _next;
    }

    public void setNext(LinkedList next)
    {
        _next = next;
    }

    public void append(LinkedList node)
    {
        if (_next == null)
            {
                _next = node;
            }
        else
            {
                _next.append(node);
            }
    }
}
```

The Manager class in Listings 7-21 and 7-22 has an _employees attribute that refers to a
LinkedList, and a method to add a new node to the list. This method traverses the list until it
finds the end and adjusts references so that the new node becomes the end of the list. The
Employee class is the one we used previously.

Listing 7-21. *The Manager Class in C#*

```csharp
// C#
namespace com.db4o.dg2db4o.chapter7
{
    class Manager : Employee
    {
        LinkedList _employees;
```

```
        public Manager(string name, string phoneNumber, string email, int
            employeeNumber, string dob) :
            base(name, phoneNumber, email, employeeNumber, dob)
        {
        }

        public LinkedList Employees
        {
            get
            {
                return _employees;
            }
        }

        public void addEmployee(Employee newEmployee)
        {
            LinkedList newNode = new LinkedList(newEmployee);
            if (_employees == null)
            {
                _employees = newNode;
            }
            else
            {
                _employees.append(newNode);
            }
        }

        public override string ToString()
        {
            return base.Name + " (Manager)";
        }
    }
}
```

Listing 7-22. *The Manager Class in Java*

```
// JAVA
package com.db4o.dg2db4o.chapter7;

public class Manager extends Employee
{
    LinkedList _employees;

        public Manager(String name, String phoneNumber, String email, int
            employeeNumber, String dob)
        {
            super(name, phoneNumber, email, employeeNumber, dob);
        }
```

```
        public LinkedList employees()
        {
                return _employees;
        }

        public void addEmployee(Employee newEmployee)
        {
            LinkedList newNode = new LinkedList(newEmployee);
            if(_employees==null)
            {
                _employees = newNode;
            }
            else
            {
            _employees.append(newNode);
            }
        }

        public String toString()
        {
            return super.getName() + " (Manager)";
        }
}
```

Let's create a Manager and give her eight Employees (some of them can be CasualEmployees). The number is chosen to exceed db4o's default activation depth of 5.

```
// C# & JAVA
Employee e1 = new Employee("Michael", "1234", "michael", 101, "10/5/1975");
Employee e2 = new Employee("Anne", "5432", "anne", 102, "8/5/1980");
Employee e3 = new Employee("Jane", "5753", "jane", 103, "10/6/1985");
Employee e4 = new Employee("Franz", "8765", "anne", 104, "6/5/1980");
CasualEmployee c1 = new CasualEmployee("Tim", "5544", "tim", 105, "7/6/1986");
CasualEmployee c2 = new CasualEmployee("Eva", "4433", "eva", 106, "11/3/1984");
CasualEmployee c3 = new CasualEmployee("Jan", "4455", "jan", 107, "7/9/1976");
CasualEmployee c4 = new CasualEmployee("Elle", "3344", "elle", 108, "12/3/1982");
Manager m1= new Manager("Sue", "1111", "sue", 109,"1/1/1981");

m1.addEmployee(e1);
m1.addEmployee(e2);
m1.addEmployee(e3);
m1.addEmployee(e4);
m1.addEmployee(c1);
m1.addEmployee(c2);
m1.addEmployee(c3);
m1.addEmployee(c4);
```

```
// C#
db.Set(m1);
```

```
// JAVA
db.set(m1);
```

Storing the Manager object causes the whole list to be stored. Now, in a separate transaction, let's retrieve the Manager with a simple QBE, and print the results. The following code traverses the list of Employees, printing each one as it goes.

```
// C#
Manager managerExample = new Manager("Sue", null, null, 0, null);
results = db.Get(managerExample);
Manager man = (Manager)results.Next();
Console.WriteLine(man);
LinkedList list = man.Employees;
while(list!=null){
    Console.WriteLine(list.Item);
    list = list.Next;
}
```

```
// JAVA
Manager managerExample = new Manager("Sue", null, null, 0, null);
results = db.get(managerExample);
Manager man = (Manager)results.next();
System.out.println(man);
LinkedList list = man.employees();
while(list!=null){
    System.out.println(list.getItem());
    list = list.getNext();
}
```

The output is as follows:

```
Sue (Manager)
Michael (Employee)
Anne (Employee)
Jane (Employee)
null (Employee)
```

We've only got three out of the eight the Employees. Setting a breakpoint and looking at man in the Locals window shows why (Figure 7-9). Each level in the tree display corresponds to one level of activation. The last Employee whose name is printed correctly is Jane, who is at the fifth level. The next LinkedList node is activated, but the Employee object it contains is not activated, so a null value is printed. No further nodes are activated.

Figure 7-9. *Manager object (man) in memory after query (default activation depth)*

Activating the Whole Graph

What activation depth would be needed to access all the Employees? Well, you need one for the Manager, one for each node in the list, and one more to activate the Employee item in the last node, resulting in 10. Remember that the activation depth must be set before the ObjectContainer is opened.

```
// C#
Db4o.Configure().ActivationDepth(10);
```

```
// JAVA
Db4o.configure().activationDepth(10);
```

The output now shows all the Employees:

```
Sue (Manager)
Michael (Employee)
Anne (Employee)
Jane (Employee)
Franz (Employee)
Tim (CasualEmployee)
Eva (CasualEmployee)
Jan (CasualEmployee)
Ellen (CasualEmployee)
```

Figure 7-10 shows man again in the Locals window. This time you can see that the object has been activated to the full depth of the graph.

This worked, but it set the global activation depth to a higher value than the default, and now all objects are activated to that depth. Alternatively, you can configure maximum or minimum activation depths for specific classes, so that other classes are not affected. These configurations override the global setting for the specified classes. For example, you could set the minimum activation depth for the Manager class to be 10, which would give the same output as earlier.

```
// C#
Db4o.Configure().ObjectClass(typeof(Manager)).MinimumActivationDepth(10);
```

```
// JAVA
Db4o.configure().objectClass(Manager.class).minimumActivationDepth(10);
```

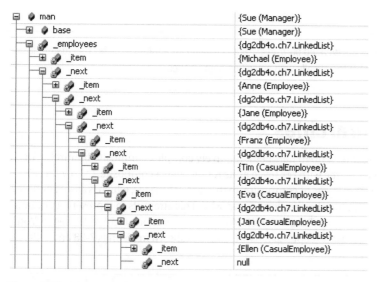

Figure 7-10. *Manager object (man) in memory after query (activation depth = 10)*

Neither solution is actually very good. Both work fine for the list of eight Employees, but what happens if more Employees are added? We really want to get all the Employees, no matter how many are added. This can be achieved by configuring the database to cascade activation for the required class:

```
// C#
Db4o.Configure().ObjectClass(typeof(Manager)).CascadeOnActivate(true);
```

```
// JAVA
Db4o.configure().cbjectClass(Manager.class).cascadeOnActivate(true);
```

Alternatively, with the database open, you can dynamically activate the next node in turn as you traverse the list. Note that you need to activate each node to a depth of 2 so that the node itself and the contained Employee are activated.

```
// C#
while(list!=null){
    Console.WriteLine(list.Item);
    db.Activate(list.Next, 2);
    list = list.Next;
}
```

```
// JAVA
while(list!=null){
    System.out.println(list.getItem());
    db.activate(list.getNext(), 2);
    list = list.getNext();
}
```

■**Note** The db4o developers are working on *transparent activation* for a future release. This feature is expected to allow db4o to deal automatically with activation depth issues.

Composite Hierarchies

As a final example we look at how db4o handles a relatively complex composite hierarchy. In Figure 7-1 you can see that the tree with Employee as its root is such a composite. Employees can be simple, in the case of CasualEmployee, or composite, in the case of Manager, which is associated with many Employees, which can in turn be simple or composite. This attempts to represent an organization with line managers at several different levels. A Department has one top-level Manager. You have already seen all these classes except Department, which is shown in Listings 7-23 and 7-24.

■**Note** The Department class looks like a simple structured object, as it has a single-valued reference to a Manager. However, because Manager is quite complex, then a Department object can be at the top level of a deep graph.

Listing 7-23. *The Department Class in C#*

```
// C#
namespace com.db4o.dg2db4o.chapter7
{
    class Department
    {
        string _name;
        Manager _manager;

        public Department(string name, Manager manager)
        {
            _name = name;
            _manager = manager;
        }
```

```
    public string Name
    {
        get
        {
            return _name;
        }
        set
        {
            _name = value;
        }
    }

    public Manager Manager
    {
        get
        {
            return _manager;
        }
        set
        {
            _manager = value;
        }
    }

    public override string ToString()
    {
        return Name + " (Department)";
    }
    }
}
```

Listing 7-24. *The Department Class in Java*

```
// JAVA
package com.db4o.dg2db4o.chapter7;

public class Department
{
    String _name;
    Manager _manager;

    public Department(String name, Manager manager)
    {
        _name = name;
        _manager = manager;
    }
```

```
    public String getName()
    {
        return _name;
    }
    public void setName(String value)
    {
        _name = value;
    }


    public Manager getManager()
    {

        return _manager;
    }

    public void setManager(Manager value)
    {
        _manager = value;
    }

    public String toString()
    {
        return _name + " (Department)";
    }
}
```

Let's build up a small department. Sue is the departmental manager, and Franz and Nicole report directly to her. Erich is a line manager, with Michael, Anne, and Dan reporting to him, and Erich himself reports to Sue. Just because we can, everyone except the head honcho, Sue, is assigned to at least one project, although this information is not used in the query in this example. Remarkably, all of these objects can all be stored by calling Set on the Department object d1.

```
// C# & JAVA
Manager m1 = new Manager("Sue", "9876", "sue", 101, "3/8/1982");
Manager m2 = new Manager("Erich", "6543", "erich", 102, "10/1/1963");
Employee e1 = new Employee("Michael", "1234", "michael", 103, "10/5/1975");
Employee e2 = new Employee("Anne", "5432", "anne", 104, "8/5/1980");
Employee e3 = new Employee("Franz", "3456", "franz", 105, "11/8/1985");
CasualEmployee c1 = new CasualEmployee("Nicole", "4321", "nicole", 106,
    "12/12/1987");
CasualEmployee c2 = new CasualEmployee("Dan", "3690", "dan", 107, "1/1/1986");
m1.addEmployee(m2);
m1.addEmployee(e3);
m1.addEmployee(c1);
m2.addEmployee(e1);
m2.addEmployee(e2);
m2.addEmployee(c2);
Department d1 = new Department("Software", m1);
```

```
Project p1 = new Project("Finance System", "C01");
Project p2 = new Project("Web Site", "C02");
p1.assignEmployee(m2);
p1.assignEmployee(e1);
p1.assignEmployee(e2);
p1.assignEmployee(c1);
p2.assignEmployee(e1);
p2.assignEmployee(c1);
```

```
// C#
db.Set(d1);
```

```
// JAVA
db.set(d1);
```

Now let's try a query—list all Managers, and for each one, list their Employees. Think about how you would do this in a relational database as you look at the next piece of code. The query itself is very simple—it's just a QBE to find all managers. Then you just iterate through the list of Employees for each Manager that the query retrieves. It really is very simple.

```
// C#
Manager managerExample = new Manager(null, null, null, 0, null);
results = db.Get(managerExample);
while (results.HasNext())
{
    Manager man = (Manager)results.Next();
    Console.WriteLine("MANAGER: " + man);
    LinkedList list = man.Employees;
    while (list != null)
    {
        Console.WriteLine(list.Item);
        db.Activate(list.Next, 2);
        list = list.Next;
    }
}
```

```
// JAVA
Manager managerExample = new Manager(null, null, null, 0, null);
results = db.get(managerExample);
while (results.hasNext()) {
    Manager man = (Manager)results.next();
    System.out.println("MANAGER: " + man);
    LinkedList list = man.employees();
    while (list != null) {
        System.out.println(list.getItem());
        db.activate(list.getNext(),2);
        list = list.getNext();
    }
}
```

The output is as follows:

```
MANAGER: Erich (Manager)
Michael (Employee)
Anne (Employee)
Dan (CasualEmployee)
MANAGER: Sue (Manager)
Erich (Manager)
Franz (Employee)
Nicole (CasualEmployee)
```

This clearly shows the composite structure of the data, which was stored in the database with exactly the same relationships as it was created. This clearly shows how db4o takes a great deal of the effort out of persistence for complex structured objects that can be found in an object-oriented domain model.

OBJECTS AND GRANULARITY

You have seen in this chapter that db4o can store an entire graph of objects with one call to Set, and retrieve a whole graph with one query. The *granularity*, or number of objects that are stored or retrieved at any one time, is an important design choice when using an object database. This comes with experience, and it's quite different from the way you would work with a relational database.

Here are a couple of examples of situations, based on the classes we have being using in this chapter and shown in Figure 7-1, where the choice of granularity is inappropriate:

- **Too many objects at a time**: The example in the "Composite Hierarchies" section in this chapter showed that by storing a single Department object, we also store Managers, Employees, and Projects. We could do the same for retrieving objects. Querying for a Department will, assuming we deal correctly with activation, return a whole object graph including Managers, Employees, and Projects. We could execute a query like this, update a Manager or two, and call Set using the Department again to store the updated objects. This would probably work, but it would store the whole object graph again. It is an approach that is too coarse-grained—too many objects, taking too much time, with the majority not actually involved in the transaction. If you store too many objects at a time, there is also the possibility in some applications that you will end up saving objects that do not contain any significant data, such as event-handling objects.

- **Too few objects at a time**: A Manager object can contain a list of Employees. We can choose to query for specific Employees, do updates, and store the updated objects. However, if the application needs to manipulate a Manager and the associated Employees as a unit, then it would require fewer queries and less code simply to query for and save the parent Manager object. With db4o, the Employee objects are also automatically retrieved and saved. The problem with being too fine-grained is that you can end up with a lot of unnecessary code.

You need to get the balance right—try getting a printout of the UML class model and thinking carefully about these questions:

- Which classes contain actual data that really does need to be stored?

- Which classes will be processed together in one pass for a specific task?

Summary

In this chapter you have seen how db4o deals with complex structured objects, and learned how to store, retrieve, update, and delete these objects. You have also seen that the concept of object activation becomes particularly important when working with complex objects. It is worth noting that since the db4o data model is essentially the same as the domain object model, it is relatively straightforward to handle even quite complex structures that would be difficult to deal with if you were to use a relational database for persistence.

Up to this point in Part II we have been using db4o as a standalone, single-user database. The next chapter shows how it can be used as a client/server database to provide concurrent access for many users or processes. It is worth remembering that all the techniques you have seen so far work the same way regardless of the mode of access to the database.

CHAPTER 8

■■■

Client/Server Mode

Up to this point, you have been using db4o as a simple standalone database in local mode, and have been accessing the database by directly opening the database file. In this mode, db4o acts as an embedded database for applications where access is restricted to one user, process, or thread at a time. However, db4o can do more than this, providing support for a wider range of application scenarios through its client/server modes.

Introduction to db4o Client/Server Modes

In general, a client/server system consists of clients that interact with a central server. The server provides a service using a daemon to listen for and accept connections. Clients then connect to the server via this daemon to perform tasks such as data retrieval, updates, deletions, and general administration.

The db4o API includes functionality to let db4o run as a server, and allows you to write clients that interact with the server, as illustrated in Figure 8-1. In a distributed environment you might choose this methodology to accept connections from a computer, or from PDAs, handheld devices, or cell phones.

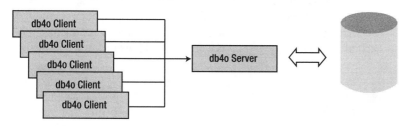

Figure 8-1. *Several db4o clients connecting to a db4o database server*

db4o supports three varieties of client/server interaction, which are introduced here and discussed in later sections:

- The first mode is the **networking mode**, which you have probably used when working with other database solutions. Here, remote clients open a TCP/IP connection to transfer, query, insert, modify, and delete instructions to, and data from, the db4o server. This mode works in db4o exactly as you would expect it to.

- db4o also supports an **embedded mode**, which doesn't involve a distributed system, although the client and the server are quite distinct objects. Instead, both the client and the server are run on the same virtual machine. The communication between the server and the client is the same as in networking mode, but in this mode you work entirely within one virtual machine, which is extremely useful in some applications. One example application for this mode could be the design of a desktop application that uses db4o as storage. If the application is later redesigned to work in a distributed mode, then it is very simple to convert to work in network mode—all you have to do is specify an IP address or hostname and TCP port number for the server.

- The last mode is used for "out-of-band" communications with the server. In this mode the information sent does not belong to the db4o protocol, and does not consist of data objects, but instead is completely user-defined. You can send objects to the server and the server can do with them whatever is needed. This is extremely useful for sending messages to the server like: "do a defragment", "stop yourself", "perform a savecopy", and so forth.

Figure 8-2 depicts all three modes operating in a single environment.

Working in a client/server mode introduces the need for access control and authentication. Up to this point you have not had to think about these issues with db4o, but you are probably familiar with the need for users to log in to gain access to other databases. As you will see, db4o's access control is pretty simple compared to most others.

On the other hand, virtually everything you have learned from the preceding chapters transfers directly over to client/server mode. Storing, updating, and deleting objects, and the query mechanisms, all work exactly the same way whichever mode you are working in.

Let's explore how each of the client/server modes works by looking at a few examples.

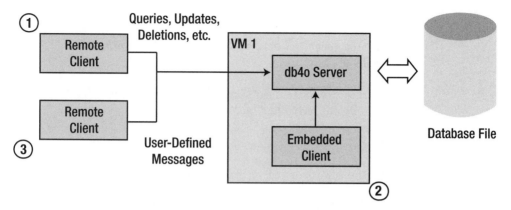

Figure 8-2. *db4o in embedded, networking, and out-of-band-modes*

Networking Mode

Consider a scenario where your customer wants to manage a database consisting of the names, addresses, and contact information of certified C# and Java developers. What you need is a db4o server that hosts this database.

Server

The following code starts a db4o server running, ready to accept connections from clients:

```
// C#
using System;
using com.db4o;

namespace com.db4o.dg2db4o.chapter8
{
    class RunServer
    {
        private bool stop = false;

        private void Run()
        {
            lock (this)
            {
                Console.WriteLine("Starting server...");
                ObjectServer server = Db4o.OpenServer("C:/netserver.yap", 8732);
                server.GrantAccess("user1", "password");
                server.GrantAccess("user2", "password");
```

```
            try
            {
                // stop condition will be defined in a later example
                while (!stop)
                {
                    Console.WriteLine("SERVER: Server is listening ...");
                    Monitor.Wait(this, 60000);

                }
            }
            catch (ThreadInterruptedException tie)
            {
                Console.WriteLine("Thread Error!" + tie);
            }
            finally
            {
                server.Close();
            }
        }
        Console.WriteLine("Server ends...");
    }

    }
}


// JAVA
package com.db4o.dg2db4o.chapter8;

import java.io.*;
import com.db4o.*;

public class RunServer implements Runnable
{
    private boolean stop = false;

    public void run()
    {
        synchronized (this)
        {
            ObjectServer server = Db4o.openServer("c:/netserver.yap", 8732);
            server.grantAccess("user1", "password");
            server.grantAccess("user2", "password");
```

```
        try
        {
            // stop condition will be defined in a later example
            while (!stop)
            {
                System.out.println("SERVER:[" +
                    System.currentTimeMillis()
                    + "] Server's running... ");
                this.wait(60000);
            }
        }
        catch (Exception e)
        {
            e.printStackTrace();
        }
        finally
        {
            server.close();
        }
    }
  }
}
```

Note As you've seen in earlier chapters, note that no schema or table creation is required! Any objects your client sends will be stored by the server without problems. This is one of the key strengths of a "zero administration" server, but of course, your clients need to be reliable and send only "correct" data.

In our case this would mean the clients should send Person objects containing _name and _age fields. However, even if the clients decide one year later to "upgrade" their Person objects to include addresses, db4o will quietly execute the necessary schema changes. We'll further discuss this matter in Chapter 12.

Now let's have a look what the previous code does. You can see that you simply open a server with Db4o.OpenServer: this simply means that an extra thread is started automatically that listens for incoming requests from clients. Requests for database operations to be executed are fulfilled using the database file specified in the call to OpenServer. The filename parameter refers to exactly the same kind of db4o database file you might use if db4o were running in local mode. The second parameter is the TCP port on which you wish your server to listen. You should make sure you use an unassigned port number—see www.iana.org/assignments/port-numbers for a list of port number assignments. You should also make sure your port number is not used by any other application in your environment or another db4o server.

The next step is to grant access to the server. You can grant access to as many users as you wish, using GrantAccess to set the access username and password for each one. Each client will then have to supply valid credentials in order to connect. If you forget to grant access with a password and a user, then no client will be able to connect.

Once the server has started, and before entering the try/catch block, you might want to set the priority of the thread in which this code runs to a low value, because the db4o server establishes its own high-priority thread. In the while loop we continue until the boolean flag stop is set. The example code does not define a stop condition: it simply loops until the thread or process is interrupted. You can either insert your own condition here, which will set stop to true, or you can use out-of-band signaling, which is explained later on this chapter.

This code does nothing more than communicate to you that the server is alive every minute. Of course, the real purpose of the server is to listen for and process client requests. And this is indeed what the server quietly does in the background. To try this out, we need some clients.

Clients

Returning to the project requirements, we need some way to enter data into the database. Let's create a client that connects to the server and allows data to be stored:

```
// C#
using System;
using com.db4o;

namespace com.db4o.dg2db4o.chapter8
{
    class AddClient
    {
        private ObjectContainer aClient;
        private bool stop = false;

        public void Run()
        {
            Console.WriteLine("Starting add client...");
            aClient = Db4o.OpenClient("localhost", 8732, "user1", "password");
            while (!stop)
            {
                Console.WriteLine("ADDCLIENT: Please enter a name: ");
                String name = Console.ReadLine();
                Console.WriteLine("ADDCLIENT: Please enter an age: ");
                int age = Convert.ToInt32(Console.ReadLine());
                aClient.Set(new Person(name, age));
                aClient.Commit();
            }
            aClient.Close();
        }

    }
}
```

```java
// JAVA
package com.db4o.dg2db4o.chapter8;

import java.util.Scanner;
import com.db4o.*;

public class AddClient implements Runnable
{
    private boolean stop = false;
    ObjectContainer aClient = null;
    Scanner sc = new Scanner(System.in);

    public void run()
    {
        try
        {
            aClient = Db4o.openClient("localhost", 8732, "user1", "password");
            while (!stop)
            {
                System.out.print("\nADDCLIENT:Enter the developer's
                    name and age (e.g. 'Tom 44'): ");
                aClient.set(new Person(sc.next(), sc.nextInt()));
                aClient.commit();
            }
        }
        catch (Exception e)
        {
            e.printStackTrace();
        }
        finally
        {
            aClient.close();
        }
    }
}
```

This code looks suspiciously incomplete, but it really has all you need. You open a client with Db4o.openClient, passing the hostname or IP address of the computer on which the server is running. In the listing, the host is "localhost", which means that the server and client are on the same computer (although not necessarily the same virtual machine)—in a live network environment this would be a resolvable hostname or a network IP address. You also specify the server's port number, and a set of valid username and password credentials.

The OpenClient call returns a client ObjectContainer reference, which can then be used exactly as you have used ObjectContainers in local mode.

Next, we loop continuously, entering a name and an age each time to create a new Person object, and saving this person in the client ObjectContainer, meaning these objects will also be saved to the db4o database. We call Commit on the ObjectContainer each time to make sure the object is written to the database. (Chapter 9 will explain the idea of committing transactions in more detail.) Again the listing does not include a way of setting the stop flag—you can add your own condition to test in the while loop to determine when to set the flag.

So what is missing? This is supposed to be a multiuser database server, so let's give it another user to deal with. We can create another client capable of simply viewing the database content:

```csharp
// C #
using System;
using com.db4o;

namespace com.db4o.dg2db4o.chapter8
{
    class ListClient
    {
        ObjectContainer lClient = null;
        private bool stop = false;

        public void Run()
        {
            lock (this)
            {
                Console.WriteLine("Starting list client...");
                try
                {
                    lClient = Db4o.OpenClient("127.0.0.1", 8732, "user2",
                        "password");
                    while (!stop)
                    {
                        ListResult(lClient.Get(new Person()));
                        Monitor.Wait(this, 10000);
                    }
                }
                catch (ThreadInterruptedException tie)
                {
                    Console.WriteLine("Thread Error!" + tie);
                }
                finally
                {
                    lClient.Close();
                }
            }
        }
```

```
        private static void ListResult(ObjectSet result)
        {
            Console.WriteLine ("LISTCLIENT: Listing...");
            while (result.HasNext())
            {
                Console.WriteLine("LISTCLIENT:" + result.Next() + "\n");
            }
        }


    }
}
```

```
// JAVA
package com.db4o.dg2db4o.chapter8;

import com.db4o.*;

public class ListClient implements Runnable
{
    private boolean stop = false;
    ObjectContainer rClient = null;

    public void run()
    {
        synchronized(this){
            try
            {
                rClient = Db4o.openClient("127.0.0.1", 8732, "user2", "password");
                while (!stop)
                {
                    listResult(rClient.get(new Person()));
                    Thread.sleep(15000);
                }
            }
            catch (Exception e)
            {
                e.printStackTrace();
            }
            finally
            {
                aClient.close();
            }
        }
    }
```

```
    public static void listResult(ObjectSet result)
    {
        System.out.println("LISTCLIENT: Listing...");
        while (result.hasNext())
        {
            System.out.println("LISTCLIENT:" + result.next());
        }
    }
}
```

This client opens the network connection to the server with OpenClient as before. To show that you can use the IP address, this example has been written to connect to the local host using the loopback IP address, 127.0.0.1. Then it enters the while loop, where it periodically queries the database and lists the results.

Running the Example

You can try out this example in a number of different ways. You can run the three classes listed as separate threads within one virtual machine; you can run them as three separate processes on the same computer; or, to give the best representation of a real network server environment, you can run them on three separate networked computers so that you have real remote clients. In the latter case, you need to specify the correct hostname or IP address for your clients to connect to.

■**Caution** You need to make sure that the server and client processes all have the data classes in their classpath. If you are running this example with remote clients, you need to remember to deploy the Person class file to the remote computers. In a real client/server scenario you can package your data classes in a DLL or JAR library and include this library in your client *and* server applications.

To run as processes, you will need to create separate main methods to instantiate each class, and to call Run for each instance. You can run these on the same computer, or separate networked computers—it's more fun if you do it over a real network!

To run as threads, you will need to create a class with a main method that starts the threads, as shown here:

```
// C#
public static void Main(string[] args)
{
    RunServer s = new RunServer();
    Thread serverThread = new Thread(new ThreadStart(s.Run));
    serverThread.Priority = ThreadPriority.Highest;
    AddClient a = new AddClient();
    ListClient l = new ListClient();
    Thread addThread = new Thread(new ThreadStart(a.Run));
    Thread listThread = new Thread(new ThreadStart(l.Run));
```

```
    serverThread.Start();
    addThread.Start();
    listThread.Start();
}
```

```
// JAVA
public static void main(String[] args)
{
    Thread s = new Thread(new RunServer(),"server");
    Thread a = new Thread(new AddClient(), "add client");
    Thread l = new Thread(new ListClient(), "list client");
    s.setPriority(Thread.MAX_PRIORITY);
    s.start();
    a.start();
    l.start();
}
```

If you start the threads in the normal way, as in the previous listing, it is not 100 percent guaranteed that the server thread will start first. The following variations, using a System. Threading.Timer in C# and a java.util.concurrent.ScheduledExecutorService in Java (you need Java 5.0), delay the start of the client threads by a specified time to let the server get started:

```
// C#
public static void Main(string[] args)
{
    RunServer s = new RunServer();
    Thread serverThread = new Thread(new ThreadStart(s.Run));
    serverThread.Start();

    AutoResetEvent autoEvent = new AutoResetEvent(false);
    ThreadStarter threadStart = new ThreadStarter();
    // the TimerCallback delegate specifies the methods
    // associated with a Timer object
    TimerCallback timerDelegate = new TimerCallback(threadStart.StartClients);
    Timer delay = new Timer(timerDelegate, autoEvent, 5000, 0);
    autoEvent.WaitOne(10000, false);
    delay.Dispose();
}

namespace com.db4o.dg2db4o.chapter8
{
    class ThreadStarter
    {
```

```
            // This method is used by the timer delegate.
            public void StartClients(Object stateInfo)
            {
                AutoResetEvent autoEvent = (AutoResetEvent)stateInfo;
                RunAddClient a = new RunAddClient();
                RunListClient l = new RunListClient();
                Thread addThread = new Thread(new ThreadStart(a.Run));
                Thread listThread = new Thread(new ThreadStart(l.Run));
                addThread.Start();
                listThread.Start();
                autoEvent.Set();
            }
        }
}


// JAVA
public static void main(String[] args)
{
    Thread s = new Thread(new RunServer(),"server");
    Thread a = new Thread(new RunAddClient(), "add client");
    Thread l = new Thread(new RunListClient(), "list client");
    ScheduledExecutorService scheduler = Executors.newScheduledThreadPool(3);
    System.out.println("MAIN: Created Scheduler ...");
    ScheduledFuture<?> fs = scheduler.schedule(s,0,TimeUnit.SECONDS);
    ScheduledFuture<?> fa = scheduler.schedule(a,5,TimeUnit.SECONDS);
    ScheduledFuture<?> fl = scheduler.schedule(l,5,TimeUnit.SECONDS);
    while(!fs.isDone()){
        try
        {
            Thread.currentThread().sleep(1000);
        }
        catch(InterruptedException ie)
        {
            ie.printStackTrace();
        }
    }
    fl.cancel(true);
    scheduler.shutdown();
}
```

Output

If you run the example in any of these ways, you can watch the client/server interaction live.
The server runs, the AddClient takes all your input and sends Person objects to the server database, and the ListClient periodically shows the full content of the database.

Let's see what the output of this example would look like (the Java version is shown).
We will look separately at the output from the server and each client. First, the server:

```
[db4o 5.0.010   2006-02-14 23:38:15]
 Server listening on port: '8732'
SERVER:[1139960296015] Server's running...
[db4o 5.0.010   2006-02-14 23:38:21]
 Client 'user1' connected.
[db4o 5.0.010   2006-02-14 23:38:25]
 Client 'user2' connected.
SERVER:[1139960356015] Server's running...
SERVER:[1139960416015] Server's running...
```

As we started the server first, it shows us each minute that it is alive. Every client connection is also listed. The first connection is the AddClient and the second connection is the ListClient. Let's look now at their output. First, the AddClient:

```
ADDCLIENT:Enter the developer's name and age (e.g. 'Tom 44'):
Michael 31
ADDCLIENT:Enter the developer's name and age (e.g. 'Tom 44'):
Sue 24
ADDCLIENT:Enter the developer's name and age (e.g. 'Tom 44'):
Tim 21
```

And now the ListClient:

```
LISTCLIENT: Listing...
LISTCLIENT:[Michael;31]
LISTCLIENT: Listing...
LISTCLIENT:[Michael;31]
LISTCLIENT:[Sue;24]
LISTCLIENT: Listing...
LISTCLIENT:[Michael;31]
LISTCLIENT:[Sue;24]
LISTCLIENT:[Tim;21]
```

The first time around, ListClient shows nothing in the database as the user was still typing in the details of the first developer in AddClient. You can then see the developers being added one by one to the database.

If you run in threads rather than separate processes, the output will be interleaved.

Embedded Mode

Running db4o in embedded mode is conceptually no different from running it in networking mode, except that you are running both the client and the server in the same virtual machine. If you do plan to use a server within a multithreaded application on a single machine, you will

get better performance in embedded mode than in networking mode, as you avoid the over-
heads introduced by networking protocols. Communicating in networking mode, with the
local host or loopback, uses your machine's TCP/IP protocol stack.

There are some differences you need to be aware of. First, the use of 0 for the port number
is taken by db4o as a indication that no networking is to take place (the Internet Assigned
Numbers Authority has reserved TCP/UDP Port 0 so that it has no specific purpose). This is
simply a matter of specifying the port value 0 in the call to OpenServer. Second, user authentication is not required, since everything is taking place within the same application—clients
will not be accessing the server via remote connections.

Finally, and most significantly in terms of coding, you need to have an ObjectServer
reference directly available in order to create a database client. Compare the code to create a
client in each mode:

```
// C#
ObjectContainer networkClient = Db4o.OpenClient("localhost", 8732, "user1", "pwd");
ObjectContainer embeddedClient = server.OpenClient(); // 'server' is an ObjectServer
```

```
// JAVA
ObjectContainer networkClient = Db4o.openClient("localhost", 8732, "user1", "pwd");
ObjectContainer embeddedClient = server.openClient(); // 'server' is an ObjectServer
```

In general, the embedded case is probably more difficult. In networking mode you just
specify the host and port, and let the network protocols take care of finding the server. As long
as there is a server listening at the specified destination, everything will work. In embedded
mode, each thread that wants to open a client will have to have an ObjectServer reference to
the server object that is instantiated, possibly in a different thread, by a call to OpenServer.

This is very easy to do if your server and all your clients are created within the same thread.
This is not a very useful scenario, though, and offers no real advantage over a standalone database in local mode (although in Chapter 9 we will do this, for a very specific reason). Usually,
you want concurrent access to the server from different threads.

To illustrate the differences, let's modify the example of the "developers" database to work
in embedded mode rather than networking mode.

Starting the Server

Previously, we simply opened the server in the RunServer process/thread. Now, we want to
register the server in such a way that all clients can look up a *server registry* to obtain the right
server reference. The server is to be started at the time of registration.

A ServerRegistry class that allows this is listed here. ObjectServer references are held in a
Hashtable or HashMap.

```
//C#
using System;
using System.Collections;
using System.IO;
using com.db4o;
```

```
namespace com.db4o.dg2db4o.chapter8
{
    class ServerRegistry
    {
        private Hashtable servers;

        public ServerRegistry()
        {
            servers = new Hashtable();
        }

        public ObjectServer RegisterServer(String filename, String id)
        {
            lock (this)
            {
                ObjectServer server = Db4o.OpenServer(filename, 0);
                servers.Add(id, server);
                return server;
            }
        }

        public ObjectServer GetServer(String id)
        {
            lock (this)
            {
                return (ObjectServer)servers[id];
            }
        }
    }
}

// JAVA
package com.db4o.dg2db4o.chapter8;

import com.db4o.*;
import java.io.File;
import java.util.Map;
import java.util.HashMap;

public class ServerRegistry
{
    private Map<String, ObjectServer> servers;

    public ServerRegistry()
    {
        servers = new HashMap<String, ObjectServer>();
    }
```

```
    public synchronized ObjectServer registerServer(String filename, String id)
    {
        ObjectServer server = Db4o.openServer(filename, 0);
        servers.put(id, server);
        return server;
    }

    public synchronized ObjectServer getServer(String id)
    {
        return servers.get(id);
    }
}
```

The main method that starts the application running now creates a registry, registers a server with the id "myserver", and passes the registry to all the threads that it starts:

```
// C#
public static void Main(string[] args)
{
    ServerRegistry sr = new ServerRegistry();
    sr.RegisterServer("C:/embeddedserver.yap", "myserver");
    RunEmbeddedServer s = new RunEmbeddedServer(sr);
    RunEmbeddedAddClient a = new RunEmbeddedAddClient(sr);
    RunEmbeddedListClient l = new RunEmbeddedListClient(sr);
    Thread serverThread = new Thread(new ThreadStart(s.Run));
    Thread addThread = new Thread(new ThreadStart(a.Run));
    Thread listThread = new Thread(new ThreadStart(l.Run));
    serverThread.Start();
    addThread.Start();
    listThread.Start();
}


// JAVA
public static void main(String[] args)
{
    ServerRegistry sr = new ServerRegistry();
    sr.registerServer("C:/embeddedserver.yap", "myserver");
    Thread s = new Thread(new RunEmbeddedServer(sr),"monitor server");
    Thread a = new Thread(new RunEmbeddedAddClient(sr), "add client");
    Thread l = new Thread(new RunEmbeddedListClient(sr), "list client");
    s.start();
    l.start();
    a.start();
}
```

Server and Client Threads

We also need to create new versions of the server and client threads that make use of the registry. Each client now needs an `ObjectServer` instance variable and a constructor that uses a `ServerRegistry` to initialize this variable. The relevant code for the new `RunEmbeddedServer` class is shown next. The `Run` method is identical to `RunServer`, shown previously, except that it does not open a new server. This thread now simply monitors the server, rather than having responsibility for starting it. The `using`/`import` statements are the same as for the network mode classes, and are not shown here explicitly.

```csharp
// C#
namespace com.db4o.dg2db4o.chapter8
{
    class RunEmbeddedServer
    {
        private ObjectServer server;
        private bool stop = false;

        public RunEmbeddedServer(ServerRegistry sr)
        {
            server = sr.GetServer("myserver");
        }

        private void Run()
        {
            ...
```

```java
// JAVA
package com.db4o.dg2db4o.chapter8;

public class RunEmbeddedServer implements Runnable
{
    private ObjectServer server;
    private boolean stop = false;

    public RunEmbeddedServer(ServerRegistry sr)
    {
        server = sr.getServer("myserver");
    }

    public void run()
    {
        ...
```

Similarly, the new `RunAddEmbeddedClient` needs to get its reference to the server from the registry, and uses this to create a client `ObjectContainer`. The `Run` method is otherwise the same as that in `AddClient` earlier.

```csharp
// C#
namespace com.db4o.dg2db4o.chapter8
{
    class RunEmbeddedAddClient
    {
        private ObjectServer server;
        private ObjectContainer aClient;
        private bool stop = false;

        public RunEmbeddedAddClient(ServerRegistry sr)
        {
            server = sr.GetServer("myserver");
        }

        public void Run()
        {
            lock (this)
            {
                try
                {
                    aClient = server.OpenClient();
                    ...
```

```java
// JAVA
package com.db4o.dg2db4o.chapter8;

public class RunEmbeddedAddClient implements Runnable
{
    ObjectServer server;
    ObjectContainer aClient = null;
    private boolean stop = false;

    public RunEmbeddedAddClient(ServerRegistry sr)
    {
        server = sr.getServer("myserver");
    }

    public void run()
    {
        synchronized(this){
            try {
                aClient = server.openClient();
                ...
```

The modifications to the new RunEmbeddedListClient are similar. The output is identical to the networking mode example. You would expect a performance increase, although you will not detect this in a simple example like this.

Using a Singleton Registry

The previous example demonstrated one way of making server references available to clients—you can probably think of other ways of doing this. A variation on the previous example is to use the well-known singleton design pattern to ensure that there is only one instance of ServerRegistry in memory at any time. This means that client threads can obtain the singleton, and do not need to have a ServerRegistry instance explicitly passed to them. The ServerRegistry is modified to contain the following static variable and method:

```csharp
// C#
private static ServerRegistry theInstance;

public static ServerRegistry GetInstance()
{
    if (theInstance == null)
        theInstance = new ServerRegistry();

    return theInstance;
}
```

```java
// JAVA
private static ServerRegistry theInstance;

public static ServerRegistry getInstance()
{
    if (theInstance == null)
        theInstance = new ServerRegistry();

    return theInstance;
}
```

In this case, the main method creates the registry by calling GetInstance, rather than with new:

```csharp
ServerRegistry sr = ServerRegistry.GetInstance();    // C#
```

```java
ServerRegistry sr = ServerRegistry.GetInstance();    // JAVA
```

Client threads are intialized with default constructors. They can get the singleton registry simply by calling the GetInstance method. RunEmbeddedAddClient is shown as an example:

```csharp
// C#
public void Run()
{
    ServerRegistry sr = ServerRegistry.GetInstance();
    server = sr.GetServer("myserver");
    try
    {
        aClient = server.OpenClient();
        ...
```

```java
// JAVA
public void run() {
    ServerRegistry sr = ServerRegistry.getInstance();
    server = sr.getServer("myserver");
    try {
        aClient = server.openClient();
        ...
```

Out-of-Band Signaling

There is one problem with the examples you have seen so far in this chapter: there is no way to stop them (other than by interrupting the processes with brute force). We did include the flag stop in each class, but so far we have not provided a way to set any flags so that anything does actually stop. This is where out-of-band signaling comes in useful.

Running db4o in networking or embedded mode means that the client ObjectContainer is communicating with the server. This communication is defined by the set of 11 methods that the API defines for the ObjectContainer, although there are more if you use the ExtObjectContainer (see Chapter 10 for details). These commands are as follows:

- Database modification commands: Delete and Set

- Querying commands: Get and two types of Query (see Chapters 5 and 6)

- Transactional commands: Commit and Rollback (see Chapter 9)

- Commands for object activation: Activate and Deactivate (see Chapter 7)

- Two management commands: Close and Ext (see Chapters 5 and 10)

This is a bit limiting for working in client/server mode. In many cases more communication is needed between the client and the server. For example, with these commands there is no way for a client to tell the server:

- To shut down.

- To perform a defragment to increase performance and decrease the database file size.

Note that in client/server mode the Close method of ObjectContainer just closes the client ObjectContainer, not the server.

In order to address this need, db4o provides two useful interfaces that can help to send any message from the client to the server, in a separate stream from the data, using a mode known as *out-of-band signaling*.

The first one is the MessageSender:

```csharp
// C#
public interface MessageSender
{
    public void Send(Object obj);
}
```

```
// JAVA
public interface MessageSender
{
    public void send(Object obj);
}
```

■**Caution** These interfaces in the .NET version of db4o do not, at the time of this writing, follow typical naming conventions—if you are a .NET programmer you would probably expect this to be called IMessageSender.

This is a very simple interface, and it implies that a MessageSender object can send an object—this can be any object at all. So where does this object get sent to? Not surprisingly, it is sent to a MessageRecipient, which implements the following interface:

```
// C#
public interface MessageRecipient
{
    public void ProcessMessage(ObjectContainer con, Object message);
}
```

```
// JAVA
public interface MessageRecipient
{
    public void processMessage(ObjectContainer con, Object message);
}
```

A MessageRecipient simply processes the message object. Processing can be defined to involve anything you like, including calling the Close method of a *server*. Both interfaces can be found in the namespace/package com.db4o.messaging.

Let's show how this all works by modifying the scenario you have seen throughout this chapter so that the server will shut down in response to a user request issued in the "add" client. We could add a completely separate client just for this purpose, but the "add" client is already dealing with user input, so it will do just fine for this demonstration.

The modifications will work the same way in either networking mode or embedded mode—we'll specifically show networking mode here as this is a more useful scenario. The new features will be as follows:

1. There will be a stop condition in the "add" client, so that when the user enters the string *"stop"* when prompted for a name, the stop flag is set to true and the while loop is exited.

2. At this point, the "add" client will send message to tell the server to stop.

3. The process that is monitoring the server will receive the message, and respond by stopping the server.

Sounds simple enough—so how do we do it? The process is illustrated in Figure 8-3, and explained in the following sections.

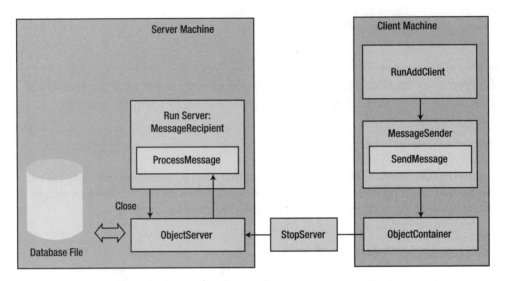

Figure 8-3. *Out-of-band signaling example*

Sending the Message

The basic idea is that the client thread or process gets a `MessageSender` instance from its `ObjectContainer`—messages sent using this will go to the server to which it is connected (by a network or in-process connection). The modified `Run` method, in `RunAddClient` in this example, looks like this:

```csharp
// C#
public void Run()
{
    try
    {
        aClient = Db4o.OpenClient("localhost", 8732, "user1", "password");
        while (!stop)
        {
            Console.WriteLine("\nADDCLIENT: Please enter a name: ");
            String name = Console.ReadLine();
            if (name.Equals("stop"))
            {
                stop = true;
            }
```

```
            else
            {
                Console.WriteLine("\nADDCLIENT: Please enter an age: ");
                int age = Convert.ToInt32(Console.ReadLine());
                aClient.Set(new Person(name, age));
                aClient.Commit();
            }
        }
    }
    catch (ThreadInterruptedException tie)
    {
        Console.WriteLine("Thread Error!" + tie);
    }
    finally
    {
        MessageSender messageSender = aClient.Ext().Configure()
            .GetMessageSender();
        messageSender.Send(new StopServer("ADDCLIENT says stop!"));
        aClient.Close();
    }
}


// JAVA
public void run()
{
    try
    {
        aClient = Db4o.openClient("localhost", 8732, "user1", "password");
        while (!stop)
        {
            System.out.print("\nADDCLIENT:Enter the developer's name and age (e.g.
                'Tom 44'): ");
            String name = sc.next();
            if(name.equals("stop"))
            {
                stop = true;
            }
            else
            {
                aClient.set(new Person(name, sc.nextInt()));
                aClient.commit();
            }
        }
    }
```

```
        catch (Exception e)
        {
            e.printStackTrace();
        }
        finally
        {
            MessageSender messageSender = aClient.ext().configure()
                .getMessageSender();
            messageSender.send(new StopServer("\nADDCLIENT says stop!"));
            aClient.close();
        }
    }
}
```

The MessageSender is obtained using the GetMessageSender method that belongs to the ObjectContainer, named aClient in this code (you will understand the Ext().Configure() part of this method call when you have read Chapters 9 and 10, but it doesn't matter exactly how this works here).

Once obtained, the MessageSender is used to send an object that is an instance of a class called StopServer. This class is simply a holder for a string that allows the client to send a comment with the message. The fact that this particular message is intended to stop the server is indicated by the class of object sent. StopServer is pretty simple, but for completeness, here is a listing:

```
// C#
namespace com.db4o.dg2db4o.chapter8
{
    class StopServer
    {
        private string _info;

        public StopServer(string info)
        {
            _info = info;
        }

        public override string ToString()
        {
            return _info;
        }
    }
}
```

```
// JAVA
package com.db4o.dg2db4o.chapter8;

public class StopServer {
    private String _info;
```

```
    public StopServer(String info) {
        _info = info;
    }

    public String toString(){
        return _info;
    }
}
```

■Note You can, if you wish, specify much more information or functionality in a message object than this. In some cases it might be useful to implement the Command design pattern, in which actions and their parameters are encapsulated into command objects. This is one of the "Gang of Four" design patterns, described in *Design Patterns: Elements of Reusable Object-Oriented Software* by Erich Gamma, Richard Helm, Ralph Johnson, and John Vlissides (Addison-Wesley, 1995).

Processing the Message

Now that the message object has been sent, you will want to process it—that is, check that it is an instance of StopServer and if so, stop the server and print out the comment it contains. You do so by making the thread or process that is monitoring the server implement the MessageRecipient interface by providing a ProcessMessage method.

Crucially, the thread or process must also register itself with the actual ObjectServer as the MessageRecipient for messages sent to that server by its clients. It does so by calling the SetMessageRecipient method that belongs to the ObjectServer, passing a this reference to itself as the parameter.

The class declaration, of RunServer in this example, is now:

```
class RunServer : MessageRecipient    // C#
```

```
class RunServer implements MessageRecipient, Runnable    // JAVA
```

The modified Run method and the new ProcessMessage method look like this:

```
// C#
private void Run()
{
    Console.WriteLine("Starting server...");
    ObjectServer server = Db4o.OpenServer("c:/netserver.yap", 8732);
    server.GrantAccess("user1", "password");
    server.GrantAccess("user2", "password");
    server.Ext().Configure().SetMessageRecipient(this);
    lock (this)
    {
```

```
        try
        {
            while (!stop)
            {
                Monitor.Wait(this, 60000);
                Console.WriteLine("SERVER: Server is listening ...");
            }
        }
        catch (ThreadInterruptedException tie)
        {
            Console.WriteLine("Thread Error!" + tie);
        }
        finally
        {
            server.Close();
        }
    }
    Console.WriteLine("Server ends...");
}

public void ProcessMessage(ObjectContainer con, Object message)
{
    lock (this)
    {
        if (message is StopServer)
        {
            Console.WriteLine("\nSERVER:" + message);
            stop = true;
            Monitor.PulseAll(this);
        }
    }
}

// JAVA
public void run() {
    System.out.println("Starting server...");
    ObjectServer server = Db4o.openServer("c:/netserver.yap", 8732);
    server.grantAccess("user1", "password");
    server.grantAccess("user2", "password");
    server.ext().configure().setMessageRecipient(this);
    synchronized (this) {
        try {
            while (!stop) {  // Out of band messages here later...
                System.out.println("\nSERVER:[" + System.currentTimeMillis()
                + "] Server's running... ");
                this.wait(60000);
            }
```

```
        } catch (Exception e) {
            e.printStackTrace();
        } finally {
            System.out.println("\nSERVER:[" + System.currentTimeMillis()
            + "] Server's stopped! ");
            server.close();
        }
    }
}


public void processMessage(ObjectContainer con, Object message) {
    synchronized (this) {
        if(message instanceof StopServer){
            System.out.println("\nSERVER:" + message);
            stop = true;
            this.notify();
        }
    }
}
```

When the message is received by the server, the ProcessMessage method is executed. If the object that was sent was indeed a StopServer object, the stop flag is set. The thread is notified so that the stop condition is evaluated immediately and it breaks out of the while loop, finally calling Close on the server.

Here's an example of the output from a test run (Java version), showing the output from the server and a client. First, the server:

```
[db4o 5.0.010    2006-02-16 09:33:05]
 Server listening on port: '8732'
SERVER:[1140082385708] Server's running...
[db4o 5.0.010    2006-02-16 09:33:10]
 Client 'user1' connected.
[db4o 5.0.010    2006-02-16 09:33:14]
 Client 'user2' connected.
SERVER:[1140082435708] Server's running...
SERVER:ADDCLIENT says stop!
[db4o 5.0.010    2006-02-16 09:33:30]
 Connection closed by client 'user1'.
[db4o 5.0.010    2006-02-16 09:33:30]
 'c:/netserver.yap' close request
[db4o 5.0.010    2006-02-16 09:33:30]
 'c:/netserver.yap' closed
```

And now the AddClient:

```
ADDCLIENT:Enter the developer's name and age (e.g. 'Tom 44'):
Michael 31
ADDCLIENT:Enter the developer's name and age (e.g. 'Tom 44'):
Sue 24
ADDCLIENT:Enter the developer's name and age (e.g. 'Tom 44'):
Tim 20
ADDCLIENT:Enter the developer's name and age (e.g. 'Tom 44'):
stop
```

Note that the next time the "list" client tries to access the server it will fail to do so, and will close after handling the resultant exception. It would be nice to be able to have the server send messages to all connected clients—for example, to warn them that it is about to shut down—but sending messages from server to clients is not supported at the time of this writing.

Summary

You have seen that the client/server mode in db4o is quite simple. Everything is done via configuration in the code. The networking mode allows connections, with authentication, from remote clients, whereas the embedded mode works for concurrent access by multiple clients within the same virtual machine. Finally, you have learned how a client can communicate with the server "out of band."

In the real world a lot of companies use these kinds of client/server communication features. For example, MR Controls, based in Calgary, uses this db4o feature extensively. They build SCADA (Supervisory Control and Data Acquisition) systems for power utilities and the gas and oil industry.

In the next chapter you will learn about database transactions in db4o, and in particular about how they work in the case of concurrent clients.

CHAPTER 9

■■■

Transactions

The job of a database is to provide for persistent data storage. It's usually expected that the database will do this job in a robust manner: making sure that the data that is stored is the correct data, that it hasn't been corrupted either by failures or by different users trying to change the same data at the same time. These requirements are met by the ACID properties of a database:

Atomicity is the ability to treat a group of operations as a single "atomic" operation. This means that the operations are grouped together into an operation that can't be subdivided by the database. The result is an "all or nothing" effect—if one of the individual operations fails for any reason, then the whole group of operations is aborted, or rolled back. The atomic operation is called a *transaction*. The operations in a transaction are all *committed* to the database together, or, if any operations fail, the entire transaction is *rolled back*—as far as the database is concerned, none of them ever happened.

Consistency is the requirement that changes to data in one part of a database be consistent with changes elsewhere in the database. For example, if the database holds the details of your bank accounts, and you transfer money from one account to another, then you hope that the database will be consistent. If one account is debited $1,000, then you really want $1,000 to be credited to the other. If only the debit operation is successful, and for some reason the credit operation fails, then the database has become inconsistent, and, more important, you have become $1,000 poorer.

Isolation is an important factor in ensuring consistency when multiple clients are accessing a database concurrently. It is important to isolate one user from the changes that are being made at the same time to the same data by the other user.

Durability is the ability of the database to recover the data in the event of a hardware or software failure. A database should be able to recover committed data even if there is a system failure during the commit process.

None of the ACID properties is coupled closely to the data model that is used to store the data. In this area, object databases are no different from relational ones. db4o provides ACID features, including transactions and transaction isolation, in standalone and client/server configurations. In this chapter you will look at some examples that illustrate db4o's support for transactions.

Working with Transactions

You've already been doing this! db4o begins transaction handling when you open a standalone database with a call to OpenFile, or when you create a client with a call to OpenClient. The transaction ends when the ObjectContainer that encapsulates the database or client is closed with a call to Close. Updates to any objects, through calls to Set, during the transaction are by default not committed until the end of the transaction. You will have been aware of this behavior already: in the examples in previous chapters that updated the database, we were always careful to start a new transaction when checking that the database was updated correctly.

You can also explicitly commit the updates during a transaction explicitly with a call to Commit. This doesn't end the transaction, but it does make sure that all updates up to that point are written to the database. Alternatively, you can roll back the transaction with a call to RollBack (surprisingly enough), which causes all updates since the last commit to be discarded.

Let's look at some examples of transaction handling in db4o. These examples make use of the classes shown in the UML class diagram shown in Figure 9-1.

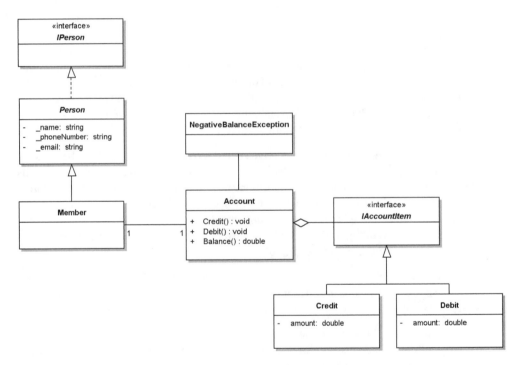

Figure 9-1. *Classes for transaction examples*

The Member class represents a member of an online payment service that allows members to make payments to other members, possibly for items bought through an online auction. The member class extends the Person abstract class and associated interface that were listed in Chapter 7. Each member has an Account, which stores a collection of AccountItem objects, each of which is either a Credit or a Debit. The account balance is calculated by a method Balance, which sums the values of the AccountItems. The Debit class has some simple built-in business logic—payments that would result in a member having a negative account balance are not permitted, and an exception is thrown.

A payment between two members is accomplished in two steps. The member who is being paid has a Credit added to his Account, while the member who is paying has a Debit added. The total sum of money in the two accounts must remain constant—money should remain within the system, simply being transferred from one member to another.

The classes in this scenario are shown in Listings 9-1 and 9-2.

Listing 9-1. *The Payment System Classes in C#*

```csharp
// C#
namespace com.db4o.dg2db4o.chapter9
{
    class Member : Person
    {
        Account _account;

        public Member(string name, string phoneNumber, string email) :
            base(name,phoneNumber,email)
        {
            _account = new Account();
        }

        public Account Account
        {
            get
            {
                return _account;
            }
            set
            {
                _account = value;
            }
        }

        public override string ToString()
        {
            return base.Name + " (Member): " +
                System.String.Format("{0:C}",_account.Balance()) ;
        }
    }
}
```

```csharp
// C#
using System.Collections.Generic;

namespace com.db4o.dg2db4o.chapter9
{
    class Account
    {
        IList<IAccountItem> _accountItems;

        public Account(){
            _accountItems = new List<IAccountItem>();
        }


        public void Credit(double amount)
        {
            _accountItems.Add(new Credit(amount));
        }

        public void Debit(double amount)
        {
            _accountItems.Add(new Debit(amount));
            if (Balance() < 0.0)
            {
                throw new NegativeBalanceException(Balance());
            }
        }

        public double Balance()
        {
            double balance = 0.0;
            foreach(IAccountItem accountItem in _accountItems){
                balance += accountItem.Amount;
            }
            return balance;
        }
    }
}
```

```csharp
// C#
namespace com.db4o.dg2db4o.chapter9
{
    class NegativeBalanceException : Exception
    {
        double _balance;
```

```csharp
        public NegativeBalanceException(double balance)
        {
            _balance = balance;
        }

        public override string ToString()
        {
            return "NegativeBalanceException (Balance = $" +
                System.String.Format("{0:C}",_balance) + ")";
        }
    }
}


// C#
namespace com.db4o.dg2db4o.chapter9
{
    interface IAccountItem
    {
        double Amount {get;}
    }
}


// C#
namespace com.db4o.dg2db4o.chapter9
{
    class Credit : IAccountItem
    {
        double _amount;

        public Credit(double amount)
        {
            _amount = amount;
        }

        public double Amount
        {
            get
            {
                return _amount;
            }
        }
    }
}
```

```csharp
// C#
namespace com.db4o.dg2db4o.chapter9
{
    class Debit : IAccountItem
    {
        double _amount;

        public Debit(double amount)
        {
            _amount = amount;
        }

        public double Amount
        {
            get
            {
                return -(_amount);
            }
        }
    }
}
```

Listing 9-2. *The Payment System Classes in Java*

```java
// JAVA
package com.db4o.dg2db4o.chapter9;

import java.text.NumberFormat;

public class Member extends AbstractPerson
{
    Account _account;

    public Member(String name, String phoneNumber, String email)
    {
        super(name,phoneNumber,email);
        _account = new Account();
    }

    public Account getAccount()
    {
        return _account;
    }
```

```java
    public void setAccount(Account value)
    {
        _account = value;
    }

    public String toString()
    {
        return _name + " (Member): " +
            NumberFormat.getCurrencyInstance().format(_account.balance());
    }
}
```

```java
// JAVA
package com.db4o.dg2db4o.chapter9;

import java.util.List;
import java.util.ArrayList;

public class Account
{
    List<AccountItem> _accountItems;

    public Account()
    {
        _accountItems = new ArrayList<AccountItem>();
    }

    public void credit(double amount) {
        _accountItems.add(new Credit(amount));
    }

    public void debit(double amount) throws NegativeBalanceException
    {
        _accountItems.add(new Debit(amount));
        if (balance() < 0.0)
        {
            throw new NegativeBalanceException(balance());
        }
    }
```

```java
    public double balance()
    {
        double balance = 0.0;
        for(AccountItem accountItem : _accountItems)
        {
            balance += accountItem.getAmount();
        }
        return balance;
    }
}
```

```java
// JAVA
package com.db4o.dg2db4o.chapter9;

import java.text.NumberFormat;

public class NegativeBalanceException extends Exception
{
    double _balance;

        public NegativeBalanceException(double balance)
        {
            _balance = balance;
        }

        public String toString()
        {
            return "NegativeBalanceException (Balance = " +
                NumberFormat.getCurrencyInstance().format(_balance) + ")";
        }
}
```

```java
// JAVA
package com.db4o.dg2db4o.chapter9;

public interface AccountItem
{
    double getAmount();
}
```

```java
// JAVA
package com.db4o.dg2db4o.chapter9;

public class Credit implements AccountItem
{
    double _amount;
```

```
    public Credit(double amount)
    {
        _amount = amount;
    }

    public double getAmount()
    {
        return _amount;
    }
}
```

```
// JAVA
package com.db4o.dg2db4o.chapter9;

public class Debit implements AccountItem
{
    double _amount;

    public Debit(double amount)
    {
        _amount = amount;
    }

    public double getAmount()
    {
        return -(_amount);
    }
}
```

Committing a Transaction

This example demonstrates a simple transaction that contains the operations needed to transfer funds from one member to another. Two Member objects are created and given a starting balance of $200 each. This means that the total assets of these two members are $400. In all the examples in this chapter, the only transfer of funds will be between these two members, so that that total must remain constant at $400; otherwise the database is inconsistent. After being initialized, the objects are stored in a db4o database, as shown in the following listings. Assume that db is a reference to an ObjectContainer.

```
// C#
Member m1 = new Member("Gary", "408 123 4567", "gary@example.net");
Member m2 = new Member("Rebecca", "408 987 6543", "rebecca@example.com");
m1.Account.Credit(200.00);
m2.Account.Credit(200.00);
db.Set(m1);
db.Set(m2);
db.Commit();
db.Close();
```

```
// JAVA
Member m1 = new Member("Gary", "408 123 4567", "gary@example.net ");
Member m2 = new Member("Rebecca", "408 987 6543", "rebecca@example.com ");
m1.getAccount().credit(200.00);
m2.getAccount().credit(200.00);
db.set(m1);
db.set(m2);
db.commit();
db.close();
```

It doesn't matter which database mode we use for this example. Single transactions work exactly the same way for standalone and client/server database access. The ObjectContainer reference could be obtained either by a call to OpenFile or a call to OpenClient. The calls to Commit and Close are shown explicitly here so that you know exactly where the transaction ends. You don't actually need the Commit call here, as Close commits and ends the transaction, but using explicit Commit calls is a good practice as it makes it absolutely clear in your code where commits are occurring.

The payment process involves a call to Credit on the Account of the first Member, and a call to Debit, for the same amount, on the Account of the second Member. Two database update operations are needed to store the updated state of the two Member objects.

Let's try making a payment of $100 from Rebecca to Gary. In the following, db is again an ObjectContainer reference, and this is a new transaction.

```
// C#
double amount = 100.00;
try
{
    member1 = (Member)db.Get(new Member("Gary", null, null)).Next();
    member2 = (Member)db.Get(new Member("Rebecca", null, null)).Next();
    member1.Account.Credit(amount);
    db.Set(member1);
    member2.Account.Debit(amount);
    db.Set(member2);
}
catch (Exception e)
{
    Console.WriteLine(e.ToString());
    db.Rollback();
}
finally
{
    db.Commit();
}
Console.WriteLine(member1);
Console.WriteLine(member2);
double total = member1.Account.Balance() + member2.Account.Balance();
Console.WriteLine("TOTAL: $" + System.String.Format("{0:C}". total));
db.Close();
```

```java
// JAVA
double amount = 100.00;
try
{
    member1 = (Member)db.get(new Member("Gary", null, null)).Next();
    member2 = (Member)db.get(new Member("Rebecca", null, null)).Next();
    member1.getAccount().credit(amount);
    db.set(member1);
    member2.getAccount().debit(amount);
    db.set(member2);
}
catch (Exception e)
{
    System.out.println(e.ToString());
    db.rollback();
}
finally
{
    db.commit();
}
System.out.println (member1);
System.out.println (member2);
double total = member1. getAccount().balance() + member2. getAccount().balance();
System.out.println ("TOTAL: " +
    NumberFormat.getCurrencyInstance().format (total));
db.Close();
```

The output looks like this:

```
Gary (Member): $300.00
Rebecca (Member): $100.00
TOTAL: $400.00
```

This looks good: the payment has been made and the total is still $400.

■Caution If you want to update an object, make sure that you use a query to get a reference that is connected to that object. References lose that connection when a transaction ends. If you open a new transaction, and there is still a reference used in a previous transaction within scope, then calling Set with that reference will add a new object to the database rather than updating the existing one. Remember that there are no primary keys in an object database to prevent this.

Rollback and Refresh

Let's run the same code, with the starting balances reset to $200 each, with a larger payment of $300. This payment should cause a NegativeBalanceException to be thrown by Gary's Account, and the database should roll back so that neither member is updated. The output now looks like this:

```
NegativeBalanceException (Balance = -$100.00)
Gary (Member): $500.00
Rebecca (Member): -$100.00
TOTAL: $400.00
```

This is a bit unexpected. The transaction is supposed to have rolled back, but it looks like the business logic has been ignored and Rebecca has been allowed to store a negative balance.

In fact, the transaction has rolled back successfully—you just have to be careful what you are looking at. The output statements print details of the objects member1 and member2. These are still connected to the relevant objects in the database, as they were returned by queries earlier in the transaction. However, once objects are activated, local cached copies are held in memory, which is what you are looking at in the output here. Rolling back only affects the database objects, not the cached copies. Of course, you could close the transaction, start a new one, and query to find the stored objects. Alternatively, to see what is actually in the database while the transaction is still active, you need to *refresh* the member1 and member2 references. The following lines can be added to the previous code before the call to Close:

```csharp
// C#
db.Ext().Refresh(member1, int.MaxValue);
db.Ext().Refresh(member2, int.MaxValue);
Console.WriteLine("STATE WITHIN TRANSACTION AFTER REFRESH");
Console.WriteLine(member1);
Console.WriteLine(member2);
double total = member1.Account.Balance() + member2.Account.Balance()
Console.WriteLine("TOTAL: $" + System.String.Format("{0:C}". total));
```

```java
// JAVA
db.ext().refresh(member1, Integer.MAX_VALUE);
db.ext().refresh(member2, Integer.MAX_VALUE);
System.out.println("STATE WITHIN TRANSACTION AFTER REFRESH");
System.out.println (member1);
System.out.println (member2);
double total = member1. getAccount().balance() + member2. getAccount().balance();
System.out.println ("TOTAL: " +
    NumberFormat.getCurrencyInstance().format (total));
```

The second parameter of the Refresh method is the member depth to which refresh will cascade—set to cascade as far as possible here by specifying MaxValue. The output now shows that the rollback has done its job: no payment has been made and the database is consistent.

```
NegativeBalanceException (Balance = $100.00)
Gary (Member): $500.00
Rebecca (Member): -$100.00
STATE WITHIN TRANSACTION AFTER REFRESH
Gary (Member): $200.00
Rebecca (Member): $200.00
TOTAL: $400.00
```

Note The Ext method of ObjectContainer returns an ExtObjectContainer, which is essentially an ObjectContainer with a richer range of capabilities, one of which is the ability used here to refresh live objects. It is expected that some or all of the additional capabilities of ExtCbjectContainer will be added to ObjectContainer in a future version of db4o. In this case, the call would become something like db.Refresh(member1, int.MaxValue)—you should check the API documentation for the version of db4o you are using to find out what methods are supported.

Note that rolling back only causes all operations since the last commit to be discarded. If you commit at the wrong time, the database can become inconsistent. To demonstrate this, let's imagine there is a call to Commit immediately after the first member is updated, that is, after db.Set(member1). The output now, with payment amount still $300 and the starting balances reset to $200 before running, is:

```
NegativeBalanceException (Balance = -$100.00)
Gary (Member): $500.00
Rebecca (Member): -$100.00
STATE WITHIN TRANSACTION AFTER REFRESH
Gary (Member): $500.00
Rebecca (Member): $200.00
TOTAL: $700.00
```

Rebecca's account is rolled back but Gary's isn't, so now there is $700 in the system instead of $400, according to the database. The developer who put the Commit call in the wrong place may well end up $300 poorer . . .

Concurrent Transactions

The transactions acting on a standalone db4o database are important as they provide atomicity and consistency in that context. In standalone mode, only one client can access a database file at a time. In client/server mode, on the other hand, there may be more than one transaction acting concurrently on a single database. The transactions may be initiated by clients in separate threads in an embedded server environment, or by separate network clients in a network server environment. The isolation between concurrent transactions becomes an important issue in these situations.

Isolation Level

With concurrent transactions, there is the possibility that one transaction may try to read or modify an object in the database during the lifetime of another transaction that is also acting on that object. A strategy is required so that the database knows what to do in this situation. The strategy is known as the *isolation level*. Isolation is one of the ACID properties. The database implements the isolation level by *locking* entities to restrict access to them. In simple terms, if an object is locked by one transaction, then no other transaction can get at it until the first transaction finishes. So, if one client is processing a payment from Rebecca to Gary, then another client that at the same time wants to process a payment from Gary to someone else can't do anything until the first client commits its transaction.

In practice, this kind of locking, known as *pessimistic locking*, can be a bad idea. It does ensure that the database remains consistent and that the data that any client reads is accurate and up-to-date. However, performance can suffer, especially if transactions act on a lot of objects, or take a long time to complete. This can lead to severe limitations on the practicable number of simultaneous users.

In multiuser environments, it's often better to be a bit more optimistic with locking. Optimistic locking assumes that, for example, it is unlikely that two transactions involving Gary will occur at the same time, so each transaction does not get to lock the object exclusively. Of course, it is possible to get collisions, where two transactions try to access the same objects. You then need to understand what effect each transaction will have on the other, and have a strategy to deal with any problems that may arise.

The isolation level describes the effects of the database's locking behavior. The commonly used isolation levels are:

Read Uncommitted: This means that there is effectively no locking, except while a transaction is actually being committed. It's possible for one transaction to read data that has been modified by another concurrent transaction that has not yet committed its updates. This data could be inaccurate, because it may include updates that will never actually be committed to the database if the transaction is rolled back. This is known as an *overly optimistic lock*, and is only appropriate in single-user situations.

Read Committed: This uses optimistic locking, and allows one transaction to read data that has been modified and committed by another concurrent transaction. This can lead to an *unrepeatable read*: if the same object is retrieved at different times during the transaction, its state may have changed from one time to the next by another transaction committing updates.

Repeatable Read and **Serializable**: These use more pessimistic locking to prevent unrepeatable reads and provide a greater degree of isolation. Serializable is the most restrictive and additionally prevents the introduction of new inserts into a locked range of data.

Many database systems allow the isolation level to be selected by a transaction but use Read Committed as the default, which gives the best compromise between performance and data integrity in a multiuser environment. db4o takes a very straightforward approach:

all transactions are Read Committed. It is possible to enforce stricter locking explicitly in your application if necessary. An example of this is shown later in this chapter.

Looking at Transaction Isolation

To demonstrate transaction isolation we need to have two transactions that access the same objects concurrently.

Code and Output

The following example starts a network server and creates two clients. The initial data in the database file is the same as in the previous example. In a real situation, the clients would be created on separate network hosts or in separate threads. Here, the two clients are created within the same thread; this means that it is easy to control the exact order of events. As far as the database is concerned, this scenario is indistinguishable from one with two separate remote clients. For simplicity, exception handling is omitted from this code. For clarity, the output is shown in stages, immediately following the relevant sections of code. The results were obtained with the value of amount equal to $100:

```
// C#
ObjectServer server = Db4o.OpenServer(Util.DbFileName, 8732);
server.GrantAccess("user1", "password");
server.GrantAccess("user2", "password");

// Create clients
client1 = Db4o.OpenClient("localhost", 8732, "user1", "password");
client2 = Db4o.OpenClient("localhost", 8732, "user2", "password");

// client 1 gets two Member objects and makes payment from Rebecca to Gary
double amount = 100.00;
member1_1 = (Member)client1.Get(new Member("Gary", null, null)).Next();
member2_1 = (Member)client1.Get(new Member("Rebecca", null, null)).Next();
member1_1.Account.Credit(amount);
client1.Set(member1_1);
member2_1.Account.Debit(amount);
client1.Set(member2_1);

// client 2 gets two Member objects
member1_2 = (Member)client2.Get(new Member("Gary", null, null)).Next();
member2_2 = (Member)client2.Get(new Member("Rebecca", null, null)).Next();

Console.WriteLine("CLIENT1:" + member1_1);
Console.WriteLine("CLIENT1:" + member2_1);
Console.WriteLine("CLIENT2:" + member1_2);
Console.WriteLine("CLIENT2:" + member2_2);
```

The output is:

```
CLIENT1:Gary (Member): $100.00
CLIENT1:Rebecca (Member): $300.00
CLIENT2:Gary (Member): $200.00
CLIENT2:Rebecca (Member): $200.00
```

Now client1 commits its running transaction:

```
client1.Commit();

Console.WriteLine("READ AFTER COMMIT");
Console.WriteLine("CLIENT1:" + member1_1);
Console.WriteLine("CLIENT1:" + member2_1);
Console.WriteLine("CLIENT2:" + member1_2);
Console.WriteLine("CLIENT2:" + member2_2);
```

The output is:

```
READ AFTER COMMIT
CLIENT1:Gary (Member): $100.00
CLIENT1:Rebecca (Member): $300.00
CLIENT2:Gary (Member): $200.00
CLIENT2:Rebecca (Member): $200.00
```

Then all objects are refreshed so that we see the current database contents:

```
// refresh all objects to get current database contents
client1.Ext().Refresh(member1_1, int.MaxValue);
client1.Ext().Refresh(member2_1, int.MaxValue);
client2.Ext().Refresh(member1_2, int.MaxValue);
client2.Ext().Refresh(member2_2, int.MaxValue);
Console.WriteLine("READ AFTER REFRESH");
Console.WriteLine("CLIENT1:" + member1_1);
Console.WriteLine("CLIENT1:" + member2_1);
Console.WriteLine("CLIENT2:" + member1_2);
Console.WriteLine("CLIENT2:" + member2_2);
double total = member1_2.Account.Balance() + member2_2.Account.Balance()
Console.WriteLine("TOTAL: $" + System.String.Format("{0:C}". total));
```

The output is:

```
READ AFTER REFRESH
CLIENT1:Gary (Member): $100.00
CLIENT1:Rebecca (Member): $300.00
CLIENT2:Gary (Member): $100.00
CLIENT2:Rebecca (Member): $300.00
TOTAL: $400.00
```

CHAPTER 9 ■ TRANSACTIONS 239

Finally, we'd better not forget to close everything down:

```
client1.Close();
client2.Close();
server.Close();
```

// JAVA
```
ObjectServer server = Db4o.openServer(Util.DbFileName, 8732);
server.grantAccess("user1", "password");
server.grantAccess("user2", "password");

// Create clients
client1 = Db4o.openClient("localhost", 8732, "user1", "password");
client2 = Db4o.openClient("localhost", 8732, "user2", "password");

// client 1 gets two Member objects and makes payment from Rebecca to Gary
member1_1 = (Member)client1.get(new Member("Gary", null, null)).next();
member2_1 = (Member)client1.get(new Member("Rebecca", null, null)).next();
double amount = 100.00;
member1_1.getAccount().debit(amount);
client1.set(member1_1);
member2_1.getAccount().credit(amount);
client1.set(member2_1);

// client 2 gets two Member objects
member1_2 = (Member)client2.get(new Member("Gary", null, null)).next();
member2_2 = (Member)client2.get(new Member("Rebecca", null, null)).next();

System.out.println("CLIENT1:" + member1_1);
System.out.println("CLIENT1:" + member2_1);
System.out.println("CLIENT2:" + member1_2);
System.out.println("CLIENT2:" + member2_2);
```

The output is:

```
CLIENT1:Gary (Member): $100.00
CLIENT1:Rebecca (Member): $300.00
CLIENT2:Gary (Member): $200.00
CLIENT2:Rebecca (Member): $200.00
```

Now client1 commits its running transaction:

```
client1.commit();

System.out.println("READ AFTER COMMIT");
System.out.println("CLIENT1:" + member1_1);
System.out.println("CLIENT1:" + member2_1);
System.out.println("CLIENT2:" + member1_2);
System.out.println("CLIENT2:" + member2_2);
```

The output is:

```
READ AFTER COMMIT
CLIENT1:Gary (Member): $100.00
CLIENT1:Rebecca (Member): $300.00
CLIENT2:Gary (Member): $200.00
CLIENT2:Rebecca (Member): $200.00
```

Then all objects are refreshed so that we see the current database contents:

```
client1.ext().refresh(member1_1, Integer.MAX_VALUE);
client1.ext().refresh(member2_1, Integer.MAX_VALUE);
client2.ext().refresh(member1_2, Integer.MAX_VALUE);
client2.ext().refresh(member2_2, Integer.MAX_VALUE);
System.out.println("READ AFTER REFRESH");
System.out.println("CLIENT1:" + member1_1);
System.out.println("CLIENT1:" + member2_1);
System.out.println("CLIENT2:" + member1_2);
System.out.println("CLIENT2:" + member2_2);
double total = member1_2.getAccount().balance() + member2_2.
    getAccount().balance();
System.out.println ("TOTAL: " +
    NumberFormat.getCurrencyInstance().format (total));
```

The output is:

```
READ AFTER REFRESH
CLIENT1:Gary (Member): $100.00
CLIENT1:Rebecca (Member): $300.00
CLIENT2:Gary (Member): $100.00
CLIENT2:Rebecca (Member): $300.00
TOTAL: $400.00
```

Finally, we'd better not forget to close everything down:

```
client1.close();
client2.close();
server.close();
```

Commentary

Note that client2 queries the database after client1 has updated its objects, but before client1 has committed those updates. client2 does not see the updated versions of the objects until after client1 has committed, and client2 refreshes to see up-to-date data. The effect is that client2 can give its user information that does not include the changes that the user of client1 has input, which is the behavior you would expect with Read Committed isolation. If client1's update fails and rolls back, client2 is unaffected.

Collisions

What if client2 doesn't just read the data, but also updates it? To simulate this collision situation, the following code can be inserted immediately after the queries on client2, so that client2 is attempting to record a payment of $50 at the same time as client1 is recording a payment of $100. client2 commits its update only at the end of its transaction.

```
// C#
member1_2.Account.Credit(50);
client2.Set(member1_2);
member2_2.Account.Debit(50);
client2.Set(member2_2);
```

```
//Java
member1_2.getAccount().credit(50);
client2.set(member1_2);
member2_2.getAccount().debit(50);
client2.set(member2_2);
```

The output this time looks like this:

```
CLIENT1:Gary (Member): $100.00
CLIENT1:Rebecca (Member): $300.00
CLIENT2:Gary (Member): $250.00
CLIENT2:Rebecca (Member): $150.00
READ AFTER COMMIT
CLIENT1:Gary (Member): $100.00
CLIENT1:Rebecca (Member): $300.00
CLIENT2:Gary (Member): $250.00
CLIENT2:Rebecca (Member): $150.00
READ AFTER REFRESH
CLIENT1:Gary (Member): $100.00
CLIENT1:Rebecca (Member): $300.00
CLIENT2:Gary (Member): $250.00
CLIENT2:Rebecca (Member): $150.00
TOTAL: $400.00
```

Now, both clients have their own viewpoint of the result of their update. Even after client1 commits and client2 refreshes, client2 is only aware of its own updated data. So which one wins? Well, if you open the database again after both clients have closed, and list the actual stored data, you get this:

```
Gary (Member): $250.00
Rebecca (Member): $150.00
TOTAL: $400.00
```

---

client2 "wins": because its updates were committed after those of client1, those are the ones which are stored. It's as if client1 never made any updates. Note that the database is consistent (the total is $400), but a whole transaction has been lost without a trace as a result of the collision.

If it is likely that collisions will occur, and the consequences are problematic, then you need to have a strategy for dealing with them. Two possible strategies are to simply detect and decide what to do about it, or to prevent them from happening in the first place.

Collision Detection

The basic idea of collision detection is to check before committing a transaction that the object in the database has not changed since the transaction started. In the example here, you can check that the account balance has not changed. The balance can be stored in a temporary variable immediately after the initial query, for example:

```
double startBalance = member1_2.Account.Balance();     // C#
```

```
double startBalance = member1_2.getAccount().balance();     // JAVA
```

Immediately before committing, you need to check what the value for this object is in the database. A call to Refresh will not work: as you saw earlier, refreshing an object within a transaction that has modified that object gives you the modified version. Instead, another ExtObjectContainer method, PeekPersisted, lets you look directly at the persisted object in the database. You can then compare the initial balance in the transaction with the balance of the persisted object. If they are not the same, then the object is likely to have been modified by a concurrent transaction. There is then a choice of ways to deal with this, including rolling back the current transaction and logging the collision, or giving the user a warning and a choice of what to do.

Let's add collision detection for one of the clients. This code, if inserted immediately before client2 is closed, simply prints a warning message and rolls back:

```
// C#
Member persisted = (Member) client2.Ext().PeekPersisted(member1_2, 10, true);
if (persisted.Account.Balance() != startBalance)
{
    Console.WriteLine("Object in database has changed during transaction");
    client2.Rollback();
}
```

```java
// JAVA
Member persisted = (Member) client2.ext().peekPersisted(member1_2, 10, true);
if (persisted.getAccount().balance() != startBalance)
{
    System.out.println("Object in database has changed during transaction");
    client2.rollback();
}
```

The object returned by PeekPersisted has no connection with the database. The parameters are: a reference in the current transaction that is connected with the object in the database; the depth to which the object is to be instantiated; and a boolean that specifies whether the object to be returned is the committed object (true) or the object that may have been set without having been committed (false). The result is that the changes made by client1 survive in the database, and those made by client2 are discarded—the difference from the previous example is that the user is told about it.

Collision Avoidance with Semaphores

Collisions can be avoided with db4o by explicitly locking objects during a transaction rather than relying on the database's own locking strategy. One way of doing this is to use *semaphores*.

A semaphore in db4o is a simple named flag that can be used to protect critical sections of code from being executed by more than one client or transaction at the same time, much like the lock and synchronized keywords in C# and Java, respectively. A database can only set one semaphore with a particular name. Many semaphores with different names can be set.

Once a particular semaphore is set out, any attempts to set a semaphore with the same name will fail until the first client releases it. For example, the following code creates a critical code section. The second parameter of SetSemaphore is the time, in milliseconds, that the database should wait for the semaphore to be released.

```csharp
// C#
if (objectContainer.Ext().SetSemaphore("MY SEMAPHORE", 1000)
{
    // Critical code section
    ...
    // Release after critical section
    objectContainer.Ext().ReleaseSemaphore("MY SEMAPHORE");
}
```

```java
// JAVA
if (objectContainer.ext().setSemaphore("MY SEMAPHORE", 1000)
{
    // Critical code section
    ...
    // Release after critical section
    objectContainer.ext().releaseSemaphore("MY SEMAPHORE");
}
```

The name of the semaphore is simply a string, which can be completely arbitrary, or it can be given a specific meaning. A useful example of a meaning is to associate it with a specific object in the database. It's just a string, though, so how do we do this? One way is to include the OID of the object in the string. For example, if obj is an object reference that is connected to a database object, the following code will create a semaphore specific to that object. Code that updates that object can be placed within the critical section protected by that semaphore.

```
// C#
long id = _objectContainer.GetID(obj);
objectContainer.SetSemaphore("Semaphore:" + id, 1000);
```

```
// JAVA
long id = _objectContainer.getID(obj);
objectContainer.setSemaphore("Semaphore:" + id, 1000);
```

For example, the class, ObjectLock, shown in Listings 9-3 and 9-4, provides a simple implementation of object locking.

Listing 9-3. *The ObjectLock Class in C#*

```
// C#
using com.db4o;

namespace com.db4o.dg2db4o.chapter9
{
    public class ObjectLock
    {
        private string SEMAPHORE_NAME = "Semaphore: ";

        public Boolean Lock(Object obj, ObjectContainer objectContainer)
        {
            long id = objectContainer.Ext().GetID(obj);
            Console.WriteLine("Attempting to get semaphore: " +
                SEMAPHORE_NAME + id);
            return objectContainer.Ext().SetSemaphore(
                SEMAPHORE_NAME + id, 1000);
        }

        public void Release(Object obj, ObjectContainer objectContainer)
        {
            long id = _objectContainer.Ext().GetID(obj);
            Console.WriteLine("Releasing semaphore: " + SEMAPHORE_NAME + id);
            objectContainer.Ext().ReleaseSemaphore(SEMAPHORE_NAME + id);
        }
    }
}
```

Listing 9-4. *The ObjectLock Class in Java*

```
// JAVA
package com.db4o.dg2db4o.chapter9;

import com.db4o.ObjectContainer;

public class ObjectLock
{
    private String SEMAPHORE_NAME = "Semaphore: ";

    public boolean lock(Object obj, ObjectContainer objectContainer)
    {
        long id = objectContainer.ext().getID(obj);
        System.out.println("Attempting to get semaphore: " +
            SEMAPHORE_NAME + id);
        return objectContainer.ext().setSemaphore(
            SEMAPHORE_NAME + id, 1000);
    }

    public void release(Object obj, ObjectContainer objectContainer)
    {
        long id = objectContainer.ext().getID(obj);
        System.out.println ("Releasing semaphore: " + SEMAPHORE_NAME + id);
        objectContainer.ext().releaseSemaphore(SEMAPHORE_NAME + id);
    }
}
```

Any client that needs to update objects must be well behaved: it must use an ObjectLock to lock those objects before updating. For example, client1 must lock its Member objects before attempting to make a payment:

```
// C#
ObjectLock objectLock = new ObjectLock ();

// Get two member objects
member1_1 = (Member)client1.Get(new Member("Gary", null, null)).Next();
member2_1 = (Member)client1.Get(new Member("Rebecca", null, null)).Next();

// make payment
if (objectLock.Lock(member1_1, client1) && objectLock.Lock(member2_1, client1))
{
    double amount = 100.00;
    member1_1.Account.Credit(amount);
    db.Set(member1_1);
    member2_1.Account.Debit(amount);
    db.Set(member2_1);
    objectLock.Release(member1_1, client1);
```

```
        objectLock.Release (member2_1, client1);
}
else
{
    Console.WriteLine("Cannot update - object lock timed out");
    client1.Rollback();
}
```

// JAVA
```
ObjectLock objectLock = new ObjectLock(client1);

// Get two member objects
member1_1 = (Member)client1.get(new Member("Gary", null, null)).next();
member2_1 = (Member)client1.get(new Member("Rebecca", null, null)).next();

// make payment
if (objectLock.lock(member1_1, client1) && objectLock.lock(member2_1, client1))
{
    double amount = 100.00;
    member1_1.getAccount().credit(amount);
    db.set(member1_1);
    member2_1.getAccount().debit(amount);
    db.set(member2_1);
    objectLock.release (member1_1, client1);
    objectLock.release (member2_1, client1);
}
else
{
    System.out.println("Cannot update - object lock timed out");
    client1.rollback();
}
```

If another client has already locked these objects, then this code will wait the specified time
(1,000 milliseconds here, but you can adjust this to suit the transaction times in your application)
for the existing lock to be released. If it is not released in that time, the calls to Lock will return
false and the transaction will be rolled back.

■**Tip** In this example we created a separate semaphore for each individual object. In most cases it would
be more efficient to create "tasks" that involve entire graphs of objects, and to create a semaphore for each task.

Failures and Durability

The one ACID property we haven't discussed much is *durability*, which requires that any data that has been committed to the database must not be lost. This is straightforward after commit: db4o database files can easily be backed up, or the data can be replicated (see Chapter 11).

If a failure occurs while a transaction is actually being committed, db4o uses a resume-commit-on-crash strategy to ensure durability. The commit will resume the next time the database file is opened. db4o does this by writing all objects to the database file immediately when they are stored or updated. The existing objects also remain in the database at this point. When a transaction is committed, pointers in the database are modified to point to the new objects. A list of pointers that are to be modified during commit is written to the database file, which is then switched into "in-commit" mode, after which the pointers are actually modified in the database file. Finally, the database file is switched to "not-in-commit" mode. If a failure occurs while the database file is "in-commit," the commit is restarted. All pointers are read from the "pointers to be modified" list and are modified to the state they are intended to have after commit.

Summary

db4o can operate as a multiuser database with ACID properties. These properties are not a function of the data model, and in fact, db4o is much like any other DBMS here, though clearly not as sophisticated as some. The usual concepts, such as transaction isolation, apply. Some examples of working with transactions in db4o have been given here—a discussion of db4o transactions in comparison with RDBMSs, and further technical issues associated with them, can be found in Chapter 13 of this book.

In the next chapter you will learn about db4o's many configuration and tuning options, and you will see more examples of the use of the ExtObjectContainer, which was briefly introduced in this chapter.

CHAPTER 10

■■■

Configurations and Tuning

This chapter describes a wide range of ways in which you can configure db4o to make it work your way. db4o includes a configuration interface, found in the `com.db4o.config` package, that defines ways in which you can control the behavior of db4o and its `ObjectContainers`.

Some configurations deal with the db4o objects you manage. For instance, you might wish to set the activation/update depth discussed in Chapter 7. Or you might wish to generate Unique Universal IDs (UUIDs), which are needed for replication or for long-term external references.

There are also configuration options that affect the performance of database operations. These mostly control aspects of the db4o database file or the way db4o uses reflection. One example of a file-related configuration is the block size you can set for the db4o file. This controls the overall chunk size, and thus the file size, of the database. Or you might want to encrypt your database file and send it secure via email or FTP. Reflection-related configurations mostly deal with the way db4o accesses and manages your classes. For example, you might wish to determine whether to use constructors or reflection when instantiating objects.

A further group of configuration options deals with communication settings. You have already learned in Chapter 8 that you can set up a networking communication between the client and the server, and also that you can set up your own communication between them using out-of-band signaling. This is done via the configuration interface, and is one of the many communications configurations.

In fact, there are many more configuration options than those mentioned here: some are illustrated in examples elsewhere in this book, but this chapter aims to provide you with a comprehensive overview. If you read the following chapter with your own particular applications in mind, you may well find precisely the configurations that will help you get the most out of db4o.

In addition to configuration options, db4o provides some external tuning and diagnostic tools that are not part of the db4o library for performing actions such as defragmenting the database. These tools are also described in this chapter.

Note that this chapter features extensive references to method names that are identical in C# and Java apart from capitalization of the first letter. Where this is the *only* difference, they are shown in C# form—in Java, the first letter changes to lowercase. Code listings are shown in both languages as usual, apart from one exceptional case where the example is only relevant to C#. Actually, C# programmers might find the use of method calls rather than properties for many of the configurations a bit surprising. It is likely that a future .NET version of db4o will adopt more typical .NET syntax for configurations.

Using Configurations

To apply a configuration you can call the Db4o.Configure static method of the Db4o class, which gives you a reference to an object that implements the Configuration interface. You then apply the desired configuration by calling the appropriate method of the Configuration object, BlockSize(8) for instance:

```
Configuration conf = Db4o.Configure();
conf.BlockSize(8);
```

Alternatively, you can do this in a single line of code:

```
Db4o.Configure().BlockSize(8);
```

When a configuration is set, it is saved in a static Configuration object in the Db4o class (actually an instance of a class called Config4Impl that implements the Configuration interface). When a new ObjectContainer is subsequently created by opening a file or connecting to a db4o server, this global Configuration object is cloned and copied to the new ObjectContainer. The same Configuration can be copied to many ObjectContainers. When a new ObjectContainer is subsequently created by opening a file or connecting to a db4o server, this global Configuration object is cloned and copied to the new ObjectContainer (see Figure 10-1). Keep in mind that any configuration calls made *after* opening an ObjectContainer have no effect on the open ObjectContainer.

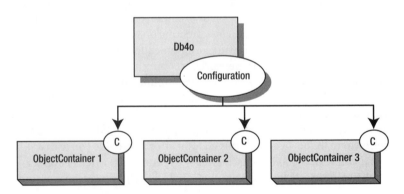

Figure 10-1. *Configurations being cloned to each ObjectContainer*

Here are some examples of calls that apply globally. They are object-related calls that have no effect on already open ObjectContainers but are applied to any that are created subsequently. The purpose of each of these configurations will be described in detail later in this chapter.

```
Configuration conf = Db4o.Configure();    // Db4o is capitalized in Java too
conf.ObjectClass(typeof(Person)).ObjectField("name").Indexed(true);
conf.CbjectClass(typeof(Person)).CascadeOnDelete();
conf.GenerateUUIDs(Int32.MaxValue);
conf.GenerateVersionNumbers(Int32.MaxValue);
conf.AutomaticShutDown(false);
conf.LockDatabaseFile(false);
```

```
conf.SingleThreadedClient(true);
conf.WeakReferences(false);
```

Note that `typeof(Person)` becomes `Person.class` in Java.

The following configuration examples have an influence on the database file—they all change the structure or content of the database file in some way:

```
Configuration conf = Db4o.Configure();
conf.BlockSize(8);
conf.Encrypt(true);
conf.Io(new XTeaEncryptionFileAdapter("password"));
conf.Password("password");
conf.Unicode(false);
```

There are also a number of configuration options that are intended to be applied directly to an individual open `ObjectContainer` or `ObjectServer`. Setting a configuration this way modifies the `Configuration` context for that `ObjectContainer` or `ObjectServer`, but does not affect the global `Configuration`.

However, because an `ObjectContainer` does not have a method to access its `Configuration`, it cannot be configured directly. It can, however, be configured through an `ExtObjectContainer`, which is a bit like an `ObjectContainer` on steroids—it can do everything an `ObjectContainer` can (it implements the same interface) and more. The intention is that `ExtObjectContainer` will provide a sandbox for the development of capabilities that may in the future be included in `ObjectContainer`, but it also makes those capabilities available now. You get an `ExtObjectContainer` that lets you configure a particular `ObjectContainer` by calling its `ext` method. You can get the `ExtObjectContainer` and apply the configuration in one line of code, as shown here. Similarly, an individual `ObjectServer` can be configured through an `ExtObjectServer`.

```
myObjectContainer.Ext().Configure()
myObjectServer.Ext().Configure()
```

It is important to understand that these configurations are *not* stored in the db4o database. This means that your code has to manage the configurations. If you decide on a particular configuration to use with your database, you should not call code that results in running with different configurations unless you are extremely confident that configuration changes are intended. If you are developing a client/server application, you should also ensure that both client and server use the same configuration settings! It might be a good idea to share these configurations in a (singleton) class that can be accessed from the server and from any client.

The Configuration Interface

While db4o offers the developer a tremendous amount of leeway regarding configuration options, chances are you're not going to require every one of them. However, it is useful to know about them. For quick reference, an alphabetical list is presented in Table 10-1. We then describe their purposes and uses in more detail. To help make sense of the wide range of

options, we will organize the configurations into six groups: object-, file-, reflection-, commu-
nication-, and logging-related options.

Table 10-1. *Alphabetic Configurations Overview*

Configuration Method	Short Description
ActivationDepth	Controls the level of object activation in deep objects
AutomaticShutDown	Switches on/off the automatic shutdown hook
BlockSize	Sets storage block size and hence maximum database size
Callbacks	Specifies whether to call callbacks on your objects
CallConstructors	Specifies whether to call default constructors to avoid slow reflection
ClassActivationDepthConfigurable	Specifies whether to allow individual class settings for activation depth
DetectSchemaChanges	Enables/disables detect schema changes (slow) on startup
DisableCommitRecovery	Enables/disables commit recovery after failure
Encrypt	Encrypts the database file using a simple algorithm
ExceptionsOnNotStorable	Specifies whether an exception will be thrown if the object cannot be stored
FlushFileBuffers	Specifies whether file buffers can be flushed during commits
Freespace	Lets you configure use of free space in the database
GenerateUUIDs	Specifies whether to generate unique identifiers
GenerateVersionNumbers	Specifies whether to generate version numbers for each object stored
GetMessageSender	Allows the client to send messages to the server
Io	Allows you to configure your own input/output (I/O) adapter (e.g., in RAM or encryption)
LockDatabaseFile	Specifies whether file locking can be enabled if single access is guaranteed
MarkTransient	Marks a field from a class as transient
MessageLevel	Sets the logging message level
ObjectClass	Gets a class definition and configures it for db4o
OptimizeNativeQueries	Turns NQ optimization on or off
OptimizeNativeQueries	Checks if NQ optimization is on or off
Password	Sets the password for simple file encryption
ReadOnly	Specifies whether ObjectContainers will be opened in read-only mode

Table 10-1. *Alphabetic Configurations Overview*

Configuration Method	Short Description
ReflectWith	Specifies whether to use another reflector (super advanced feature)
RefreshClasses	Reanalyzes all classes if changed classes are available
ReserveStorageSpace	Lets the database file be in one chunk on the disk
SetBlobPath	Specifies the path for BLOB entries
SetClassloader	Defines a new classloader for db4o
SetOut	Sets the print stream for db4o logging messages
SingleThreadedClient	Configures single or multithreaded clients
TestConstructors	Allows/prevents creating test instances of classes at startup
TimeoutClientSocket	Sets how long the client waits for a server response
TimeoutPingClients	Specifies the period of client inactivity after which the server checks client connections
TimeoutServerSocket	Specifies the regular interval at which the server read threads check if the server has been shut down
Unicode	Turns Unicode off to store strings smaller and faster
WeakReferences	Turns the weak reference management system on or off
WeakReferencesCollectionInterval	Sets the interval to detect unused weak references

Object-Related Configurations

These configurations are associated with the actual objects that db4o stores. Note that parameter types shown here are for C#. There are some slight differences in Java; for example, bool becomes boolean.

ActivationDepth(int depth)

The concept of activation depth was described in detail in Chapter 7. That chapter showed you how important it is to control the activation of your subobjects. Here is a short summary to refresh your knowledge. If you search for objects and access them by iterating through the ObjectSet, you cannot assume that all referenced child objects will be instantiated automatically. Let's assume you have an object person that contains object references to a depth of 5. Assume also that the ActivationDepth configuration has the value 3. To find a field called field5, you might have to follow object references like person.field1.field2.field3.field4.field5. If you retrieve the object by extracting it from an ObjectSet, you will receive the objects person, field1, field2, and field3 as valid objects, but field3 is not activated. This means you cannot get access to field4 (and thus not to field5). Additionally, you should keep the following two points in mind:

- The default activation level is 5. You can adjust this to the needs of your particular object model.

- If you then need the object field3 activated because you need access to its members, you can call myObjectContainer.Activate(field3, DEPTH) and the same for field5.

Callbacks(bool flag)

Callbacks provide a way to get your own object methods called in response to certain database events (update, delete, etc.). These methods will be detected via reflection at runtime, and thus decrease the performance of your application. Therefore, if your application does not use callbacks, you should set the flag to false to increase the performance. Some uses of callbacks are described in Chapter 12.

ClassActivationDepthConfigurable(bool flag)

Activation is one of the options that can be controlled for individual classes as well as globally (see ObjectClass). This method turns individual class MaximumActivationDepth configuration on and off. true is the default, and means that classes can be configured individually using the following:

```
Db4o.Configure().ObjectClass(typeof(Person)).MaximumActivationDepth(10);    // C#
Db4o.configure().objectClass(Person.class).MaximumActivationDepth(10);    // JAVA
```

false means that the previous declaration has no effect. This means that the update depth must be defined globally with ActivationDepth(int depth).

Generateuuids(int setting)

This setting configures the container to use long object IDs that are entirely unique. The generation of Unique Universal IDs (UUIDs) is important for replication, and is explained in Chapter 11. You can configure the UUID generation for all ObjectContainers or for specific classes only, which is shown in the second line using ObjectClass:

```
Db4o.Configure().generateUUIDs(Int32.MaxValue);
Db4o.Configure().objectClass(typeof(Person)).generateUUIDs(true);
```

UUID generation should only be switched on if necessary because it consumes space and performance.

Generateversionnumbers(int setting)

This is similar to UUIDs. db4o can store version numbers for each object that will be stored. If you set this configuration setting to -1, version number generation will be off. If you set the maximal value of your integer (e.g., Int32.MaxValue), then all classes will get a version number. Alternatively, you can set the value to 1. This means that you will set the versioning for classes individually (see ObjectClass).

MarkTransient(string attributeName)

This setting is used to mark certain fields as transient. Please note that this configuration is for .NET users only!

Normally if your field is marked as transient (Java) or [NonSerialized] (C#), db4o will not store the values. Therefore, if you store and retrieve classes you will get null values in these fields. On the other hand, if you don't want to change the original class to specify that a field is NonSerialized, but you want only certain fields to be managed by db4o, you can use the MarkTransient configuration.

This feature makes use of C# *attributes*. C# allows you to define declarative tags, called attributes, that you can place on items in your source code to specify additional information. Attributes allow separation of concerns with your code. In this case the decision on whether or not to save is known as a *cross cut concern* as it can apply to many different classes or fields. In contrast, behavior that is specific to a class is known as a *core concern*. The same attribute can be used in deciding whether or not to save many different fields. Attributes are sometimes referred to as *aspects*.

Consider a scenario where you have a class that has a lot of fields. One field is a file object or a file handle. As a result, you would never wish to save this object because of its large size or changing content.

Here is an example of using MarkTransient:

1. An attribute is actually defined as a class, which can optionally contain custom code, so define your own attribute class or use an existing one:

   ```csharp
   // C#
   namespace com.db4o.dg2db4o.chapter10
   {
       [AttributeUsage(AttributeTargets.Field)]
       public class MyTransient : Attribute
       {
       }
   }
   ```

2. Tell db4o that this attribute should be used to mark fields transient:

   ```csharp
   Db4o.Configure().MarkTransient("com.db4o.dg2db4o.chapter10.MyTransient");
   ```

3. Then use this attribute in your .NET classes to mark transient fields:

   ```csharp
   // C#
   public class MyClass {
   [com.db4o.dg2db4o.chapter10.MyTransient]
       string transientField;
       string persistentField;
   }
   ```

ObjectClass(object clazz)

We already have seen many examples where you might want to make a configuration not for all classes in db4o but for each class individually. This configuration returns the ObjectClass for a specified class. This class is a db4o representation of your class. It can be used to perform several more configurations on the object such as CascadeOnActivate(...), CascadeOnDelete(...), Compare(...), GenerateUUIDs(...), GenerateVersionNumbers(...), Rename(...), UpdateDepth(...), and many more.

It also contains the method ObjectField to return an ObjectField reference. This in turn can be used to configure the field of the class (e.g., to set indexing). This might sound like the usual reflection methods to you.

You have already seen some examples of the use of ObjectClass.

Unicode(bool flag)

db4o is able to support Unicode as a storage format for strings. So, if you need Unicode support, you should call Unicode(true) before opening an ObjectContainer. Once created the database keeps its file format. The advantage of setting Unicode(false) is that space can be saved (8 instead of 16 bits per character) and the system will be faster.

UpdateDepth(int depth)

Earlier we mentioned the ActivationDepth configuration that denotes the level to which objects will be instantiated in a deep object graph. The configuration Updatedepth is the same for updates (i.e., changing and calling Set) on objects.

You can set this configuration globally or for specific classes:

```
Db4o.Configure().UpdateDepth(5);
Db4o.Configure().ObjectClass(typeof(Person)).UpdateDepth(5);    // C#
Db4o.Configure().objectClass(Person.class).updateDepth(5);    // JAVA
```

GETTING THE UPDATE DEPTH RIGHT

The default value for updateDepth is 1. This often is the root cause for many errors. Here's an example: you are storing a Project object that contains a collection of Persons who are a part of the project. In your application life cycle you read the project. This works fine because the activation depth level is 5 by default. All Persons will be stored. Then another Person joins the project. You add this Person to your collection. And finally you update the entire project. Guess what happens? If you reload the project, the size() of the Persons collection still has the old value! Of course, this is because the project was written with an update level of 1, which means that only the project has been updated while the collection with the new Person has not. If you remember to set the update depth a little deeper, everything works fine.

WeakReferenceCollectionInterval(int milliseconds)

With this configuration, you can configure the interval at which the weak-reference collector will check the reference tree for garbage-collected references and clean them out. The default time is 1000ms. If you set this time to 0, the weak reference management thread is turned off. If you don't have loads of objects and you have plenty of memory, you can set this value even higher. See `WeakReferences` for more information.

WeakReferences(bool flag)

You can turn the weak reference check system on or off before opening the `ObjectContainer`. The default for this configuration is `true`. You have seen previously that db4o is able to hold weak references to objects you have stored or retrieved. A weak reference is the way in which db4o memorizes objects. The opposite of weak references are hard references, meaning a direct reference to the object. So if you turn weak references off, then db4o has to hold hard references.

This approach is fast but consumes memory because any garbage collector cannot clean unused objects away. In this case, you have to call `ExtObjectContainer.purge(object);` manually for every unused object to remove the reference. This does a job that you might expect something with a name like `object.Close` to do: deleting the object by discarding the references. But there is no such method as `Close` for objects in db4o or in C#/Java. You have to use `Purge` to detach objects manually. After calling `Purge` the object is not known by the current `ObjectContainer` and will not be changed and set or saved. If you do store an object, purge it, and store it again after the purge, you will end up with a duplicate object, because the `ObjectContainer` has lost the connection between the in-memory object and the stored object.

With weak-reference management on, an extra thread will collect weak references and you don't need to worry about purging objects to save memory.

File-Related Configurations

This section takes a closer look at configurations that are related to the interaction between db4o and the database file. For example, you might want to encrypt the file, save BLOBs, or give db4o database hints for better optimization.

BlockSize(int bytes)

This byte value will set the data block size for the database file. The value can be a number from 1 to 127, but should be a multiple of 8 because of the lengths of internal pointers. The default value is 1, and with this value the database file is allowed to grow up to 2GB. db4objects recommends a value of 8 for this configuration, which means a database file up to 16GB. But be aware that if you double the block size you might not be able to store twice the data. The data you store often has to be padded to a specific length depending on the block size, which means that space can be lost if the block size is large.

For example, in a test of writing 1,000 random objects to the file system, we produced a 73KB database with the default setting of 1. The size was 77KB with the default setting of 8, and 214KB with a block size of 64.

■Tip If you have a huge number of objects belonging to different classes with no relationships between them, it might be a good idea to use different ObjectContainers in parallel (instead of a big one). These different ObjectContainers can even share objects by moving, copying, or replicating them between the containers.

DisableCommitRecovery()

This parameterless command indicates that commit recovery must be enabled on startup. Therefore, when the database file is opened no unfinished commits will be written.

db4o processes transactions using a two-phase commit protocol. In the first phase, the transaction data is written in the database file into the transaction commit record. In the second phase, the transaction data is transferred to its final destination. If the transaction is interrupted in the second phase, it will be resumed on restarting the database and all transactions will be completed normally. But there may be a rare case where even the complete transaction record is corrupted and can cause harm because the commit recovery on startup won't work. In this case, you can call this configuration to prevent db4o from performing the commit recovery. If you have opened the database without recovery, you will still be able to work with the database using uncommitted data.

Encrypt(bool flag)

db4o provides two encryption algorithms. The simple one can be turned on using this encryption configuration. You have to set the password after setting encryption:

```
Db4o.Configure().Encrypt(true);
Db4o.Configure().Password("yourPwd");
```

The security provided by this encryption mechanism is not high. This is acceptable if you don't expect attacks or your data is not that valuable and high-speed encryption is necessary. An alternative is to use the XTEA encryption file adapter described in Chapter 12.

FlushFileBuffers(bool flag)

If set to true, the file buffers will be flushed during transaction commits. db4o ensures Atomicity, Consistency, Isolation, and Durability (ACID) properties by using a resume-commit-on-crash approach. If a transaction commits, db4o performs the following tasks:

1. db4o writes a list to the database that includes a list of pointers that have to be modified.

2. db4o sets a flag in the database file called in-commit.

3. db4o then modifies the pointers in the database.

4. db4o switches the database flag from in-commit to not-in-commit.

The database will have the following states if crashes occur at the following points:

- Before step 2: All objects will be in the state as they were before the commit.

- Between steps 2 and 4: When the database is opened again after the crash, the commit will be started again. The pointer will be read again from the list and they will be put in the state they should have after the commit.

- After step 4: The transaction can be completed as intended and all changes will be committed.

Normally, operating systems will not use in-memory file caches. That's why the default setting is false. Thus file buffers will not be flushed by db4o, which has a good impact on the performance. On the other hand, some operating systems might use in-memory file caching to achieve better file I/O performance. However, this might change the order in which writes are written to the medium and could lead to an incorrect database. If this is the case, then this configuration must be set to true even if it has a negative performance effect.

Io(IoAdapter adapter)

This configuration allows you to configure your own I/O adapter. See Chapter 12 for more details on the pluggable file I/O capability. You can write your own I/O adapters here or you can use the ones provided by db4o, which you'll find in com.db4o.io. The two favorites are

```
Db4o.Configure().Io(new XTeaEncryptionFileAdapter("password"));
Db4o.Configure().Io(new MemoryIoAdapter());
```

The first one encrypts the data with an XTEA cipher, while the second creates an in-memory adapter. In both cases, you would open an ObjectContainer after configuring the adapter and start working.

LockDatabaseFile(bool flag)

If you set this flag to false, there will be no locking of the database file. This is faster, of course, but you have to be sure that no concurrent access on the file will take place. For example, you can use the database in the read-only mode: Db4o.Configure().ReadOnly(true).

If it is set to true (the default), the file may be locked by db4o. This can be done either via the virtual machine (e.g., Java 1.4.1 NIO locking) or via file information or timestamps that are written to the file. This prevents other processes from accessing the file.

■**Caution** If you set this flag to false and there are multiple threads or processes accessing the database file, the file can be seriously damaged.

Password(string pass)

This configuration belongs to the simple encryption mechanism (see Chapter 12). Before opening the ObjectContainer, you simply set encryption to true and set your password:

```
Db4o.Configure().Encrypt(true);
Db4o.Configure().Password("yourEncryptionPasswordHere");
```

Don't forget that this is a weak encryption. If you have valuable data, then you should encrypt it with the XTeaEncryptionFileAdapter.

ReadOnly(bool flag)

This flag allows you to configure db4o to run in a read-only mode. true means that all ObjectContainers that are opened with Db4o.openFile(String filename) will be in read-only mode. This configuration can have a positive performance effect if multiple reading processes access the database. In this case, the LockDatabaseFile configuration can be set to disable (slow) file locking. If you are reading from non-writable media such as CD-ROMs, you would use this mode.

■**Caution** db4o will not throw any exceptions here if you try to write data in read-only mode. This has the advantage that any client can use the database in any mode without adding any try/catch blocks to the code. But you should never write in read-only mode. Subsequent reads in read-only mode might throw FileFormatIncompatible exceptions.

ReserveStorageSpace(long byteCount)

This configuration is a tuning feature. When you call this method, the expected size of your database file is the parameter you should pass. The advantage is that one file block with this size will be reserved right from the start and filled with your database data. This in turn means that your database file will not be fragmented on the disk by the operating system and thus it will be accessed faster. The default size is 0, so db4o will reallocate the file size if needed, which could lead to a huge defragmentation.

To increase performance, you should determine the anticipated file size in a test. Then set the ReserveStoraceSpace a little bigger than the anticipated file size. If you are already running the database, call this method before a defragment call (see the section "External Tools" later in this chapter) and again set the size slightly above the expected database size.

■**Note** If you have allocated a specific amount of storage space and the database engine crashes, all your allocated space is lost. If you run the defragment program, you can recover this lost space.

SetBlobPath(string path)

This configuration tells db4o where to store your binary large object (BLOB) data. BLOB fields are a feature of most databases, and can be used to store large pieces of binary data, such as images. db4o provides some useful features to help performance when working with BLOBs. Of course, you can always simply define a byte[ ]array in your object to hold a BLOB, but db4o provides an extra class for this specific purpose: com.db4o.types.Blob. You can use this class as a field type in your classes, in which case BLOB data is stored independently of the main database. In client/server mode, db4o carries out all BLOB operations in a separate thread on a dedicated socket, resulting in asynchronous operation—your application can continue to access the database while a BLOB is transferred. The `Blob` class has some useful methods, as shown in Table 10-2.

Table 10-2. *Blob Class Methods*

Method	What It Does
GetFilename	Returns the filename under which this BLOB was stored
GetStatus	Gives you status information from the last read or write operation
ReadFrom	Reads a file from the file system into the db4o `Blob` type
ReadLocal	Reads from the local file system
WriteLocal	Writes the stored BLOB data locally into your file
WriteTo	Writes the stored BLOB data into your file

If you are working in a client/server environment, using `ReadLocal` or `WriteLocal` means that you will read or write on the client side if the client issues this command. On the other hand, if you issue `ReadFrom` and `WriteTo`, then db4o will open a socket thread to transfer the data.

Note This is one of the rare options that can throw an I/O exception if you pass a wrong path! Accordingly, all the methods we've described here that deal with filenames will throw this exception as well.

The status information gained by `GetStatus` helps you to track the completion of the process. db4o will return the status information shown in Table 10-3.

Table 10-3. *Blob Status*

Value	Meaning
Status.UNUSED	No data was ever stored to the BLOB field.
Status.AVAILABLE	Available data was previously stored to the BLOB field.
Status.QUEUED	An operation was triggered and is waiting for its turn in the BLOB queue.
Status.COMPLETED	The last operation on this field was completed successfully.
Status.PROCESSING	For internal use only.
Status.ERROR	The last operation failed.

The default path is `/blobs` in your virtual machine's (VM) execution root, which is " . " Let's look at a short example, kindly provided by Carl Rosenberger:

```csharp
// C#
namespace com.db4o.dg2db4o.chapter10
{
    class PicBlobWrapper
    {
        Blob blob;

        public static void Main(String[] arguments)
        {
            // write the blob file to db
            ObjectContainer con = Db4o.OpenFile("blobtest.yap");
            PicBlobWrapper picWrapper = new PicBlobWrapper();
            con.Set(picWrapper);
            picWrapper.blob.ReadFrom(new j4o.io.File("test.png"));
            con.Close();
            Console.WriteLine("stored...");

            // read the blob file
            con = Db4o.OpenFile("blobtest.yap");
            ObjectSet set = con.Get(new PicBlobWrapper());
            PicBlobWrapper picWrapperOut = (PicBlobWrapper)set.Next();
            picWrapperOut.blob.WriteTo(new j4o.io.File("testOut.png"));
            con.Close();
            Console.WriteLine("done...");
        }
    }
}
```

```java
// JAVA
package com.db4o.dg2db4o.chapter10;
public class PicBlobWrapper {
    Blob blob;
    public static void main(String[] arguments) throws Exception
    {

        // write the blob file to db
        ObjectContainer con = Db4o.openFile("blobtest.yap");
        PicBlobWrapper picWrapper = new PicBlobWrapper();
        con.set(picWrapper);
        picWrapper.blob.readFrom(new File("test.png"));
        con.close();
        System.out.println("stored...");

        // read the blob file
        con = Db4o.openFile("blobtest.yap");
        ObjectSet set = con.get(new PicBlobWrapper());
        PicBlobWrapper picWrapperOut = (PicBlobWrapper) set.next();
```

```
        picWrapperOut.blob.writeTo(new File("testOut.png"));
        con.close();
        System.out.println("done...");
    }
}
```

blobtest.yap is the database file that will be written in your VM's root. test.png must be present in the same root and will be written in the first phase to ./blobs/test.png. In the second phase the image will be retrieved and written to the newly created file testOut.png in your root again. If the same filename already exists in the blob directory, then it will be saved with a numbered name (e.g., test_0.png).

Reflection-Related Configurations

To store and restore objects, db4o relies on several reflection mechanisms. db4o has to check that the objects in the database match the objects in your classpath, so it can analyze the class structure. Other examples deal with constructors and query optimization. The latter not only uses reflection but advanced libraries to read your code and transform your code on runtime. However, all the subsequent configurations inspect your objects or your code.

CallConstructors(bool flag)

If you are using a modern .NET or Java virtual machine, then it can be possible to instantiate the objects without calling constructors. Both Java and C# / .NET offer *reflection* features to create your objects. If you want to make use of this, you should add a public default constructor, with no arguments, for every object you store and set this configuration value to false. Then you will retrieve your objects faster, as benchmarks on .NET have shown. If you want to decide this per class, then you might set the flag to false (meaning that reflection is used all the time) but turn on calling the constructor for specific classes that have them. In that case you would use:

```
Db4o.Configure().ObjectClass(typeof(Foo)).CallConstructors(true);   // C#
Db4o.configure().objectClass(Foo.class).CallConstructors(true);   // JAVA
```

DetectSchemaChanges(bool flag)

Normally if you open a database file, db4o will analyze the classes and detect schema changes, such as changed fields. This consumes a lot of time and means a slow startup. If you want a fast startup and you are sure that the database file is "in schema sync" with the classes on your classpath, you should call DetectSchemaChanges(false).

■Note Another option that can provide flexibility in the way you optimize database startup is to use multiple database files. This can be more flexible and faster on startup. If you are working in a client/server environment, you can use ((ExtClient) objectContainer).switchToFile(databaseFile); to switch between different database files from the client side.

OptimizeNativeQueries()

This configuration without any parameter simply returns the Native Queries optimization settings. As you might expect, `true` will tell you that optimization is on and `false` means it is off.

OptimizeNativeQueries(bool optimizeNQ)

As Chapter 6 explains, native queries are translated to SODA queries, and optimized if possible. If you don't want to optimize queries—or, with Java, if you do not have the libraries required for optimization (see Chapter 6 for details)—you should set this configuration value to `false`. On the other hand, if the required libraries are in your classpath, you can set `true` and your queries will be optimized dynamically. `true` is the default value.

ReflectWith(Reflector reflector)

This configuration allows you to set an alternative reflector. If you are using Java, for example, then by default `java.lang.reflect` is used. Unfortunately, this package doesn't exist on some platforms, such as a Java 2 Micro Edition (J2ME) environment—in this case you would need to reimplement the functionality that reflection offers to get db4o running on devices, such as many mobile phones, that only support J2ME. Once you have implemented this, you can configure db4o to use your reflector.

As you might imagine, this is really an advanced feature, most likely to be used by db4objects' own developers. Providing support for J2ME by implementing a suitable reflector is at the time of this writing on the db4o roadmap for future developments.

RefreshClasses()

This configuration enforces that all classes be reanalyzed again. We have mentioned before that on system startup db4o performs initialization tasks in order to find stored classes with callback methods and more.

If the classpath environment or the classes or libraries have changed due to classloader activities, they could be analyzed anew. If this method is called on the global configuration context, the classes in all db4o sessions will be refreshed. But in an `ObjectContainer` configuration context, only the classes of the respective `ObjectContainer` will be refreshed.

SetClassLoader(ClassLoader classLoader)

This configuration sets a new classloader. db4o usually runs with the default classloader and knows its classes from its classpath. The configuration of the classloader or a new classloader might become an issue if, for example, you want to change your classes, or if you are working with a plug-in architecture, or in an application server where db4o is used as a shared library. The tutorial that comes with db4o has an excellent overview of this topic.

TestConstructors(bool flag)

This configuration method is tightly coupled to the `CallConstructors` configuration. You can implement a public constructor and set `CallConstructors` to `true` to achieve better performance. The `TestConstructors` configuration goes a step further. Upon startup, db4o tries to instantiate all classes to see if everything works fine. So if you have public constructors that you are sure will never fail, then you can set this flag to `false` to prevent this time-consuming instantiation process.

Communication-Related Configurations

The following configuration methods deal with client/server communications. So, the following methods are used to establish the out-of-band communication described in detail in Chapter 8. More methods are described here to check the connection status.

GetMessageSender()

If you have a client that wishes to send any information to the server (for example instructions to defragment or shut down), then it uses this configuration to obtain from the `ObjectContainer` a context for sending such a message:

```
MessageSender messageSender = objectContainer.Ext().Configure().GetMessageSender();
```

The `ObjectServer` gives a `MessageRecipient` context for processing the message. The discussion in Chapter 8 of out-of-band-signaling gives detailed information about this configuration.

SetMessageRecipient(MessageRecipient messageRecipient)

This is the complement to the `GetMessageSender()` configuration. The context for receiving messages is obtained using this configuration:

```
db4oServer.Ext().Configure().SetMessageRecipient(this);
```

Here you can define any class or your class to be a message recipient. This in turn means that this class has to implement the method `processMessage(ObjectContainer con, Object message)`.

SingleThreadedClient(bool flag)

This is a client/server configuration setting. In a client/server environment, the client and server might wish to communicate. This communication might involve data access in the networking or embedded mode, or messages in the out-of-band signaling mode. If you set this configuration value to `true`, you will get a single-threaded client. This is could be suitable for systems with small resources as only one thread covers resources. But of course, asynchronous messaging could be slow when using this setting.

On the other hand, a configuration flag set to `false` enables the client to be multithreaded, which is fast for asynchronous message exchange but uses a little more resources. The default value is `false`.

The exception is that the default is `true` on the .NET Compact Framework, because the Compact Framework is designed for programming on limited resources as PDAs, mobile phones, and set-top boxes and thus a single-threaded client is better because it will consume fewer resources.

TimeoutClientSocket(int milliseconds)

This timeout configuration is used to configure the client side to wait only a specific time for a server response. The default time is 300,000ms, which is 5 minutes. If your server and the network are stable, you might want to set this value higher; otherwise set it lower.

TimeoutPingClients (int milliseconds)

The server is constantly watching its clients to see if they are alive or not. By doing this, the server is able to release resources from the clients as semaphores. If a client is not answering the server messages, the server sends a "PING" message to the client and waits for an "OK" response. This is done five times, and if they are all unsuccessful, then the connection is closed. The default value is 180,000ms, which is 3 minutes after the last communication, when the server starts questioning its clients again. If you have single-threaded clients (see the SingleThreadedClient configuration), then you might increase this value because they are not able to answer quickly.

TimeoutServerSocket(int milliseconds)

To receive messages, the server starts multiple socket-read threads. These threads might then be active although the server has already been shut down. Thus you can refine the time when these threads check if the server is still alive. The default value is 5,000ms, which is 5 seconds. Thus, if you have a stable server running for a long time, you might want to configure this value higher.

Logging-Related Configurations

db4o does not have a perfect logging integration yet. Up to version 5.2 there is no perfect way to use famous logging frameworks in the core of db4o. But if you use something like Jakarta Commons Logging or something equivalent for C# in your code, then you can use the db4o internal logging system to gain insights to what db4o is doing. This logging system is small and not all-embracing configurable. In our experience, it is mostly used when db4o is not doing what you expect. In this case, you can see how far db4o is getting before exceptions occur. However, this should be a rare case and we hope you are just using this feature to learn more how db4o works and leave the logging system quiet due to performance aspects.

MessageLevel(int level)

One of the easiest configurations, you have already seen this in Chapter 5. This configuration sets the message level of the db4o logging. The usage is as you would expect:

```
Db4o.Configure().MessageLevel(0);
```

You have four levels to choose from:

Level 0: No messages will be logged.

Level 1: Only open and close messages will be logged.

Level 2: New, update, and delete actions will be logged too.

Level 3: Messages for activation and deactivation will be printed as well.

Level 0 effectively means silence, while 3 means noisy. You can configure your print stream using SetOut(j4o.io.PrintStream) for C# or setOut(java.io.printStream) for Java (see the next section).

SetOut(PrintStream outStream)

We mentioned SetOut() in relation to the MessageLevel configuration earlier. SetOut() lets you select a print stream for db4o logging, either the console or some other stream. For example, the following prints out to the console, which is the default:

```
Db4o.Configure().SetOut(new j4o.io.PrintStream(System.Console.Out));    // C#
Db4o.configure().setOut(System.out);    // JAVA
```

The following logs to a specified file:

```
Db4o.Configure().SetOut(new j4o.io.PrintStream(new StreamWriter("log.txt")));    // C#
Db4o.configure().setOut(new PrintStream(new File("log.txt")));    // JAVA
```

■**Note** The j4o namespace for .NET is included with db4o, and provides classes that adapt some db4o API calls to use .NET system classes, reflecting db4o's Java origins.

Miscellaneous Configurations

Let's have a look at configurations that don't fall under any category.

AutomaticShutDown(bool flag)

This configuration value is true by default, meaning that the ObjectContainer will perform a shutdown if the JDK terminates or it has no references and it is garbage collected.

In Java, if this happens, a shutdown hook (defined using Runtime.addShutdownHook) is called and the ObjectContainer will be closed. If you set this flag to false, then the automatic shutdown of the container is omitted.

Normally you should close the containers using `Close`, which means that all database files will be closed normally, avoiding problems with the lock on the database files. If you are using a rare virtual machine that has problems with any shutdown hook methods, you should set the `automaticShutDown` flag to `false`.

ExceptionsOnNotStorable(bool flag)

Whether or not an object can be instantiated depends on the availability of the constructors and on the virtual machine used. Consider the case where you have a limited virtual machine (that does not allow you to instantiate via reflection without using constructors) and also no constructors. This could be the case, for example, if you have a class that has only a private default constructor and is instantiated only from within itself and persists itself. In this case the virtual machine might throw an exception to indicate that the object cannot be stored.

You can use this configuration to suppress these exceptions if you set the value to `true`. If you pass `false`, then an `ObjectNotStorableException` would be thrown. On the other hand, if you implemented constructors, db4o will try them all using `null` values if the constructors have arguments.

Freespace()

This configuration returns the free space configuration interface. This interface has three interesting methods:

```
UseRamSystem()
UseIndexSystem()
DiscardSmallerThan(int byteCount)
```

So what's happening here? By default the index-based system is used, and unused space is marked and managed in lists on the file system so that it can be reused. This allows adjacent entries to be merged. Because this list is managed on the file system, no free space can get lost after a (file) system crash, and the memory footprint is lower. On the other hand, free space management is naturally slower on the disk than on RAM because free space information is written with every commit.

However, it might be useful to keep the free space management in your RAM. This gives you the best performance if you have enough space available. On the other hand, if your system crashes, the free space information is lost and your database will grow. Then you should defragment and restart.

The last method, `DiscardSmallerThan`, is a little tricky, so have a look at Figure 10-2 first. Let's assume your db4o is running and heavily writing, deleting, and updating data. By default, the `DiscardSmallerThan` value is set to zero bytes. This means that all free space that occurs in the database will be managed and reused. What you can do now is to set the value to the largest integer value your system allows, e.g., `Int32.MaxValue` (C#) or `Integer.MAX_VALUE` (Java). This means that no free space—no matter how large it might be—will be managed. This in turn means that your system will be lightning fast, but the database file will also grow faster. db4objects recommends that you set a value between 10 or 50. Of course, it is up to you to run tests and determine the optimum value for your database.

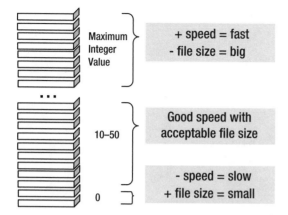

Figure 10-2. *Adjusting the byteCount that the free space manager should discard*

A Glimpse into the ExtObjectContainer

As you have seen, the ExtObjectContainer class is a kind of sandbox for commands whose usefulness is still to be proved before they are promoted to the "real" ObjectContainer class.

Because of this, the API of ExtObjectContainer might not be as stable as that of ObjectContainer, whose members are proven mainstream methods whose interfaces will not change in future versions of db4o. However, the ExtObjectContainer includes a number of highly useful capabilities right now:

- Backup: Use this command to back up a database to another file. The following code shows a simple backup operation. Changes that are made to the ObjectContainer while the backup is in progress will be applied to both the open ObjectContainer and to the backup. The following lines show that we open a database file as usual and then call the backup method to create the second database file:

```csharp
// C#
System.IO.File.Delete("c:/primary.yap");
System.IO.File.Delete("c:/secondary.yap");
ObjectContainer db = Db4o.OpenFile("c:/primary.yap");
db.Set(new Person("Lincoln", 56));
db.Commit();
try
{
    db.Ext().Backup("c:/secondary.yap");
}
catch (Exception e)
{
    Console.WriteLine(e.StackTrace);
    db.Close();
}
db.Close();
```

```java
// JAVA
new File("c:/primary.yap").delete();
new File("c:/secondary.yap").delete();
ObjectContainer db = Db4o.openFile("c:/primary.yap");
db.set(new Person("Lincoln", 56));
db.commit();
try
{
    db.ext().backup("c:/secondary.yap");
}
catch (IOException e)
{
    e.printStackTrace();
    db.close();
}
db.close();
```

- Bind: Called as Bind(Object, id), this methods loads the object with the id into memory and replaces this memory reference with the object that has been given as a parameter. After this, you should make a Set call to store the new object. This method is useful for exchanging objects after a database has been closed and reopened.

- GetByID: Gets an object when passing the long ID.

- GetByUUID: Gets an object when passing the UUID.

- GetID: Gets the ID when passing the object.

- GetObjectInfo: Returns an object information object that can be used to get the UUID and the transactional version number.

- IsActive: Tests if an object is active (true). If it is not stored within the object container, then false will be returned.

- IsCached: Tests if the object behind the passed ID is cached.

- IsClosed: Tests if the object container has been closed before (true).

- IsStored: Tests if the object is already stored in this container.

- KnownClasses: Returns an array of all known classes. This array is of the type ReflectClass, but you might want to use GetName on each element to obtain all the names of the classes in the database.

- Purge: Has been discussed previously—used to remove objects from the reference system if weak reference is turned off.

- ReleaseSemaphore/SetSemaphore: Works with semaphores (see examples in Chapters 9 and 12).

- ReplicationBegin: Prepares a replication with another ObjectContainer (see Chapter 11).

- Set: This is used as set(object obj, int depth) and allows the update depth to be specified manually.

- Version: Returns the transactional serial number.

External Tools

db4o provides a further set of tools in the form of classes in the namespace/package com.db4o. tools. This package is not actually included in the db4o DLL or JAR library. Instead, these classes are provided with the distribution as source code. This means that you need to embed this source code into your application in order to use the tools.

Defragment

Defragment deletes unused fields and management information. The resulting database file is smaller and ready for faster access.

There are two ways to initiate a defragmentation. First, the Defragment class has a Main method, so it can be executed directly from the command line. Alternatively, you can initiate it programmatically by calling

```
new Defragment().Run("db.yap", true);
```

The first argument is the file to defragment. The second one is a Boolean that indicates whether or not the original file should be deleted. If this is true, only one file will be there after the Defragment command. false means that you will have a second file called <filename>.bak after the defragment.

Statistics

This class simply prints statistics about a database file. Again, it can be run from the command line or programmatically using the Run method:

```
new Statistics().Run("db.yap");
```

Here's an example of statistics for a very small database that contains a single Person object:

```
************* STATISTICS **************
File: c:/db.yap


*************** CLASSES ***************
Number of objects per class:
com.db4o.dg2db4o.chapter10.Person: 4
com.db4o.MetaClass: 0
com.db4o.MetaField: 0
com.db4o.MetaIndex: 1
com.db4o.P1Object: 0
com.db4o.PBootRecord: 0
```

```
com.db4o.StaticClass: 0
com.db4o.StaticField: 0
com.db4o.ext.Db4oDatabase: 1


*************** SUMMARY ***************
File: c:/nq.yap
Stored classes: 9
Total number of objects: 6
```

Logger

This class simply logs the objects in a database file. Again, it can be run from the command line. The following Java command, for example, logs all stored objects in the specified database. Alternatively, you can specify a particular class to log.

```
java com.db4o.tools.Logger db.yap
```

Here's an example of logging for a very small database that contains four Person objects:

```
com.db4o.db2db4o.chapter10.Person
    .Person._name: Mandela
    .Person._age: 86
com.db4o.db2db4o.chapter10.Person
    .Person._name: Teresa
    .Person._age: 86
com.db4o.db2db4o.chapter10.Person
    .Person._name: Lincoln
    .Person._age: 56
com.db4o.db2db4o.chapter10.Person
    .Person._name: Gandhi
    .Person._age: 79


Log complete.
Objects: 4
```

Tuning for Speed

Let's finish this chapter by briefly describing some key "dos and don'ts" you should take into account when tuning db4o for speed. Most, though not all, of these involve configurations.

- Set the activation and deletion depth exactly to match the size of your needs. Activating a deep object graph is time consuming if you don't need the subobject-graph.

- Turn weak references off. If you only write or query, then you may well not need them.

- Set DetectSchemaChanges to false because your classes probably don't change often.

- The same should be done for TestConstructors because you often do not need to check the classes on startup for the availability of a zero-parameter constructor.

- Set field indexes to enable really fast search on your most used objects (see Chapter 12).

- Set the free space management to RAM or to an appropriate value.

- Use multiple object containers. Do you really need your data to be all in one file? If not, try to group objects and use multiple containers.

- Optimize your native queries. Make sure you have bloat.jar nqopt.jar in your classpath if you are using Java. C# users will always get optimized results.

There is an endless list of further hints, such as avoid callbacks; generate no UUIDS (if you don't need them or don't need replication); mark transient wherever you can; don't use a big block size if you don't need a huge database file (use 8 bytes or try to test your best block size); use defragment when the database is not in use; don't encrypt unless you really need to; leave FlushFileBuffers set to false; and use the database in read-only mode.

Summary

In this chapter you have seen many configurations and tools that you can use to tune your db4o databases. These configurations are important if you want to tune db4o up to maximum speed, or to adjust the settings to fit your application scenario. In the former case, nearly all the reflection-related and all the file-related configurations can be adjusted to make db4o very fast.

The next chapter will show you how to replicate your objects between db4o servers and between db4o and relational databases.

CHAPTER 11

■■■

Replication

Replication is defined by wikipedia.com as "the provision of redundant resources (software or hardware components) to improve reliability and fault-tolerance." In our context, replication deals with software—more precisely, the data we store in our db4o databases.

The participants in the replication process are known as masters, or publishers, where the data initially changes, and clients, or subscribers, that receive the changes at some time afterward. Several forms of data replication exist with db4o:

- **Snapshot Replication** is akin to taking a picture of the data in its present state and synchronizing the data with one or more database servers. Additional snapshots can be taken periodically in accordance with a specific schedule or in response to events. db4o supports this form of replication using a query that detects all (new) objects.

- **Transactional Replication** detects objects that have changed during the course of a transaction and moves them from the master to the clients (or from the publisher to the subscribers, if you prefer that terminology). Typically, transactional replication starts with synchronized databases, and as the master database is modified its changes will be replicated immediately to the other servers.

- **Merge Replication** aggregates data from different servers to create a single central database. Any changes to a subscriber database will be updated on the central publisher either transactionally or on a periodic basis. Later the other subscribers will be updated to reflect the new data from the first subscriber. This scenario typically occurs when the subscribers might be occasionally offline but will synchronize with the central server upon their return.

Unlike most database systems, where replication can be done on an administrative level, the db4o replication mechanism is provided as an API, which has to be coded into a C# or Java application. While this sounds difficult, you'll soon find it's actually fairly simple to implement with just a few lines of code.

■**Caution** Replication will not guarantee that all databases are synchronized at all times. Processes might be slow, or there might be connection delays or other unforeseen incidents. Therefore, replication is not suitable replacement for a sound backup policy. However, db4o makes backups easy for you: just manually make a backup copy of the database file, or let a scheduler like Quartz and a build tool like ant, nant, or rake "make" the copy for you.

---

db4o Replication Mechanisms

db4o has been capable of replication since version 4.0. However, version 5.1 brought with it support for a redesigned mechanism, known as the db4o Replication Service (dRS), which has some important new features. Currently (version 5.2), both mechanisms are supported. There are significant differences between the two:

- **db4o core replication**: This is included as part of the standard distribution in .NET and Java versions, and allows replication between db4o databases.

- **db4o Replication Service (dRS)**: This is a separate download, and is currently available in a Java version only. dRS allows replication between db4o databases, and also replication to and from a wide range of relational databases, providing the capability to migrate data from db4o to, for example, MySQL.

It's probable that db4o's developers will concentrate their future efforts on dRS and that a .NET version will be released. If so, then the core replication mechanism may well not be supported in future releases. Nevertheless, we will include coverage of both mechanisms here as the core mechanism is at the time of this writing the only one that provides direct .NET support.

Configuring db4o Core Replication

db4o core replication transfers data between peer `ObjectContainers`. These peers can be local database files, or they can be clients that communicate with db4o servers that are working in networking or embedded modes, as described in Chapter 8. The replication process is configured in the same way regardless of the operating modes of the peers.

You can choose to replicate some or all of the current data from one peer to another (snapshot replication) or to replicate data as it is changed in one peer into another (transactional replication). Merge replication is configured as a variation of snapshot replication, except that there are multiple peers.

Implementing db4o replication requires three steps: generating unique IDs and version numbers, creating a `ReplicationProcess` object, and replicating objects.

Generating Unique IDs and Version Numbers

db4o replication involves moving objects between database files. db4o needs to be able to distinguish between objects that originated in different databases. Objects in a db4o database file are usually identified by an ID that is unique *within that file*. However, replication could potentially result in objects with the same ID trying to coexist in the same file, which would cause conflicts when accessing the objects.

Unique universal identifiers (UUIDs) provide a way to ensure that all objects have different IDs no matter their origin. The format of UUIDs has been standardized by the Open Software Foundation for use in distributed computing environments. A UUID is a 128-bit number, which in db4o's implementation contains a database signature generated by an algorithm that concatenates the hostname, the network address, the current timestamp value, and two random long values. UUIDs are stored as instances of the class Db4oUUID, which contains a "signature part" as a byte[] array and a "long part," which identifies the object within the database, as a long value.

db4o also needs to keep track of changes to objects, which it does by looking at their *version numbers*. The database itself has a version number, which starts at zero and is incremented every time a transaction is committed. When an object is modified, its version number changes to the version number of the database at that time.

These features are not enabled by default. They incur some overhead in terms of database size and performance, and they are not necessary unless objects will be transferred between databases. To enable them you need to call the following configuration methods before you open the database:

```
// C#
Db4o.Configure().GenerateUUIDs(Int32.MaxValue);
Db4o.Configure().GenerateVersionNumbers(Int32.MaxValue);
```

```
// JAVA
Db4o.configure().generateUUIDs(Integer.MAX_VALUE);
Db4o.configure().generateVersionNumbers(Integer.MAX_VALUE);
```

Interestingly, you can also restrict replication to specific classes. Here's how to specify that UUIDs and version numbers be generated for the class Foo:

```
// C#
Db4o.Configure().ObjectClass(typeof(Foo)).GenerateUUIDs(true);
Db4o.Configure().ObjectClass(typeof(Foo)).GenerateVersionNumbers(true);
```

```
// JAVA
Db4o.configure().objectClass(Foo.class).generateUUIDs(true);
Db4o.configure().objectClass(Foo.class).generateVersionNumbers(true);
```

Creating a ReplicationProcess Object

A ReplicationProcess defines the peers for the replication, and also allows you to define how conflicts will be handled. A conflict arises when the same object has been modified in both databases. The following code shows an example of creating a ReplicationProcess:

```
// C#
ReplicationConflictHandler conflictHandler = new MyReplicationConflictHandler();
ReplicationProcess replication =
    db_A.Ext().ReplicationBegin(db_B,conflictHandler);
```

```
namespace com.db4o.dg2db4o.chapter11
{
    class MyReplicationConflictHandler : ReplicationConflictHandler
    {
        public Object ResolveConflict(
                    ReplicationProcess replicationProcess, Object a, Object b)
        {
            return a;
        }
    }
}
```

```
// JAVA
ReplicationProcess replication =
    db_A.ext().replicationBegin(db_B, new ReplicationConflictHandler()
    {
        public Object resolveConflict(
            ReplicationProcess replicationProcess, Object a, Object b)
        {
            return a;
        }
    }
);
```

This code enables you to begin replication between peer ObjectContainers called db_A and db_B. It uses the ReplicationBegin method of the first ObjectContainer (called through the associated ExtObjectContainer, as described in Chapter 10), which takes the second ObjectContainer as a parameter. By default, both peers are treated equally; thus the order is arbitrary.

ReplicationBegin also requires an additional parameter: an object that implements an interface called ReplicationConflictHandler. This object defines how to deal with conflicts that occur when the same object has been updated in both peer databases. In Java you can use an anonymous inner class, but in C# you must define a named handler class (the class has a single method, resolveConflict, but db4o does not currently support the use of a delegate here). The handler class here defines a simple rule, namely that db_A is the master and its value takes precedence. You can define any rule you like here, though. For example, you could prompt the user and ask which is the "right" version of the object. If the resolveConflict method returns null, then no changes are made to the object in either database.

The replication is bidirectional by default. What if you only want changes to be propagated in one direction? In this case you can configure the replication mode to be "directed" like this:

```
replication.SetDirection(db_A, db_B);    // C#
```

```
replication.setDirection(db_A, db_B);    // JAVA
```

Replicating Objects

For each object you want to replicate, you need to call the `replicate` method of your `ReplicationProcess`. The following code replicates a single object called `myObject`:

```
// C#
replication.replicate(myObject);
replication.Commit();
```

```
// JAVA
replication.Replicate(myObject);
replication.commit();
```

For transactional replication you would do this as you update objects. For snapshot replication, though, you don't want to do it quite like this. For example, suppose you have a database with a million or so objects, and you have changed 100,000 objects. You only want to replicate exactly the objects that have changed.

You do this by defining a query, actually a SODA query (see Chapter 6), and constrain it to only return changed objects. `ReplicationProcess` has a useful method, `whereModified`, which can add this constraint to a query. You can constrain the query any other way you like too—for example, let's say you want to only replicate objects of class `Foo`. The following code creates and constrains a query as described, and executes the query to get the set of objects that are to be replicated. It then iterates through the set and replicates each object.

```
// C#
Query q = objectContainer.Query();
q.Constrain(typeof(Foo));
replication.WhereModified(q);
ObjectSet replicationSet = q.Execute();
while (replicationSet.HasNext()) {
    replication.Replicate(replicationSet.Next());
}
replication.Commit();
```

```
// JAVA
Query q = objectContainer.Query();
q.Constrain(Foo.class);
replication.whereModified(q);
ObjectSet replicationSet = q.execute();
while (replicationSet.hasNext()) {
    replication.replicate(replicationSet.next());
}
replication.commit();
```

Putting It Together—A Complete Example

Let's consider an example where a process is making changes to a standalone database with the filename represented by the constant `LOCALFILE` in local mode. In fact, it simply reads in name and age values, creates new instances of the `Person` class we used in Chapter 5 and elsewhere, and adds these to the database. Each time a new object is added, it is replicated to a db4o network server with configuration represented by HOST:PORT. We'll call this process the *replicator*.

To make this work, you'll need to start the server. We'll call the process that does this the *server*. Let's also have another process that accesses the server independently at set intervals and lists its contents, which lets you check that replication has taken place. This process populates the server database with a couple of Person objects initially. We'll call this process the *client*.

The architecture for this example is depicted in Figure 11-1, and the code for the three processes is given in Listing 11-1 (C#) and Listing 11-2 (Java). This is quite similar to the example that was used to illustrate db4o in networking mode in Chapter 8, and can similarly be run as separate threads or separate processes. You can refer to Chapter 8 to see how to do so. Note that in the example here we are using an abstract class/interface ServerConfiguration simply as a convenience for specifying constant values, such as filenames, host, port, and so on, which are shared between the processes.

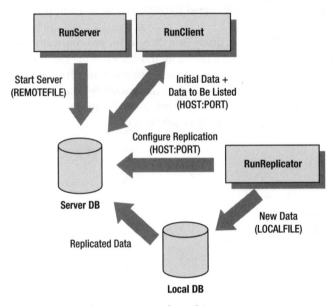

Figure 11-1. *Replication example architecture*

Listing 11-1. *Replication Example Complete Code in C#*

```csharp
// C#
namespace com.db4o.dg2db4o.chapter11
{
    public abstract class ServerConfiguration
    {
        public string HOST = "127.0.0.1";
        public string REMOTEFILE = "C:/remote.yap";     // gets changes
        public string LOCALFILE = "C:/local.yap";       // produces changes
        public int PORT = 8732;
```

```
        public string USER = "myName";
        public string PASS = "myPwd";
    }
}


// C#
using System;
using com.db4o;

namespace com.db4o.dg2db4o.chapter11
{
    class RunServer : ServerConfiguration
    {
        private bool stop = false;

        private void Run()
        {
            lock (this)
            {
                Console.WriteLine("Starting server...");
                // start server and grant access to one user
                ObjectServer server = Db4o.OpenServer(REMOTEFILE, PORT);
                server.GrantAccess(USER, PASS);
                try
                {
                    // see Chapter 8 for example of setting stop condition
                    while (!stop)
                    {
                        Monitor.Wait(this, 60000);
                        Console.WriteLine("SERVER: Server is listening ...");
                    }
                }
                catch (ThreadInterruptedException tie)
                {
                    Console.WriteLine("Thread Error!" + tie);
                }
                finally
                {
                    server.Close();
                }
            }
            Console.WriteLine("Server ends...");
        }
    }
}
```

```csharp
// C#
using System;
using com.db4o;
using com.db4o.replication;

namespace com.db4o.dg2db4o.chapter11
{
    class RunReplicator : ServerConfiguration
    {
        private bool stop = false;

        public void Run()
        {
            lock (this)
            {
                ObjectContainer remoteServer = null;
                ObjectContainer localProducer = null;
                Console.WriteLine("Starting replicator...");
                // configure for replication - will apply to all databases opened
                Db4o.Configure().GenerateUUIDs(Int32.MaxValue);
                Db4o.Configure().GenerateVersionNumbers(Int32.MaxValue);
                try
                {
                    // open remote server to accept replicated data
                    remoteServer = Db4o.OpenClient(HOST, PORT, USER, PASS);
                    // open local file which will originate data
                    localProducer = Db4o.OpenFile(LOCALFILE);
                    // create ReplicationProcess with conflict handling
                    ReplicationConflictHandler conflictHandler =
                        new MyReplicationConflictHandler();
                    ReplicationProcess replication =
                        localProducer.Ext().ReplicationBegin(
                            remoteServer, conflictHandler);
                    replication.SetDirection(localProducer, remoteServer);

                    while (!stop)
                    {
                        // get data from console and create Person object
                        Console.WriteLine("REPLICATOR: Please enter a name: ");
                        String name = Console.ReadLine();
                        Console.WriteLine("REPLICATOR: Please enter an age: ");
                        int age = Convert.ToInt32(Console.ReadLine());
                        Person p = new Person(name, age);
                        // store object to local database
                        localProducer.Set(p);
```

```
                            // replicate to remote server
                            replication.Replicate(p);
                            replication.Commit();
                        }
                    }
                    catch (ThreadInterruptedException tie)
                    {
                        Console.WriteLine("Thread Error!" + tie);
                    }
                    finally
                    {
                        localProducer.Close();
                        remoteServer.Close();
                    }
                }
            }
        }
    }
}
```

```
// C#
namespace com.db4o.dg2db4o.chapter11
{
    class MyReplicationConflictHandler : ReplicationConflictHandler
    {
        public Object ResolveConflict(
                ReplicationProcess replicationProcess, Object a, Object b)
        {
            return a;
        }
    }
}
```

```
// C#
using System;
using com.db4o;

namespace com.db4o.dg2db4o.chapter11
{
    class RunClient : ServerConfiguration
    {
        private ObjectContainer db;
        private bool stop = false;
```

```csharp
public void Run()
{
    lock (this)
    {
        Console.WriteLine("Starting client...");
        try
        {
            // configure for replication opened
            Db4o.Configure().GenerateUUIDs(Int32.MaxValue);
            Db4o.Configure().GenerateVersionNumbers(Int32.MaxValue);
            // connect to remote server and store some initial data there
            db = Db4o.OpenClient(HOST, PORT, USER, PASS);
            db.Set(new Person("Bob", 35));
            db.Set(new Person("Alice", 29));
            db.Commit();
            // repeatedly list remote server database contents
            while (!stop)
            {
                ListResult(db.Get(new Person()));
                Monitor.Wait(this, 10000);
            }
        }
        catch (ThreadInterruptedException tie)
        {
            Console.WriteLine("Thread Error!" + tie);
        }
        finally
        {
            db.Close();
        }
    }
}

private static void ListResult(ObjectSet result)
{
    while (result.HasNext())
    {
        Console.WriteLine("CLIENT:" + result.Next());
    }
}
```

Listing 11-2. *Replication Example Complete Code in Java*

```java
// JAVA
package com.db4o.dg2db4o.chapter11;

public interface ServerConfiguration
{
    public String HOST = "localhost";
    public String REMOTEFILE = "C:/remote.yap";  // gets changes
    public String LOCALFILE = "C:/local.yap";    // produces changes
    public int PORT = 8732;
    public String USER = "myName";
    public String PASS = "myPwd";
}


// JAVA
package com.db4o.dg2db4o.chapter11;

import java.io.*;
import com.db4o.*;

public class RunServer implements Runnable, ServerConfiguration
{
    private boolean stop;

    public void run()
    {
        synchronized (this)
        {
            new File(REMOTEFILE).delete();
            // start server and grant access to one user
            ObjectServer server = Db4o.openServer(REMOTEFILE, PORT);
            server.grantAccess(USER, PASS);
            try
            {
                // see Chapter 8 for example of setting stop condition
                while (!stop)
                {
                    System.out.println("SERVER:[" + System.currentTimeMillis()
                        + "] Server's running... ");
                    this.wait(60000);
                }
            }
            catch (Exception e)
            {
                e.printStackTrace();
            }
```

```
                    finally
                    {
                        server.close();
                    }
                }
            }
        }

// JAVA
package com.db4o.dg2db4o.chapter11;

import com.db4o.*;
import com.db4o.replication.*;
import java.util.Scanner;

public class RunReplicator implements Runnable, ServerConfiguration
{
    private boolean stop = false;

    public void run()
    {
        ObjectContainer remoteServer = null;
        ObjectContainer localProducer = null;
        // configure for replication - will apply to all databases opened
        Db4o.configure().generateUUIDs(Integer.MAX_VALUE);
        Db4o.configure().generateVersionNumbers(Integer.MAX_VALUE);
        try
        {
            // open remote server to accept replicated data
            remoteServer = Db4o.openClient(HOST, PORT, USER, PASS);
            // open local file which will originate data
            localProducer = Db4o.openFile(LOCALFILE);
            // create ReplicationProcess with conflict handling
            ReplicationProcess replication = localProducer.ext().
                replicationBegin(remoteServer, new ReplicationConflictHandler()
            {
                public Object resolveConflict(
                        ReplicationProcess replicationProcess, Object a, Object b)
                {
                    return a;
                }
            });
            replication.setDirection(localProducer, remoteServer);
            Scanner sc = new Scanner(System.in);
            while(!stop)
            {
```

```
            // get data from console and create Person object
            System.out.print("REPLICATOR: Enter next
                surname and age (e.g. 'Tom 44'): ");
            Person p = new Person(sc.next(), sc.nextInt());
            // store object to local database
            localProducer.set(p);
            // replicate to remote server
            replication.replicate(p);
            replication.commit();
        }
        sc.close();
    }
    catch (Exception e)
    {
        e.printStackTrace();
    }
    localProducer.close();
    remoteServer.close();
    }
}


// JAVA
package com.db4o.dg2db4o.chapter11;

import com.db4o.*;

public class RunClient implements Runnable, ServerConfiguration
{
    private boolean stop = false;
    ObjectContainer db = null;

    public void run()
    {
        synchronized(this)
        {
            try
            {
                // configure for replication
                Db4o.configure().generateUUIDs(Integer.MAX_VALUE);
                Db4o.configure().generateVersionNumbers(Integer.MAX_VALUE);
                // connect to remote server and store some initial data there
                db = Db4o.openClient(HOST, PORT, USER, PASS);
                db.set(new Person("Bob", 35));
                db.set(new Person("Alice", 29));
```

```
                // repeatedly list remote server database contents
                while (!stop)
                {
                    listResult(db.get(new Person()));
                    Thread.sleep(15000);
                }
            }
            catch (Exception e)
            {
                e.printStackTrace();
            }
            finally
            {
                db.close();
            }
        }
    }

    public static void listResult(ObjectSet result)
    {
        System.out.println("CLIENT: Listing...");
        while (result.hasNext())
        {
            System.out.println("CLIENT:" + result.next());
        }
    }
}
```

When you start the server, it simply reports that it's running. The output from the Java version is as follows:

```
[db4o 5.2.002    2006-03-26 22:03:21]
Server listening on port: '8732'
SERVER:[1131461334875] Server's running...
SERVER:[1131461354875] Server's running...
```

Once the server is running, the client process or thread starts, creates, and stores two Person objects ("Bob" and "Alice") and lists the contents of the server's database, which will consist only of these two objects at this point.

```
CLIENT: Listing...
CLIENT:[Alice;29]
CLIENT:[Bob;35]
```

Once the replicator process or thread starts, you are prompted to enter the details for a new Person, for example:

```
REPLICATOR: Enter next surname and age (e.g. 'Tom 44'): William 21
```

The client periodically lists all the objects in the server's database, including those that have been added to the local database file by the replicator process and also replicated to the server. The following output shows an example of the client doing this after one object has been replicated into the database:

```
CLIENT: Listing...
CLIENT:[William;21]
CLIENT:[Alice;29]
CLIENT:[Bob;35]
```

Other replication scenarios may be more complex than this example but will be based on the same technique. For example, multiple clients could be replicating their data to be merged at the server, and a similar replication could be run in the opposite direction to transfer data added by one client into all the other client databases.

Note that db4o imposes no architecture or outside configuration on your application in terms of replication. Wherever changed objects in your code might occur, you can replicate them to other databases. In fact, you can set up as many replication process objects as you like in order to distribute your objects to other databases.

Replication with Existing Databases

What if you want to replicate existing database files that were not originally configured for replication, and so you don't have UUIDs and version numbers? You can achieve retrospective generation of UUIDs and version numbers using the Defragment tool described in Chapter 10. You need to first enable replication either with the GenerateUUIDs and GenerateVersionNumbers configuration, or using a per-class configuration method called EnableReplication as shown in the following example, and then run the defragment procedure.

```
// C#
Db4o.Configure().ObjectClass(typeof(Person)).EnableReplication(true);
new Defragment().Run("db.yap", delete);
```

```
// JAVA
Db4o.configure().objectClass(Person.class).enableReplication(true);
new Defragment().Run("db.yap", delete);
```

The db4o Replication System

Version 5.1 of db4o introduced support for the db4o Replication System (dRS). dRS is an ambitious replication solution, which bridges the divide between db4o and relational databases. With dRS you can have single- or bidirectional replication of data between peer db4o databases, between db4o and a wide range of relational databases, and even between relational databases.

Although it is closely associated with db4o, dRS also allows you to create replication applications for other databases. Support for working with relational databases within an object-oriented application is provided by Hibernate. Since Hibernate is a Java API, the initial release of dRS only supports Java, although it is likely that a .NET release will follow. If it does, it may be based on NHibernate, the .NET port of Hibernate.

HIBERNATE

Hibernate is a widely used open source object-relational mapping framework for Java, which uses XML configuration files to map objects onto database tables. In Chapter 1 we talked about Hibernate as an alternative to db4o, but in this scenario they are working as partners.

Hibernate is a mature framework with support for a large number of database products, including as of version 3 DB2, Firebird, FrontBase, HSQLDB, Informix, Ingres, InterBase, Mckoi SQL, Microsoft SQL Server, MySQL, Oracle, PointBase, PostgreSQL, Progress, SAP DB, and Sybase.

Installing dRS

dRS can be downloaded from the db4o Download Center (www.db4o.com/community/ontheroad/downloadcenter/—free registration is required before you can access this site). The version described here is dRS 1.1. Clicking the dRS link lets you download the file dRS-1.1.zip. After you have unpacked the zip file you will see a set of folders with the same names as those in the main db4o distribution: doc, lib, and src.

The src folder contains the dRS sources. The doc directory contains the API and a useful tutorial. Finally, the lib directory contains all the libraries needed to run replication applications. There are quite a few of these: some of the most important ones are:

- dRS-core.jar: The core dRS library.

- hibernate3.jar: The Hibernate configuration classes.

- commons*.jar: The well-known Commons libraries from Apache are required by Hibernate. Several other open source third-party libraries are also required by Hibernate, including Xerces for XML parsing and log4j for logging.

- hsqldb.jar: The HSQLDB database is one example of a tiny but powerful relational database that can be used out-of-the-box for testing dRS. If you are using another database, then you might have to include JDBC driver libraries in your project. Basically, whatever you would need to work with your database using Hibernate, you also need for dRS.

The dRS distribution also includes db4o-5.2-java5.jar, the db4o Java library, as db4o classes are used when replicating db4o databases.

■ Note JDBC is an API that provides connectivity to a wide range of SQL databases, allowing SQL statements to be executed from within Java applications. JDBC drivers are available for most popular databases.

dRS Replication Between db4o Databases

Like db4o, dRS is an API rather than an application—you can use it to create your own application to perform whatever replication process you require. You need to include the relevant dRS libraries in your project's classpath: at the very least, dRS-core.jar and hibernate 3.jar are needed. The latter has to be included even if you want to replicate between db4o databases and so are not using Hibernate. You'll probably find that you need to include more than just these two, though.

Let's look at a simple example that works with db4o databases only. This example is based on the scenario described in the white paper by Eric Falsken[1] where a handheld device aggregates data while disconnected. When the device is connected to a network, its database file is copied across, and the data from this device and others is merged into another database on a desktop PC. From the point of view of the handheld, its own database file is the local file, while the desktop database is the remote file.

This job could also be done using db4o core replication as described in the first part of this chapter. However, it's worth using dRS whenever you can, as it provides a consistent interface no matter what kind of databases you are using.

The example is straightforward to run, as it simply replicates between two database files that are in standalone mode for this purpose—no clients or servers are involved, although the replication process can equally well be done in client/server mode. The description that follows shows the stages of the process—all of the code shown can be placed in a single method to be executed.

■**Note** All the code in this example is in Java as dRS does not support C# at the time of this writing.

As we did for db4o core replication, we need to configure db4o to generate UUIDs and version numbers for all objects:

```
Db4o.configure().generateUUIDs(Integer.MAX_VALUE);
Db4o.configure().generateVersionNumbers(Integer.MAX_VALUE);
```

or for specified classes:

```
Db4o.configure().objectClass(Person.class).generateUUIDs(true);
Db4o.configure().objectClass(Person.class).generateVersionNumbers(true);
```

Next we open the two databases, and put a couple of objects (Person objects again) into each:

```
new File("c:/local_db.yap").delete();
ObjectContainer handheld = Db4o.openFile("c:/local_db.yap");
handheld.set(new Person("Gandhi", 79));
handheld.set(new Person("Lincoln", 56));
new File("c:/remote_db.yap").delete();
ObjectContainer desktop = Db4o.openFile("c:/remote_db.yap");
```

---

1. See www.db4o.com/about/productinformation/whitepapers/.

We now create the ReplicationSession that defines the source and destination. This is roughly equivalent to the ReplicationProcess in db4o core replication. It is created by calling the static begin method of the dRS Replication factory class:

```
ReplicationSession replication = Replication.begin(handheld, desktop);
```

This is the simplest way to create a ReplicationSession. However, the begin method is overloaded, so that you can define different types of source and destination. You can also add a ConflictResolver if you will need to deal with data that has changed in both the source and the destination. Table 11-1 shows all the combinations of parameter types allowed by Replication.begin.

Table 11-1. *Parameters of the begin Method Used to Open a ReplicationSession*

First Parameter	Second Parameter	Third Parameter
org.hibernate.cfg.Configuration	org.hibernate.cfg.Configuration	
org.hibernate.cfg.Configuration	org.hibernate.cfg.Configuration	ConflictResolver
com.db4o.ObjectContainer	org.hibernate.cfg.Configuration	
com.db4o.ObjectContainer	org.hibernate.cfg.Configuration	ConflictResolver
com.db4o.ObjectContainer	com.db4o.ObjectContainer	
com.db4o.ObjectContainer	com.db4o.ObjectContainer	ConflictResolver
ReplicationProvider	ReplicationProvider	
ReplicationProvider	ReplicationProvider	ConflictResolver

As Table 11-1 shows, these are all simply combinations of two instances of any of the following: a Hibernate Configuration object (the use of Hibernate will be described in the next section); a db4o ObjectContainer; or an implementation of the interface com.db4o. ReplicationProvider. The last of these represents a façade for persistence systems that provide replication support. The overloading of the begin method explains why you need to have the Hibernate library in the classpath even when not using Hibernate for replication.

The first two rows of Table 11-1 have a Hibernate Configuration for each of source and destination. The implication of this is that you can use dRS for replication even when no db4o databases are involved.

■**Note** In the façade design pattern, an object hides the details of one or more other objects, making them easier to use. dRS provides implementations of ReplicationProvider, which can act as façades for db4o ObjectContainers and Hibernate Configurations.

The ConflictResolver interface is very similar to the db4o core replication ConflictHandler described earlier, and is used by writing an anonymous inner class that defines the rule for dealing with conflicts. The following call to Replication.begin specifies that the replication process will handle conflicts by giving precedence to objects in the source database:

```
ReplicationSession replication = Replication.begin(handheld, desktop,
    new ConflictResolver()
{
    public Object resolveConflict(ReplicationSession session,
        Object a, Object b)
    {
        return a;
    }
});
```

Next we want to detect all new objects in the handheld (source) ObjectContainer and replicate them to the desktop (destination) ObjectContainer:

```
ObjectSet changed = replication.providerA().objectsChangedSinceLastReplication();
while (changed.hasNext())
    replication.replicate(changed.next());
replication.commit();
replication.close();
```

The method replication.providerA returns the source ReplicationProvider (which is actually an ObjectContainer here). If you want bidirectional replication, you can insert the same lines for providerB.

Let's add some further code to list the contents of the databases to demonstrate that this replication has worked correctly. We'll wait a while to let the replication finish, and then query the databases and list the results. To help see what is happening, we can print the UUID and the version for each object—these can be accessed using the getObjectInfo method of the database's ExtObjectContainer.

```
try
{
    Thread.sleep(5000); // Wait 5 seconds...
}
catch (Exception e)
{
    e.printStackTrace();
}

ObjectSet localdata = handheld.get(new Person()); // using the handheld container
while (localdata.hasNext())
{
    Person p = (Person) localdata.next();
    System.out.println("Local:" + p + ", " + "UUID:" +
        handheld.ext().getObjectInfo(p).getUUID().getSignaturePart() +
        "." + handheld.ext().getObjectInfo(p).getUUID().getLongPart() +
        ", version:" + handheld.ext().getObjectInfo(p).getVersion());
}
```

```
ObjectSet remotedata = desktop.get(new Person()); // using the desktop container
while (remotedata.hasNext())
{
    Person p = (Person) remotedata.next();
    System.out.println("Local:" + p + ", "   + "UUID:" +
        desktop.ext().getObjectInfo(p).getUUID().getSignaturePart() +
        "." + desktop.ext().getObjectInfo(p).getUUID().getLongPart() +
        ", version:" + desktop.ext().getObjectInfo(p).getVersion());
}
handheld.close();
desktop.close();
```

The output of this program is as follows, showing that the two Person objects have been replicated. The UUIDs and version numbers are retained when the objects are transferred between databases.

```
Local:[Lincoln;56], UUID:[B@cdfc9c.1939274514499143370, version:1
Local:[Gandhi;79], UUID:[B@cdfc9c.1939274514499143369, version:1

Remote:[Gandhi;79], UUID:[B@cdfc9c.1939274514499143369, version:1
Remote:[Lincoln;56], UUID:[B@cdfc9c.1939274514499143370, version:1
```

Replicating Back to the Original Database

Now we'll add a few extra lines so that after the first replication some changes are made to the desktop database, and these are replicated back to the handheld database. Two new objects are added, and one is updated.

```
desktop.set(new Person("Teresa", 87));
desktop.set(new Person("Mandela", 86));
Person update = (Person)desktop.get(new Person("Gandhi",0)).next();
update.setAge(80);
desktop.set(update);
desktop.commit();

ReplicationSession replication = Replication.begin(handheld, desktop,
    new ConflictResolver()
{
    public Object resolveConflict(ReplicationSession session,
        Object a, Object b)
    {
        return a;
    }
});
```

```
ObjectSet changed2 = replication.providerB().objectsChangedSinceLastReplication();
while (changed2.hasNext())
    replication.replicate(changed2.next());
replication.commit();
replication.close();
```

With these additions, the output looks like the following. Note that the UUID signature part identifies which database each object was originally created in, and that the version number is higher for the new and updated objects. The version number for "Gandhi" in the local database does not change as it was not updated in that database.

```
Local:[Mandela;86], UUID:[B@750159.-4752372636586212024, version:4
Local:[Teresa;87], UUID:[B@750159.-4752372636586212025, version:4
Local:[Lincoln;56], UUID:[B@1abab88.2455213756814525349, version:1
Local:[Gandhi;80], UUID:[B@1abab88.2455213756814525348, version:1

Remote:[Mandela;86], UUID:[B@750159.-4752372636586212024, version:4
Remote:[Teresa;87], UUID:[B@750159.-4752372636586212025, version:4
Remote:[Gandhi;80], UUID:[B@1abab88.2455213756814525348, version:4
Remote:[Lincoln;56], UUID:[B@1abab88.2455213756814525349, version:1
```

Selective Replication

The previous example replicated *all* the objects that had changed. Alternatively, you can apply any condition you like to select particular objects to be replicated. For example, let's change the initial (forward replication only) version of the previous example to replicate only Persons that have an even number value of age:

```
while (changed.hasNext())
{
    Person p = (Person) changed.next();
    if(p.getAge()%2 == 0)
        replication.replicate(p);
}
```

The result will be that Gandhi, with age equal to 79, would not be replicated to the desktop:

```
Local:[Lincoln;56], UUID:[B@cdfc9c.1939274514499143370, version:1
Local:[Gandhi;79], UUID:[B@cdfc9c.1939274514499143369, version:1

Remote:[Lincoln;56], UUID:[B@cdfc9c.1939274514499143370, version:1
```

Replicating with Hibernate

With db4o, the database is closely integrated within an application, and can't be accessed easily in other ways. Often this is not a problem, as db4o is mainly targeted at embedded use and packaged applications. However, sometimes you may need to make the data accessible to other applications and tools. Diversity of access is a feature lacking in db4o but offered by virtually any relational database. This means that there is a need for a way to replicate data from db4o to RDBMSs. dRS enables the replication of objects to relational databases.

dRS needs to be able to work with objects and relational databases together. Hibernate is considered to be the most suitable tool to achieve this result. Because it's based on Hibernate, dRS can immediately take advantage of Hibernate's extensive support for popular RDBMSs. Note that Hibernate 3 is required as the API and some package names changed between versions 2 and 3. Figure 11-2 depicts the environment for the examples.

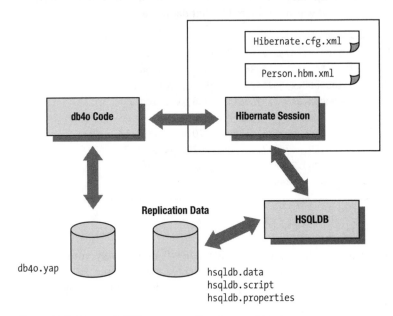

Figure 11-2. *Example Hibernate replication architecture*

Setting Up Hibernate

You can download Hibernate from www.hibernate.org. Alternatively, you can use the libraries that are provided in the dRS/lib directory, which is probably simpler. To set up a dRS project to use Hibernate, you need to do the following:

- Either include all the libraries distributed with dRS or make sure you include Hibernate's lib folder in your IDE's classpath.

- Also include your database's JDBC driver library in your classpath. We have chosen to use HSQLDB because no installation of the database is necessary (as with db4o, you just need to include the library). Any of the aforementioned databases could have been used instead, though. dRS includes the HSQLDB library, hsqldb.jar, or you can download it from www.hsqldb.org.

Next you'll need to configure Hibernate. Create a Hibernate configuration file, which must be named `hibernate.cfg.xml`, in your top-level class directory above the package directories, with the following content:

```xml
<?xml version='1.0' encoding='utf-8'?>
<!DOCTYPE hibernate-configuration PUBLIC
    "-//Hibernate/Hibernate Configuration DTD//EN"
    "http://hibernate.sourceforge.net/hibernate-configuration-3.0.dtd">

<hibernate-configuration>
    <session-factory>

        <property name="hibernate.connection.driver_class">
                org.hsqldb.jdbcDriver</property>
        <property name="hibernate.connection.url">
                jdbc:hsqldb:hsql://localhost</property>
        <property name="hibernate.connection.username">
                 sa</property>
        <property name="hibernate.connection.password"></property>
        <property name="dialect">org.hibernate.dialect.HSQLDialect</property>
        <property name="show_sql">false</property>
        <property name="hibernate.hbm2ddl.auto">update</property>

        <!-- Mapping files -->
        <mapping resource="com/db4o/dg2db4o/chapter11/Person.hbm.xml"/>

    </session-factory>
</hibernate-configuration>
```

As you can see from this example, you have to configure the driver and the connection URL exactly as you would to access HSQLDB using JDBC in a Java program. HSQLDB has similar operating modes to those of db4o. Here, the URL declares that we are accessing a network server (using `jdbc:hsqldb:hsql://localhost` as the URL). You can also access HSQLDB using an in-memory mode, `jdbc:hsqldb:mem:replication`, which doesn't store data permanently (although it is fast!), or using a standalone in-process mode, `jdbc:hsqldb:file:replication`.

Next you provide the default HSQLDB credentials (username "admin" and an empty password), which allow connection to the database without any preliminary configuration of users. You then have to configure the Hibernate dialect to be HSQLDB. If you've decided to use another database, MySQL for instance, change these settings as necessary. The `show_sql` property allows you to view or hide Hibernate SQL commands. This can be useful for debugging, although the SQL statements that are shown aren't particularly helpful as they don't include any of the actual values passed to the database.

Finally, you need to specify what class or classes will be stored in the HSQLDB database. Each class needs a mapping configuration file—`Person.hbm.xml` in this case for the `Person` class—and Hibernate needs to be told about these, which is what the `<mapping>` element does. You need one `<mapping>` for each class to be replicated.

■**Note** Creating mapping files for classes can be quite tricky if you are not fluent with Hibernate. There are several settings you can use in the XML files. Subtle differences exist in the dialects used for different databases, which means that you can't be sure that a mapping file that works fine with HSQLDB will work unchanged with MySQL, for example. You can refer to the Hibernate documentation for help, and some trial and error is often needed.

The mapping file for the `Person` class is as follows:

```xml
<?xml version="1.0"?>
<!DOCTYPE hibernate-mapping PUBLIC
    "-//Hibernate/Hibernate Mapping DTD 3.0//EN"
    "http://hibernate.sourceforge.net/hibernate-mapping-3.0.dtd">

<hibernate-mapping default-access="field" default-lazy="false"
        default-cascade="all">
    <class name="com.db4o.dg2db4o.chapter11.Person">
        <!--Primary key column-->
        <id column="PersonID" type="int">
            <generator class="native"/>
        </id>
        <property name="name"/>
        <property name="age"/>
    </class>
</hibernate-mapping>
```

This assumes that fields have the same names in the objects and in the tables, and also that you have added an additional `id` field in your `Person` class. The `id` is needed as a primary key in HSQLDB, although it is not necessary for db4o. If you create objects in the db4o database with `null` values for `id`, then the mapping file `<generator>` tag instructs the database to automatically generate values in the HSQLDB database.

You can add other parameters if you like. For instance, if the fields in your database don't match the class fields, then you can write more verbose definitions like this:

```xml
<property name="name" type="string" update="true" insert="true" column="name" />
```

This file should be named `Person.hbm.xml` and should reside in the same directory as the class itself or within the top-level class directory: the location should be specified precisely in the Hibernate configuration file.

■**Caution** If you don't have a local copy of the DTD referred to in your mapping file, your system will retrieve it from the actual Hibernate DTD Internet URL. If there is neither a local copy nor Internet access, then an exception may be thrown.

Creating the HSQLDB Database

You don't actually need to do anything else to create the database, because Hibernate can use mapping files to work out how to create empty tables for you. If the tables already exist in the database, Hibernate simply works with those tables.

If you want to create tables manually, perhaps if you want to put in some initial data before replicating, then you have several options for creating and populating your database.

HSQLDB provides a database console you open by executing the following from the command line:

```
java org.hsqldb.util.DatabaseManager.
```

You can open this console and enter your SQL CREATE TABLE and INSERT commands to create your initial data:

```
CREATE TABLE Person (id INTEGER PRIMARY KEY, name CHAR(10), age INTEGER);
INSERT INTO Person Values (100, 'Tom', 34);
INSERT INTO Person Values (101, 'Steve', 28);
INSERT INTO Person Values (102, 'Jim', 36);
INSERT INTO Person Values (103, 'John', 44);
SELECT * FROM Person;
```

You can also specify an HSQLDB file containing the previous SQL from the command line (the first line in the following code), or start a command session (second line) to enter your data:

```
java -jar $HSQLDB_HOME/lib/hsqldb.jar urlid \i file.sql

java -jar $HSQLDB_HOME/lib/hsqldb.jar urlid -
```

The final option is to write some simple Java code to add some data using JDBC:

```
try
{
    Class.forName("org.hsqldb.jdbcDriver");
}
catch (ClassNotFoundException e)
{
    System.out.println("Cannot load Driver!");
    e.printStackTrace();
    System.exit(0);
}

System.out.println("JDBC Driver loaded.");
Connection con = DriverManager.getConnection(
    "jdbc:HSQLDB:C:/HIB/replication.db", "sa", "");
System.out.println("Connection established!");

Statement stmt = con.createStatement();
```

```
String sqlQuery = "CREATE TABLE Person (
    id CHAR(10) PRIMARY KEY, name CHAR(10), age INTEGER)";
ResultSet rs = stmt.executeQuery(sqlQuery);

sqlQuery = "INSERT INTO Person VALUES ('id0','Tom',34)";
rs = stmt.executeQuery(sqlQuery);
sqlQuery = "INSERT INTO Person VALUES ('id1',Steve,28)";
rs = stmt.executeQuery(sqlQuery);
sqlQuery = "INSERT INTO Person VALUES ('id2','Jim',36)";
rs = stmt.executeQuery(sqlQuery);
sqlQuery = "INSERT INTO Person VALUES ('id3','John',44)";
rs = stmt.executeQuery(sqlQuery);

sqlQuery = "SELECT * FROM Person";
rs = stmt.executeQuery(sqlQuery);
while (rs.next()) {
    System.out.println(counter++ + ". Set Number:");
    String id = rs.getString("id");
    System.out.println("\t[id=" + id + "]");
    String name = rs.getString("name");
    System.out.println("\t[name=" + name + "]");
    int age = rs.getInt("age");
    System.out.println("\t[age=" + age + "]\n");
}
con.close();
System.out.println("Ready!");
```

Now that the initial configuration is complete, we can look at the code that performs the replication.

Running Hibernate Replication with dRS

To show Hibernate replication in action, we can build on the example we used to show basic dRS replication. Look at the following line from that example:

```
ReplicationSession replication = Replication.begin(handheld, desktop);
```

Previously both participants in the replication were db4o databases, one on the handheld device and one database on the desktop PC. Now our goal is to replace the desktop db4o database with a relational database. This can be done by exchanging the second parameter (which is an ObjectContainer) with a Hibernate Configuration object. This object encapsulates the information in the Hibernate configuration file hibernate.cfg.xml, which specifies all the relevant details of the relational database. Apart from this one change, the code for Hibernate replication is the same as that for db4o-to-db4o replication:

```
Configuration hibernate = new Configuration().configure("hibernate.cfg.xml");
ReplicationSession replication = Replication.begin(handheld, hibernate);
```

▓**Note** The Configuration class here is the one from the org.hibernate.cfg namespace, and should not be confused with the class of the same name in com.db4o.config, or with other any other class having that name.

The file hibernate.cfg.xml is read from your classpath. Therefore, it should usually reside at the top level in your project above the packages. The second line uses this configuration to tie the db4o handheld database and the Hibernate/HSQLDB together.

A Complete Example

Let's put what we've learned into action by creating a simple application that uses dRS. Before we start replicating, we need to make sure that we can connect to the HSQLDB database. To run an HSQLDB server, you can execute the following command at the command line in the directory where you want your database files to be stored:

```
java -cp ../lib/hsqldb.jar org.hsqldb.Server -database.0 replicate ➥
-dbname.0 replication
```

Depending on where you run the command from, you may have to modify the path to the hsqldb.jar file.

Alternatively, you can start the server using a Java process from your IDE by executing the class shown in Listing 11-3.

Listing 11-3. *The StartHsqlServer Class*

```
public class StartHsqlServer
{
    public static void main(String[] args)
    {
        String serverProps;
        String url;
        String user = "sa";
        String password = "";
        Server server;
        try
        {
            serverProps = "database.0=file:c:/HIB/replicate";
            url = "jdbc:hsqldb:hsql://localhost";
            server = new Server();
            server.putPropertiesFromString(serverProps);
            server.setLogWriter(null);
            server.setErrWriter(null);
            server.start();
        }
```

```
        catch (Exception e)
        {
            System.out.println("Error starting server: " +
                    e.toString());
        }
    }
}
```

Now let's have a look at the code to run the replication (see Listing 11-4).

Listing 11-4. *The Class HibRep, the Complete Hibernate Replication Example*

```java
public class HibRep
{
    private static final String handheld_DB = "c:/local_db.yap ";

    public static void main(String[] args)
    {
        new HibRep().run();
    }

    private void run(){
        Db4o.configure().generateUUIDs(Integer.MAX_VALUE);
        Db4o.configure().generateVersionNumbers(Integer.MAX_VALUE);
        new File(handheld_DB).delete();
        ObjectContainer handheld = Db4o.openFile(handheld_DB);
        handheld.set(new Person("Ghandi", 79));
        handheld.set(new Person("Lincoln", 56));
        handheld.commit();

        Configuration hibernate = new Configuration().
                    configure("hibernate.cfg.xml");
        ReplicationSession replication = Replication.begin(handheld, hibernate);

        //Query for objects changed from db4o
        ObjectSet changed =
            replication.providerA().objectsChangedSinceLastReplication();
        while (changed.hasNext())
        {
            Person p = (Person) changed.next();
            replication.replicate(p);
        }
        replication.commit();
        replication.close();
        handheld.close();
    }
}
```

This will replicate "Gandhi" and "Lincoln" into the HSQLDB database.

UUIDs and Version Numbers

The previous example shows replication from db4o to HSQLDB using Hibernate. It doesn't tell the full story of what dRS is doing, though. As you already know, db4o replication requires that objects be stored with UUIDs and version numbers. If we want to replicate in the other direction, from the relational database to a db4o database, then the same information needs to be available in the relational database. Without this information, there is no way to track changes that take place in the HSQLDB database.

dRS makes this possible by using Hibernate to create some extra fields in your tables, and some extra tables, to store and organize object identity and versioning. Each data table is modified to have three extra fields: drs_provider_id, drs_uuid_long_part, and drs_version, which correspond to the UUID signature, long part, and version number stored in db4o, respectively.

Along with creating additional fields, dRS creates a set of tables to assist the replication process. These include the following:

- REPLICATIONPROVIDERSIGNATURE: This table contains the database identifier part of the UUID for each db4o database, known as *providers*. In this example there is only one db4o provider, but you can have multiple db4o databases replicating into the same relational database. The drs_provider_id field in a data table is actually a foreign key, which relates a data row to an entry in this table. The HSQLDB database itself is regarded as a provider as well, and has an entry in this table.

- REPLICATIONRECORD: This table contains the current version number associated with each db4o provider database.

If you update a row of the Person table in the HSQLDB, then you need to update the version number accordingly. For example, if you update the age of "Gandhi", you need to update the drs_version value for the affected row so that it is greater than the highest version value in the REPLICATIONRECORD table. The update could be done with a SQL statement like this:

```
UPDATE Person
SET
age = 80,
drs_version = (select max(version) from replicationrecord) + 1
WHERE Person.name = 'Gandhi';
```

If the version numbers are correct, then reverse replication with Hibernate is done in exactly the same way as it was with basic dRS replication. We just specify that we want to replicate objects changed in provider B rather than provider A.

Detecting RDBMS Updates Made via Hibernate

In some situations, the relational database may be modified by an application that is also using Hibernate. In that case, it is possible to use dRS—using its ReplicationConfigurator class—within that application to install an event listener. This listener detects updates or inserts done through Hibernate, and automatically updates the drs_version field in the same way as in the SQL example in the previous section. It can also generate version numbers and UUIDs for data inserted with Hibernate. The dRS listener transparently ensures that Hibernate updates can be correctly replicated back to db4o.

The following listing shows installation of a listener and then an example of a Hibernate transaction, which updates a single object (actually it updates the RDBMS table row which represents the object). The object to be updated is first retrieved using Hibernate's query language, HQL. The listener updates the drs_version field for that object in the RDBMS,

```
// Configure Hibernate and install listener
Configuration cfg = new Configuration().configure("hibernate.cfg.xml");
ReplicationConfigurator.configure(cfg);
SessionFactory sessionFactory = cfg.buildSessionFactory();
Session session = sessionFactory.openSession();
ReplicationConfigurator.install(session, cfg);

// Hibernate transaction retrieves and updates an object
Transaction tx = session.beginTransaction();
List result = session.createQuery(
    "from Person person where person.name = 'Gandhi'").list();  // HQL query
Iterator it = result.iterator();
while(it.hasNext())
{
    Person pers = (Person)it.next();
    pers.setAge(80);
    session.save(pers);
}
tx.commit();
session.close();
```

dRS, Hibernate, and Structured Objects

The examples we have considered so far replicated simple objects that had no relationships with any other objects. In more realistic situations, the objects you want to replicate will be structured, meaning that they have fields that are themselves objects. The current version of dRS supports replication of some forms of object relationships, including one-to-one, one-to-many, and collections. Collections support is currently limited to arrays, lists, sets, and maps. Multidimensional arrays or collections other than the ones listed are not yet supported.

One-to-One Relationships

Let's have a look at a simple one-to-one example, where a class references a single instance of another class. In this and the following examples, the field that defines a relationship is highlighted.

```
public class Person
{
    private long id;
    private String name;
    private int age;
    private Address adr;
```

```
    // and the usual getters, setters, constructors and
    // toString methods that were introduced in chapter 5
}

public class Address
{
    private long id;
    private String location;
    // with getters, setters, etc.
}
```

First we need to change the `hibernate.cfg.xml` file and include two mapping files, for Person and Address:

```
<mapping resource="com/db4o/dg2db4o/chapter11/Person.hbm.xml"/>
<mapping resource=" com/db4o/dg2db4o/chapter11/Address.hbm.xml"/>
```

Then we have to change the `Person` class mapping file in order to declare the one-to-one mapping:

```
<hibernate-mapping default-access="field" default-lazy="false"
            default-cascade="all">
    <class name="com.db4o.db4db4o.chapter11.Person">
        <id column="id" type="int">
            <generator class="native"/>
        </id>
        <property name="name"/>
        <property name="age"/>
        <one-to-one name="address" lazy="false"/>
    </class>
</hibernate-mapping>
```

The `Address` mapping file is similar to the original `Person.hb.xml` example with only the class and attribute names changed.

Collections

In this section we'll take a brief look at the techniques for mapping relationships that involve arrays and collections. If you want to learn more about the details of Hibernate mappings for collections, take a look at Chapter 7 of the Hibernate documentation, where they are covered in detail.

Array

First let's have a look at an example of array mapping.

```
public class Person
{
    private long id;
    private String name;
    private int age;
    private Address[]adr;      // Array
}
```

The Person.hbm.xml file includes the following mapping for the array, using an <array> tag that is included inside the <class> tag:

```
<array name="adr" table="adr" cascade="all">
    <key column="personId"/>
    <list-index column="sortOrder"/>
    <one-to-many class="com.db4o.dg2db4o.chapter11.Address"/>
</array>
```

Note that we need a key column in the Address table. Furthermore, an index is needed for arrays or lists. It is always defined as list-index and is created as an integer. These properties are actually defined in the Person mapping file.

List

The following code shows an example of a List field in the Person class, and the <list> tag, which is added to the Person mapping file:

```
public class Person
{
    private long id;
    private String name;
    private int age;
    private List adr;    // List
}
<list name="adr" table="adr">
    <key column="personId"/>
    <list-index column="sortOrder"/>
    <one-to-many class="com.db4o.dg2db4o.chapter11.Address"/>
</list>
```

Map

The Map is similar to the List except that a <map-key> tag is used instead of <list-index>:

```
public class Person
{
    private long id;
    private String name;
    private int age;
    private Map adr;     // Map
}
```

```
<map name="adr" table="adr">
   <key column="personId"/>
   <map-key type="string"/>
   <one-to-many class="com.db4o.dg2db4o.ch11.Address"/>
</map>
```

Set

Finally, the mapping of a Set doesn't need the `<list-index>` tag:

```
public class Person
{
    private long id;
    private String name;
    private int age;
    private Set adr;    // Set
}
```

```
<set name="adr" table="adr">
   <key column="personId"/>
   <one-to-many class="com.db4o.dg2db4o.ch11.Address"/>
</set>
```

Summary

In this chapter you learned about the two forms of replication that are supported. First, we examined the basic replication between db4o `ObjectContainers`. This is a straightforward process that only requires UUIDs, versions, a conflict handler, and a replication object to get your objects replicated. The second form is provided by the dRS (db4o Replication System), which also lets you connect db4o to relational databases. You have seen a simple example that writes objects from a local db4o database to a relational database system using Hibernate.

The application areas for dRS are wide. The obvious scenario is that of mobile, disconnected, or partially connected devices that capture data in a db4o database, and then later replicate this data into their RDBMS in the office. There are many more possible scenarios: for example, dRS has been used by companies to transfer specific content between different RDBMSs. Give some thought to dRS and see what might it be able to do for you.

The next chapter rounds off Part II of this book by giving you a tour of some of the advanced features of db4o, from indexing to encryption and pluggable input/output.

CHAPTER 12

Advanced Issues

This chapter covers important issues that you might not need at first but can be useful as you go further with db4o. It starts with a discussion of object IDs and when you need to make use of them. We then go on to consider a diverse range of topics that might be of interest to you:

- **IDs**: Using object IDs and Unique Universal IDs

- **Indexing**: Giving object fields an extra internal description for fast access

- **Callbacks**: Defining methods to be called in response to database actions such as activating or updating an object

- **Semaphores**: Applications of flags that protect critical sections of code

- **Web environments**: Using db4o as the back-end for web applications

- **Mixed environments**: Using the same database in .NET and Java

- **Schema evolution**: Dealing with changes in the data model

- **Pluggable file I/O**: Using custom adapters to control how data is written to the database file (or files)

- **Encryption**: Simple encryption and using custom I/O adapters to achieve stronger encryption of the database file.

- **The Generic Reflector**: Reading data without having the original classes

We close this chapter with a bit of crystal-ball gazing, by trying to predict features that db4o may acquire in the future.

IDs

Any object you store will get a unique internal object ID, which looks, at first glance, like a key that is unique within the entire db4o database. Object IDs that have been written to the database are cached by the `ObjectContainer`. These cached IDs are known as *weak references*. The concept of weak references is important for updates, as an update is just a change to an object with a weak reference followed by a `Set` of the object. This mechanism also ensures that every object is only instantiated once when an entire object graph is retrieved from the database.

It is possible to think of applications where you might have the objects but no connection to the database. This could be the case in stateless network applications without a session. Consider the example illustrated in Figure 12-1.

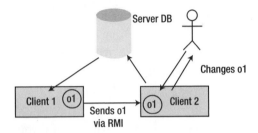

Figure 12-1. *ID scenario*

Client 1 retrieves an object o1 from the db4o server, and has to send this object to client 2 via Java Remote Method Invocation (RMI) or some similar mechanism. Client 2 receives this object, but now this object is not connected to any ObjectContainer. Therefore it has no weak references in any container cache.

Now the user attached to client 2 wishes to change the object. Client 2 might send the changes back to client 1, which creates no problem at all. But what if client 2 itself is supposed to store the object back to the same db4o server?

Now client 2 somehow needs the ID of the object if the user wants to change. Client 1 can obtain the ID of the object by calling

```
long anID = db1.Ext().GetID(object);    // C#
long anID = db1.ext().getID(object);    // JAVA
```

Here, db1 is client 1's ObjectContainer reference. Client 1 passes the ID to client 2. Client 2 can then bind its copy of the object to the stored object:

```
db2.Ext().Bind(o1, anID);    // C#
db2.ext().bind(o1, anID);    // JAVA
```

db2 is client 2's ObjectContainer reference. Now the changes can be applied by client 2. The object is known by the container and can subsequently be written to the server by calling Set.

Before you try this, you should be aware that there are other ways of achieving a similar result. For example, client 1 might do better by just sending the ID of the object and letting client 2 retrieve the correct object from the server by ID:

```
Object o1 = db2.Ext().GetByID(anID);    // C#
Object o1 = db2.ext().getByID(anID);    // JAVA
```

Alternatively, the architecture of this example could be improved. It might, for example, be better to use replication (see Chapter 11). Sending objects over a network between clients should probably be avoided when using db4o. Instead, try to attach each client to its own database.

COMMON PROBLEMS WITH IDS

You should be particularly careful with the following issues when working with IDs:

- The method GetByID() does not activate the object! If you want to work with the object you have just retrieved in that way, you have to activate the object by calling objectContainer. Activate(object, depth).

- A problem that arises with GetID() and Bind() in practice is that when your object is actually a deep graph, you need to traverse the graph to get the ID of every object in the graph and then individually bind each one.

- Normally db4o IDs do look like primary keys within the entire db4o database. They are unique for every object. Even if the ObjectContainer is closed and reopened, nothing changes. One case when IDs might change occurs if you use the Defragment tool, which is described in Chapter 10. Hence it's always a good idea to avoid relying on IDs because they can change over time, and so are not in fact like fixed primary keys.

UUIDs

You have already seen another kind of ID in this book. Replication, which was introduced in Chapter 11, needs Unique Universal IDs (UUIDs), which were described in that chapter.

```
// C#
Db4o.Configure().GenerateUUIDs(int MaxValue);
Db4o.Configure().ObjectClass(typeof(Person)).GenerateUUIDs(true);
```

```
// JAVA
Db4o.configure().generateUUIDs(Integer.MAX_VALUE);
Db4o.configure().objectClass(Person.class)).generateUUIDs(true);
```

These UUIDs are guaranteed to stay unique even if the objects are moved from one ObjectContainer to another. The previous example code shows that you can turn on UUID generation for a specific class. Now you need the respective methods to retrieve the UUIDs and to retrieve the object by a UUID. db here is the ObjectContainer reference, so db.Ext() is an ExtObjectContainer.

```
// C#
ObjectInfo oi = db.Ext().GetObjectInfo(object)
Db4oUUID uuid = oi.GetUUID();

Person person = (Person) db.Ext().GetByUUID(uuid);
```

```
// JAVA
ObjectInfo oi = db.ext().getObjectInfo(object)
Db4oUUID uuid = oi.getUUID();

Person person = (Person) db.ext().getByUUID(uuid);
```

■**Tip** Before designing your application, you should think about the architecture. Will you need unique object IDs for each server? If this is the case, then you have to configure UUIDs manually at the start because this is not done by default. The activation of UUIDs might be useful in some circumstances, but their management results in overhead in performance and storage space. Hence, if you don't need (unique) object IDs, then you should avoid UUIDs and use the normal db4o IDs.

Indexes

Indexing is a common way to improve performance of databases. In an RDBMS it allows fast access to rows in tables. The information of several rows is taken, aggregated in some way, and put into a new row. As a result the index is much smaller than the original row and can be optimized for fast search algorithms using, for example, balanced B-trees. If you have an ADDRESSES table containing a STREET column, and you are searching for a street like "High Road," you would have to look up all rows to find those that match. This is called a *full table scan*. If you had a balanced tree on this column, you would simply be able to follow the tree and thus being able to get the information in logarithmical time.

In a similar scenario in an object database, you can similarly use a balanced tree index to avoid doing a *full object scan*.

In general you gather some kind of "meta"-information about the database. In db4o you will select the field on which an index should be created. Indexes can improve the query performance dramatically. On the other hand, the index has to be stored and so the database becomes larger, so storage and update performance will be reduced. As a result you should test your application with a typical load of data to determine if the performance increase outweighs the penalties of size growth and Set/Delete performance decrease.

To turn indexing on, you have to configure this on your ObjectContainer before it is opened. Configuring will simply set the internal flag i_indexed to true on the object field you selected. If you then start working with the database and the index does not exist, it will be created. On the other hand, if the index does exist and the flag is set to false before opening the ObjectContainer, the index will be dropped.

■**Note** You have learned in previous chapters about configurations. These configurations have no permanent representation in the database. Thus if you write objects with one configuration and reopen the database with another configuration, only the configuration before opening the actual container is valid. Indexes represent the only configuration that will persist in the database.

Let's look at an example. We'll use the Person class, which was listed in Chapter 5. It has two fields, _name and _age. Let's set an index on the field _name with the following code:

```
// C#
Db4o.Configure().ObjectClass(typeOf(Person)).ObjectField("_name").Indexed(true);
```

```
// JAVA
Db4o.configure().objectClass(Person.class).objectField("_name").indexed(true);
```

Take care to use the correct name of the field! db4o will not throw an `illegal argument exception` if the field does not exist. Instead, it will do nothing—in other words, simply create no index.

You can remove the index with the following code—remember that the index is not dropped until an `ObjectContainer` is opened and you start working with the data.

```
// C#
Db4o.Configure().ObjectClass(typeOf(Person)).ObjectField("_name").Indexed(false);
```

```
// JAVA
Db4o.configure().objectClass(Person.class).objectField("_name").indexed(false);
```

If you want to create an index on a large number of objects you have two choices:

- You might store all objects using an `ObjectContainer` where indexing is turned on. You set and commit your objects. This will keep memory consumption low.

- On the other hand, you can store all objects with indexing off. Then you configure the index and reopen the `ObjectContainer` again. Then if you use or attach your classes again, an index will be created. This is much faster than the first case.

Tip Have a look how db4o creates and drops indexes by simply setting the message level to 1 with `Db4o.configure().messageLevel(1)`. In this case db4o will tell you something like: `[db4o 5.2.008 2005-11-25 13:27:33] creating index com.db4o.dg2db4o.chapter12.Person._name.`

So now let's see how the index will improve the database search performance when one trivial object has to be retrieved. The results of a set of tests that were run using the Java version of db4o are shown in Table 12-1.

Table 12-1. *Performance and File Size for Database Objects When Using the Index*

Objects in db	Indexing	Performance	File Size
101	false	16 ms	10 KB
101	true	0–16 ms	11 KB
1,001	false	32 ms	73 KB
1,001	true	0–16 ms	85 KB
10,001	false	172 ms	706 KB
10,001	true	0–16 ms	824 KB
100,001	false	1062 ms	7,034 KB
100,001	true	0–16 ms	8,206 KB

The test scenario was as follows: the database initially contained 100 objects, with one object to search. The test query was run with indexing and without indexing. The result was that the file size increased 16 percent with indexing in this simple scenario. The same test was repeated with increasing numbers of objects in the database, as you can see in the table.

The database was consistently 16 percent larger each time. The significant result, however, was that the search time to find the one element in the database stayed nearly constant.

You can easily reproduce the scenario using, for example, the Jakarta Commons libraries for random string creation and timing measurement, or you can simply download the test program from the Apress website.

In conclusion, when defining your object model to use with db4o, you should always mark the fields that will be heavily searched. Creating an index on them using the ObjectContainer is usually a good idea as this can improve performance significantly.

Callbacks

db4o callbacks are methods in your objects that are called by db4o in response to database events. db4o defines a set of callback methods in the ObjectCallBacks interface. Let's have a look at this interface (Listing 12-1).

Listing 12-1. *The ObjectCallbacks Interface in C# and Java*

```
// C#
namespace com.db4o.ext
{
    public interface ObjectCallbacks
    {
        bool ObjectCanActivate(com.db4o.ObjectContainer container);
        bool ObjectCanDeactivate(com.db4o.ObjectContainer container);
        bool ObjectCanDelete(com.db4o.ObjectContainer container);
        bool ObjectCanNew(com.db4o.ObjectContainer container);
        bool ObjectCanUpdate(com.db4o.ObjectContainer container);

        void ObjectOnActivate(com.db4o.ObjectContainer container);
        void ObjectOnDeactivate(com.db4o.ObjectContainer container);
        void ObjectOnDelete(com.db4o.ObjectContainer container);
        void ObjectOnNew(com.db4o.ObjectContainer container);
        void ObjectOnUpdate(com.db4o.ObjectContainer container);
    }
}

// JAVA
package com.db4o.ext;

public interface ObjectCallbacks {
    public boolean objectCanActivate(ObjectContainer container);
    public boolean objectCanDeactivate(ObjectContainer container);
    public boolean objectCanDelete(ObjectContainer container);
```

```
    public boolean objectCanNew(ObjectContainer container);
    public boolean objectCanUpdate(ObjectContainer container);

    public void objectOnActivate(ObjectContainer container);
    public void objectOnDeactivate(ObjectContainer container);
    public void objectOnDelete(ObjectContainer container);
    public void objectOnNew(ObjectContainer container);
    public void objectOnUpdate(ObjectContainer container);
}
```

You can implement any of these methods in your classes. For example, you might include a method ObjectOnDelete in a class, and store an instance on that class in the database. If you then delete that object from the database, this method will automatically be called by db4o. You can include code in the method to perform some action in response to the deletion: for example, you might want to log delete operations.

■**Note** The ObjectCallBacks interface doesn't have to be implemented by your own class, which is good, as in that case you would have to provide implementations for *all* the methods. db4o uses reflection to search your class, and thus it knows whether or not these methods are present. You can add any number of the methods declared in ObjectCallBacks and they will be called in response to the relevant events.

There are two distinct groups of callback methods. Any method that includes Can in its name (e.g., objectCanUpdate) is called before this event or action. The method returns a Boolean value. If you choose to return false, then that event will not be allowed to happen.

Every method in the second group, each of which is prefaced by On, is called after the action.

If you return false in these methods, it can be a very useful behavior, but also a very dangerous one. For example, if you activated cascade on delete and you need to ensure that some objects will never be deleted, the false return for those objects can be very useful. On the other hand, the application can show unexpected behavior if you forget that some actions are disallowed in this way.

Callback Example—Recording or Preventing Updates

Let's try an example to see a callback in action. This example shows an object in a database keeping its own history of update events.

The object is an instance of the class Fruit (Listings 12-2 and 12-3). A Fruit object represents a type of fruit, and holds the amount that a trader needs to order of that fruit. The amount to be ordered is updated regularly. Note that the Fruit class is unlike most of the domain classes we have looked at in that it needs to know something about how it is persisted: to detect updates, it needs to include db4o API references and calls.

Listing 12-2. *The Fruit Class with Callback Method in C#*

```csharp
// C#
using System;
using System.Collections.Generic;
using com.db4o;
using com.db4o.ext;

namespace com.db4o.dg2db4o.chapter12
{
    class Fruit
    {
        private string _name;
        private int _amount;
        private IList<String> amountHistory;

        public Fruit(String name, int amount)
        {
            _name = name;
            _amount = amount;
            amountHistory = new List<String>();
        }

        public bool ObjectCanUpdate(ObjectContainer container)
        {
            amountHistory.Add(
                    DateTime.Now.Ticks.ToString()
                    + ", " + _amount);
            Console.WriteLine("I was updated!");
            return true; // Can be updated!
        }

        public override string ToString()
        {
            String ret = "Name=" + _name + "\nAmount=" + _amount;
            foreach (string s in amountHistory)
            {
                ret += "\nModified at:" + s;
            }
            return ret;
        }

        // Name and Amount property definitions omitted
    }
}
```

Listing 12-3. *The Fruit Class with Callback Method in Java*

```java
// JAVA
package com.db4o.dg2db4o.chapter12;

import com.db4o.ext.ObjectCallbacks;
import com.db4o.ObjectContainer;
import java.util.List;
import java.util.ArrayList;

public class Fruit {
    private String _name;
    private int _amount;
    private List<String> amountHistory;

    public Fruit(String name, int amount){
        _name = name;
        _amount = amount;
        amountHistory = new ArrayList<String>();
    }

    public boolean objectCanUpdate(ObjectContainer container){
        amountHistory.add(
                new Long(System.currentTimeMillis()).toString()
                + ", " + _amount);
        System.out.println("I was updated!");
        return true; // Can be updated!
    }

    public String toString(){
        String ret="Name=" + _name + "\nAmount=" + _amount;
        for (String s :  amountHistory) {
            ret += "\nModified at:" + s;
        }
        return ret;
    }

    // getters and setters omitted
}
```

Now let's try storing a Fruit and updating it a couple of times. The code to do this is shown next. Note that the value of _amount in the live object is changed three times, to 250, 300, and finally 400. The object is only stored with calls to Set twice, when _amount is 300 and then when it is 400. Note also that we refresh the object before output so we see the actual stored object.

```csharp
// C#
Db4o.Configure().ObjectClass(typeof(Fruit)).CascadeOnUpdate(true);
ObjectContainer db = Db4o.OpenFile("C:/ch12.yap");
Fruit mac = new Fruit("Macintosh Red", 200);
db.Set(mac);
mac.Amount = 250;
mac.Amount = 300;
db.Set(mac);
Thread.Sleep(2000);
mac.Amount = 400;
db.Set(mac);
db.Commit();
db.Ext().Refresh(mac, 3);
Console.WriteLine(mac);
db.Close();
```

```java
// JAVA
Db4o.configure().objectClass(Fruit.class).cascadeOnUpdate(true);
ObjectContainer db = Db4o.openFile("C:/ch12.yap");
Fruit mac = new Fruit("Macintosh Red", 200);
db.set(mac);
mac.setAmount(250);
mac.setAmount(300);
db.set(mac);
Thread.sleep(2000);   // need to throw or catch InterruptedException
mac.setAmount(400);
db.set(mac);
db.commit();
db.ext().refresh(mac,3);
System.out.println(mac);
db.close();
```

The output is as follows:

```
I was updated!
I was updated!
Name=Macintosh Red
Amount=400
Modified at:1139415800301, 300
Modified at:1139415802309, 400
```

The stored history shows the two database updates. The change to 250 was not set to the database, so it is not recorded.

If you change the return value of the callback to false, you get a different result. The following output shows this. This time, there were output statements *before* and *after* the refresh:

```
I was updated!
I was updated!
Name=Macintosh Red
Amount=400
Modified at:1139416152324, 300
Modified at:1139416154329, 400
Name=Macintosh Red
Amount=200
```

The callback protects the object from update, so it has prevented the value of Amount being updated, and has prevented the history from being stored.

Other Possible Use Cases for Callbacks

Some uses of callbacks are fairly obvious: for example, informing the user about specific operations and avoiding deletion of particular objects in cascading deletes. There are, however, many more situations where you might wish to use callbacks. Here are some examples:

- **Setting default values after refactorings**: If you refactor objects, they sometimes have to be newly instantiated and initialized. In some cases it is difficult to obtain the correct or old values, so methods like CanNew would help here.

- **Checking the object integrity before storing objects**: This means that you can, for example, include assertions within CanNew or CanUpdate to check if values or fields are correct, and return false if they are not.

- **Setting transient fields**: When instantiating objects from a database, db4o searches for an appropriate constructor (it needs to be one that accepts null or 0 values for its parameters without throwing an exception). If no suitable constructor is available in the class, then it can bypass unsuitable constructors or instantiate without a constructor. In some cases this can cause problems if the class has transient fields that are not stored in the database and that need to be initialized by a constructor. A callback can provide an alternative way of doing this.

- **Restoring the connected state when objects are activated**: This could involve a show or visible method for a GUI, or opening files or network connections.

- **Creating special indexes**: For example, if an object is updated often, and therefore must be queried often, the object itself might make a request for an index on its important query fields.

■**Caution** In a client/server environment, ObjectOnDelete and ObjectCanDelete are called on the server, not the client. All other callback methods are called on the client and behave as they do for an embedded database.

Semaphores

Most people think of a *semaphore* as a flag of some kind that carries a signal—the term is derived from the Greeks words for "sign" and "carry." Semaphores have long been used for communication at sea, and the concept has been well known for a long time in computer science as a data structure to synchronize processes. The idea is to schedule access to resources. db4o supports the concept of semaphores.

Semaphores in db4o were briefly introduced in Chapter 9. To recap, a db4o semaphore is a simple named flag that can be used to protect *critical sections* of code from being executed by more than one client or transaction at the same time. The first works of Dijkstra defined a critical section, and the number of processes or threads that are allowed to "use" or enter this section of code. Many languages have a keyword for this, including the lock and synchronized keywords in C# and Java, respectively. In db4o, the major difference from the classical definition is that the number of processes, or more accurately, transactions that can enter the exclusive code block is always limited to one.

■**Note** It is important to realize that db4o semaphores are not some mystical db4o container service but simply an abstract signal that you have to breathe life into. This means that it is your responsibility to define your semaphore and to make sure that all the clients you implement use this semaphore in the same way and don't break the rules you impose. In fact, you don't even have to use the db4o mechanism. There are many semaphore implementations in C# and Java (for example, java.util.concurrent.semaphore in the Java API), or you can even write your own. However, db4o offers some useful features with its own semaphore implementation: for example, in a client/server environment, which is where you would want to control concurrent access, semaphores are released automatically when a client disconnects. Furthermore, the server monitors the client connections and releases semaphores if a client cannot be detected any more.

One common use of semaphores is to enforce transaction isolation in a client/server environment, and this was illustrated in Chapter 9.

However, you can do a variety of other things with them. You can use semaphores to control access to any resource you like in db4o. For example, you can control client logins to a server by ensuring that only one client can log in with a particular username at one time, or by limiting the total number of clients that can log in at a time.

The latter use case is interesting, because it makes use of db4o's ability to release semaphores automatically and it shows that with a bit of ingenuity you can limit access to a number of clients that you choose, not just to one client.

Semaphore Example—Limiting Number of Clients

In the following example, a client gets access to the server through an instance of a class LoginManager (Listings 12-4 and 12-5) instead of directly calling OpenClient.

Listing 12-4. *The LoginManager Class in C#*

```
// C#
using com.db4o;

namespace com.db4o.dg2db4o.chapter12
{
    class LoginManager
    {
        string _host;
        int _port;
        static int MAXIMUM_USERS = 4;

        public LoginManager(String host, int port)
        {
            _host = host;
            _port = port;
        }

        public ObjectContainer Login(String username, String password)
        {
            ObjectContainer objectContainer;
            try
            {
                objectContainer = Db4o.OpenClient(_host, _port, username, password);
            }
            catch (System.IO.IOException e)
            {
                return null;
            }

            bool allowedToLogin = false;

            for (int i = 0; i < MAXIMUM_USERS; i++)
            {
                String semaphore = "login_limit_" + (i + 1);
                if (objectContainer.Ext().SetSemaphore(semaphore, 0))
                {
                    allowedToLogin = true;
                    Console.WriteLine("Logged in as " + username);
                    Console.WriteLine("Acquired semaphore " + semaphore);
                    break;
                }
            }
        }
    }
}
```

```
                if (!allowedToLogin)
                {
                    Console.WriteLine("Login not allowed for " + username + ": max
                        clients exceeded");
                    objectContainer.Close();
                    return null;
                }

                return objectContainer;
            }
        }
    }
```

Listing 12-5. *The LoginManager Class in Java*

```
// JAVA
package com.db4o.dg2db4o.chapter12;

import com.db4o.ObjectContainer;
import com.db4o.Db4o;
import java.io.IOException;

public class LoginManager {
    String _host;
    int _port;
    static final int MAXIMUM_USERS = 4;

    public LoginManager(String host, int port) {
        _host = host;
        _port = port;
    }

    public ObjectContainer login(String username, String password){

        ObjectContainer objectContainer;
        try {
            objectContainer = Db4o.openClient(_host, _port, username, password);
        } catch (IOException e) {
            return null;
        }

        boolean allowedToLogin = false;
```

```
    for (int i = 0; i < MAXIMUM_USERS; i++) {
        String semaphore = "login_limit_" + (i+1);
        if(objectContainer.ext().setSemaphore(semaphore, 0)){
            allowedToLogin = true;
            System.out.println("Logged in as " + username);
            System.out.println("Acquired semaphore " + semaphore);
            break;
        }
    }

    if(! allowedToLogin){
        System.out.println("Login not allowed for " + username + ": max clients
            exceeded");
        objectContainer.close();
        return null;
    }

    return objectContainer;
    }
}
```

Every time a `LoginManager` is asked to log in to a server, it first opens a client with `OpenClient`. If the connection and user details are correct, this should succeed and it opens an `ObjectContainer` as a client. Next, it tries to set a named semaphore. It does this in a `for` loop, and successively tries names from `login_limit_1` up to `login_limit_4` (as `MAX_USERS` is set to 4), breaking out of the loop as soon as it succeeds in setting a semaphore. If no other clients are connected, it should succeed in setting semaphore `login_limit_1`. If there is one other client connected, it should succeed in setting semaphore `login_limit_2`, and so on. If the maximum number of clients is already connected, it will fail to set `login_limit_4`, and will give up and close the `ObjectContainer` it opened initially and return `null`.

The following code tests the `LoginManager` class. It starts a server (on localhost) and grants access to five users. To simulate concurrent clients, the next section of code simply creates a set of `LoginManager` objects, and uses each one to try to log in to the server and obtain an `ObjectContainer` reference. Note that, as stated earlier, you must ensure that all your code obeys the rules you define: the `LoginManager` class only limits clients who use it to log in—it doesn't stop "rogue" clients that call `OpenClient` directly.

Note the sequence of events:

1. Server is started.

2. Four clients connect.

3. Fifth client tries to connect.

4. One connection is closed, and client 5 tries again—it should succeed now.

5. The server is closed, disconnecting all clients, and one of the clients reconnects.

```
// C#
// Start server
ObjectServer server = Db4o.OpenServer("c:/ch12.yap", 8732);
server.GrantAccess("user1", "password");
server.GrantAccess("user2", "password");
server.GrantAccess("user3", "password");
server.GrantAccess("user4", "password");
server.GrantAccess("user5", "password");

// Concurrent clients
Console.WriteLine("MAX 4 CLIENTS ALLOWED");
Console.WriteLine("----------------------");
Console.WriteLine("FIRST 4 CLIENTS CONNECT");

LoginManager loginManager1 = new LoginManager("localhost", 8732);
ObjectContainer client1 = loginManager1.Login("user1", "password");

LoginManager loginManager2 = new LoginManager("localhost", 8732);
ObjectContainer client2 = loginManager2.Login("user2", "password");

LoginManager loginManager3 = new LoginManager("localhost", 8732);
ObjectContainer client3 = loginManager3.Login("user3", "password");

LoginManager loginManager4 = new LoginManager("localhost", 8732);
ObjectContainer client4 = loginManager4.Login("user4", "password");

Console.WriteLine("-------------------------");
Console.WriteLine("CLIENT 5 TRIES TO CONNECT");
LoginManager loginManager5 = new LoginManager("localhost", 8732);
ObjectContainer client5 = loginManager5.Login("user5", "password");

Console.WriteLine("--------------------------------------");
Console.WriteLine("CLIENT 2 CLOSED THEN CLIENT 5 CONNECTS");
client2.Close();
client5 = loginManager5.Login("user5", "password");

Console.WriteLine("--------------------------------------");
Console.WriteLine("SERVER CLOSED THEN CLIENT 4 CONNECTS");
client1.Close();
client3.Close();
client4.Close();
client5.Close();
server.Close();
server = Db4o.OpenServer("c:/ch12.yap", 8732);
client4 = loginManager4.Login("user4", "password");

server.Close();
```

```java
// JAVA
// Start server
ObjectServer server = Db4o.openServer("c:/ch12.yap", 8732);
server.grantAccess("user1", "password");
server.grantAccess("user2", "password");
server.grantAccess("user3", "password");
server.grantAccess("user4", "password");
server.grantAccess("user5", "password");

// Concurrent clients
System.out.println("MAX 4 CLIENTS ALLOWED");
System.out.println("----------------------");
System.out.println("FIRST 4 CLIENTS CONNECT");

LoginManager loginManager1 = new LoginManager("localhost", 8732);
ObjectContainer client1 = loginManager1.login("user1", "password");

LoginManager loginManager2 = new LoginManager("localhost", 8732);
ObjectContainer client2 = loginManager2.login("user2", "password");

LoginManager loginManager3 = new LoginManager("localhost", 8732);
ObjectContainer client3 = loginManager3.login("user3", "password");

LoginManager loginManager4 = new LoginManager("localhost", 8732);
ObjectContainer client4 = loginManager4.login("user4", "password");

System.out.println("-------------------------");
System.out.println("CLIENT 5 TRIES TO CONNECT");
LoginManager loginManager5 = new LoginManager("localhost", 8732);
ObjectContainer client5 = loginManager5.login("user5", "password");

System.out.println("--------------------------------------");
System.out.println("CLIENT 2 CLOSED THEN CLIENT 5 CONNECTS");
client2.close();
client5 = loginManager5.login("user5", "password");

System.out.println("--------------------------------------");
System.out.println("SERVER CLOSED THEN CLIENT 4 CONNECTS");
client1.close();
client3.close();
client4.close();
client5.close();
server.close();
server = Db4o.openServer("c:/ch12.yap", 8732);
client4 = loginManager4.login("user4", "password");

server.close();
```

The output looks like the following. db4o messages are shown here in normal typeface, while output from the previous code is shown in bold.

```
[db4o 5.0.010    2006-02-09 01:00:53]
 Server listening on port: '8732'
MAX 4 CLIENTS ALLOWED
----------------------
FIRST 4 CLIENTS CONNECT
[db4o 5.0.010    2006-02-09 01:00:53]
 Client 'user1' connected.
Logged in as user1
Acquired semaphore login_limit_1
[db4o 5.0.010    2006-02-09 01:00:53]
 Client 'user2' connected.
Logged in as user2
Acquired semaphore login_limit_2
[db4o 5.0.010    2006-02-09 01:00:53]
 Client 'user3' connected.
Logged in as user3
Acquired semaphore login_limit_3
[db4o 5.0.010    2006-02-09 01:00:53]
 Client 'user4' connected.
Logged in as user4
Acquired semaphore login_limit_4
------------------------
CLIENT 5 TRIES TO CONNECT
[db4o 5.0.010    2006-02-09 01:00:53]
 Client 'user5' connected.
Login not allowed for user5: max clients exceeded
[db4o 5.0.010    2006-02-09 01:00:53]
 Connection closed by client 'user5'.
------------------------------------
CLIENT 2 CLOSED THEN CLIENT 5 CONNECTS
[db4o 5.0.010    2006-02-09 01:00:53]
 Connection closed by client 'user2'.
[db4o 5.0.010    2006-02-09 01:00:53]
 Client 'user5' connected.
Logged in as user5
Acquired semaphore login_limit_2
--------------------------------------
SERVER CLOSED THEN CLIENT 4 CONNECTS
[db4o 5.0.010    2006-02-09 01:00:53]
 'c:/ch12.yap' close request
[db4o 5.0.010    2006-02-09 01:00:53]
 'c:/ch12.yap' closed
[db4o 5.0.010    2006-02-09 01:00:53]
 Client 'user5' timed out and closed.
```

```
[db4o 5.0.010    2006-02-09 01:00:53]
 Client 'user3' timed out and closed.
[db4o 5.0.010    2006-02-09 01:00:53]
 Server listening on port: '8732'
[db4o 5.0.010    2006-02-09 01:00:53]
 Client 'user4' connected.
Logged in as user4
Acquired semaphore login_limit_1
```

Note that the first four clients acquire semaphores with names in numerical order. When client 2 closes, db4o automatically releases its semaphore login_limit_2, which can then be set by client 5. When the server restarts, all semaphores are released, so the first client to attempt to log in gets login_limit_1. Closing a client effectively logs the user out—the LoginManager class does not need a Logout method.

In conclusion, db4o semaphores are useful in client/server environments, where they can be used to lock objects or control access to other resources. db4o's own semaphore mechanism is simple, but offers an important advantage over other C# or Java semaphores that you could possibly use instead: db4o itself manages and checks the validity of its own semaphores.

Web Environments

Although db4o's main target is embedded applications, it can also be suitable for web applications. The following points indicate why db4o is a good choice for some web environments:

- db4o always runs in a thread-safe mode. Even if you call db4o from, for example, a Java servlet, which can and will be accessed by many threads, the transactional calls to the db4o core will be executed in a thread-safe manner.

- db4o is just a library you have to plug into your web application (for example in WEB-INF/lib in a J2EE application). You then just need to ensure that the server is started up and closed correctly.

- db4o again will save the objects as they are. You don't have to care about containers, mappings, data sources, and other complications. It suits the development style that is fostered by lightweight frameworks such as Spring. Nevertheless, even in EJB environments db4o can be used as a persistence layer for session beans.

To learn more about running db4o in a web environment, think about this: Why shouldn't we open a container the standard way by simply calling ObjectContainer webDb = Db4o.OpenFile("???"). Well, we would have some problems with this.

The first obvious issue is the path to the database file. This is important as the application may be deployed on different servers. This means that it is unwise to specify an absolute path within the file system. But what should the relative path look like?

The second problem is that we need to make the database available to all web pages in the application. How can you do this?

In Chapter 8 you learned that there are several modes for running db4o. The networking mode is probably not appropriate because you don't need "real" clients that are distributed over the network. You are more likely to have one application server, and all the clients are basically threads running on the same machine. This means that the embedded "server" mode may be suitable for this problem. The configuration is illustrated in Figure 12-2.

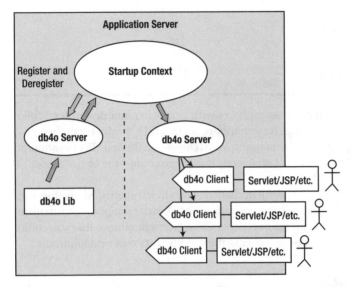

Figure 12-2. *Running db4o within an application server for web apps*

So, what you essentially need is a consistent way to start up the db4o server and to shut it down. The way you do this will depend on the application server you are using. Let's look at basic examples using Active Server Pages (ASP.NET) on Windows Internet Information Services (IIS) 6.0, and in a Java environment using JavaServer Pages (JSP)/servlets on a Tomcat application server. In other environments the same concepts will apply but the details will differ. A full description of the use of ASP.NET and JSP/servlets is beyond the scope of this book. If you need more background information on these technologies, we recommend some useful titles at the end of this book.

In both cases, the web application will display a form to allow the user to enter details about a person (name and age). Submitting the form will cause a Person object to be stored in a db4o database, and a further page allows the user to retrieve a list of the stored objects. The Person class is the one we have used in several places in this book, and is listed in Chapter 5.

ASP.NET Example

ASP.NET processes page requests using a set of extensible objects called the HTTP Pipeline. The extensibility lets you add support for db4o to an ASP.NET web application. An HTTP module is a .NET component that serves as a point of extensibility. HTTP modules implement the IHttpModule interface. Listing 12-6 shows an HTTP module, Db4oHttpModule, which provides ways for an ASP.NET application to start and stop db4o servers, and to make the database available to pages within the application. This code was kindly provided by Simone Busoli.

Listing 12-6. *The Db4oHttpModule Class in C# for ASP.NET*

```csharp
using System;
using System.Configuration;
using System.Web;
using com.db4o;

public class Db4oHttpModule : IHttpModule
{
    private static readonly string KEY_DB4O_FILE_NAME = "db4oFileName";
    private static readonly string KEY_DB4O_CLIENT = "db4oClient";
    private static ObjectServer objectServer = null;

    public void Init(HttpApplication application)
    {
        application.EndRequest += new EventHandler(Application_EndRequest);
    }

    private static ObjectServer Server
    {
        get
        {
            HttpContext context = HttpContext.Current;
            if (objectServer == null)
            {
                string yapFilePath =
                    context.Server.MapPath(ConfigurationSettings.
                    AppSettings[KEY_DB4O_FILE_NAME]);
                objectServer = Db4o.OpenServer(yapFilePath, 8732);
                OnServerOpened();
            }
            return objectServer;
        }
    }

    public static ObjectContainer Client
    {
        get
        {
            HttpContext context = HttpContext.Current;
            ObjectContainer objectClient =
                context.Items[KEY_DB4O_CLIENT] as ObjectContainer;
            if (objectClient == null)
            {
                objectClient = Server.OpenClient();
                context.Items[KEY_DB4O_CLIENT] = objectClient;
                OnClientOpened();
            }
```

```csharp
            return objectClient;
        }
    }

    private void Application_EndRequest(object sender, EventArgs e)
    {
        HttpApplication application = (HttpApplication)sender;
        HttpContext context = application.Context;

        ObjectContainer objectClient =
            context.Items[KEY_DB4O_CLIENT] as ObjectContainer;
        if (objectClient != null)
        {
            objectClient.Close();
            objectClient = null;
            context.Items[KEY_DB4O_CLIENT] = null;
            OnClientClosed();
        }
    }

    public void Dispose()
    {
        if (objectServer != null)
        {
            objectServer.Close();
            objectServer = null;
            OnServerClosed();
        }
    }

    public static string HashCodes
    {
        get { return "Server HashCode: " +
            Server.GetHashCode() + " Client HashCode: " + Client.GetHashCode();}
    }

    #region Events
    public delegate void ClientOpenedEventHandler(object sender, EventArgs e);
    private static ClientOpenedEventHandler _clientOpenedEventHandler = null;

    public event ClientOpenedEventHandler ClientOpened
    {
        add { _clientOpenedEventHandler += value; }
        remove { _clientOpenedEventHandler -= value; }
    }
```

```csharp
public delegate void ServerOpenedEventHandler(object sender, EventArgs e);
private static ServerOpenedEventHandler _serverOpenedEventHandler = null;

public event ServerOpenedEventHandler ServerOpened
{
    add { _serverOpenedEventHandler += value; }
    remove { _serverOpenedEventHandler -= value; }
}

public delegate void ClientClosedEventHandler(object sender, EventArgs e);
private static ClientClosedEventHandler _clientClosedEventHandler = null;

public event ClientClosedEventHandler ClientClosed
{
    add { _clientClosedEventHandler += value; }
    remove { _clientClosedEventHandler -= value; }
}

public delegate void ServerClosedEventHandler(object sender, EventArgs e);
private static ServerClosedEventHandler _serverClosedEventHandler = null;

public event ServerClosedEventHandler ServerClosed
{
    add { _serverClosedEventHandler += value; }
    remove { _serverClosedEventHandler -= value; }
}
#endregion

#region Event raising
protected static void OnClientClosed()
{
    if (_clientClosedEventHandler != null)
        _clientClosedEventHandler(typeof(Db4oHttpModule), null);
}

protected static void OnClientOpened()
{
    if (_clientOpenedEventHandler != null)
        _clientOpenedEventHandler(typeof(Db4oHttpModule), null);
}

protected static void OnServerOpened()
{
    if (_serverOpenedEventHandler != null)
        _serverOpenedEventHandler(typeof(Db4oHttpModule), null);
}
```

```
    protected static void OnServerClosed()
    {
        if (_serverClosedEventHandler != null)
            _serverClosedEventHandler(typeof(Db4oHttpModule), null);
    }
    #endregion
}
```

The methods that you should look primarily at here are the ones whose names are high-lighted in bold in the listing:

- The Server property, which returns a reference to the db4o server that will be used by the web application. Starts the server up if necessary.

- The Client property, which returns a reference to a client that will be shared by sessions in the application. Opens the client by connecting to the db4o server if it is not already open

- Application_EndRequest, which responds to an end request event by closing the client.

- Dispose, which disposes with resources at application shutdown by closing the db4o server.

Most of the remaining code in Db4oHttpModule is concerned with providing the capability within the HTTP Pipeline to execute code in response to events such as opening or closing the db4o server.

Configuration

The ASP.NET application needs to be configured to use the Db4oHttpModule class. This is done in the web.config file. This is an XML file that contains elements for various types of configuration. The web.config file for this example application is shown in Listing 12-7. The <httpModules> element allows you to specify the class and name of an HTTP module. The file shown also has an <appSettings> element, which stores the db4o database filename, in the web application root directory in this case. This information is used by the Server property in Db4oHttpModule.

■**Tip** In a real application you would probably have the Db4oHttpModule class in a specific namespace, for example: type="Db4oUtilities.Db4oHttpModule, Db4oUtilities", where the name after the comma represents the assembly name. An assembly is the basic logical unit of code in a .NET application.

Listing 12-7. *The web.config File*

```
<?xml version="1.0"?>
<configuration>
  <appSettings>
    <add key="db4oFileName" value="newwebdb.yap" />
  </appSettings>
```

```
  <system.web>
    <httpModules>
      <add type="Db4oHttpModule" name="Db4oHttpModule" />
    </httpModules>
  </system.web>
</configuration>
```

If you wish, you can add handlers for events defined in Db4oHttpModule in the file global.asax in the web application root directory, although we are not making use of this in our simple example. global.asax normally contains handlers for Application_Start and Application_End events. If you want to run some custom code when a client is opened, for example, the handler would look like this:

```
protected void Db4oHttpModule_OnClientOpened(Object sender, EventArgs e)
{
    // CUSTOM CODE GOES HERE
}
```

Using the Database in a Web Page

A reference to the client can be obtained from the HTTP module in any page in the application, using the Client property. Listing 12-8 shows a page Store.aspx, with a code-behind file Store.aspx.cs, which displays a data entry form. When the submit button is clicked, the Store_Object method is called. This method gets the client reference (the relevant line is highlighted in bold). A Person object is constructed using the data in the form, and the client stores it in the database.

Listing 12-8. *Data-Entry Form Store.aspx with Code-Behind Class Store.aspx.cs*

STORE.ASPX

```
<%@ Page Language="C#" AutoEventWireup="true" CodeFile="Store.aspx.cs"
    Inherits="Store" %>

<!DOCTYPE html PUBLIC "-//W3C//DTD XHTML 1.0 Transitional//EN"
    "http://www.w3.org/TR/xhtml1/DTD/xhtml1-transitional.dtd">
<html xmlns="http://www.w3.org/1999/xhtml">
<head runat="server">
    <title>Store Person</title>
</head>
<body>
    <form id="form1" runat="server">
        <div>
            <h1><asp:Label ID="Label1" runat="server"➥
                    Text="Store Person object"></asp:Label> </h1>
```

```
        <p><asp:Label ID="Label2" runat="server"➥
                Text="Name: "></asp:Label><asp:TextBox ID="TextBox1"
                runat="server"></asp:TextBox></p>
        <p><asp:Label ID="Label3" runat="server"➥
                Text="Age: "></asp:Label><asp:TextBox ID="TextBox2"
                runat="server"></asp:TextBox></p>
        <p><input type="button" value="store" onserverclick="Store_Object"➥
                id="Button1" runat="server"></p>
        <p><a href="/dg2db4oweb/Retrieve.aspx">Retrieve stored objects</a></p>
    </div>
  </form>
</body>
</html>
```

Store.aspx.cs

```csharp
using com.db4o;   // standard web/data namespace definitions omitted

public partial class Store : System.Web.UI.Page
{
    protected void Page_Load(object sender, EventArgs e){}

    protected void Store_Object(object sender, EventArgs e)
    {
        ObjectContainer db = Db4oHttpModule.Client;
        string name = TextBox1.Text;
        int age = Convert.ToInt32(TextBox2.Text);
        Person p1 = new Person(name,age);
        db.Set(p1);

        Label2.Visible = false;
        Label3.Visible = false;
        TextBox1.Visible = false;
        TextBox2.Visible = false;
        Button1.Visible = false;
        Label1.Text = "Person object stored";
    }
}
```

■**Tip** This example uses a client that is shared by all user sessions (known as the "shared transaction" mode). This can give high performance, since db4o needs to cache objects only once. You can also use "session transaction" mode, where each session opens a new client so that each user has a separate object cache. To change to the latter mode, you would need to make the Server property in Db4oHttpModule public, and use the following code to open a client in Store.aspx.cs: ObjectContainer db = Db4oHttpModule.Server.OpenClient();.

Viewing Data in a Web Page

The same approach is used in another page, Retrieve.aspx with code-behind class Retrieve.
aspx.cs, shown in Listing 12-9, to open another client on the same server and retrieve the data.
This example shows, in a very basic way, that a db4o ObjectSet can be bound as a DataSource
to an ASP.NET Web Forms control, a GridView in this case. The same is true for Windows Forms
controls too, by the way.

Listing 12-9. *Retrieve.aspx with Code-Behind Class Retrieve.aspx.cs*

Retrieve.aspx

```
<%@ Page Language="C#" AutoEventWireup="true"
    CodeFile="Retrieve.aspx.cs" Inherits="Retrieve" %>

<!DOCTYPE html PUBLIC "-//W3C//DTD XHTML 1.0 Transitional//EN"
    "http://www.w3.org/TR/xhtml1/DTD/xhtml1-transitional.dtd">
<html xmlns="http://www.w3.org/1999/xhtml">
<head runat="server">
    <title>Untitled Page</title>
</head>
<body>
    <form id="form1" runat="server">
        <div>
            <h1>Person objects retrieved</h1>
            <p><asp:GridView ID="GridView1" runat="server"></asp:GridView></p>
            <p><a href="/dg2db4oweb/Store.aspx">Store another object</a></p>
        </div>
    </form>
</body>
</html>
```

Retrieve.aspx.cs

```
using com.db4o;  // standard web/data namespace definitions omitted

public partial class Retrieve : System.Web.UI.Page
{
    protected void Page_Load(object sender, EventArgs e)
    {
        ObjectContainer db = Db4oHttpModule.Client;
        ObjectSet results = db.Get(new Person());
        GridView1.DataSource = results;
        GridView1.DataBind();

    }
}
```

The store and retrieve pages are shown in action in Figure 12-3.

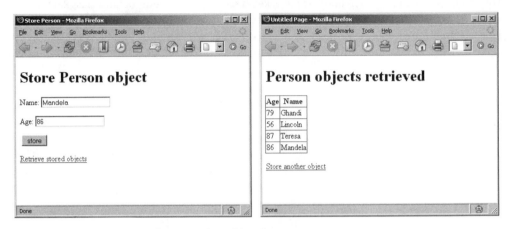

Figure 12-3. *ASP.NET example pages viewed in a browser*

ASP.NET COMPILATION

Dynamic ASP.NET compilation causes problems for db4o, as the assembly name assigned to classes in the web application changes each time you modify a class, if the class files are in the App_Code folder where Visual Studio encourages you to put classes which are not related to specific web pages. The result is that db4o will not be able to find previously stored objects as the new assembly name will not match the previous one. Full class names, which in .NET include the assembly name, are crucial for db4o.

You need to use the ASP.NET compiler, which can be run from the command line or accessed graphically through the Publish Web Site tool in Visual Studio 2005, to create an application with fixed assembly names. Alternatively, you can create another project which contains all the classes you need to store, and reference this project from your ASP.NET project. The free Visual Web Developer Express edition does not allow you to do either, and so is not currently suitable for developing ASP.NET applications with db4o. Version 5.3 of db4o will introduce a feature called Class Aliases, which is designed to help with .NET assembly name issues and should provide a solution for this problem.

JSP/Servlet Example

In a J2EE environment, the preferred place to start and stop the server is in a *context-listener* class. Each J2EE web application has its own *servlet context*, which is an object containing servlet information about the web application. Application events (such as server startup and shutdown, application deployment, and so on) provide notifications of a change in state of the servlet context. You can write event listener classes that respond to these changes in state, and deploy these listeners in the web application.

Setting Up a Servlet Context Listener

The example application described here includes a listener class, Db4oServletContextListener. This is not a db4o API class, but it is provided in the tutorial that is part of the db4o distribution.

The full example here builds on this to make a working web application. To run the example, you will need to create the Db4oServletContextListener class using the listing given in the db4o tutorial. The contextInitialized method of this class is called automatically by the application server (also referred to as the *servlet container*) when the web application is initialized. A db4o server is opened, and a reference to this server is stored as an attribute of the servlet context. This example was tested on a Tomcat 5.5 servlet container.

Every servlet inherits the getServletContext method from the GenericServlet class. This servletContext object allows any servlet to retrieve the server reference using the method getAttribute.

In order for this listener to work, it needs to be *registered* with the servlet container. This is done using an entry in the configuration file web.xml, which is located in the WEB-INF directory inside the web application's root directory. This simply tells the container that it should recognize Db4oServletContextListener as a listener class:

```
<listener>
    <listener-class>com.db4o.db2db4oweb.Db4oServletContextListener</listener-class>
</listener>
```

One more bit of configuration is needed. Note that the physical path to where the database file is located depends on the configuration of the application server, and is retrieved at runtime using the getRealPath method of the servlet context. The location of the database file within the web application is inside a directory called db in the WEB-INF directory. The actual database filename, dg2db4oweb.yap, is configured as a context parameter in web.xml—the advantage of this is that it can be reconfigured without recompiling any Java code.

```
<context-param>
    <param-name>db4oFileName</param-name>
    <param-value>dg2db4oweb.yap</param-value>
</context-param>
```

■**Caution** You need to make sure that the db4o JAR is available to your application server at runtime. If you are using Tomcat (tomcat.apache.org), for example, the JAR file can be placed in the web application's WEB-INF/lib directory.

Using the Database in a Servlet

A reference to the server can be obtained within any servlet from the servlet context using the key db4oserver. Listing 12-10 shows a servlet, StoreServlet, which gets the server reference and opens a client for that server. A Person object is constructed using values for name and age passed to the servlet in its HttpRequest, and the client stores it in the database. The values can be passed in the query string or from a form in a JSP. A suitable JSP would look exactly the same in the browser as the ASP.NET data entry form in Figure 12-3.

Listing 12-10. *The StoreServlet Class*

```java
package com.db4o.dg2db4oweb;

import com.db4o.*;   // standard servlet imports omitted

public class StoreServlet extends HttpServlet
{
    protected void processRequest(HttpServletRequest request,
        HttpServletResponse response)
        throws ServletException, IOException
    {
        response.setContentType("text/html;charset=UTF-8");
        PrintWriter out = response.getWriter();
        String name = request.getParameter("name");
        int age= Integer.parseInt(request.getParameter("age"));
        ServletContext context = getServletContext();
        ObjectServer server=(ObjectServer)context.getAttribute("db4oServer");
        ObjectContainer db = server.openClient();

        Person p1= new Person(name,age);
        db.set(p1);
        db.close();
        // output
        out.println("<html>");
        out.println("<head>");
        out.println("<title>Servlet StoreServlet</title>");
        out.println("</head>");
        out.println("<body>");
        out.println("<h1>Person object stored</h1>");
        out.println("<a href=\"/dg2db4oweb/RetrieveServlet\">
            Click here to retrieve</a>");
        out.println("</body>");
        out.println("</html>");
        out.close();
    }

    protected void doGet(HttpServletRequest request, HttpServletResponse response)
        throws ServletException, IOException
    {
        processRequest(request, response);
    }

    protected void doPost(HttpServletRequest request, HttpServletResponse response)
        throws ServletException, IOException
    {
        processRequest(request, response);
    }
}
```

Viewing Data

The same approach is used in another servlet, RetrieveServlet, shown in Listing 12-11, to open another client on the same server and retrieve and output the data.

Listing 12-11. *The RetrieveServlet Class*

```
package com.db4o.dg2db4oweb;

import com.db4o.*;  // standard servlet imports omitted

public class RetrieveServlet extends HttpServlet
{
    protected void processRequest(HttpServletRequest request,
        HttpServletResponse response)
        throws ServletException, IOException
    {
        response.setContentType("text/html;charset=UTF-8");
        PrintWriter out = response.getWriter();
        ServletContext context = getServletContext();
        ObjectServer server=(ObjectServer)context.getAttribute("db4oServer");
        ObjectContainer db = server.openClient();

        ObjectSet results = db.get(new Person());
        db.close();
        // output
        out.println("<html>");
        out.println("<head>");
        out.println("<title>Servlet RetrieveServlet</title>");
        out.println("</head>");
        out.println("<body>");
        out.println("<h1>Person objects retrieved</h1>");
        while (results.hasNext()){
            Person person = (Person)results.next();
            String name = person.getName();
            int age = person.getAge();
            out.println("<p>Name: " + name + "<br/>");
            out.println("Age: " + age + "</p>");
        }
        out.println("<a href=\"/dg2db4oweb/index.jsp\">Click
            here to store another Person</a>");
        out.println("</body>");
        out.println("</html>");
        out.close();
    }

// doGet and doPost methods same as in StoreServlet listing
}
```

The output from RetrieveServlet is shown in Figure 12-4.

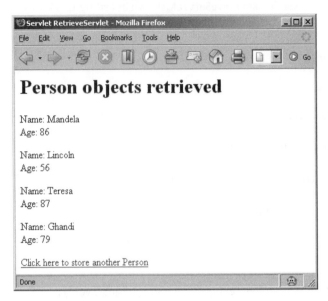

Figure 12-4. *Servlet example viewed in a browser*

One question might occur to you at this point: what if you want to access the db4o server from a class that is not a servlet? There's no problem in JSPs (JSPs are compiled to servlets, and the servletContext is available to a JSP through the built-in application object).

What about plain Java classes, though? It is quite common to use a framework where the persistence layer is contained in classes that are not servlets. In this case it should be possible for you to register and deregister the server object in an object of your own that is accessible from your Java code. This might, for example, be a singleton class that can hold the server object and provide it to clients when required and also to the application when it wants to close the server.

■**Caution** If db4o is used as a library shared between J2EE web applications, there could be classloader problems, which could result in classes not being found. If you deploy db4o as part of the web application, there should be no problem. If it is a shared library, db4o has to be configured to use the same classloader as the classes in your web application. You configure, as usual, before opening an ObjectContainer.

Web Environments: Wrapping Up

To sum up, whatever the details for a particular application server, the key point about using db4o in a web application is that you simply have to find out how to start up a db4o server and register it in some way, how to access the registered server, and how to shut down and deregister the server.

> **Note** Web application frameworks for Java are becoming popular—for example, Spring (www.springframework.org). There is an ongoing project that is developing db4o-Spring integration—see http://db4o-spring.dev.java.net for more information.

Working in a Mixed .NET/Java Environment

db4o stores native .NET or Java objects, but can you read objects stored from a .NET application into a Java application, or vice versa? The answer is a qualified "yes." If you have classes with the same names, and field names and types that are equivalent, you can work with the same database in a mixed .NET/Java environment.

db4o stores the full class name with each object in the database. Class names are crucial for db4o. Unless it can find objects in the database that have exactly the same name as the target object, it will not return any results from a query. The full name includes the .NET namespace or Java package name. Therefore, your .NET and Java applications must have matching namespace/package names. Even then, though, there is one complication, as .NET and Java classes are named slightly differently. In Java, the full name is just

```
package_name.class_name
```

For example:

```
com.db4o.dg2db4o.chapter12.Person
```

However, in .NET, classes also have the name of the assembly that they belong to appended to the name, like this:

```
namespace_name.class_name, assembly_name
```

For example:

```
com.db4o.db2db4o.chapter12.Person, dg2db4o
```

This assumes the .NET Person class is in an assembly called dg2db4o.

> **Note** A .NET assembly is a logical unit of code that can contain one or more files. It is the basic building block of a .NET application. By default, compiling .NET code generates an assembly that is an EXE file or a DLL.

The result is that a Java db4o application will not recognize .NET objects because it cannot match the stored class name to any classes in the application, and vice versa. It's not too difficult to get around this, though. It is fairly straightforward to check the names of the stored classes in the database when you first access it. If the current stored names match your environment (the assembly name is present for .NET, but not present for Java), then you can query the database and retrieve objects. If the stored names and environment don't match, you can change the names.

Listing 12-12 shows a very simple C# application, MixedExample, which checks the stored class names, found by calling db.Ext().StoredClasses(), where db is the ObjectContainer. If any stored class exists in the namespace specified in the call to ConvertClassNames, and does not have a comma in its name, then the specified assembly name is appended to make it .NET compatible (the application must be in an assembly with that name: in Visual Studio the default assembly name is usually the same as the project name). The application then reads all instances of the Person class and allows the user to add new Person objects to the database. The Person class is the one we have used in several places in this book, and is listed in Chapter 5.

Listing 12-12. *The MixedExample Class in C#*

```
//C#
using System;
using com.db4o;
using com.db4o.ext;

namespace com.db4o.dg2db4o.chapter12
{
    class MixedExample
    {
        private string DBFILENAME = "c:/mixed.yap";

        public static void Main(String[] args)
        {
            MixedExample mixed = new MixedExample();
            mixed.ConvertClassNames("com.db4o.dg2db4o.chapter12", "dg2db4o");
            mixed.ReadAll();
            mixed.AddData();
            mixed.ReadAll();
            Console.WriteLine("--------------");
            Console.WriteLine("Ending program");
            Console.ReadLine();

        }

        public void ReadAll()
        {
            Console.WriteLine("Reading database in .NET");
            ObjectContainer db = Db4o.OpenFile(DBFILENAME);
            ObjectSet results = db.Get(new Person());
            while (results.HasNext())
            {
                Console.WriteLine(results.Next());
            }
            db.Close();
        }
```

```csharp
public void AddData()
{
    bool stop = false;
    Console.WriteLine("Adding new data in .NET");
    ObjectContainer db = Db4o.OpenFile(DBFILENAME);

    while (!stop)
    {
        Console.WriteLine("Please enter a name: ");
        String name = Console.ReadLine();
        if (name.Equals("stop"))
            break;
        Console.WriteLine("Please enter an age: ");
        int age = Convert.ToInt32(Console.ReadLine());
        Person p = new Person(name, age);
        db.Set(p);
    }
    db.Close();
}

public void ConvertClassNames(string classNamespace, string assembly)
{
    Console.WriteLine("Checking class names in .NET");
    ObjectContainer db = Db4o.OpenFile(DBFILENAME);
    // get stored classes as an array
    StoredClass[] classes = db.Ext().StoredClasses();
    // check each class name and convert if necessary
    for (int i = 0; i < classes.Length; i++)
    {
        StoredClass storedClass = classes[i];
        String name = storedClass.GetName();
        String newName = null;
        int pos = name.IndexOf(",");
        // if there is no comma in the name then it's not a .NET name
        if (pos == -1)
        {
            pos = name.IndexOf(classNamespace);
            // only convert if it's in the specified namespace
            if (pos == 0)
            {
                newName = name + ", " + assembly;  // add assembly name
                storedClass.Rename(newName);
                Console.WriteLine("Renaming " + name + " to " + newName);
            }
        }
    }
}
```

```
            db.Close();
        }
    }
}
```

Listing 12-13 shows the equivalent Java application, again as a class called MixedExample. The main difference from the C# version is that the name needs to be converted if it *does* include a comma. The conversion is simple: the comma and everything after it is removed to make the name Java compatible. In C#, we needed to specify a namespace and the relevant assembly name for that namespace: in the Java version we don't need to do this, as we are simply stripping off all assembly names.

Listing 12-13. *The MixedExample Class in Java*

```
// JAVA
package com.db4o.dg2db4o.chapter12;

import com.db4o.*;
import com.db4o.ext.*;
import java.util.Scanner;

public class MixedExample {
    private final String DBFILENAME = "c:/mixed.yap";

    public static void main(String[] args){
        MixedExample mixed = new MixedExample();
        mixed.convertClassNames();
        mixed.readAll();
        mixed.addData();
        mixed.readAll();
    }

    public void readAll() {
        System.out.println("Reading database in Java");
        ObjectContainer db = Db4o.openFile(DBFILENAME);
        ObjectSet results = db.get(new Person());
        while (results.hasNext()) {
            System.out.println(results.next());
        }
        db.close();
    }

    public void addData() {
        boolean stop = false;
        System.out.println("Adding new data in Java");
        ObjectContainer db = Db4o.openFile(DBFILENAME);
        Scanner sc = new Scanner(System.in);
```

```java
        while (!stop) {
            System.out.print("\nEnter the developer's name and age
                (e.g. 'Tom 44'): ");
            String name = sc.next();
            if(name.equals("stop"))
                stop = true;
            else {
                db.set(new Person(name, sc.nextInt()));
                db.commit();
            };
        }
        db.close();
    }

    public void convertClassNames() {
        System.out.println("Checking class names in Java");
        ObjectContainer db = Db4o.openFile(DBFILENAME);
        // get stored classes as an array
        StoredClass[] classes = db.ext().storedClasses();
        // check each class name and convert if necessary
        for (int i = 0; i < classes.length; i++) {
            StoredClass storedClass = classes[i];
            String name = storedClass.getName();
            String newName = null;
            int pos = name.indexOf(",");
            // simply strip off anything after a comma
            if(pos > 0){
                newName = name.substring(0, pos);
                storedClass.rename(newName);
                System.out.println("Renaming " + name + " to " + newName);
            }
        }
        db.close();
    }
}
```

Let's look at the output from a test run, which will show the same database being read and updated from Java and C#. The first part of the test creates a new database in Java and adds two objects. No conversions are necessary because there are no objects in the database initially.

```
Checking class names in Java
Reading database in Java
Adding new data in Java
Enter the developer's name and age (e.g. 'Tom 44'):
Tom
44
```

```
Enter the developer's name and age (e.g. 'Tom 44'):
Bill
32
Enter the developer's name and age (e.g. 'Tom 44'):
stop
Reading database in Java
[Bill;32]
[Tom;44]
```

The next part of the test opens the same database file in C#. It needs to convert the name of the Person class, and once it has, we can read the existing data and add two more objects.

```
Checking class names in .NET
Renaming com.db4o.dg2db4o.chapter12.to com.db4o.dg2db4o.chapter12.Person, dg2db4o
Reading database in .NET
[Bill;32]
[Tom;44]
Adding new data in .NET
Please enter a name:
Joe
Please enter an age:
90
Please enter a name:
Eve
Please enter an age:
21
Please enter a name:
stop
Reading database in .NET
[Joe;90]
[Bill;32]
[Tom;44]
[Eve;21]
--------------
Ending program
```

Finally, the database file is opened in Java again, and this time conversions are needed. The Person class is converted, and so are some internal db4o classes. All the data added in both Java and C# is read, and new data can be added.

```
Checking class names in Java
Renaming com.db4o.dg2db4o.chapter12.Person, dg2db4o to ➥
    com.db4o.dg2db4o.chapter12.Person
Renaming com.db4o.MetaField, db4o to com.db4o.MetaField
Renaming com.db4o.MetaClass, db4o to com.db4o.MetaClass
```

```
Renaming com.db4o.StaticField, db4o to com.db4o.StaticField
Renaming com.db4o.StaticClass, db4o to com.db4o.StaticClass
Reading database in Java
[Joe;90]
[Bill;32]
[Tom;44]
[Eve;21]
Adding new data in Java
Enter the developer's name and age (e.g. 'Tom 44'):
Sue
29
Enter the developer's name and age (e.g. 'Tom 44'): Reading database in Java
Stop
Reading database in Java
[Joe;90]
[Bill;32]
[Tom;44]
[Eve;21]
[Sue;29]
```

■**Tip** If you open the database file in the ObjectManager, you will see that the class names are in the format used by either .NET or Java, depending on which platform the file was most recently opened. Object IDs are not changed during the conversion.

Caveats

There are a couple of issues that you should take into account if you are thinking of using db4o in a mixed environment. First, the conversion process makes a significant change to the database schema so that one type of application can read the data. Concurrent access by .NET and Java clients is not likely to be reliable.

Second, converting class names is only helpful if the same namespaces and packages are available in .NET and Java. This is the case for the namespace in the example, and also for db4o API classes (which in .NET are in the assembly db4o). However, other classes, such as collection classes and dates, are completely different in the two environments. You can, however, make collections convertible if you use the db4o collections classes, which are in the com.db4o.types namespace. These are database-aware collections, which can be useful, but they introduce a dependency on db4o in your entity classes. db4o collections are described in Chapter 7. To ensure compatibility for db4o API class names in C#, you need to add a further call to ConvertClassNames:

```
mixed.ConvertClassNames("com.db4o", "db4o");    // C#
```

■**Note** Look out for the Class Aliases feature to be introduced in version 5.3 of db4o. This feature should simplify working in a mixed environment.

Schema Evolution

Schema evolution in relational databases is very much an active research area. It is also referred to as database refactoring. The idea is that schema changes may occur in every project lifetime. As schema changes are always a big obstacle, the developers should be given as much support as possible to achieve the task. In object-oriented systems that rely on relational databases, a schema change can be particularly awkward, because all object/relational (O/R) mappings must be changed, which is difficult if the environment is not highly automated.

■Tip If you are interested in further reading on RDBMS schema refactoring, take a look at Scott Ambler's recent book on this topic,[1] and especially the catalog that is included there. This catalog gives you a very detailed listing of possible refactorings for a relational database.

Schema refactoring for OODBMSs is quite different, and a lot easier because in the RDBMS world you have two items: the class and the table. In OODBMSs you just have one: the class. Thus you only have to consider changes in the class. This comparison is illustrated in Figure 12-5. Of course, the disadvantage is that you cannot have different classes that might evolve but still map onto a stable (relational) data model.

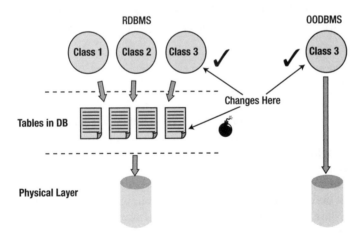

Figure 12-5. *Schema changes in RDBMS and OODBMS*

The refactoring or schema evolution scenario in db4o is as follows: you have your project already running, with a working database. Suddenly you realize the need to change one of your persistent classes. How can db4o help you in this case?

---

1. *Refactoring Databases: Evolutionary Database Design,* by Scott W. Ambler (Addison-Wesley 2006)

Common Refactoring Scenarios

Let's look at what sort of things could change in your class as your application evolves:

Changes to the interface that a class implements: This means that the methods that have to be implemented change their signature. Of course, this usually has little effect on data storage because only the "data," i.e. the attributes, will be stored. Things might be different with static fields that come from the interface. OODBMS vendors handle this issue differently. As described in Chapter 7, db4o does not store static fields.

Removing a field: You might decide to delete a field in your class. An example would be an Address class with streetFirstLine and streetSecondLine fields. If you delete the latter field from the class, and store more new Address objects in the database, then db4o will store the new object automatically in the new format. Old objects will not be changed. And if you run queries that return old Address objects, you receive the results as instances of the new Address class. The old field streetSecondLine is simply ignored.

Adding a field: Adding a field is quite similar to deleting a field. db4o simply works with the new class. Any queries that return the old class will have the new field set to zero or null.

Changing the field type: Imagine you have a product amount that is int and you wish to change this to long. db4o will then create this as a new field. The old field will still be present in the database but is hidden from queries. If you "undo" this schema refactoring and switch to the old version, the values will still be there. The fact that db4o creates and adds a complete new field in the database means that any type changes for the field can be handled. If you had a field named length of the type double and you change this to be a string, then you can continue to work with the new definition without any trouble. But of course if you have old double values that should continue to be used in the new class structure as strings, then you have to write a few lines of code that migrate this data.

Renaming a field: If you want to rename a field and you simply change it in your class, db4o assumes the old field should be deleted and a new inserted. You can manage this change explicitly with a call similar to this:

```csharp
// C#
Db4o.Configure().ObjectClass(typeof(MyClass).
    objectField("oldField").rename("newField");
```

```java
// JAVA
Db4o.configure().objectClass("MyClass.class").
    objectField("oldField").rename("newField");
```

After this command the field oldField in the database will be renamed for all objects.

Renaming a class: To rename the class for all objects in the database simply use:

```csharp
// C#
Db4o.Configure().ObjectClass(typeof(MyClass).
    rename("NewClass");
```

```
// JAVA
Db4o.configure().objectClass("Mypackage.MyClass").
    rename("NewPackage.NewClass)
```

There are more refactorings that are not yet supported by db4o, although db4o is working on this area. It is possible to implement tools that perform these operations (for example, with a transfer class):

Merging fields: Two fields from the same class should be merged. The common example is the string `firstname` and string `lastname` fields in classes representing people—these could be merged to a single field `name`.

Splitting a field: This is the reverse of the previous operation: for example, a single `name` field is split into fields named `firstname` and `lastname`.

Moving a field: This involves moving a field from class A to class B.

Merging and splitting fields can also occur between different classes. A helper program would use a transfer class to copy all the unchanged fields to the transfer class and perform the calculations needed to achieve the required merge, split, or move operations. A second helper program would then be started with the new class, which gets all the fields copied from the transfer class.

■**Caution** In the previous list of refactoring scenarios, we mentioned that renaming a field or changing the type creates a completely new field and hides the old one. If you defragment the database, these old fields will be swept away. All the values they had will be lost.

Inheritance Evolution

Finally, there is one last important refactoring: the evolution of the inheritance structure. db4objects, Inc. is developing tools to change any inheritance structure that occurs, including deletions from, insertions into, or modifications of the inheritance structure.

For example, consider a very difficult case: an inheritance tree

A ➤ C ➤ B ➤ M ➤ N ➤ X ➤ Y

changes to

A ➤ K ➤ C ➤ B ➤ Y ➤ X ➤ M

This means that class A is still the root, and all others are subclasses of A and of the classes before them in the tree. However, the following changes have occurred:

- Classes have changed their position in the tree; for example, X ➤ Y has changed to Y ➤ X (this kind of change is very rare).

- A class has been deleted; N ➤ X has become just X.

- A new classes has been inserted; A ➤ C has changed to A ➤ K ➤ C.

There already are refactoring tools for performing this change if the objects are plain or have no references in the database from other objects. These tools will create a typeless transfer database (where you switch your classpath manually), or they will load the old and the new classpath dynamically to perform your class inheritance changes. db4objects, Inc. can support you if you have this particular problem, directly or through the community forums.

Pluggable File I/O

db4o was redesigned in version 4 to direct all file input/output (I/O) through a *file adapter*. A file adapter is an object that controls exactly how I/O operations on the database are executed. File adapters are *pluggable*, which means you can choose which adapter to use. This allows you to use special I/O implementations to meet specific requirements; for example, to maximize performance, to provide encryption, for read-after-write checks, and for mirrored write. You can use adapters that are provided or you can, if you wish, write your own custom adapters.

The Standard Adapter

db4o initially is provided with a standard adapter called RandomAccessFileAdapter. This file adapter writes and reads all the requests from the db4o core to a file on the disk that you specify when opening the ObjectContainer or the server. If you look at the source code, you can find a line in com.db4o.Config4Impl that represents a part of db4o's settings:

```
IoAdapter i_ioAdapter = new RandomAccessFileAdapter();
```

The basic component of pluggable I/O is the abstract class IOAdapter, which is partially listed here:

```
// C#
namespace com.db4o.io
{
    public abstract class IoAdapter
    {
        private int _blockSize;
        ... // several methods concerning the block size
        ... // methods like copy, exists, sync, etc.
        public abstract void Close();
        public abstract com.db4o.io.IoAdapter Open(string path, bool lockFile, long
            initialLength);
        public abstract int Read(byte[] bytes, int length);
        public abstract void Seek(long pos);
        public abstract void Write(byte[] buffer, int length);
        ... // and some more
    }
}
```

```java
// JAVA
package com.db4o.io;

public abstract class IoAdapter {
    private int _blockSize;
    ... // several methods concerning the block size
    ... // methods like copy, exists, sync, etc.
    public abstract void close() throws IOException;
    public abstract IoAdapter open(String path, boolean lockFile, long initialLength)
        throws IOException;
    public abstract void seek(long pos) throws IOException;
    public abstract int read(byte[] bytes, int length) throws IOException;
    public abstract void write(byte[] buffer, int length) throws IOException;
    ... // and some more
}
```

This class is the basis of all file I/O. You can look at the source code of this file, then have a look at the RandomAccessFileAdapter class that extends the IoAdapter. This is the standard implementation as mentioned earlier. Taking one example method, you will see that the RandomAccessFileAdapter class overwrites the write(byte[] buffer) method like this:

```csharp
// C#
public override void Write(byte[] buffer, int length)
{
    _delegate.Write(buffer, 0, length);
}
```

```java
// JAVA
public void write(byte[] buffer, int length) throws IOException {
    _delegate.write(buffer, 0, length);
}
```

What's happening here? db4o delegates the call to a delegate class, which implements its own Write(buffer, 0, length) method.

The delegate used by RandomAccessFileAdapter for Java is an instance of java.io. RandomAccessFile. This means that the RandomAccessFileAdapter basically redirects to the standard Java I/O. The .NET version eventually redirects to System.IO, via the class j4o.io. RandomAccessFile, which is included with db4o. There are some quirks for other operating systems like Symbian OS that we will not discuss here.

Alternative Adapters

The general idea is that you should be able to handle the I/O stream however you like by changing the I/O adapter. Besides changing the type of I/O stream you use, you might want to redirect the I/O stream to another location. This could be a shadowing application where you write two *.yap files in order to have a second equivalent database. This is just one idea—more ideas may come to you the longer you work with db4o.

In the next section we will look at encryption, which is an important application of pluggable I/O. Here, we illustrate using the adapters with the example of MemoryIoAdapter. This adapter allows db4o to run in an in-memory mode. Many databases, HSQLDB for example, have an in-memory mode that provides incredibly high performance, albeit with no permanent storage.

The following code configures the use of this adapter. It illustrates the general approach: a call to the Io method of the database Configuration object. As usual, configuration is done before opening the ObjectContainer.

```csharp
// C#
Db4o.Configure().Io(new MemoryIoAdapter());
ObjectContainer db = Db4o.OpenFile("C:/mem.yap"); // Or any string as name
db.Set(new Person());
db.Close();
```

```java
// JAVA
Db4o.configure().io(new MemoryIoAdapter());
ObjectContainer db = Db4o.openFile("C:/mem.yap"); // Or any string as name
db.set(new Person());
db.close();
```

If you run this example, you will see that no file C:/mem.yap is created (so actually you can use any string you like). The name string is just used to put the actual MemoryIoAdapter into a hashtable. db4o defines its own hashtable class, Hashtable4, which can resize dynamically. The write method of MemoryIoAdapter actually calculates the position where it should write the bytes it is given in memory and does an array copy.

To sum up: the db4o pluggable file I/O principle easily allows changes of the I/O mechanism. Figure 12-6 shows that db4o runs with a RandomAccessFileAdapter by default. However, you can exchange these with the MemoryIoAdapter or the XteaEncryptionFileAdapter (described in the next section), or you can invent more adapters quite easily (such as a shadowing adapter) to address any specific needs you have.

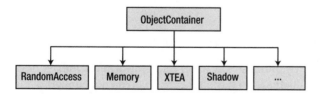

Figure 12-6. *Pluggable file I/O options*

Encryption

Since its early versions, db4o has included a simple encryption mechanism for database files, which will be described in the next section. With version 5.1 a stronger encryption mechanism was introduced. Both encryption mechanisms cover the encryption of the database file only. This means that the communication between a client and a server is not yet secured, as indicated in Figure 12-7.

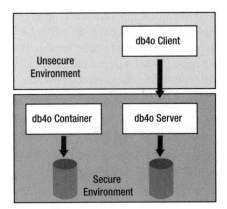

Figure 12-7. *Encryption in db4o*

The main purpose of db4o encryption is to secure the file I/O and to encrypt the database itself. In practice, users find it useful to transfer databases—meaning one or many *.yap files— via the Internet. The encryption methods used by db4o are described here, and we also show how you can integrate even stronger security.

Simple Encryption

The simple db4o encryption is a very unsecure encryption, actually not much stronger than a simple Caesar cipher, although a little trickier. The intention is simply to prevent anyone from opening the database file in a hex editor and being able to view content right away. To enable this encryption, you call the following methods:

```
// C#
Db4o.Configure().Encrypt(true);
Db4o.Configure().Password("yourEncryptionPasswordHere");
```

```
// JAVA
Db4o.configure().encrypt(true);
Db4o.configure().password("yourEncryptionPasswordHere");
```

Encryption must be enabled in exactly the same way when you create a new database *and* when you access an existing encrypted database. In the latter case, if you do not configure encryption, or if you supply the wrong password, the database cannot be opened and db4o will give an error message. As with other configurations in db4o, you call the configuration methods before opening the `ObjectContainer`.

Strong Encryption

The stronger encryption method included since version 5.1 uses the pluggable file I/O feature, described in the preceding section, which can be configured to integrate any encryption you need.

As a basic implementation, and to provide an example of how to create an encrypting adapter, db4o decided to integrate the eXtended Tiny Encryption Algorithm (XTEA) encryption algorithm, a public domain block cipher.[2] The advantage of this algorithm is that it is tiny and very fast. In fact, you will only see an average 15 percent performance decrease if you run db4o with XTEA at the recommended 32-cycle mode. In this mode, the encryption is at least as secure as DES or IDEA.

So, if you are using db4o version 5.1 or higher, you have several possible ways to enable encryption. A class XTeaEncryptionFileAdapter is included (it's in the com.db4o.io.crypt namespace/package). The following code shows how to configure a database to use it. This is simply a case of specifying the appropriate I/O adapter class:

```
Db4o.Configure().Io(new XTeaEncryptionFileAdapter("password")); // C#
```

```
Db4o.configure().io(new XTeaEncryptionFileAdapter("password")); // JAVA
```

Again, encryption needs to be configured in exactly the same way when you create a new database and when you access an existing encrypted database. You can use any password you like. There are no restrictions on the password, although if you pass an empty string an illegal parameter, an exception will be thrown. Even if you pass one space character, the password will be converted to a 128-bit field using an MD5 hash.

As you might imagine, XTeaEncryptionFileAdapter acts as a wrapper that encrypts data and then calls the standard I/O adapter to store the encrypted data. If you open an ObjectContainer after configuring this wrapper and store some objects, then everything is encrypted in the file.

There are a number of ways to use this adapter. The next example shows that you can pass it an iteration parameter:

```
// C#
Db4o.configure ().io(new XTeaEncryptionFileAdapter("password", XTEA.ITERATIONS16));
```

```
// JAVA
Db4o.configure ().io(new XTeaEncryptionFileAdapter("password", XTEA.ITERATIONS16));
```

The iteration parameter defines the number of cycles that XTEA uses to "shake" the input to make it harder to obtain the original. This is also well known from algorithms like DES, which operates in 16 rounds by default. XTEA uses two rounds per cycle. When using XTEA in db4o, you can choose along the values 8, 16, 32, and 64 (you should use the constants XTEA.ITERATIONS8, XTEA.ITERATIONS16, XTEA.ITERATIONS32, and XTEA.ITERATIONS64, which are defined in the IterationSpec class). Other values (like 24) are not allowed and will lead to wrong results because of wrong offsets. If you choose a small number of rounds, the encryption will be faster than the standard 32 rounds, which is the default but, of course, a little less secure (although still hard to crack). And similarly, if you decide to choose even higher security with 64 rounds, the database file will have the highest level of security, but db4o will be about 20 percent slower compared to its performance with no encryption.

---

2. XTEA was invented in 1997 by Roger Needham and David Wheeler. XTEA operates on a fixed block length using 64-bit blocks for the data and a 128-bit key.

Finally, you can use db4o's encryption together with your own I/O adapter. If you have created an adapter called `MyIoAdapter`, which might implement one of the ideas suggested in the previous section, you can wrap it with an encryption adapter (this is an example of the well-known decorator pattern[3]):

// C#
```
Db4o.Configure().Io(new XTeaEncryptionFileAdapter(new MyIoAdapter(),"password"));
```

// JAVA
```
Db4o.configure().io(new XTeaEncryptionFileAdapter(new MyIoAdapter(),"password"));
```

■**Note** As you might guess, your password is important once you have written encrypted data to the database. If you lose the password, your data is likely to be lost. There is no way to change the password on the file—it is part of the file. The only way to change or remove the password is to write a new program that reads all your data with the old password and writes the data to another file with a new password or no password.

---

db4objects, Inc. encourages you to implement new encryption algorithms and new file adapters, and to share these with the community.

To integrate new encryption algorithms you simply do the following:

1. Read the `com.db4o.io.RandomAccessFileAdapter` carefully and find the constructor, the parameters, and the read and write methods.

2. Write your own encryption class that implements the `IOAdapter` interface. It should probably delegate raw file I/O to another adapter.

3. Implement your `read` and `write` methods in which you perform your tasks. Then, call the original read and write methods.

4. Plug in your adapter by using `Db4o.configure().io(new MyEncryptionAdapter())`.

In fact, step 3 is a little tricky as db4o writes changes to the disk in small amounts. This means you have to do a little alignment to always encrypt a fixed block length that is small enough for db4o but large enough for your algorithm. Trace the `seek` methods and the `length` parameter in the `RandomAccessFileAdapter` to get a feeling for what is happening there.

The Generic Reflector

In version 4.5, the `reflect`, `generic` and `jdk` namespaces and packages were added to db4o. The basic idea was a little like the DynaBeans[4] introspection utilities from Jakarta Commons: the purpose is to deal with situations where you need classes that are not known at compile

---

3. *Design Patterns: Elements of Reusable Object-Oriented Software* by Erich Gamma, Richard Helm, Ralph Johnson, John Vlissides (Addison-Wesley, 1995)
4. `http://struts.apache.org/struts-action/userGuide/preface.html`

time. DynaBeans have been used in the Struts Framework to capture form information, which is then handed over to be transformed into model data.

db4o has a similar requirement: what if you send to a customer a db4o full of valuable data, and the customer can't read the data because he doesn't have the original classes? RDBMSs seem to have an advantage here because the data itself is neutral and unbound. db4o might have a disadvantage, because the data is tied to the class. Thus, no class, no data!

But since version 4.5 this has changed. Now db4o can handle stored objects as classes without knowing their "real" classes, using *generic reflection*. One good example that you have seen is the ObjectManager graphical database browser, described in Chapter 5. We mentioned in that chapter that the ObjectManager can run in two modes: in one mode it "knows" the classes in the database because you provided them (File ➤ Preferences ➤ Add directory (or Add jar/zip file)). However, the ObjectManager can also work if the classes are not known. This is indicated by a (G) beside the objects, which stands for *Generic Class*.

Many commercial OO databases can read the information from the database file, but usually they add a lot of meta-information about the class. db4o is a little different here because there is essentially no "magic" meta-information in the database. db4o simply reads from the database and builds up generic objects.

Generic reflection has similar methods to normal Java reflection or the C# assembly methods. A class obtained by reflection implements the ReflectClass interface. If you retrieved a class ReflectClass myClass, then you are able to apply the well-known reflection operations:

```
// C#
ReflectField[] fields myClass.GetDeclaredFields() // retrieve all fields
```

```
// JAVA
ReflectField[] fields myClass.getDeclaredFields() // retrieve all fields
```

This operation gives an array containing the fields of the class, and you can iterate over them, accessing each field with a variable (i):

```
// C#
String fieldName = fields[i].GetName(); // The name of the field
ReflectClass fieldClass = fields[i].GetType(); // The type of the field
fields[i].SetAccessible(); // Grant access to private members
// and more methods available
```

```
// JAVA
String fieldName = fields[i].getName(); // The name of the field
ReflectClass fieldClass = fields[i].getType(); // The type of the field
fields[i].setAccessible(); // Grant access to private members
// and more methods available
```

Of course, ReflectClass also has well-known methods such as GetName, GetSuperclass, and many more.

■**Caution** At the time of this writing, the generic reflector packages are in the beta state, not completely tested and documented. So if you have an application area where you might need help with the generic reflector, you should ask db4objects, Inc. for assistance in the community forums.

A Look into the Future

It's not always possible to predict the future, but we would like to suggest some possible features that we would like to see in db4o. It is, of course, entirely db4objects's decision as to whether or not, or when, they implement any of these features. The company responds to the demands of its customers—so tell them what you would like to be included in future versions of db4o.

- **Native Queries**: As you have seen in Chapter 6, native queries are powerful and fun, but nothing is perfect. Native Queries has the "disadvantage" that C# or Java are not languages that are designed for database queries. You might miss some well-known SQL functions that currently you have to implement but that could possibly be integrated into db4o. Typical functions are the aggregate functions like SUM, AVG, and COUNT.

- **Transparent activation**: In Chapter 7 you learned about activation when reading or updating objects. On the one hand, this is a very powerful feature because if you control the activation level, you can strongly control performance. Deep objects you don't want to load will simply not be loaded. On the other hand, if you don't care about performance and always wish to work with the complete deep objects, then you might get irritated by the activation you have to perform. And of course activation by hand can be error prone because we humans make mistakes (we might forget the level or configure the wrong level). As a result, users might wish to work in a mode where objects are completely activated when retrieved or accessed. And updates might always be "complete and deep." So, in the future the user might be able to determine the mode to work in.

- **Client/server mode**: Although working in client/server mode is not currently the primary application area, this mode could be improved to widen the scope of db4o. For instance, there could be connection management that is visible to the user; clients might access the server and read objects without having the real classes at hand (generic reflection is required here); and many more features from the RDBMS world, such as easily configurable object locking and dirty reads.

- **Performance**: The generation of indexes using different types might be improved. Techniques such as a caching mode and faster and better support of collections would also be quite useful.

Of course, we could wish for much more, and the community forums are full of "wants," such as support for different languages (Ruby, Python, Perl, etc.). But as you would expect, features have to be prioritized due to "real" industrial needs. It's well worth keeping track of the latest developments by subscribing to the db4objects newsletter and looking at the latest release notes on the website.

Summary

In this chapter we concluded our hands-on tour of the capabilities of db4o by looking at some issues that will be of particular interest to advanced users. At the end of Part II, you should now be familiar with the techniques you need to get the best from db4o, including simple object storage, querying, client/server operation, configuration, replication, as well as the advanced issues described in this chapter. Part III looks at db4o from a different perspective: it compares the SQL and db4o ways of performing typical database operations, analyzes the performance of db4o compared with the alternatives, and discusses where db4o fits into today's database market.

PART III

■■■

db4o in the Real World

First standardized in 1986, SQL has won a huge community of followers. The reality is that most databases in today's marketplace are relational, and the wide acceptance of SQL is one of the main reasons why this is the case. It shouldn't be a surprise, then, that when faced with alternative techniques, many developers take their existing SQL experience as their reference point. In this part of the book we describe how db4o fits into this world. Chapter 13 examines db4o from the perspective of the SQL database developer and describes best practices for moving from an RDBMS to an ODBMS. The following chapters examine the performance of db4o compared to RDBMS solutions, discuss the practicalities of using db4o in different application areas, and lay out the business case for db4o.

■■■

CHAPTER 13

From RDBMS to OODBMS

Some of the most common questions asked by newcomers to OODBMS in general, and db4o in particular, are along the lines of "I can do this with SQL—how do I do it in an object database?" To answer these types of questions, we need an example scenario where we can look at the SQL way of solving problems, and show how similar problems can be solved with db4o.

It's important to emphasize a couple of things right off the bat here. First, relational and object databases are fundamentally different in the way they model data, and as a result they have different strengths. A problem that can be solved simply in one may be difficult in the other. For reference, Part I of this book describes in detail how the underlying data models differ.

Second, this chapter is largely written from a database perspective—it's intended to help the experienced SQL developer understand how familiar database operations are done in db4o. You should keep in mind, though, that db4o is not intended to be a standalone DBMS. A key strength is its ability to be seamlessly embedded into a .NET or Java application, using a data model that is the same as the application's object model and without the need for database administration. There is no need to map objects to tables, and complex object models are easily supported. The contrast will become very obvious when you start looking at the code examples, where RDBMS solutions are illustrated with SQL code, while db4o solutions are illustrated with Java code.

It should be reasonably clear how the db4o code examples work, but it's recommended that you refer also to the chapters in Part II that cover specific db4o techniques in more depth. To avoid obscuring the main theme here, which is the SQL/db4o comparison, we illustrate db4o techniques using one language only, departing from the practice in the earlier parts of the book of giving both C# and Java code. Java code is shown, but the discussion applies equally to C# and Java.

Designing the Database

The scenario we will use in this chapter is a training academy that is teaching db4o to some eager trainees. The academy employs experts to do the training. Each expert should be able to teach one or more courses. Trainees can enroll in different courses led by one of these experts.

Let's look at the Entity Relationship (ER) model, which shows the way the RDBMS developer views the scenario (see Figure 13-1). From the description it appears that the academy may be modeled by three types of entity: Expert, Trainee, and Course. However, a fourth table, Assignment, is introduced to define the relationships between the other entities. This table needs to be there because a many-to-many relationship exists between Course and Trainee. Assignment contains three foreign keys: one for each referenced table.

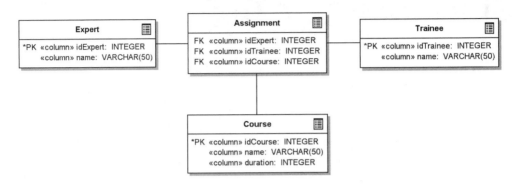

Figure 13-1. *Sample ER model*

Meanwhile, the db4o developer will model the same scenario with three classes: Course, Expert, and Trainee. Then he needs to decide which objects should know about the others. Figure 13-2 shows a possible solution in which Course has responsibility for joining the objects together—there is no need for an equivalent to the Assignment table as the object data model can handle many-to-many relationships. A Course object holds references to a single Expert and a collection of Trainee objects. We presume that the Course class is able to manage tasks such as adding a Trainee or Expert.

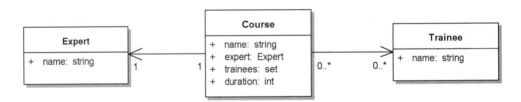

Figure 13-2. *Sample object data model*

■**Note** In C# the attributes are usually accessed through properties, while in Java we usually use getter and setter methods. These are not shown explicitly in the diagram, although they are used in the code examples. You can refer to Part II for more detailed db4o code examples showing the use of object attributes.

Once the initial design is completed, the databases need to be created. The relational database needs to be set up initially by an administrator who can then provide the necessary information to connect the database. Tables are then created using SQL CREATE TABLE statements. The db4o database, on the other hand, needs no initial administration: its schema will be created directly from the objects that are passed to it to be stored, as described in Chapter 5.

Basic SQL Statements

Now that we have defined the database schemas, we need to put some data in our databases and do some basic manipulation of the data. In the RDBMS, we do so by executing SQL statements. Let's look at some examples, and the way the equivalent operations are done with db4o.

■**Note** The SQL statements shown could be executed from any kind of database client, such as a command-line client or database administration tool. Alternatively, they might be embedded within an application. In the latter case, there is a further layer of abstraction between the database and the way the information is represented in the application. With db4o, the code shown is already part of an application.

INSERT Statements

So how do we insert some sample data into our databases? For the RDBMS, assuming we have already created all tables, the SQL commands would look something like this:

```
INSERT INTO course VALUES("1","Objects and databases");
INSERT INTO expert VALUES("1","Cooper");
INSERT INTO trainee VALUES("1","Griffin");
```

The meaning of each of these INSERT statements should be quite obvious. So far, though, we have just created the basic entities; we haven't defined any relationship between them. The following SQL statement inserts a row into the Assignments table that is needed to ensure that an Expert named Cooper teaches Trainee Griffin in the Course "Objects and databases":

```
INSERT INTO assignment VALUES("1","1","1");
```

After issuing a COMMIT command, the data is stored.

The equivalent in db4o to these INSERT statements can be written in Java as follows, assuming the classes have suitable constructors. First, the objects are created and relationships defined using the Course object itself:

```
Course course = new Course("Objects and databases");
Expert expert = new Expert("Cooper");
Trainee trainee = new Trainee("Griffin");
course.setExpert(expert);
course.addTrainee(trainee);
```

Next the objects are stored in the db4o container like so:

```
ObjectContainer container = Db4o.openFile("academy.yap");
container.set(course);
container.commit();
container.close();
```

Now that we have some structure and data to work with, we can compare some simple queries, and then move on to look at more complex situations.

SELECT Statements

The SQL query to list the names of all the Experts in the database would look like this:

```
SELECT name FROM expert;
```

Depending on the underlying architecture, a collection consisting of strings representing the stored names will be returned, for example a .NET DataSet or a Java ResultSet. We are just showing the SQL code here—for clarity we omit the code required to execute the SQL within an application.

This leads us to the first significant difference between the RDBMS and OODBMS worlds. In the object-oriented world you have to retrieve the whole objects even if you are only interested in some parts of them. The SQL query simply gave us the name attribute of each Expert. The db4o equivalent, implemented using query-by-example (QBE), gave us the Expert entities, as an ObjectSet that is basically a list of objects. If we want to print out the name value of an object, we have to extract it from the object. In C# we simply access the relevant property, while in Java we call the getter method:

```
Expert expertPrototype = new Expert(null);
ObjectSet experts = container.get(expertPrototype);
while(experts.hasNext())
{
    Expert expert = (Expert) experts.next();
    System.out.println(expert.getName());
}
```

The db4o query is approximately equivalent to the following SQL query:

```
SELECT * FROM expert;
```

■**Note** It is not possible to write a query to simply return specific attributes from objects with db4o. Other object-oriented query languages, such as ODMG OQL and Hibernate's HQL, do allow this.

The relationship between data (values) and objects (entities) is handled in a fundamentally different way by the two database types:

- SQL gives data: If we want objects we have to construct them from the data.

- db4o gives objects: If we want data we have to extract it from the objects.

The way this difference works out in practice depends on what we need to do with the database contents. We will concentrate here on the use of the database to provide persistent storage within .NET and Java applications.

The results of executing a SQL statement may be returned in the form of a RecordSet object (.NET) or ResultSet object (Java), which in many applications is bound to a data-aware GUI control to allow the user to view and update data. Using db4o in this situation is actually quite similar. A db4o query returns a collection of objects, often an ObjectSet, that implements the IList (.NET) or List (Java) interface. Many data-aware GUI controls can be bound to collections of this type. For example, in Chapter 12, we showed a simple example of binding an ASP.NET GridView control to a db4o ObjectSet. If you want to see further examples of data binding in C#, db4o developer Eric Falsken has written a great Windows Forms sample application using db4o: it's available for download from his website at www.everylittlething.net/PartsAssembly/.

Other applications are based on a *domain model*, in which the business logic is implemented by the behavior and interactions of domain objects. Here, the purpose of the database is to store and retrieve the domain objects themselves. db4o has a distinct advantage here because this is exactly what it is designed to do. Retrieving an object from a relational database involves a bit more work: we need to loop through the RecordSet or ResultSet using each row to provide the parameters required to construct a new domain object. This involves writing lots of additional code, or using an object-relational mapper such as Hibernate. The Java code that follows shows how the previous SQL query could be used to construct some Expert objects. The domain model class here needs an ID field so that an object can be matched to the correct table row in the database—db4o doesn't require this field as objects in memory are automatically matched to stored objects.

```
ResultSet rs = stmt.executeQuery("SELECT * FROM expert");
while(rs.hasNext())
{
    Expert expert = new Expert();
    expert.setId(rs.getInt(1));      // need ID field for relational database
    expert.setName(rs.getString(2));
}
```

SELECT with WHERE Clause

Building on the previous example, let's search for a specific Expert. The SQL statement looks like this:

```
SELECT * FROM expert WHERE name="Cooper";
```

Here's the equivalent db4o query (using QBE):

```
Expert expertPrototype = new Expert("Cooper");
ObjectSet experts = container.get(expertPrototype);
```

QBE is limited in its power. It can only provide an equivalent for queries with criteria that are matched exactly, and it isn't very flexible when it comes to compound criteria. Later in this chapter you will see how to simulate more complex SQL statements by harnessing the power of Native Queries.

UPDATE Statements

The ER model in Figure 13-1 shows that a Course has a duration. For instance, the course "Transactions" will require 5 days. We forgot to define the course duration when we originally executed the INSERT statements, so we need to update the information in the database. The SQL UPDATE statement might look like this:

```
UPDATE course SET duration = 5 WHERE name = "Transactions";
```

In order to change an object in db4o, we have to retrieve it first, like this:

```
ObjectSet result = container.get(new Course("Transactions"));
Course course = (Course) result.next();
```

Then we change the data through a method call on the retrieved object. The updated object is then stored with a call to set:

```
course.setDuration(5);
container.set(course);
```

DELETE Statements

Let's conclude this brief introduction by expelling a lazy trainee:

```
DELETE FROM trainee WHERE name = "Fizzle";
```

The process of deleting an object is quite similar to that involved when performing an update. First retrieve the object, and then get rid of it:

```
ObjectSet result = container.get(new Trainee("Fizzle"));
Trainee ex = (Trainee) result.next();
container.delete(ex);
```

What if there is more than one trainee with the name "Fizzle"? The SQL DELETE statement shown will automatically delete all occurrences for "Fizzle". This might not be the desired behavior, of course. If we want to make sure that only one trainee is deleted then we'd be more likely to delete based on the primary key field.

With db4o, on the other hand, the delete method always deletes one object only. If more than one object is retrieved by the query, we have to iterate through the list of result objects and delete them separately, as shown here:

```
ObjectSet result = container.get(new Trainee("Fizzle"));
while (result.hasNext())
{
    Trainee ex = (Trainee) result.next();
    container.delete(ex);
}
```

Similarly, SQL can update many table rows with one statement, while we need to iterate through the query results for multiple updates in db4o.

If we want to delete exactly one specific object from a db4o database we need to make sure that the objects have a field that contains a value that is unique within the extent of the class in the database. db4o does not have primary keys or auto-increment fields, so it is up to the application to enforce the rules here. This issue is discussed further in the section "Constraints and Referential Integrity," later in this chapter.

Complex SQL Statements

So far we have looked at some simple database operations. In this section we'll look at more complex operations, such as joins, subqueries, operators, sorting, views, and aggregations. For some of these, db4o provides equivalent functionality, although expressed quite differently. For other operations, as you will see, db4o does not provide direct support, although they can often be implemented in the application code. db4o is typically used for reasons other than its analytic query capability. It is instructive, though, to see just how far we can go in emulating the capabilities of SQL, and how much effort is required to do so. This comparison provides some useful insight into the practicalities of the object data model.

Joins

Let's say we need to find which courses a particular expert is currently leading. In SQL you would typically join the three appropriate tables in order to do so:

```
SELECT c.name
FROM course c, expert e, assignment a
WHERE
    e.idEXPERT = a.fk_idEXPERT
    AND c.idCOURSE = a.fk_idCOURSE
    AND e.name = "Cooper";
```

Or, if you prefer the SQL99 syntax:

```
SELECT c.name
FROM course c
JOIN assignment a
ON (a.fk_idCOURSE = c.idCOURSE)
JOIN expert e ON (a.fk_idEXPERT = e.idEXPERT)
WHERE e.name = "Cooper";
```

This is straightforward in SQL, but this particular task can't be accomplished in an elegant way with db4o when querying by example. To accomplish this using QBE based on the object data model in Figure 13-2, we need to first get all courses, then manually iterate through the list while comparing the containing course expert's name with the given predicate.

There are two solutions to avoid this tedious task: either we change the data model and keep querying by example, or we use db4o's Native Queries. Both alternatives are described next.

Change the Data Model

The apparent problem for db4o here was that the relationship between Course and Expert is defined by a reference in the Course object. Look at Figure 13-2: this relationship has an arrow pointing from Course to Expert. We can't navigate this relationship in the opposite direction—the Expert class does not have a reference to any Course objects. So, if we retrieve our specified expert from the database, we can't simply get his list of courses.

Object databases are often described as being *navigational*, which means that queries must follow the direction of defined relationships. Use of an object database can be made easier by a well-planned data model that takes account of likely queries. Relational database developers are not used to this idea: there is no concept of direction when two tables are joined.

If we decide to change the model, a solution that of course is not appropriate for every situation, we can add a reference in Expert to Course objects. This should be a multivalued reference, in other words, a collection or list of Course objects. The initialization of the objects will be done like this:

```
Course course = new Course("Objects and databases");
Expert expert = new Expert("Cooper");
course.addExpert(expert);
expert.addCourse(course);
```

In effect, we now have matching inverse relationships between Expert and Course. With this design decision one simply has to query the Expert object for the courses.

```
ObjectSet result = container.get(new Expert("Cooper"));
Expert expert = (Expert) result.next();
List courses = expert.getCourses();
```

The need to maintain the inverses means that extra code is required, and there is more scope for making errors. This kind of relationship should probably be avoided wherever possible. Some of the previous ease in which Expert could be handled was lost in order to gain simplicity in querying for courses.

Of course, if we'd asked a different question—what is the name of the expert leading a particular course?—then there would be no need to change the data model: we could simply find the relevant Course object and then get the Expert object from it:

```
ObjectSet result = container.get(new Course("Objects and databases"));
Course course = (Course) result.next();
Expert expert = course.getExpert();
```

Joins Using Native Queries

db4o's advanced query capabilities provide ways of performing the previous operation with no need to change the data model. The concept of Native Queries (NQ), described in detail in Chapter 6, offers a particularly powerful solution. A native query expresses the criteria that target objects must match within a method of a predicate class. The query is written in the application language (Java in the following example). For each object of the required type in the database, the match method returns true if the conditions specified in the method are met, and returns false otherwise; the query itself returns a collection of the objects that matched. With some clever optimization going on behind the scenes, the query is often executed without the performance hit of having to get all the objects from the database to test.

■**Note** Native Queries, which were introduced in db4o 5.0, is now the recommended method for advanced querying. However, the advanced query method used in previous versions, Simple Object Data Access (SODA), can still be useful and is still supported. SODA is also described in Chapter 6.

The following native query delivers the desired results in an elegant manner without having to change the model. The `return` statement checks that each candidate `Course` has an `Expert` assigned (!= null) and also checks whether the expert is "Cooper". The query then returns an `ObjectSet` that implements the `IList` (C#) or `List` (Java) interface.

```
List<Course> courses = container.query(new Predicate<Course>()
{
    public boolean match(Course course)
    {
        Expert expert = course.getExpert();
        return expert != null ?
            expert.getName().equals("Cooper") : false;
    }
});
```

■**Note** This single db4o query retrieves whole `Course` objects that, depending on activation depth (see Chapter 7), can also include the associated `Expert` and `Trainee` objects. It would take a lot more code than this to construct all these objects from the results of SQL queries.

Working with Object Graphs

We get a real payoff for planning the object data model carefully when we need to work with whole object graphs in the application. To take a simple example, let's say that there is an important bit of business logic built into an interaction between a `Course` and its `Expert`, so we need to have instances of both in the application. This is simple in db4o—by retrieving a `Course` object we also retrieve the relevant `Expert` object.

With SQL we have to do a lot more work within the application. To arrive at the same point we would need to:

- Make sure the SQL query selects all the important columns in the `Course` and `Expert` tables

- Extract the field values from the `DataSet` or `ResultSet`, as shown in the "SELECT Statements" section earlier in this chapter

- Construct new objects and set the field values

We get a similar payoff when storing objects from an application. Whereas in db4o we can store a `Course` and an `Expert` with a single line of code, with SQL we need to use a separate `INSERT` statement for each table. Furthermore, these `INSERT` statements need to be laboriously built up as strings using the object field values.

Whether we are storing or retrieving, the payoff gets bigger the more complex the object model is.

> **Note** An object-relational mapper such as Hibernate similarly simplifies the process of getting objects into and out of a relational database, but at the expense of performance. Also, Hibernate does not remove the need to create tables or to work out mappings between tables and objects.

Deep Queries

A deep query is one that depends on multiple fields scattered throughout a set of entities that form a hierarchy. To illustrate this task, we'll enhance our ER model (see Figure 13-3). Every course session must be held in a classroom of some sort. A room contains various resources necessary for teaching. Therefore, we extend our model by adding a table, Room, which contains a column that references the foreign key of the course. The resources in another new table, Resource, are associated with exactly one room. A description column specifies the purpose of the resource (projector, laptop, etc.) and each one has an inventory number (invNo column).

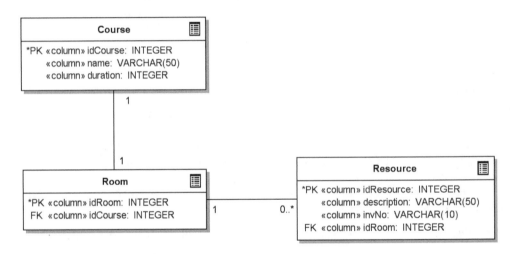

Figure 13-3. *ER model extensions*

With this in mind, if we want to determine for which courses the resource with inventory number "A11" was used, we can execute the following SQL statement:

```
SELECT c.name
FROM course c, room rm, resource re
WHERE
  c.idCOURSE = rm.fk_idCOURSE
  AND rm.idROOM = re.fk_idROOM
  AND re.invNo= "A11";
```

Once again we use three tables and join them via their keys.

Meanwhile, in the object data model, we create a class titled Room that is delegated by the Course class. The Room class in turn contains resources, so Room aggregates the Resource class (see Figure 13-4).

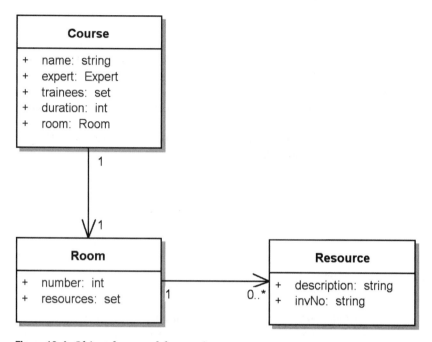

Figure 13-4. *Object data model extension*

The same query is quite tricky in the object database, again because we are starting with an attribute of Resource and trying to find the corresponding Course. Figure 13-4 shows that we are going against the directionality of two relationships.

The following native query solution takes the room attribute of each course and iterates through all the resources for that room. If it comes upon the desired inventory number, it will return true, so that this Course is returned by the query.

```
List<Course> courses = container.query(new Predicate<Course>()
{
    public boolean match(Course course)
    {
        Room room  = course.getRoom();
        for (Resource resource : room.getResources())
            if(resource.getInvNo() == "A11")
                return true;
        return false;
    }
});
```

As before, the db4o query would have been simpler if the relationships were bidirectional, at the expense of making object references more difficult to maintain. This architecture would allow a simple walkthrough of the object graph to the desired course: resource.getRoom(). getCourse(). With an object database, it is helpful to have a well-planned object data model that takes into account the likelihood of particular queries.

Subselect

Subselects are SELECT statements that are merged into other SELECT statements. You can find them in WHERE, FROM, or HAVING clauses. Subselects are required to gather data in subqueries, which then act as criteria in the enclosing query.

To see an example of this, we extend the tables Expert and Trainee. In each case we add a birthdate field.

Next we want to find out which trainees are older than an expert called "Cooper". The following SQL statement reflects these considerations:

```
SELECT name
FROM trainee
WHERE birthdate <
(
  SELECT birthdate
  FROM expert
  WHERE name = "Cooper"
);
```

This construct is called single-row, because the subquery should only return exactly one value. For multiple-row queries, you have to deal with several tuples. They are generally treated much the same. Only the operators change: IN, ANY, or ALL instead of <. We will discuss some issues concerning these operators later in this chapter.

What about the object data model? The Expert and Trainee classes are expanded to include the birthdate attribute. Like the SQL solution, the db4o query will combine two queries. However, in this case the query that is equivalent to the SQL subquery is written first. It's a simple query that can be done with QBE.

```
Expert cooperPrototype = new Expert("Cooper");
ObjectSet allCooper = container.get(cooperPrototype);
Date coopersBday = ((Expert) allCooper.next()).getBirthDate();
```

Then, a native query uses the result. A native query can use functionality provided by the programming language: the before method of the Date class is used here:

```
List<Trainee> allOlder = container.query(new Predicate<Trainee>()
{
    public boolean match(Trainee trainee)
    {
    return
      trainee.getBirthDate().before(coopersBday) ? true : false;
  }
});
```

Native queries are very flexible: you can use any functionality provided in the language API or your domain classes. In comparison, with SQL you are constrained by the functions provided by the DBMS vendor. Subqueries are arguably easier to write and more readable in db4o than in SQL since the sequence of operations is more obvious. In general, you need to gather all values that are intended to act as criteria before running the NQ. What at first glance may look not very practical for a SQL developer will lead to a reduction of work in the end. The other major advantage db4o gives us with native queries in this regard is the ease of refactoring. You do not need to edit mappings or query strings when the model changes.

Operators: LIKE, IN, BETWEEN, EXIST

Queries that use the SQL LIKE operator can be simulated with native queries. For instance, suppose we want to list all trainees whose names start with the letter A. The following SQL statement should do this:

```
SELECT * FROM trainee WHERE name LIKE "A%";
```

The equivalent db4o NQ is:

```
List<Trainee> students = container.query<Trainee>(new Predicate<Trainee>()
{
  public boolean match(Trainee trainee)
  {
    return trainee.startsWith("A");
  }
});
```

There are similar native language equivalents for the other operators. Table 13-1 compares some common cases. There are many additional third-party tools available, making tasks like this much easier (for example, Jakarta Commons Lang for String comparisons). In general, you get more functionality because you can benefit from the whole toolset that the .NET or Java community provides for you. With NQs you can include regular expressions, string comparisons, and any sophisticated operator that is available.

Table 13-1. *SQL Operators and Java Equivalents*

SQL	Java Equivalent
IN (1,20,23)	return target.contains(obj.getId())
BETWEEN 1 AND 3	return obj.getId()>=1 && obj.getId()<=3
LIKE "He%"	return obj.getString().startsWith("He")
LIKE "%en%"	return obj.getString().indexOf("en")!=-1
LIKE "%en"	return obj.getString().endsWith("en")
LIKE "li[vf]es"	return obj.getString().matches("li[vf]es")
LIKE "a-z123"	return obj.getString().matches("[a-z123]")

Sorting

Sorting results is straightforward in SQL; for example:

```
SELECT * FROM expert ORDER BY name ASCENDING;
```

In db4o, a native query can also return sorted results. Native queries make use of the programming language's own support for comparing and sorting, which gives a great deal of flexibility. We can define a Comparison (C#) or Comparator (Java) object, and within that object we define ordering in any way we like. Here's a Java example of returning all experts sorted by name (there are further C# and Java examples in Chapter 6):

```
// First define Comparator
Comparator<Expert> expertCmp = new Comparator<Expert>()
{
    public int compare(Expert e1, Expert e2)
    {
        return e1.getName().compareTo(e2.getName());
    }
};

// then use Comparator to sort Query
List< Expert > result = db.query(new Predicate< Expert >()
{
    public boolean match(Expert expert)
    {
        return true;
    }
},expertCmp);
```

■**Note** Sorting support in Native Queries was introduced in version 5.2. Prior to that, two options were available for sorting: one was to use the older SODA mechanism (see Chapter 6 for details on sorting with SODA); the second was to copy the list returned by a native query into an array and then sort that array.

Views

Views are routinely used in SQL for filtering data from one or more tables, and providing only the relevant parts of the big picture. Data that otherwise would have been gathered by using a complex join can then be queried by a simple SELECT statement. Views are often used by administrators for security purposes, as many users have no need to view every item of data in a given row. Some users can be given access permissions only on a view of the data rather than on the underlying tables.

The idea of views doesn't really fit naturally into the way db4o works. As we noted earlier, a query in db4o returns whole objects, rather than bits of objects. We can't easily hide bits of some objects, or merge bits from different objects. However, in this section we look at an example of a view in SQL, and show a programming technique that can be used with db4o to simulate some of the capabilities of this view.

Let's imagine our academy's administration department needs simply to be able to get a list of all experts and their courses. This information could be contained in the following view:

```
CREATE VIEW roster AS
SELECT e.name as expert, c.name as course
FROM course c, expert e, assignment a
WHERE
  e.idEXPERT=a.fk_idEXPERT
  AND c.idCOURSE=a.fk_idCOURSE;
```

Users in the administration department could query this view as follows:

```
SELECT * FROM roster ORDER by expert;
```

This query would give output like this:

```
Expert              Course
----------------------------------
Cooper              Transactions
Cooper              Configuration
Rocksberg           Objects and Databases
Rocksberg           Native Queries
```

These users could be granted the right to run queries on this view only, and not on the underlying tables:

```
GRANT SELECT ON roster TO adminusers;
```

This GRANT statement would give read-only access—updating and deleting data through views should be handled with care. There is danger of running into anomalies because you can't fully manipulate the data.

So, can we do something similar with db4o? Would we want to? At first sight it doesn't appear that we can, since db4o has no built-in feature equivalent to SQL views. However, the scenario here has parallels with a widely used object-oriented design pattern, the façade pattern. This simple pattern is often unconsciously utilized by developers. It describes a class that delegates a range of functions to other classes that exist deeper in the system. If you use a façade, you do not need to know about the underlying system architecture; this allows you to concentrate on the immediate requirements without having to bother with internal configuration or details of objects behind the façade. It is even possible to have two or more subsystems being utilized through one façade, as shown in Figure 13-5.

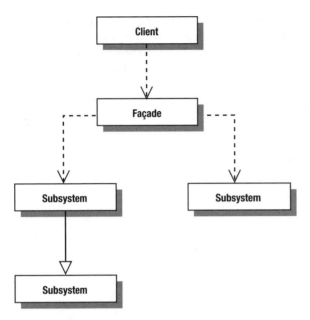

Figure 13-5. *Façade scenario*

We can use a façade to play a similar role to a view in SQL. This moves the role from the data model to the application architecture.

A façade can act like a SQL view in the following ways:

- Merge data from different objects

- Protect underlying systems from being changed without permission

- Guarantee data consistency between the façade and subsystems

It does not, however, provide a per-user or per-role security mechanism in the way that a SQL view can.

In our scenario, the entity classes, Course, Expert, and so on, would be encapsulated into a package or assembly. This would also include the Roster façade class we list in a moment.

The "admin department" application would be enclosed in a separate package or assembly that would only interact with the Roster class. The Roster class has a method getCourseExpertPairs that retrieves Course and Expert objects from the database, and builds a HashMap containing the required data.

```
public class Roster
{
    public HashMap<String, String> getCourseExpertPair(ObjectContainer container)
    {
        HashMap<String, String> result = new HashMap<String, String>();
        ObjectSet courses = container.get(new Course(null));
```

```
        while (courses.hasNext())
        {
            Course course = (Course) courses.next();
            result.put(course.getName(),
            course.getExpert() != null?course.getExpert().getName(): "unassigned");
        }
        return result;
    }
}
```

The admin department application can now query the object data as follows:

```
Roster roster = new Roster();
HashMap<String, String> output = roster.getCourseExpertPair(container);
System.out.println(output);
```

We could add methods for updating the subsystems Expert as well as Course, but we'll leave this as an exercise for the reader.

As you can see, the database container is passed into the method. This suggests that the Roster object alone is responsible for gathering and updating data—a common approach when using a small to middle-sized system utilizing an object database. Note that a Roster object does not contain any data of its own, and so we would not store Roster objects in the database.

It is worth reiterating that views are not naturally supported by db4o. However, because db4o is so closely integrated into an application, it is quite natural to build the view logic into the application architecture as shown here. db4o's role in this scenario is simply to provide a simple and efficient way to store and retrieve the domain objects.

Aggregate Functions and Grouping

These are widely used SQL operations that are not naturally supported by db4o. Although less convenient, equivalent operations can usually be implemented in the application code or by careful design of the object data model.

COUNT

In order to count the total number of rows in the database, you would execute a SELECT statement using the count() function, like this:

```
SELECT COUNT(*) FROM courses;
```

The number of objects returned by a db4o query can be found using the size method of the ObjectSet:

```
ObjectSet result = container.get(new Course());
System.out.println("Courses in academy: "+result.size());
```

It looks as if we have to instantiate all the Course objects simply to find out how many there are, which seems like an inefficient use of memory. In fact, no objects are instantiated unless you iterate through the list by calling result.next(). Only the object IDs are taken from the database. This corresponds to a memory consumption of (size*long) bytes, so you can count your results without having to worry about performance or memory issues.

SUM, AVG, MAX, and MIN

db4o does not provide any of these aggregate functions. We have to write additional code to sum or average, or to get maximum or minimum values. Take a look at this elegantly functional SQL statement, which uses the AVG function to give the average duration of all courses:

```
SELECT AVG(duration) FROM courses;
```

To do this with db4o, we need to query to get all Course objects, and iterate through the results to calculate the average of the duration field:

```
int sum = 0;
ObjectSet result = container.get(new Course());
while (result.hasNext())
{
  sum += ((Course) result.next()).getDuration();
}
System.out.println("AVG:" + (result.size() == 0 ? 0 : sum / result.size()));
```

Other functions, like MIN or MAX, must be implemented in a similar way.

GROUP BY

Grouping in SQL lets the results of a query be grouped together based on some common attribute. Grouping is often used in conjunction with the aggregate functions.

Let's look at a very simple example of grouping. It would be an easy task to determine the number of courses to which each of our experts is assigned:

```
SELECT expert, COUNT(course) FROM roster GROUP BY expert;
```

Expert	COUNT(course)
Cooper	3
Spindle	5

Due to the huge range of grouping and aggregation scenarios that can occur, it is difficult to show a best practice solution for implementing them with db4o. We will simply look at a couple of options for this particular scenario.

As was the case for the discussion of joins earlier in this chapter, one option would be to change the object model itself. To be more precise, we could add a list of Courses to the Expert class, the same change as we suggested earlier. By doing this we impose a natural grouping within the object model: Courses are directly grouped with the relevant Experts. The output from the SQL query can then be emulated by finding the size of each list:

```
System.out.println(expert.getName()+"-"+expert.getCourses().size());
```

In the original object data model, the only relationship between the classes was that a Course had a reference to one Expert. If we do not want to or can't adapt this object data model, the grouping is more tedious to accomplish. We have to manually iterate through the Course objects, keeping track of the name and a counter for each separate Expert found. This involves a lot of extra coding effort, which emphasizes again the benefits of designing an object data model to match the way it will be accessed.

```
ObjectSet result = container.get(new Course());
HashMap<Expert, Integer> groupedResults = new HashMap<Expert, Integer>
while (result.hasNext())
{
    Integer count = groupedResults.get(result.getExpert());
    groupedResults.put(result.getExpert(),(count == null ? 1 : count + 1));
}
```

In general, you can say that with every new table that takes part in the grouping function a new loop has to be written in the object world.

As we saw previously, we can benefit from thinking about likely queries when we are designing the object data model. In that way, we can avoid changing the model later or having to write awkward additional code.

Constraints and Referential Integrity

Constraints enforce rules on tables. In relational databases these constraints are directly imposed on tables. Examples of constraints include primary keys, foreign keys, and NOT NULL, and many more can be defined.

With db4o these rules can't be applied by the database and need to be defined in the application's object model. There are good reasons for this. Constraints are a necessity when working with relational tables. This artificial information must be employed in order to ensure data integrity. In the object world, you do not need this metadata because it is defined implicitly in the objects.

Let's take a closer look at some important types of constraints.

NOT NULL/CHECK/FOREIGN KEY

This group of constraints can be implemented directly by the object itself. We can catch exceptions when a field is set to a null value (NOT NULL), or enforce other rules (CHECK) with assertions in the appropriate setters of the object. If one object is directly related to another object and we want to ensure that the other object exists, we can define a constructor with the necessary objects passed in (FOREIGN KEY).

PRIMARY KEY

db4o, like most object databases, assigns a unique object ID (OID) to every object stored. The OID does not depend on the value of any field. You can store two Expert objects with the same name, for example, and db4o will regard them as different objects as the OIDs will be different.

If we want to prevent objects with duplicate values in particular fields being stored in the database, we need to query the database for matching objects first. If we get a non-null result, we need to decide what to do with the new object: for example, we can update the stored object, warn the user, or discard the new object.

ON DELETE CASCADE

Constraints can ensure data integrity. For example, the ON DELETE CASCADE constraint in a relational database is used to delete stale data (associated rows) that would be left by a deleted entry.

To see an example, let's assume that our academy leases fully equipped rooms within a business center. All resources are therefore tied to a specific room. If the academy gives up the lease for a particular room, the resources will go with it. Depending on the DBMS used, this or a similar constraint can be defined:

```
(table room)
CONSTRAINT fk_room
  FOREIGN KEY (fk_room)
  REFERENCES room (pk_room)
  ON DELETE CASCADE
```

The object data model for this scenario was shown in Figure 13-4. Now imagine that we have two rooms with some resources assigned to them:

```
Room room1 = new Room(1);
List<Resource> res = new ArrayList<Resource>();
res.add(new Resource ("Laptop R1"));
res.add(new Resource ("Projector R1"));
room1.setResource (res);

Room room2 = new Room(2);
res = new ArrayList<Resource>();
res.add(new Resource ("Laptop R2"));
res.add(new Resource ("Projector R2"));
room2.setResource (res);

container.set(room1);
container.set(room2);
```

The following code deletes a room, listing the resources in the database before and after the deletion. The method call listResources() simply iterates through the available Resource objects and prints their name.

```
System.out.println("Resources before transaction:");
listResources ();
Room room1 = (Room) container.get(new Room(1)).next();
System.out.println("Deleting Room "+room1.getNr());
container.delete(room1);
container.commit();
System.out.println("\nMaterials after transaction: ");
listResources ();
```

Unless we inform db4o about cascading, we will get the output in the left-hand column of Table 13-2. The room is deleted and all associated objects will remain in the database. If we want to change this behavior we need to make the following configuration call *before* opening the container:

```
Db4o.configure().objectClass("Room").cascadeOnDelete(true);
```

It is now guaranteed that db4o resolves all objects referenced by the room and subsequently deletes them. db4o configurations are described in detail in Chapter 10.

Table 13-2. *Output Without and with cascadeOnDelete Configured*

Without	With
Resources before transaction:	Resources before transaction:
Laptop R1	Laptop R1
Projector R1	Projector R1
Laptop R2	Laptop R2
Projector R2	Projector R2
Deleting Room 1	Deleting Room 1
Resources after transaction:	Resources after transaction:
Laptop R1	Laptop R2
Projector R1	Projector R2
Laptop R2	
Projector R2	

▓**Caution** You should be aware of the fact that db4o is not concerned about multiple object references. All objects that are referenced in the Room object are deleted regardless of whether they are referenced by any other objects. So, be careful using this feature.

Triggers

Triggers are favored instruments for automating operations in databases. Database designers can define triggers to be raised by certain actions. Triggers can catch actions such as inserts, updates, or deletes before or after they happen. Then you can prevent them from being processed, or alternatively execute other procedures in response. Triggers are useful for many situations, such as:

- Logging activities in a database.

- Enforcing data integrity.

- Assuring semantic integrity.

- Supplying clients with functionality. Once written, the code does not need to be doubled in every client application.

However, the danger of writing procedures is as great as the list of possibilities. For instance, triggers are a common reason for performance loss in complex databases. Executing an improperly written trigger could cause unintended execution of a huge amount of other code throughout the database.

In the world of db4o, you can find similar functionality. Where we define triggers for tables or rows in an RDBMS, we can attach *callbacks* to objects in db4o. A callback method can be added to any class. Listing 13-1 shows the ObjectCallBacks interface that specifies the supported callback method names.

Listing 13-1. *The ObjectCallbacks Interface in db4o*

```
public interface ObjectCallbacks
{
    public boolean objectCanActivate(ObjectContainer container);
    public boolean objectCanDeactivate(ObjectContainer container);
    public boolean objectCanDelete(ObjectContainer container);
    public boolean objectCanNew(ObjectContainer container);
    public boolean objectCanUpdate(ObjectContainer container);

    public void objectOnActivate(ObjectContainer container);
    public void objectOnDeactivate(ObjectContainer container);
    public void objectOnDelete(ObjectContainer container);
    public void objectOnNew(ObjectContainer container);
    public void objectOnUpdate(ObjectContainer container);
}
```

All objectCan* callback methods are called before the event, while all objectOn* methods are called after the event. For example, if a class has an objectOnDelete method defined, then db4o will execute the code in this method after every deletion of an instance of that class. Callbacks are described in more detail in Chapter 12.

The following method would print the value of toString for every object deleted:

```
public void objectOnDelete(ObjectContainer container)
{
    System.out.prinln("Deleted: "+this);
}
```

Table 13-3 shows how some of these callback events relate to SQL triggers. Object activation and deactivation callbacks have no direct SQL equivalents.

Table 13-3. *Comparison of Triggers and Callbacks*

Trigger	Callback
BEFORE UPDATE	objectCanUpdate
AFTER UPDATE	objectOnUpdate
BEFORE DELETE	objectOnDelete
AFTER DELETE	objectCanDelete
BEFORE INSERT	objectCanNew
AFTER INSERT	objectOnNew

Be aware that in a client/server mode, the callbacks are executed at the client. The advantage of server-side execution is missing here. Triggered work such as cleaning up data or processing large numbers of objects on the server is now stressing the client.

Compared to RDBMS triggers, callbacks differ in where they are executed, and they also offer a limited range of functionality. If you really want to execute code on the server side of a client/server mode, you should look at the db4o out-of-band message facility described in Chapter 8.

Let's look at an example of a simple trigger and an equivalent db4o callback in action. We've decided that every time a trainee leaves the academy he or she will be added to a list of alumni. We need a new table, Alumni, in our ER model, and a new Alumni class, as shown in Figure 13-6.

Figure 13-6. *Representing Alumni in the ER and object data models*

Writing into the new table will automatically be accomplished using a trigger called LOG_DISMISS. We also want to log the date of departure.

```
CREATE TRIGGER LOG_DISMISS AFTER DELETE ON trainee
  FOR EACH ROW INSERT INTO alumni SET name=OLD.name, ex=NOW();
```

With a DELETE callback we can easily do the same thing in db4o. All we need to do is add the method objectOnDelete to the class Trainee:

```
public void objectOnDelete(ObjectContainer container)
{
  Alumni alumni = new Alumni();
  alumni.setName(this.name);
  alumni.setEx(new Date());
  container.set(alumni);
  container.commit();
  System.out.println("New Alumni: " + this.name);
}
```

Now we test this functionality by dismissing the first trainee:

```
System.out.println("Alumnis before transaction:");
ObjectSet alumnis = container.get(new Alumni());
for (Object al : alumnis) {
  System.out.println(((Alumni) al).getName());
}
```

```
// query for list of trainees and delete the first one
ObjectSet trainees = container.get(new Trainee(null));
if (trainees.hasNext()) {
  Trainee trainee = (Trainee) trainees.next();
  System.out.println("Dismissing: " + trainee.getName());
  container.delete(trainee);
  container.commit();
}

System.out.println("\nAlumnis after transaction: ");
alumnis = container.get(new Alumni());
for (Object al : alumnis) {
  System.out.println(((Alumni) al).getName());
}
```

This code gives output like this with two `Trainee` objects already in the database:

```
Alumnis before transaction:

Dismissing: Griffin
New Alumni: Griffin

Alumnis after transaction:
Griffin
```

Of course, only strictly coupled object relations should be handled with callbacks. Having the persistence logic focused on one point or layer is preferable to scattering it over all objects, packages, or namespaces, which could result in performance bottlenecks or even hard-to-trace deadlocks.

Stored Procedures

In an RDBMS, a stored procedure is a group of statements that execute within the database to accomplish a task. Stored procedures can be called from client applications, but the processing takes place on the database server.

db4o is designed to integrate with client applications, and does not support procedures running within the database. As we saw in the previous section, out-of-band messaging gives some support for executing code in a db4o server process, but this is a very limited capability, and there is currently no mechanism for a server to return values in response to an out-of-band message.

Structural Changes

Many software architectures are living systems, which must be able to tolerate structural changes within the data model. Small changes, such as adding a missing description, are common, while drastic changes, such as inserting a whole new hierarchical layer, are sometimes required. SQL can handle many such refactorings.

ALTER

The ALTER statement is responsible for the following changes:

- Creating new rows (defining a default-value)

- Changing rows

- Deleting rows

Similar changes can be implemented in db4o without difficulty. If a new field is added, deleted, or changed in a persisted object, then db4o will take care of this automatically. Chapter 12 takes a closer look at the topic.

It becomes more difficult if all the class hierarchies hide behind certain table associations. Review Chapter 3 for an introduction to this topic. Schema evolution is recognized by the db4o developers, and is partially solved via tools. These tools can cope with situations such as adding new parent objects or changing an entire tree structure. However, in this special case schema evolution can be very complicated and therefore only a small set of cases has been covered so far.

■**Caution** When changing the classes' model and using a db4o server or different databases in general, you should remember to put the class changes into the classpath of the client as well as the classpath of the server. Otherwise, you will encounter strange effects such as losing updates on new fields.

DROP

Removing an entire table with the DROP statement is roughly equivalent to deleting all the objects of a particular class from a db4o database. For example, let's remove the alumni that we added in the previous section. In the RDBMS, we can do this:

```
DROP TABLE alumni
```

In db4o it's done like this:

```
ObjectSet alumnis = container.get(new Alumni());
while (alumnis.hasNext())
    container.delete(alumnis.next());
```

This is not quite the same as simply deleting all rows from a table. Since there are no Alumni objects in the db4o database, the database has no knowledge of that class, just like when the table is dropped. There is one difference, though: with db4o we don't have to define the schema—we just pass objects to it to be stored. So, we could, if we wanted to, immediately start storing Alumni objects again.

Transactions

In the world of relational databases, transactions target the principle of data consistency. A transaction consists of a series of logically dependent actions. Data inconsistency occurs when a user cancels a process or a system failure appears in the course of those actions.

In a transactional database, such an abort should result in a *rollback*. Some RDBMS solutions support so-called savepoints. These savepoints enable rollbacks to specific intermediate states even within the scope of a transaction.

When a database is used by many users with read/write access, transactions can write data concurrently to the database. The level of isolation between such transactions is important in ensuring data consistency.

Problems that can arise in concurrently writing transactions include:

- **Lost update**: See the examples in Figures 13-7 and 13-8.

- **Unrepeatable read**: Occurs when a transaction reads data, but upon reading the same data again it has been modified by another transaction.

- **Dirty read**: Occurs when a transaction reads data that has not yet been committed by another transaction.

- **Phantom read**: Occurs when new data appears between two read operations within a transaction.

The SQL standard defines several isolation levels for coping with these different anomalies. In general, the choice of isolation level involves a compromise between data consistency and performance. The isolation levels shown in Table 13-4 are supported in most of the well-known RDBMSs. Serializable provides the highest level of isolation, known as pessimistic locking, while Read Uncommitted provides the lowest, known as overly optimistic locking.

Table 13-4. *SQL Isolation Levels (X = Possible)*

Isolation Level	Dirty Read	Unrepeatable Read	Phantom Read
Read Uncommitted	X	X	X
Read Committed		X	X
Repeatable Read			X
Serializable			

Most databases use Read Committed as the default behavior. With this isolation level, you must be careful about all anomalies except dirty read. If you have a problem with data consistency, you would probably execute the following statement:

```
SET TRANSACTION ISOLATION LEVEL SERIALIZABLE
```

db4o does support concurrent access in its client/server mode (described in Chapter 8). However, there is no easy way of selecting the isolation level. db4o always operates with Read Committed isolation. This prevents dirty reads, but anomalies can still occur as a result of one or another of the problems we've described.

For example, let's demonstrate a lost update by changing the duration value of one course in two concurrent transactions. Figure 13-7 shows the SQL version, while Figure 13-8 shows the db4o equivalent. In each figure, the commands executed in the two transactions are shown side by side, together with the resultant value of duration.

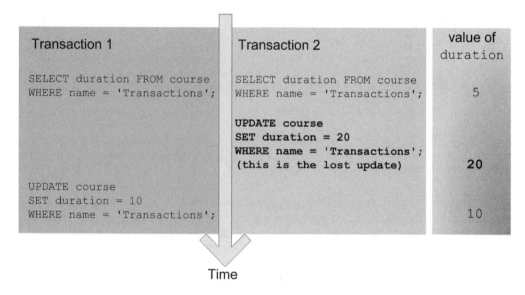

Figure 13-7. *Example of a lost update occurring with SQL*

Almost any RDBMS could prevent this lost update from happening by setting a minimum isolation level of Repeatable Read.

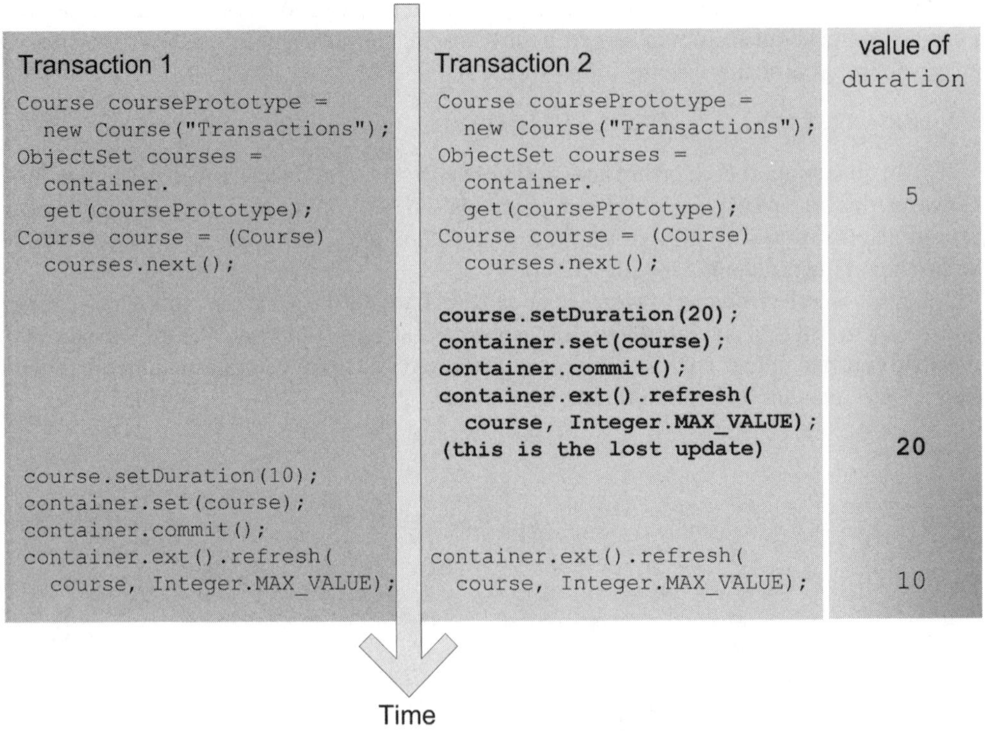

Transaction 1	Transaction 2	value of duration

`Course coursePrototype =`
`  new Course("Transactions");`
`ObjectSet courses =`
`  container.`
`  get(coursePrototype);`
`Course course = (Course)`
`  courses.next();`
	`Course coursePrototype =`
	`  new Course("Transactions");`
	`ObjectSet courses =`
	`  container.`
	`  get(coursePrototype);`
	`Course course = (Course)`
	`  courses.next();`
		5

	`course.setDuration(20);`
	`container.set(course);`
	`container.commit();`
	`container.ext().refresh(`
	`  course, Integer.MAX_VALUE);`
	`(this is the lost update)`
		20

`course.setDuration(10);`
`container.set(course);`
`container.commit();`
`container.ext().refresh(`
`  course, Integer.MAX_VALUE);`
	`container.ext().refresh(`
	`  course, Integer.MAX_VALUE);`
		10

Time

Figure 13-8. *Example of a lost update occurring in db4o*

This example also shows how db4o and Read Committed transactions work. There is no "transaction start" explicitly called. Every commit will save the objects to the container without paying attention to other running transactions (no locks). Note that you need to explicitly refresh the objects to make sure you are actually reading from the database, and not from the in-memory cache that is held during a transaction.

One thing that is reliably prevented with db4o is reading and processing a value that has been not yet been committed by a parallel transaction. It is due to the explicit commit command that you can read changes from a parallel transaction in db4o.

If you need more restrictive locking, you are forced to implement your own locking. One possibility is to use semaphores to get the concurrent processes synchronized. Transactions in db4o, and locking objects with semaphores in particular, are described in detail in Chapter 9.

Other Database Objects

We finish off this chapter by considering two further kinds of database object: sequences and indexes.

Sequence

A *sequence* is a database object that generates integer values. Usually you create primary key values with the help of sequences. Values generated by a sequence are always unique for each row in a table. In an object database, every object is assigned a unique OID. This parallels the way "live" objects are represented in memory—every one is uniquely identifiable by its memory address. Therefore, you do not need to generate special values in order to make an object unique.

In some cases, however, it's useful to be able to generate sequential values, where these have a meaning. For example, the academy might need a class to represent bookings for courses: you might want to give each new Booking a unique booking number. One simple way to do this is to store a single instance of the BookingNumber class, shown here, and to retrieve and update it each time you need get the next booking number:

```
public class BookingNumber
{
    private Long nextNumber;

    public BookingNumber()
    {
        nextNumber = new Long(1);
    }

    public void incrementNumber()
    {
        int num = nextNumber.intValue();
        num++;
        nextNumber = new Long(num);
    }

    public Long getNextNumber()
    {
        return nextNumber;
    }
}
```

Index

Indexing grants faster access to the desired data. Indexes are decoupled from tables and can be deleted without worrying about structure, although deletion of a table also results in deletion of its indexes. In contrast to most RDBMSs, db4o will not set an index for a class automatically, but you can easily configure it to create indexes.

Let's look at a simple example of creating an index. In SQL, we can index the name column of the Trainee table like this:

```
CREATE INDEX traineeNames ON trainee (name);
```

The db4o equivalent indexes the name field of the Trainee class:

```
Db4o.configure().objectClass(Trainee.class).objectField("name").indexed(true);
```

Voilà! You should experience a significant performance gain when querying using the names of trainees now. Please bear in mind that if you refactor the database you may have to manually reconfigure the indexes.

Summary

In this chapter we looked at db4o from the SQL developer's point of view by comparing a range of common SQL operations with the db4o equivalent, where available. We hope that looking at it in these terms helps you to understand how to get the best out of db4o, to identify where it provides a different way of doing the same thing, and to recognize where familiar database concepts are not appropriate. It's important to emphasize again that the strengths of db4o don't lie in its ability to replicate the capabilities of a relational database; instead, it offers a unique combination of integration with .NET and Java applications, support for complex object models with no need for object-relational mapping, low use of resources, and zero administration.

In the next chapter, we try to answer two more important questions that database developers ask when considering whether db4o is right for them: how does it perform and what can you use it for?

∎∎∎

CHAPTER 14

Technical Considerations When Using db4o

This chapter tries to answer questions that arise when deploying db4o to different target architectures. For instance, db4o is a good candidate for embedded systems, but does it also fit into other conventional system architectures? Where can db4o best be utilized, and when should we choose another option? What are the limits of db4o, and how does it perform in comparison to other DBMSs? The information and comments in this chapter should help you evaluate the suitability of db4o for your own applications.

Performance

Performance is a key factor in the choice of a database. For db4o to be an ideal choice, it should provide performance that is clearly better than the available alternatives, or that is comparable, in which case its other advantages become significant. A true test of performance requires benchmarking with your own type of application and hardware combinations. To get an initial indication of likely performance, however, general benchmarks are available that can give you a guide to the strengths and weaknesses of different persistence solutions. In this chapter we use an open source benchmark, written in Java, called PolePosition.[1] You will see pros and cons of object databases, specifically db4o, and get to know some typical behavior of OODBMSs.

After that, we discuss the issues that arise when db4o is driven to its limits: how it performs with huge objects or large numbers of objects, and how it performs in systems with large numbers of users. At the end of this section you should be able to answer the question of whether db4o has the performance to suit your needs.

Benchmarking: David vs. Goliath?

If we want to figure out the performance of an OODBMS, it is obvious that we need to compare it to well-known RDBMSs. Unfortunately, there is no way of presenting the results of benchmarks from large database vendors like Oracle without their permission due to their licensing models. Also, benchmarks that simply reflect the database itself may not be particularly meaningful when what you really want to know is what kind of performance you will get with a particular combination of database and access method. For example, the performance within a Java

---

1. www.polepos.org

application using an RDBMS may be significantly different when accessing the database using JDBC compared to using an object/relational (O/R) mapper such as Hibernate or JDO. Of course, mapping is not an issue with db4o.

The PolePosition benchmark provides some very useful information in the context of object-oriented applications. This benchmark project provides a set of benchmark tests and the results of running these tests against a variety of databases. The results that have been published in the public domain apply strictly to open source persistence solutions, although as the benchmark itself is open source, you can adapt it to run against any database you like. The published results include a rich set of measurements and comparisons between databases, including MySQL, HSQLDB, and db4o. This accounts for a representative range of database types, from enterprise-level RDBMSs to small footprint RDBMSs to OODBMSs. Most notably you will find different persistence strategies compared. In other words, "pure" db4o will compete against O/R mappers and also nonmapping direct JDBC. JDO/VOA, which is also included in Table 14-1, is an O/R mapping tool from Versant.

It's worth looking in detail at the published PolePosition results. Table 14-1 shows a brief summary of the results of a range of operations that illustrate cases where db4o performs well; we've taken one representative result from each test series. The top and bottom performers in each test are bolded in the table. By the way, tests where db4o does not perform so well are also shown, in Table 14-2. The tests that are summarized are as follows:

- **Write flat bulk**: This is a simple test that writes 10,000 objects of a single kind without further dependencies into the database.

- **Read/write/delete object tree**: This test writes/deletes and reads a complex object tree with depth 8 of simple objects into the database.

- **Query inheritance**: This test writes, reads, queries, and deletes object trees with a five-level inheritance structure. Each tree consists of five objects; the next derives from the previous and so on. The last one gets persisted. The test queries a previously indexed field in the middle of the whole inheritance structure (100 selects executed on 1,000 objects). The published results also show db4o just needs 2 milliseconds of additional time in order to execute 100 selects on 30 times more objects in the database (100 selects executed on 30,000 objects), whereas the Hibernate/HSQLDB combination needs additional time by a factor of 40! The Hibernate/MySQL combination behaves better here, however, so we should not blame the O/R mapper for this.

- **Query indexed int**: This test shows how fast you can query a single object from the database by using an indexed (integer) field (900 selects executed on 1,000 objects).

- **Retrieve object by native ID**: In contrast to the previous test, here the objects are queried by their native ID. Querying the RDBMSs is done—as usual—via the primary key. Five thousand selects are executed against 30,000 objects. Though db4o does not get pole position in this case, it is much faster than the other solutions, except HSQLDB. This advantage could be leveraged when optimizing very critical queries.

Table 14-1. *PolePosition Benchmark Results: db4o As Top Performer*

Time in ms	Write Flat Bulk	Read Object Tree	Write Object Tree	Delete Object Tree	Query Inheritance	Query Indexed Int	Retrieve Object by Native ID
db4o/4.5.200	931	25	**18**	27	**22**	**158**	236
Hibernate/MySQL	5570	127	148	258	148	1812	3306
JDBC/MySQL	3060	53	117	108	37	299	1383
Hibernate/HSQLDB	1602	120	82	157	11791	897	1134
JDBC/HQSLDB	**291**	66	19	81	14912	191	**22**
JDO/VOA/MySQL	2814	176	211	50	67	500	2403

So what do we learn from these test results? Well, probably not much you could not get from considering the characteristics of object databases. In fact, we pretty much see the results we would have expected. If there is a need to access complex object structures, then db4o is at its most impressive. RDBMSs, with or without O/R mappers, cannot compete when it comes to this kind of task. They need to access several tables with several queries and fetch operations (mostly selects) in case of deep inheritance trees as well as deep object graphs. Keep in mind that navigating an object tree instead of playing with different single values helps you to write code that is easier to understand and to maintain.

If you are accessing your data primarily through object navigation, then an object database will be superior in any case. On the other hand, if you need to query simple data values, access via SQL is likely to perform better. This is reflected in Table 14-2, which illustrates cases in which db4o shows relatively weaker performance.

Table 14-2. *db4o As Underdog*

Time in ms	Query String	Delete Flat Indiv
db4o/4.5.200	16489	414
Hibernate/MySQL	2735	973
JDBC/MySQL	1115	449
Hibernate/HSQLDB	1352	291
JDBC/HSQLDB	**477**	**34**
JDO/VOA/MySQL	1825	103

Here is how these tests worked:

- **Query string**: This test shows how fast an object can be queried using a characteristic string value as identifier (selects: 900/objects: 1,000).

- **Delete flat indiv**: Deletes 1,000 objects individually by ID.

The results from the two tables point to a simple rule of thumb: the flatter and simpler your data, the better performance you will get with SQL. Particularly when it comes to string comparisons, which have to be executed for each object, the highly optimized RDBMSs are by far superior to the native functions from Java and .NET.

Results always depend on the benchmark's environmental background. What the benchmark does not test are the more interesting behaviors, such as concurrent access to the database (parallel read and write access). This hides issues of locking and how databases perform when they are heavily utilized. We will discuss these issues later. HSQLDB delivers some astonishing results solely because it runs "in-process."

Further, db4o is running in local mode in these tests, and the tests used solely SODA queries. However, we have rewritten some tests to use native queries and discovered a slight performance increase of some 10 percent. Exchanging the db4o libraries from version 4.5.200 to version 5.0.002 gave an additional 2 percent performance gain.

The test framework is still in development, and we encourage you to have a look to the PolePosition website for further reading. You may find additional tests, including coverage of other competitors, and of course you can download the test code and run your own tests. The following sections discuss some issues that the PolePosition tests do not take into account.

Behavior with a Large Quantity of Data

In the previous section we compared the performance of different databases and persistence strategies for different scenarios (flat write, inheritance query, etc.). Now let's focus on db4o in some extreme cases of object model design.

Huge Objects

This kind of object is to be found in dynamically or script-created data models. In terms of object analysis these objects are rather evil, but they do arise in some situations. Therefore, every DBMS should be capable of storing this kind of object. db4o has no problems storing huge objects with more than 1,000 fields. During tests we found that storage time is only linearly dependent on field count (and of course, limited by heap memory), so objects can get bigger without having exponential performance loss.

Objects with Huge Fields

Large fields in objects are required for multimedia data such as pictures, documents, or simply files. It is crucial to know how this data can be accessed in the business logic. Are there files representing the data on disk, or is the data held within the object itself? In the latter case, data size is limited by the available heap space. On the other hand, db4o provides functionality to store BLOBs (Binary Large OBjects) independently of the main database file, as already seen in Chapter 10. Table 14-3 illustrates the main benefits and pitfalls of both strategies.

Table 14-3. *Comparing Strategies for Storing Huge Fields in db4o*

Property	Object with byte[ ]-field	Object with db4o-BLOB
Max size	JVM heap size	No upper limit (OS)
Code used to store data (see Chapter 10)	`container.Set(obj);`	`container.Set(obj);` `obj.blob.readFrom(File);`
Benefits	Easy access	No upper limits Objects do not need to be read at once Reading and writing takes place in an extra thread Activation depth is unimportant Data is stored separately, so backup and non-db4o access possible
Pitfalls	JVM limits size No concurrent access Activation depth is crucial for loading objects (otherwise, objects are read fully even if you only need parts of an object)	Requires special code for storing and retrieving data Additional management

■**Caution** When saving an object with a huge field via `objectContainer.Set(obj)`, all data will immediately be sent to the database. Keep this in mind when operating db4o in a client/server configuration.

db4o BLOBs are particularly interesting if you deal with huge fields. Since data is written to disk in a separate thread, you can continue to run application logic while db4o persists your object data. Therefore, you can define and store additional metadata or wrapper data in terms of fields. Optionally, you can store the data to a local file system instead of stressing the network infrastructure. This is an advantage, especially when you do not share data between applications or users.

It is not always appropriate or desirable to store large data masses in a database. The alternative is to store pointers to the location of these masses on a fast disk array. In fact, other than in certain awkward infrastructural environments, or for security reasons, there is no compelling need to store data in the database. Working with HSQLDB, MySQL, or even PostgreSQL, you would in any case prefer the solution of using pointers: if you store data masses in the database you get a performance loss by stressing the database with a very large data payload. If you have ever tried to store huge BLOBs in a MySQL database, you know how tedious this task can be.

With db4o, BLOB storage is quite useful. The simplicity of storing BLOBs with db4o, making data db4o-aware, is excellent, because you do not isolate this data from its logical background. Data can naturally be accessed through the object tree, having only a few lines of additional code. Compare this to storing file strings with external dependencies.

To sum up, we can say that storing very large objects is possible in db4o without serious performance loss. Additionally, development time can be reduced due to the simplicity of the storage mechanism.

Many Objects

The number of storable objects is only limited by the maximum database file size defined. By default it is set to 2GB but can be adjusted by the internal db4o `BlockSize` value:

```
Db4o.Configure().BlockSize(multiplier);
```

You can pick a `BlockSize` between 1 and 127 bytes. The default is 1 byte. Setting it to 8 bytes, giving a database size of 16GB, is recommended, since internal db4o pointers have this length.

Query performance drops linearly in relation to the amount of objects in the database. However, as for any DBMS, indexing single fields significantly improves query performance. In contrast, you do not need to worry about increasing object navigation time. Accessing objects in depth can be done in nearly the same time regardless of the database size or amount of stored objects.

■**Caution** After having used `Set` to store a large number of objects in the db4o container, you should issue a `Commit` before triggering new container actions. The reason is that this will clean the transactional index held in memory, which would cause the system to dramatically slow down.

Behavior with Large Numbers of Users

db4o was not intended to work with extremely high user occurrences. In spite of this, it actually scores well in stress tests of this kind. Until you reach a usage level of 10 users per second, the server is very robust. With heavier loads than this, you will find a linearly increase in processing time depending on the number of users per second. The system does not break down abruptly, even when having extremely high query frequencies or users (far above real-world occurrences).

You should be aware of the limited support for locking in db4o. There is no choice of transaction isolation levels, as shown in Chapter 9. If you need to enforce locking that is more pessimistic than that provided by Read Committed isolation, the logic must be written into your application code. It is your code that determines performance loss or gain. The way in which semaphores are set is decisive: locking too much (e.g., the root object) could result in a slow system, while locking too few objects could cause deadlocks or other transaction anomalies, which need to be detected and dealt with. DBMS vendors have dedicated years of research into these issues, and you will probably fall into several traps by doing this yourself. In fact, you should factor in a significant development time for this. Later on in this chapter we discuss further how well db4o suits distributed systems.

How Does the .NET Version Differ?

Since PolePosition is a pure Java solution, you may ask if there are differences in performance between the Java and .NET versions of db4o. This question is probably best answered by Carl Rosenberger, db4o's chief software architect, who says " . . . performance is quite similar on Java and on .NET. It certainly is in the same order of magnitude." This is borne out by the authors' experience of working with the two platforms.

However, pitfalls arise from language specifics in .NET. Using .NET structs with db4o causes problems. Structs are treated as second-class objects and are stored by value. They are not stored as part of the reference tree. To store them as first-class objects in db4o, they have to be rewritten. A second performance downfall can occur when utilizing .NET exceptions in the wrong places. Exceptions in a native query or in a callback method must be caught by db4o, causing a considerable performance loss.

Wrapping Up

The performance of db4o has been compared with a range of RDBMSs in the context of use in object-oriented applications. It behaves as you would probably expect an object database to do. It excels in operations involving complex data and large objects, while it is less compelling for very simple data and operations. db4o handles huge masses of data well, but it has limitations for large numbers of concurrent users.

Suitability of db4o for Specific System Types

No single database product is likely to be equally suitable for all types of application. For example, Oracle and PostgreSQL are excellent enterprise products, but you would not try to use them for local data storage on a handheld device. So where does db4o fit into the picture, and what types of applications are likely to benefit from its use? Performance is an issue, of course, while other factors, such as zero configuration and ease of development, are important too.

Embedded Systems

The term "embedded system" is used in different ways throughout the world of informatics. It is both a marketing slogan and a technical definition. There is one common factor—an embedded system is one in which hardware as well as software establishes a single functional unit.

The characteristics of such a unit can be narrowed down to the following:

- A clear definition exists of the systems' properties and duties.

- Resources are limited (often without peripherals such as disks, display, or keyboard).

- Prices are low as a result of large production volumes.

- Once the application is deployed, it runs without the need for an administrator who maintains the system (in other words, it's maintenance-free).

- Because of the absence of an administrator, it has to be very secure and reliable.

- Systems often run in real-time mode.

- Systems are often located on mobile devices, and sometimes also in kiosk systems or other similar stationary/standalone environments.

Examples could include a medical application running on a PDA that assists the doctor during his ward round; an industrial robot control system; or a personal assistant on your private smart phone. Also, client software such as a read-out application for wind measuring systems that runs on the laptop of an employee could be considered embedded. In this case the data will be processed immediately and temporarily stored to an internal database.

This introduces the term "embedded database." Such a database must be able to maintain its data without an extra database administration tool. The database is provided with the application. Its primary purpose is to solely act for the application, and does not need to be accessed by external events or systems.

db4o does meet these requirements to a large degree. The footprint of the database is around 400KB. Nonetheless, functionality is not limited by this tiny library size, which is achieved through source code optimization and not through the omission of features. Therefore, db4o is small enough to fit into most of the small to mid-sized applications. In comparison, SQL Server Mobile needs a memory footprint of approximately 2MB—this is a real difference given the resources available in mobile devices.

Support for Mobile Platforms

db4o runs on any Java, .NET (version 1.0 and later, including the Compact Framework), or Mono environment. Devices must be capable of utilizing at least .NET or Java (using a compact virtual machine such as CVM).

For Java this means in particular that

- J2ME-capable devices are supported if they provide the Connected Device Configuration (CDC).

- Connected Limited Device Configuration (CLDC) devices are not supported due to their lack of Java reflection and their very slow record store access. This currently rules out many Java-enabled mobile phones and PDAs.

In the latter case, however, you should note that the flexible and dynamic nature of an open source project is important. Development gets adjusted according to demands, and if demand increases significantly for CLDC devices the community will force the support for such devices. In fact, the problem of reflection absence is something the db4o team is developing, and a solution should become available during 2006.

Today's market of mobile devices is very diverse. You will find smart phones with 8MB memory limits but also PDAs with more than 256MB. In general, there is a rapid pace of development, leading to more and more power, with low prices. This progress will have a significant impact on the market for very small devices.

Platform independence is likely to become increasingly important. db4o does well here by supporting the main platforms, namely Java/.NET. Further, all common operating systems are supported: Windows Mobile 5 OS, Symbian, and SavaJe OS are all supported.

Memory

You need at least one nonvolatile data medium for long-lasting persistence, often flash memory. Given low memory capacities, auto-compression of binary data would be a nice feature to have. Fine-tuning the database would then involve decisions about which is more precious: processor time or memory. db4o does not currently provide this feature.

db4o can also work in environments where no nonvolatile data exists. Particularly in real-time systems, performance does count more than storage issues. It can be configured through its `MemoryIoAdapter` class to operate in-memory and therefore provide high-performance persistence.

Administration

The requirement of zero administration is well supported by db4o. You do not need any administration for creating or maintaining the database and schemas, management of users, roles and rights, monitoring of log files, and so on. The executing application is in full control of the database. Once started, db4o runs until termination of the parent process.

Reliability

The reliability of databases can only be verified by long-term experience. But without getting into great philosophical discussions, many people think that open source–driven products are of higher quality than their proprietary, commercial counterparts. The source code is freely accessible; many developers and users take part in the development process and therefore bugs can be found and eliminated quickly and reliably. Even though db4o is a comparatively young project, it has an active community and excellent prospects for reliability. One real-world application that exemplifies this is the control center software used for Spain's AVE high-speed bullet train system. Developed by Indra Sistemas, this system relies on db4o as a mission-critical, fail-proof, real-time object database. You can find information about other users and applications in the impressive and growing "Customers" section of the db4o website.[2]

Security

Security can be especially important on mobile devices. Just think of patient data, personal data, dates from a mobile organizer, or customer data from outdoor staff that might be held on a mobile device. This kind of information must be protected from unauthorized access. Only the application should be permitted to read from these data. As you can imagine, especially with mobile devices, it is easy to gain possession of a storage medium or the device itself. To address this issue, db4o comes with several database encryption strategies (these are described in more detail in Chapter 12):

- The `XTeaEncryptionFileAdapter` pluggable I/O adapter, which uses the eXtended Tiny Encryption Algorithm (XTEA)

- A very weak built-in encryption

- The possibility to design and implement your own encryption algorithm

Each of these three methods has the same caveat: if you embed the credentials required to access the database into your source code, you are not well protected against source code pirates. Even if the application asks every time for the credentials, you may experience eavesdropping through man-in-the-middle attacks. Of course, not using client/server mode will reduce this risk significantly.

Encryption usually affects performance. With encryption in db4o, you typically suffer a performance loss of approximately 5 percent.

---

2. www.db4o.com/about/customers/

Real Time

Real time, by definition, guarantees that an operation is processed completely by a given time window. Sun's Real-Time Specification for Java provides an environment to cope with this as does Windows Mobile/CE with .NET. In these systems, db4o will naturally run in real time.

Transaction Isolation

The weak spot whereby db4o has only one transaction isolation level (Read Committed) does not play a vital role in embedded environments. As long as you do not use several threads for accessing the database concurrently, this drawback is not particularly relevant.

Wrapping Up

db4o, with its good performance and small footprint, certainly shows its strength in the case of embedded systems.

Distributed Systems

Considering the features of db4o—small, fast, easy to embed—it seems that db4o would perfectly fit for distributed systems as well. However, many details that are needed for proper operation in a distributed system only exist in the roadmap for db4o. This is not surprising: db4objects Inc. itself states that they have not yet concentrated on this matter and therefore distributed systems are not their main playing ground. Let's assess the current situation, though.

A distributed system typically consists of the following components:

- Network

- Autonomous processing unit (client, server, peer)

- Software

In this compound structure, the application software running on the processing units communicates with the other nodes. Nodes transmit messages and interact with each other.

We can imagine at least three different ways of deploying a database in such a network, as shown in Figure 14-1:

- Databases embedded on every client/peer (peer-to-peer, or P2P)

- One server-centric database (client/server, or C/S)

- Databases on both—server and client/peer (distributed database, or DD)

An example of a peer-to-peer scenario might be the processing of CPU-intensive algorithms. Every resource in the network will be utilized for this task. The single, local databases adopt application-wide services while acting as a temporary storage medium for other nodes.

Client/server is the most widely used database application architecture, and you can probably think of many scenarios such as a browser-based web shop or a "fat client" solution like a home banking software application. An example from the enterprise market would be an enterprise resource planning (ERP) system.

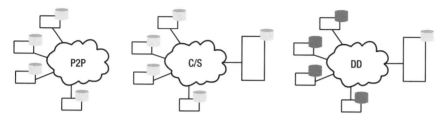

Figure 14-1. *Database deployment scenarios (peer-to-peer, client/server, distributed database)*

Distributed databases are commonly found in software solutions for outdoor staff. The agents collect data and synchronize or replicate it to a central management solution. For example, Eastern Data's successful LoanMaster home credit industry software and Mobilise Van route accounting distribution management both use db4o. In these systems, data is collected on handheld devices and collated by Eastern Data's software.

Distributed systems are affected by a number of problems that must be addressed:

- Handling of stale data

- Replication conflict management

- Locking and concurrent writing

- Performance (connecting time, amount of users, fault tolerance and handling)

- Distributed transactions (two-phase commit, etc.)

- Security

- Robustness and scalability

We do not currently recommend using db4o in distributed systems where you expect a ready-made set of security guidelines and data consistency. Leading product vendors like IBM with their "DB2 Everyplace Enterprise Edition," or Oracle with their "Lite" version, take care of these issues. You also get a simple synchronization component with which you can keep your data in sync. However, all these features come at a significant price.

Many of the problem areas mentioned earlier cannot at present be solved by db4o satisfactorily. Let's look at the ones that we consider to be most critical.

Activation/Refresh

Because of the internal db4o caching mechanism, you cannot be sure you'll get up-to-date objects when querying the container. If another process has changed an object after you have opened the container, you will get the cached version, not the changed one. You are forced to continuously refresh the object after getting it to ensure it is the latest version. However, even this approach can be clumsy and dangerous. At the very least, when your objects have complex hierarchies or deep tree structures you must set the right activation depth for the refresh command. If not, you may work with stale data without knowing. In a future version of db4o, this issue will be addressed. A feature called auto-activation will ensure that all data gets loaded by demand.

Locking

As we have already mentioned throughout this book, db4o does not support built-in locking mechanisms. It is the responsibility of the application to take care of it. With the help of semaphores, you can precisely define the level of granularity with which object data is locked. This task is not to be underestimated. It is not trivial to decide where semaphores should be set in your specific data model. Global object locks (like the root object) are secure but slow down the system significantly. Setting too fine-grained object locks can result in hard-to-find bugs or even produce deadlocks.

The next version of db4o promises to use timestamps for stored objects. That way, db4o will be able to detect changed and conflicting data through a system of versioning and then inform the application about this fact. The application will decide how to proceed—whether a rollback has to be performed or data should be merged.

Exception Handling

Distributed systems require a network connection to run. Commonly, especially when working with mobile devices, a connection breaks down. Dealing with this requires the availability of a very powerful exception handling or disaster-recovery mechanism. db4o does not have either. Hazard tests have shown that the storing application simply does not get informed that its object has not been persisted by the server if the server goes down during the saving process. Exception handling is a big issue for the next milestones in the db4o roadmap.

Scalability

db4o does not support clustering itself. Nevertheless, you can implement your own cluster architecture using the replication facilities provided by db4o since version 5.1, described in Chapter 11. Alternatives for scaling the system are basically limited to upgrading the system resources like disk space or CPU power. Other alternatives that provide the reliability of a cluster system include RAID systems and uninterruptible power supplies (UPSs). Backing up the database should yield no problem. db4o provides hot backup functionality to back up single-user databases and client/server databases while they are running. If needed, the replication facilities (direct synchronization) of db4o can also be used to develop a backup strategy.

Figure 14-2 shows a schematic diagram of a possible distributed system that includes the features described in this section.

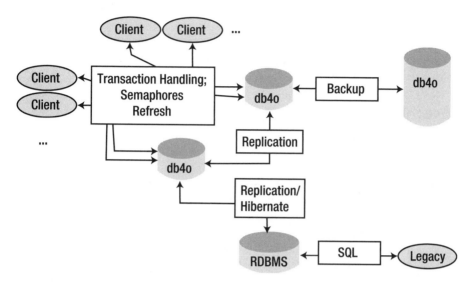

Figure 14-2. *Possible distributed scenario*

Recovery

Apart from the native file system recovery routines on which the db4o instance is running, db4o only supports one recovery mechanism at this time. db4objects Inc. calls it a resume-commit-on-crash strategy. If a system crashes during the commit of a transaction due to power loss or any other hazardous failure, the commit will be finished by the next time the container is opened. In conjunction with an improved working exception handling, this will in future versions lead to acceptable security through recovery.

Security

If security within a distributed environment is a concern, you need to implement your own adapter on top of the native, unencrypted object stream (its format is open but not particularly well documented) from db4o. You will have to dig deep into db4o internals or change your architecture.

Classes

You must take care of your classes! Objects are not interchangeable like raw data submitted to an RDBMS. Since an object database only stores the state of objects, a stored object has little meaning without a class definition. It is essential to have exactly the same classes in the class-path of all databases and clients that talk to each other. Otherwise, objects simply do not get stored—a mistake that could result in hours of bug tracing. However, if you are careful with this, you can still make use of db4o's schema evolution feature. You can get further information in Chapter 12, which describes how db4o recognizes and handles changes in the model and what you should take into account.

Wrapping Up

db4o has some significant limitations for distributed systems, but many of these either have been addressed—for example, through the replication mechanism supported by db4o 5.1—or will be addressed in future versions.

Enterprise Systems

Looking finally into the world of the time-honored enterprise software development, we get the feeling that db4o does not fit into that. It somehow seems to be too effective, too fast, and too small for this kind of "big" environment. As an example that is in some ways comparable, think about how long it took for ideas like agile software development to be adopted.

Enterprise systems are different from other systems, and make different demands. In general, and in stark contrast to embedded systems, the developer does not have to think about limited resources. The challenge here is a high abstraction level: the software architect must consider questions of portability, exchangeability, security, and availability. All these complex fields of interest must be combined into a long-term robust composition.

The techniques used to persist objects are of higher importance than in an embedded system. Different applications often need access to the same data in the same time. Furthermore, legacy systems do not even know about objects (object-oriented COBOL notwithstanding). All this implies user management: roles, groups, rights, and so on. In enterprise systems it is necessary to centralize data due to cost reduction. You also need a domain model. Every domain should manipulate only data of its own responsibilities. This is the only way to render possible a working versioning, backup, and recovery procedure and therefore avoids uncontrolled behavior and data growth.

You will find several approaches in the field of persistence strategies, including Sun's J2EE (EJB), ADO.NET, JDO, and even JDBC/ODBC access to RDBMSs. Further, much of the data processing may be done by stored procedures in the database rather than by the applications.

Can All These Demands Be Met by db4o?

The answer is: no. For the time being, db4o is no competitor for the established players in this game. Companies have invested much effort and expenditure into their preferred DBMS and simply cannot switch entirely to OODBMS solutions. It should also be remembered that DBMS vendors have spent lots of development time (over 30 years) to make complex features like replication and synchronization work. During this time they grew up with the special needs of their customers and have adapted to this environment.

So How Does db4o Fit In?

db4o does have a place in the enterprise, but it must fit into the existing infrastructures. As a first step, db4o can be used, securely kept in data access object (DAO) patterns, in the satellites of an enterprise system. There it will be responsible for local or temporary data storage. The DAO approach guarantees exchangeability and reduces the fear of a vendor lock-in. Linking up to legacy systems can be done the old-fashioned way with well-known interfaces, web services, or, in the next stage of expansion, with the Hibernate-based replication mechanism of db4o. db4o easily integrates into web applications via the application context.

We believe that the more db4o is used, the more people will notice the advantages. These advantages are addictive. Having worked without being forced to be concerned about O/R mapping, architectural design of a database, or even complex individual solutions (because in db4o the class model is the database schema), you probably do not want to go back again. However, you should keep in mind our discussion of distributed systems in this chapter. db4o's capabilities diminish with complexity of concurrent processes or the number of clients that need access to the same data.

Summary

The aim of this chapter was to help you understand the technical issues involved in deploying a persistence solution based on db4o, concentrating primarily on performance and technical requirements of different application types. The next chapter looks at the use of db4o from another, equally important point of view, discussing the business case for using db4o.

CHAPTER 15

The Business Case for db4o

Since the decline of the Internet boom several years ago, few startups in Silicon Valley have lasted the pace. db4objects, Inc. is an exception. Founded in Germany and then incorporated in the United States, the company behind db4o has drawn praise from analysts, the media, and investors. Of course, there are many database vendors in the marketplace, quite a few of them much bigger and better known than db4objects. However, the company has proven in a few short years that it is genuinely innovative, and has developed a product that has some compelling advantages within its target markets. In this chapter we take a brief look at the company, its technology and its history, at the dual-licensing model on which its business is based, at how db4o compares to today's most commonly used persistence methods, and at how changing market conditions affect the prospects for object databases. Finally, we sum up the benefits and drawbacks of using db4o and consider the business risks associated with using it.

The Technology

What is the best persistence technology for objects? Probably the one that saves development time, fits best to your development frame work, lets the persistence implementation be like the rest of the program, and handles the objects in their native form, as objects. This kind of technology will allow developers to handle persistent objects in the most natural way possible.

This seems quite obvious, and indeed the idea of an object database is far from new. With the advent of object-oriented programming in the early 1980s, discussion on the storage of objects began. It took about ten years until the first object database products were commercially available. However, what looked like a major step forward for programming technologies— although started with great expectations—turned out to suffer from some significant problems, some technical and some otherwise.

The promise of replacing relational database systems has not materialized—perhaps until now. In recent years a handful of object databases have overcome many of the important problems of persisting objects. One of them is db4o—database for objects. Today db4o is the leading open source database for objects, and is ranked among the most popular object-oriented database systems.

The Company: db4objects, Inc.

The company was founded in 2000 by Chief Architect Carl Rosenberger. A year later the first product had been released: db4o 1.0 for Java. In 2004 the company was incorporated under CEO Christof Wittig. db4objects, Inc. is held in private hands and is now located in San Mateo, California. Financial backing comes from established Silicon Valley investors, including Mark Leslie, Diane Greene, and Audrey MacLean. Due to their challenging objectives and even more so their achievements, db4objects, Inc. has become a well-regarded startup and one of the foremost technology innovators in Silicon Valley.

The rising popularity of db4o stems from a variety of factors: the simplicity of the underlying programming interface; the reliability of the product; and last but not least, for the dual-license model, including an open source license. The community of db4o supporters is continually increasing, with over 250,000 downloads and some 10,000 registered users in 2005. Over 100 commercial projects have been successfully realized with db4o so far, and it has been proven in mission-critical applications. db4o is being used by companies to drive innovation. Boeing, BMW, Hertz, and Bosch have embedded db4o in future projects with demanding requirements, in both standalone and distributed systems. db4o has positioned itself among the top products of a challenging and growing market, and future prospects look bright.

The fact that the source code has been made publicly available has enhanced the dependability of the product. In other open source projects like Linux and MySQL, the open availability of the source code has had significant benefits, including rapid discovery and elimination of flaws, and the growth of a community of users and developers, helping to assure the long-term future of the products. The existence of a reliable, affordable, and embeddable open source database for objects gives object-oriented developers the tool they need for exciting new applications and smart devices.

License Model

db4o is offered by db4objects, Inc. under a dual-license model. The product can be used either with a commercial license or the well-known GNU General Public License (GPL). The GPL requires db4o to be open source.

A dual license is very fair in terms of affordability. The software is free for some users, for example students, researchers, faculty, and community and educational projects. Their activities will enrich the open source community under GPL. For those who do their business using db4o, affordable low unit prices are offered. The pricing generally undersells conventional vendors.

The dual license has proved its sustainability as a business model with the widely used open source relational database MySQL. Offering software at no cost might appear absurd at a first glance, but in fact it is a very smart and effective long-term strategy. It helps to form an active and dynamic community that can interact with the vendor and steer the direction of the product to ensure it meets customers' need. Operational and strategic problems are discussed on a much broader stage than within only one company. Finally, the commercial users of db4o benefit from the license model as savings on the marketing and sales costs help to keep commercial license terms affordable.

The GPL

The distinction between open source software and free software is not completely clear to some people. db4o is open source: anyone can download and examine the source code. However, whether or not you can use it free of charge depends on the way that db4o is used or embedded in your software, on the commercial aspects of your project, and on the level of support you require for the project.

The General Public License provides you with the software free of charge, but has some important restrictions. The license limits the distribution and publishing of your own software. It follows the "quid pro quo," or "something for something," principle. It supports the legal concept of supplying something of value in return for receiving something of value. If the providing vendor is open source, then the user's software needs to be open source as well.

If customers' software is based on db4o software licensed under GPL terms, then GPL terms must also apply to the software in which db4o is deployed. The following four points have been specified by db4objects, Inc. to help you decide whether your software is based on db4o. Your software is considered to be based on db4o software in situations including, but not limited to, the following:

- You compile your software against the db4o software.

- Your software contains specific references to the db4o software.

- Your software requires the db4o software to work.

- Your software uses the proprietary db4o API.

In all of these situations, if you distribute or publish your software, then the source code for your software will have to be made available open source too, in addition to meeting other GPL requirements.

The trigger for the GPL obligations is redistribution. In general: no redistribution, no GPL constrains. If there is redistribution, then the resulting software should be GPL too; otherwise, a db4o commercial license is required. The decision tree shown in Figure 15-1 has been created to guide you in deciding whether you need to pay for a commercial license.

The deployment of db4o within a company for in-house projects is also allowed under the GPL terms. A commercial license is required only for redistribution. Any evaluation, development, or educational applications stay free with the GPL terms.

In cases where you choose to distribute your software within a client/server system, further criteria exist for deciding which license applies. Some technologies coalesce objects running on the client and those running on the server. The objects technically and legally can't be separated. This depends on the technology that is employed. If the clients access the server via HTTP or TCP/IP protocols, then the actual application still runs on the server side. The client only represents a view of the application via these protocols. In these circumstances the licensing criteria do not apply.

Other proprietary protocols for remote procedure calls (RPCs) involve both client and server components that work with objects. The components technically and legally can't be separated. The rule that the software references or compiles against db4o software will apply; hence a commercial license is needed.

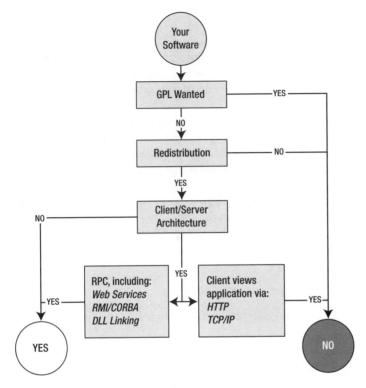

Figure 15-1. *Do you have to pay?*

Another important consideration in the decision process is the amount of support that is required when using db4o in a project. db4objects, Inc. provides detailed documentation for each release. The website also offers a community support forum in which the db4o developers are active participants and frequently answer users' questions. In projects with fixed timescales, however, more support may be considered necessary. In those cases db4o provides a Developer Network with an extended Developer Portal, available to members only. The benefits are **personalized** (you only see your own questions), **private** (privacy is guaranteed; don't worry—nobody else out there can read what you wrote), and **tracked** support (you can see the status of your question at any time). A response is guaranteed within 24 hours.

Licensing Examples

The following licensing examples illustrate some of the general principles—they are, however, not exhaustive.

Student Project

First, imagine a team of students is building a mini self-controlled robot car. They need a computing unit and decide to use a popular PDA model. They buy a remote controlled car, remove the remote units, and assemble the PDA. The tricky part starts with implementing the software system. They decide to use db4o as an easy embeddable resource accessible via Java and .NET. Clearly this academic project fully complies with GPL terms and no payments are necessary (unless the team decides to commercialize the project at a later date).

Small Web Shop

The second example (see Figure 15-2) addresses small to mid-sized business needs. Suppose a small company develops a Java or .NET web shopping application using db4o as the data store. Access to this system only takes places via web browsers, through the HTTP protocol. This web shop is definitely commercial. According to the strict interpretation, this system is clearly based on db4o. The system should be open source or a commercial license should be brought. However, as we saw earlier, the HTTP protocol separates the browser client from the server so that these two components are not coupled; therefore, no redistribution takes places and the data store does not require commercial terms.

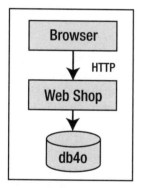

Figure 15-2. *Web shop with db4o*

Multiplayer Game

The booming cell phone market shows potential for creating new business models. For example, multiplayer games are currently in great demand. In a multiplayer game environment, the cell phones are the clients that contact the game server via a network protocol. In this case the protocol is TCP/IP (see Figure 15-3), and the game server provides features like high scores, states of the current game, and so forth. On the server side, persistence is managed by db4o. Again the actual action of the gaming application takes place on the server. The cell phone clients with their TCP/IP packages only have a view on the application. Therefore, no commercial license is needed. In practice, however, the company should probably take part in the Developer Network to ensure full support.

■**Caution** This section should be interpreted as a guide to help you understand the dual-license model, and is not an all-embracing legal statement. For detailed questions on licensing, you should contact db4objects, Inc. or your lawyer.

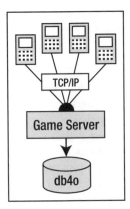

Figure 15-3. *Cell phone multiplayer game with db4o*

Commercial Terms

Product developers can purchase db4o Runtimes (dRT) for redistribution of applications with db4o embedded. As a guide, as of 2006 the unit price is $9.00 (US dollars) per license for up to 10,000 dRT licenses, and can drop to $1.00 for large volumes. However, flexibility and suitability for customers needs are essential features of the licensing plans. For this reason, customers are encouraged to request a personal free quote from db4objects, Inc.

For networking and broad support issues, db4o offers the db4o Developer Network (dDN). It has been designed for companies that develop software with db4o or run db4o applications in-house. This solution includes, for example, individual case support with maximum response time of 24 hours and a lock-in of already negotiated dRT licenses for reliable long-term budget calculations. Normally db4o requires the dDN membership to distribute dRT licenses with applications. As of December 2005 the dDN costs $1,200 per member and year.

The third license available is the db4o Server License (dSL) for in-house, non-GPL usage of db4o. This comes together with a dDN subscription for the mentioned enhanced support features.

Common Persistence Solutions

In this section we briefly review some of the more commonly used solutions for persistence in object-oriented applications, looking at the key technology and application issues. The list is not intended to be exhaustive, but covers the main persistence solution types. We then go on to analyze the place that db4o occupies in this landscape.

One feature common to almost all solutions that are currently used is that they center on the idea that one side—the application side—works with pure objects, usually Java or .NET, while the other side—the persistence side—uses pure relation sets for data in an RDBMS. The distinction between different solutions lies mainly in how they bring the two sides together. You can refer to Part I of this book for a detailed description of the object and relational models.

Design Process

The typical design process for an application is pretty much the same no matter which of the persistence solutions we describe here is used. Most object-oriented applications are designed using the Unified Modeling Language (UML), starting with a set of use cases that the application needs to implement. The use cases are broken down to pure objects, producing a class diagram with all attributes that represent the entities and the methods applied to those entities. Interaction diagrams express the behavior of these objects in implementing the use cases.

On the data side, developers need to define the data that needs to be stored. Then an Entity Relationship Diagram (ERD) is produced. Deriving the ERD from the object model requires a process known as normalization. The attributes of an entity need to be structured until only directly dependent attributes to the primary key remain. For the rest of the attributes, a new entity will be linked via foreign keys to the original entity. Constraints and triggers assure the integrity of the data.

In practice, most developers or teams are used to building data models together with their applications. Usually this goes without question simply because it is the established approach. However, looking at this approach from the viewpoint of a project manager, with a focus on timelines and budget, the process of building two models of a system represents a significant cost in designing an application. Every change in one model triggers a change or adaptation in the other.

JDBC

Java Database Connectivity (JDBC) is the industry standard for communicating with an RDBMS from within a Java application. JDBC provides an API that allows the execution of SQL commands against a database. JDBC is demanding in terms of resources for maintenance and implementation. Today it is rarely used for large projects and only affordable in that market with code generators. Nonetheless, it is well suited for small projects and offers very good performance. JDBC is a good choice in applications using embedded SQL databases such as HSQLDB.

JDBC is nowadays often used with data access objects (DAOs), as shown in Figure 15-4. With this approach, data encapsulation can be achieved with the DAO managing the data access. With a DAO architecture, it is easy to switch from one database to another. On the debit side, this means high costs for development and for change management, which has to be done through all layers: objects, DAOs, and relational model.

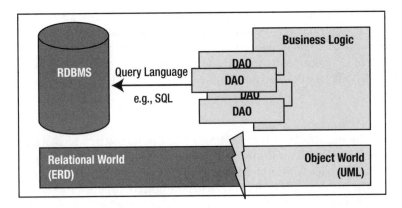

Figure 15-4. *Data access objects approach*

ADO.NET

ADO.NET is the standard data access model for .NET applications. It is based on the idea of a disconnected record set, known as a DataSet, with data adapters that fill the record set by executing SQL statements. The DataSet is not directly connected to a database, and can contain data from different kinds of data source.

The ADO.NET programming model is strongly supported by Microsoft's development tools. It does, however, largely impose a tabular representation of data within the application. ADO.NET applications tend to use the Table Module data access pattern, which is very clearly described by Martin Fowler.[1] This pattern does not sit well with object-oriented application architectures where business logic is implemented in the domain model.

Enterprise JavaBeans

On the Java side, Enterprise JavaBeans (EJB), part of the Java 2 Enterprise Edition (J2EE) architecture, were designed to meet the needs of enterprise-level applications. With so-called entity beans, persistence management can be performed by the J2EE container automatically. This can be done as container-managed persistence (CMP), or, with the implementation of a persistence manager, bean-managed persistence (BMP). Beans encapsulate and simplify data access to RDBMS. Using CMP there is no need to integrate SQL statements into application code. The most recent update is the EJB 3.0 specification. This introduces many changes, but the focus is still on object-relational mapping.

The EJB architecture is highly scalable, but relatively complex to implement. The benefits are only felt with large-scale applications.

---

1. *Patterns of Enterprise Application Architecture*, by Martin Fowler (Addison-Wesley, 2002).

Object-Relational Mapping Frameworks

Many developers have turned to alternative frameworks for persistence management, which supports automatic object-relational mapping without the need to implement the rest of the EJB architecture. A variety of frameworks and tools are available. In the Java world, Hibernate has become particularly popular.

Hibernate is an open source object-relational persistence and query service for Java. It uses XML files that contain information on how classes should be mapped to tables in the RDBMS, as illustrated in Figure 15-5. The application code deals purely with objects, while Hibernate uses the mapping information to generate SQL behind the scenes. Queries can be defined in the application using the HQL or QBC (query-by-criteria) query languages.

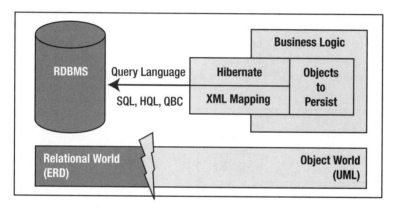

Figure 15-5. *Hibernate approach*

Hibernate allows developers to work with pure objects without the need to implement any other architecture. Although the performance is good, there is an inevitable overhead due to the fact that object-relational mapping has to occur at runtime. Implementation and change management is less time-consuming than the JDBC API or EJB approaches, but object-relational mapping still has to be done or adjusted through the Hibernate mapping files.

Currently Hibernate is the one of leading solutions for object-relational matching, an accepted product, which wraps relational database to store objects. Benchmark results reveal that this type of solution is only practicable if resources are substantial and performance is not highly important.

Similar object-relational mapping tools can be found in the .NET world. NHibernate is a .NET port of Hibernate. Other tools include TierDeveloper and RapTier—these are code generation tools that enable mapping and generation of .NET business or data objects.

Some alternative Java frameworks are based on the Java Data Objects (JDO) specification, which aimed to establish a standard, datastore-independent interface for working with persistent objects. JDO implementations are provided by different vendors, such as Kodo JDO. This makes the usage vendor dependent. Overall, JDO has had relatively low acceptance in the market.

The Alternative: db4o Persistence

With all the solutions described in the previous section, there is a lot of overhead in either development time or performance just to store data. The developer has to solve the so-called impedance mismatch himself. He needs to have expert knowledge in both worlds—the relational and the object world.

Now the db4o approach: you just design your classes with UML and implement them using the db4o API with Java or .NET. That's all. The object schema is the same as the data model. This sounds like a straightforward simplification, but it actually represents a huge step forward for object persistence. Querying uses db4o's simple query-by-example (QBE) mechanism, or the advanced Native Queries method. Figure 15-6 illustrates the pure object approach of db4o.

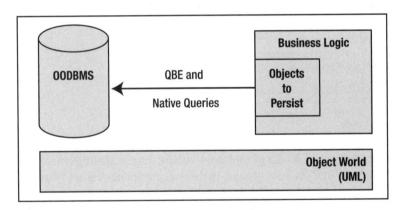

Figure 15-6. *The db4o approach*

The key advantages are that developers can work with object structures as if they were in-memory structures, while there is no performance loss associated with processing taking place behind the scenes to fit those objects into a relational database. Little additional coding is required to manage object persistence. New application features can be added to products much more quickly to gain competitive advantages. Models can be updated more easily for debugging or refactoring, or in order to apply change requirements.

Market Opportunities

In this section we look at the place of object databases in the current database market, and discuss how db4o addresses some of the main impediments to market acceptance of the technology.

One of the main reasons for the dominance of relational database systems today is the existence of legacy systems with numerous enterprise applications depending on the same data. Object-oriented database systems, although they have been commercially available for more than 15 years, have not as yet reached the mainstream market. Most proprietary vendors tried to fit into a vertical market niche, and established themselves for certain industry sectors such as healthcare or defense. This highly focused approach led to complicated interfaces with expensive support practices, limited know-how among developers, and costly commercial terms.

A major shift in the database market in recent years is the emergence of embedded database management systems. The market for these grew 15 percent in 2004 to a total of $1.86 billion.[2] The demand is focused on standalone systems that work out-of-the-box with zero database administration. The types of application range form large server-based to small mobile and desktop applications. IDC,[3] a global provider of market intelligence and advisory services, expects the market to continue growing at least for the next five years. The demand is driven by smaller businesses that require affordable software and lower software engineering efforts.

The embedded database market represents a significant new opportunity for object databases. Modern systems are facing new challenges mainly related to distributed network architectures. The industrial focus is on mobility and availability. At the same time, object-oriented programming languages like Java and C# have become increasingly dominant. In this context traditional RDBMS technology is driven to its limits in terms of handling objects. db4o is a solution that can handle a large number of complex objects, offers powerful replication and querying capabilities, and greatly reduces development time.

Addressing Perceived Problems with Object Databases

Many decision makers either have no knowledge of object databases, or have a view based on some common perceptions. db4o provides some new answers to those concerns. One prejudice concerns the performance of object systems. However, as benchmarks have shown, db4o can achieve better results than commonly used object-relational mappers. These performance benchmarks are described in detail in Chapter 14.

Another widely held view of object data stores is the low volume of data that can be handled. In the case of db4o, the database is able to handle up to 254GB of data. For whole enterprise data stores with multimedia content this might not be enough, but for most small to mid-sized applications this more than meets the requirements.

Although object databases are a growing market they still lack accepted standards to match SQL. The Object Data Management Group (ODMG) standards developed in the 1990s failed to address this problem. Because of this, there are nonproprietary object database development tools. With db4o this problem does not apply since the API can be integrated into any Java or .NET IDE.

---

2. "Worldwide Embedded Database Management Systems 2005–2009 Forecast," IDC, May 2005.
3. A subsidiary of the Information Data Group (IDG).

A further common criticism of object systems is the lack of query languages. Many proprietary approaches exist among object databases. db4o has powerful support for querying, particularly with the introduction of the Native Query (NQ) mechanism, described in Chapter 6. The concept of integrating queries into the programming language has been validated by Microsoft's LINQ (.NET Language Integrated Queries) project and seems to pilot an important industry trend.

Benefits and Pitfalls of db4o

We have tried in this book to demonstrate that db4o has many exciting and unique capabilities. However, there is no universal solution to the problem of persistence in object-oriented systems: the features that make db4o an ideal solution for some applications make it unsuitable for others. Here we briefly summarize some of the benefits and pitfalls that have been identified in the preceding chapters.

Benefits

- db4o is a full-featured, embeddable database engine for devices; for mobile, desktop, and server platforms in object-oriented environments; and for applications with multimedia content or complex data structures.

- The binary has a tiny size, around 400KB, and can be integrated easily in the same memory process as the application—even in devices with limited resources.

- db4o is a zero-administration database.

- It eliminates the need for tools and code that are required for object-relational mapping. Using db4o reduces code complexity and resource consumption compared with common 3-tier approaches, leading to savings in development time and cost.

- It greatly simplifies refactoring in data-aware applications.

- db4o offers a high level of cross-platform support, including for mobile platforms, as it is available for Java, .NET, and Mono.

- Replication to relational databases using the db4o Replication Service allows migration of data to legacy data stores.

Pitfalls

- An object database should not be deployed when data independence is required. Without the application or exactly the same class model, the data cannot be accessed unless the data is migrated to an alternative data store.

- If your environment consists of older systems that are relational-based, then an object database will not be the answer.

- The lifetime of the data and the application should be considered—in many cases the data lives longer than the actual application.

- To date db4o does not offer database clustering.

- db4o does not provide functionality to control rights for individual users or roles. If these are needed, the application itself needs to implement a rights management.

- Though db4o complies with ACID principles, transaction support and recovery are not as comprehensive as those in many RDBMSs.

- Object databases are new to business systems and are a long way from being as established as relational systems. Consequently, there is a lack of third-party products such as embeddable tools for data mining, tuning, and reporting.

These factors lead to some conclusions about where db4o is most useful. Its suitability for some key application areas was discussed in detail in Chapter 14. Briefly, the target environments for db4o are persistence architectures where there is no database administrator and no RDBMS legacy. It can successfully be deployed embedded in devices, in mobile and desktop clients, and in the middleware. db4o can be used in enterprise data centers, but is used less often here due to the prevalence of legacy data and systems. db4o customers can be found in many industries, including transportation, networks, natural sciences, industrial, consumer and enterprise applications.

Risk Analysis

When selecting a new technology, evaluation should focus strongly on the risk to your business that might arise. In this final section, we take at look at some potential risks associated with selecting db4o, and describe how we think those risks are addressed.

Technology

Clearly, a major risk factor is that db4o is a new technology competing with relational database systems that have been under constant development and refinement for over 30 years. Perceptions will also be affected by the failure of previous object database systems to have any significant impact in the mainstream. It's important to recognize that db4o, as an embeddable native object database, is a totally different proposition from previous products, and competes in a changed marketplace where embedded databases are increasingly important. db4o stands a very good chance of proving the sustainability of the object database concept

Availability of developer skills is an issue that needs to be considered. There are many highly skilled database developers who will be resistant to any move away from the well-known technology. In fact, db4o development is more likely to be done by .NET and Java programmers than traditional database developers, and those programmers are likely to become comfortable with db4o very easily.

Industry standards are a key issue, and SQL has been a strong factor in the success of relational databases. Attempts to establish similar standards for object databases have been largely unsuccessful. db4o handles this issue by standardizing on .NET and Java. The programming language is used to create databases, store data, and run queries.

The Vendor

Apart from technological considerations, a key risk factor is the business continuity of the vendor. Will the product succeed, and will third-party vendors or the open source community enrich the product with additional tools?

Compared to the main vendors of relational database systems, like Oracle, IBM, Microsoft, and so on, db4objects, Inc. is a small company. It is, however, a growing, dynamic and innovative company with solid, long-term financial backing. The pace of development over the past year or two has been highly impressive, and db4o remains highly innovative while turning rapidly into a mature product.

The license model is a strong plus. The source code is publicly available, so the product will not vanish from one day to another. An active community is following developments, sharing advice and experience, and contributing to the product quality. Open source software has been criticized for lack of support and documentation. However, the success of projects such as MySQL has proved that open source can be at least as reliable as commercial systems. MySQL in particular has demonstrated the benefits of a dual-licensing model similar to that adopted for db4o.

Industry Acceptance

The final risk factor can be summed up by the question "so who else uses it?" db4o's client list includes some pretty impressive companies: Boeing, Bosch, Hertz, BMW, and more, and some very successful projects have been implemented using db4o. For example, the safety-critical Integrated Control System (IRC) of the Spanish AVE High-Speed Train system, developed by Indra Sistemas, relies on db4o. Other success stories can be found on the db4o website.

One of the most interesting things about the customer stories listed at the site is the diversity of applications. Although targeted primarily at specific types of systems, db4o is clearly making a compelling argument for itself across a broad range of market sectors. If you have an application that needs to work with persistent objects, the experience of these users suggests that you should give db4o some pretty serious consideration.

■ ■ ■

Working with the ObjectManager

In Chapter 5 we briefly introduced db4o's graphical database browser, the ObjectManager. In this appendix, we examine in more detail what you can do with it. Before we do that, let's be clear about exactly what it is, and also what it isn't.

As you probably know, many graphical database administration tools are available for relational databases. Some are specific to one RDBMS—for example, MySQL Administrator (www.mysql.com/products/tools/administrator/). Others will, given suitable database drivers, interface with pretty much any RDBMS. Modern IDEs such as Visual Studio, Eclipse, and NetBeans have integrated database administration tools. With any of these tools, you can expect to be able to create schemas and tables; to define columns, indexes, and keys in tables; and to view, insert, edit, and delete data. These functions are carried out either by using graphical controls or by executing SQL statements and viewing the results graphically.

None of these tools will interface with db4o because, as should have become clear throughout this book, the underlying data model is fundamentally different. This is not a problem, as db4o is intended to be tightly integrated into applications that will usually have exclusive responsibility for interfacing with the database. Administration tasks, such as creating schemas, are also embedded within the applications, so there is no need for external administration tools.

However, it is often very useful to be able to look into a db4o database in an ad hoc way, by browsing or running queries for specific objects, even if only to check that your application has stored its data correctly. The ObjectManager allows you to do exactly this, and little more than this. It does not let you alter the database schema, or to insert or delete objects. It does allow a very basic level of updating: you can only edit the values of numeric and string fields in any object in a database. It's a simple, but very useful, tool.

Installing and Running

This appendix describes ObjectManager version 1.7 for db4o 5.2. The ObjectManager is separate from the main db4o distribution, and is available as a Java application only, written using the Standard Widget Toolkit (SWT) for its graphical user interface. This doesn't mean that C# developers can't use it. The generic reflector, described in Chapter 12, allows db4o to read .NET objects from databases, and the ObjectManager itself is supplied in a version that can run on .NET without the need to install Java. It can be obtained from the Download Center area of the db4objects website (www.db4o.com/community/ontheroad/downloadcenter/). Free registration is required to get access to this area. Versions are available for both Windows and Linux. You have two choices on Windows:

- **ObjectManager for Windows no Java VM**: Use this version if you have a Java Virtual Machine (JVM) installed.

- **ObjectManager for Windows IKVM**: IKVM is an implementation of Java that runs on top of the .NET Framework and Mono. It includes a JVM and a .NET implementation of the Java class libraries, and allows you to run ObjectManager as a standalone application on a system without a Java installation, which may well appeal to .NET developers.

Installation is simply a matter of extracting the files from the archive you download: a `.zip` archive on Windows and a `.tar.gz` archive on Linux. You then run the program as follows:

- **Windows**: Run the file `objectmanager.bat` in the root folder, which is the folder where your `zip` file was located. If your operating system path does not include the `bin` folder of your Java installation, then you will need to edit `objectmanager.bat` to include the full path.

- **Linux**: Run the file `objectmanager.sh` script file in the root directory, which is the folder where your `zip` file was located. You will need to set permissions so that this script file is executable: `chmod +x objectmanager.sh`. If your path does not include the `bin` folder of your Java installation, then you will need to edit `objectmanager.sh` to include the full path at `export VMEXE`.

Opening and Browsing a Database

When you start the ObjectManager you will see the main window with no open database, as shown in Figure A-1. On Windows, a command prompt window will open first and display startup messages—you don't need to interact with this; just wait for the main window to open.

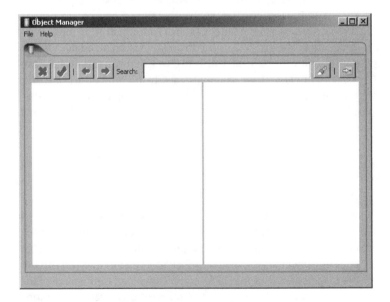

Figure A-1. *The ObjectManager main window*

Opening a File

To open a database file directly, select the File ➤ Open menu option and browse for the file. If the database file is encrypted, use the File ➤ Open "Encrypted" File option, which displays a dialog box that allows you to browse for the file and also asks you to enter a password, as shown in Figure A-2.

Figure A-2. *The Open "encrypted" file dialog box*

Note that this option only works with files encrypted using simple db4o encryption. The ObjectManager does not currently support the stronger encryption provided in db4o by the XTeaEncryptionFileAdapter pluggable I/O adapter described in Chapter 12 (or, for that matter, any other custom I/O adapter). This seems like an obvious development for future versions of the ObjectManager.

■**Caution** Opening a database file in ObjectManager will lock the file, so if you try to run an application that accesses the same file while it is still open in the ObjectManager, you will get a Database File Locked exception. You need to close the database with File ➤ Close All Databases or shut down the ObjectManager before running the application.

Connecting to a Server

Alternatively, you can connect to a database server that is running in network mode. In this case, other clients can have concurrent access to the database while it is open in the ObjectManager. You can't connect to a server running in embedded mode. Use the File ➤ Connect to Server option, which opens the dialog box shown in Figure A-3.

Figure A-3. *The Connect to db4o Server dialog box*

Displaying Objects

The method used to access the database makes no difference to the way the contents are displayed. Figure A-4 shows the main window after opening the database used in Chapter 6. This simple database contains only one type of object: it has four instances of the class Person.

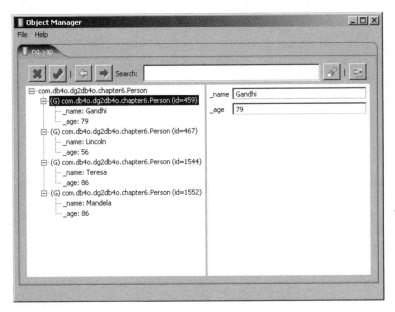

Figure A-4. *The main window with an open database*

The way the database contents are displayed strongly emphasizes the difference between an object database and a relational database. Where an RDBMS query browser tool would have a tabular display, the ObjectManager displays the stored objects as a tree, in the left pane. At the top level are the classes. Expanding a class shows the extent of that class, that is, all the objects of that class. Each object has its OID displayed alongside it. Expanding an object displays its fields, and their values if they are simple numeric or string fields. Fields that are themselves objects can be further expanded—you will see examples of that later in this appendix.

Selecting an object in the left pane displays the details of that object in the right pane.

Updating Fields

Field values that are displayed in the right pane in text boxes can be edited directly. You can update the stored object by clicking the Save button, or roll back changes by clicking Cancel.

Adding Your Classes to the Classpath

The objects shown in Figure A-4 have a (G) symbol beside them. This indicates that db4o does not have access to the actual class files corresponding to the objects in the database, and is using the generic reflector to work out what fields to display. You can give it a bit of help by adding the original class files to the ObjectManager's classpath. This is one of the options in the

Preferences dialog box, shown in Figure A-5, which is accessed using the File ➤ Preferences menu option.

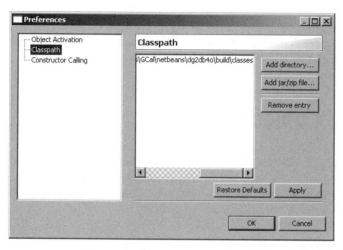

Figure A-5. *Setting classpath preference*

You can add directories or archives. When adding a directory, make sure that you specify the root classes directory of your project so that namespace and package names can be resolved correctly. With the classpath correctly set, the database is displayed as shown in Figure A-6. Two differences that are immediately apparent are that the (G) symbol is no longer displayed, and that the ToString method is being used in the display of objects in the left pane.

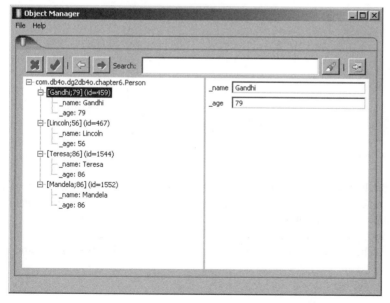

Figure A-6. *Database displayed with original classes available*

Also, any static fields, which are not stored in the database, will be displayed if the class file is made available in this way.

Calling Constructors

The Constructor Calling option in the Preferences dialog box allows you to specify classes for which constructors are called when the database is opened. This can be useful if you want to display transient fields that are not stored in the database but that are initiated by constructors.

Browsing Complex Objects

Figure A-7 shows the ObjectManager displaying a database with a more complex object structure, which includes collections and inheritance. The classes in this example are defined in Chapter 7. Note that all stored classes are displayed in the left pane, including collection classes, superclasses, and abstract classes. As described in Chapter 7, the extent of a class includes any instances of that class and any of its subclasses.

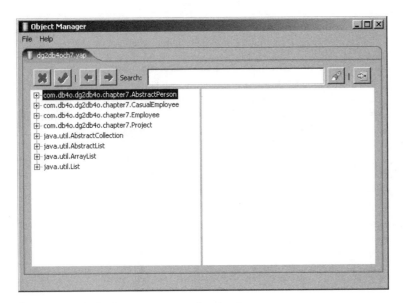

Figure A-7. *Displaying a more complex database*

You can browse the database by expanding tree nodes. Figure A-8 shows the Employee node expanded, and the "Michael" node further expanded. Michael is an Employee, and has a reference to a collection of Project objects. Note that OIDs of related objects, such as the "Finance System" Project, are shown, and that the same object can appear in more than one place in the object tree. The Finance System appears as part of Michael's list of Projects, and also within the Project extent.

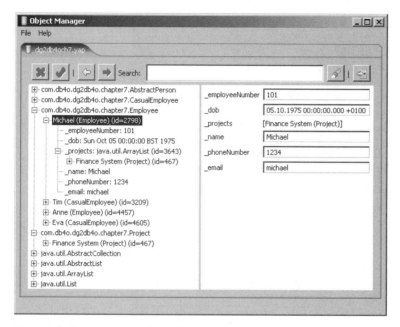

Figure A-8. *Browsing complex objects*

You can set the activation depth used by the ObjectManager in the Preferences dialog box. The concept of activation depth was explained in Chapter 7.

Querying

If your database has only a few objects, then you can probably find whatever information you are looking for simply by browsing. The Search box lets you do a quick search for text in currently displayed objects, which can be useful if you have a large object tree displayed. Simply type some text in the box and click the Search button. If your text is matched, the relevant object or field will be highlighted in the object tree.

When there are many objects in the database, it is generally better to run queries. The ObjectManager lets you build queries graphically. Let's look at an example. The database contains some objects of the class Customer defined in Chapter 7. A Customer object has a field that is an instance of the class Address.

To define a query, you need to click the New Query button, or use the File ➤ Query menu option. The Query a Type dialog box opens. This displays a list of the classes stored in the database, from which you should select one. This is equivalent to specifying a class in the predicate for a Native Query or in a SODA query constraint, as described in Chapter 6. A new tab opens in the ObjectManager main window, as shown in Figure A-9. You can open as many query tabs as you like on a single database. In the figure, we have chosen to query for Customer objects.

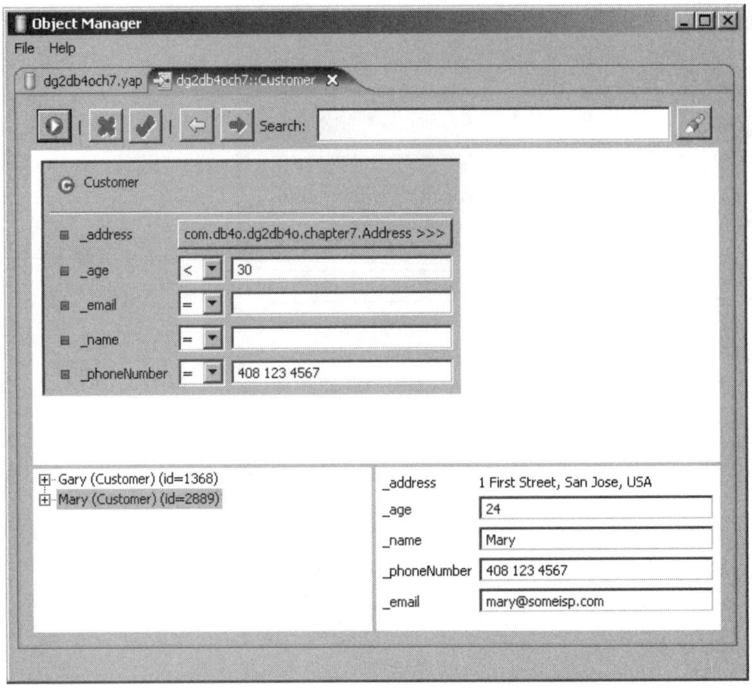

Figure A-9. *A query tab*

The fields of the Customer class are listed, with select and text boxes that allow you to build a query by constraining them. If you leave a text box empty, then that field is not constrained. The constraint type options (=, >, <, etc.) are roughly equivalent to the SODA constraint keywords listed in Chapter 6. Multiple constraints are combined with the logical AND—you can't specify a logical OR. To execute the query, you need to click the Run Query button. The figure shows a query that finds "Customers with age less than 30 who have the phone number 408 123 4567".

The ~ constraint type is similar to the SODA Like constraint, except that it matches characters anywhere in a string. For example, specifying "~ ry" for the _name field will return Customers with names Gary and Mary. Specifying "~ Ga" will return Customers with names Gary and Garth.

Polymorphism

A query will search for instances in the database of the class you specify, and also of its subclasses. You could find Customer objects by specifying its superclass, AbstractPerson, as the query type. This would allow a query to find at the same time instances of Customer and of any other subclass of AbstractPerson. However, query criteria could then only be specified for the fields defined in the superclass.

Deep Queries

The _address field of Customer is an object reference, not a simple value. In Figure A-9 you can see that the _address field is represented by a button with the class name displayed. Clicking this button lets you descend to the Address class and specify constraints on that class, in much the same way as you can descend within a SODA query. This allows you to build deep queries. In Figure A-10, the query is finding "Customers aged less than 25 whose address is in San Jose".

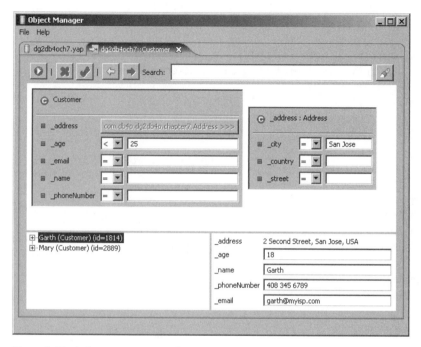

Figure A-10. *A deep query example*

Export to XML

The ObjectManager allows you to export a db4o database as XML. This might be useful if you want to store a copy of the data in a form that is not dependent on the application which created it. The XML data could be parsed and used by another application, or could possibly be imported into a relational database. However, before you choose to use this facility, you may wish to think about whether the replication service described in Chapter 11 better meets your needs.

To export, choose the File ➤ Export to XML menu option, and select a filename for export. The data is exported as a set of XML elements, rather than a complete well-formed document. No XML version tag, for example <?xml version="1.0"?>, is included, and the elements are not enclosed in a root element. Also, no schema or Document Type Definition (DTD) is created. If you want to open the exported data in a web browser or parse it as a complete document, you will need to edit the file and insert the XML version tag at the start. You also need to add a root element.

An example of exported XML follows. The XML was created by exporting the database we queried earlier, which contains Customer and Address objects. Each element that represents an object has the OID as attribute. Note that each Customer element has a child element that represents an Address object. The third Customer has the same Address as the first, and the Address child element contains only an OID attribute, as the field values for the corresponding object have been specified earlier in the XML code. The lines in bold were added manually to create a well-formed document.

```xml
<?xml version="1.0"?>
<!-- db4odata is the root element -->
<db4odata>
<com.db4o.dg2db4o.chapter7.Customer id="1368">
    <_address id="1376" className="com.db4o.dg2db4o.chapter7.Address">
       <_street>1 First Street</_street>
       <_city>San Jose</_city>
       <_country>USA</_country>
    </_address>
    <_age>23</_age>
    <_name>Gary</_name>
    <_phoneNumber>408 123 4567</_phoneNumber>
    <_email>gary@example.net</_email>
</com.db4o.dg2db4o.chapter7.Customer>
<com.db4o.dg2db4o.chapter7.Customer id="1814">
    <_address id="2709" className="com.db4o.dg2db4o.chapter7.Address">
       <_street>2 Second Street</_street>
       <_city>San Jose</_city>
       <_country>USA</_country>
    </_address>
    <_age>18</_age>
    <_name>Garth</_name>
    <_phoneNumber>408 345 6789</_phoneNumber>
    <_email>garth@example.net</_email>
</com.db4o.dg2db4o.chapter7.Customer>
<com.db4o.dg2db4o.chapter7.Customer id="2889">
    <_address reference="1376"/>
    <_age>24</_age>
    <_name>Mary</_name>
    <_phoneNumber>408 123 4567</_phoneNumber>
    <_email>mary@example.com</_email>
</com.db4o.dg2db4o.chapter7.Customer>
</db4odata>
```

Looking Ahead

db4o was always intended to be used mainly within applications, and the ObjectManager is a relatively recent addition. It is at an early stage of development, and its future direction will be driven by how helpful db4o users find it to be, and by what further needs they identify. Here are a few of our ideas for capabilities that might be nice to see in future versions:

- Inserting and deleting objects

- Starting and stopping db4o networking mode servers

- Interactive testing of Native Query expressions and optimization

- Interactive control of database replications

- Producing reports

- Supporting pluggable I/O adapters

If you have other ideas or requirements for the ObjectManager, then you should let db4objects, Inc. know about them!

■■■

Quick Reference

This appendix gives you quick access to example code for the most commonly used basic db4o operations. It is split into C# and Java sections so that you can quickly find the commands for your preferred language. Each operation has a reference to the chapter where it is described in detail.

C# Reference

Open a Database File (Chapter 5)

```
File.Delete("mydata.yap");    // Might want to delete before test run
ObjectContainer db = Db4o.OpenFile("mydata.yap");
```

db is an ObjectContainer referenced throughout this appendix.

Storing Data (Chapter 5)

```
db.Set(new Person("Gandhi", 79)); // Store an object
db.Set(new Person("Lincoln", 56));
db.Commit() // Always remember to commit
```

Person is an ordinary C# class used as an example throughout this appendix.

Searching Data: Query by Example (Chapters 5 and 6)

All Objects of a Specified Class

```
ObjectSet result = db.Get(new Person());  // or typeof(Person)
ListResult(result);
```

Iterating Through an ObjectSet

```
ListResult(ObjectSet result)
{
   while (result.HasNext())
      Console.WriteLine(result.Next());
}
```

All Objects That Match a Template Object

```
Person p = new Person();
p.Name = "Lincoln";
ObjectSet result = db.Get(p);
```

Modifying Data (Chapter 5)

```
ObjectSet result = db.Get(new Person("Gandhi"));  // Use QBE to find object
Person p = (Person) result.Next();   // First object in ObjectSet
p.Age = 90;      // Modify
db.Set(p);       // Store
db.Commit()
```

Deleting Data (Chapter 5)

```
Person p = (Person) db.Get(new Person("Gandhi")).Next();
db.Delete(p);
```

Searching Data: Native Queries (Chapter 6)

Search Using Query Expression

```
IList<Person> result = db.Query<Person>(delegate(Person person)
{
    return person.Age > 60;    // Query expression
});
foreach(Person person in result)    // List results
{
    Console.WriteLine(person);
}
```

Native Query with Sorting

```
Comparison<Person> personCmp = new Comparison<Person>(    // Comparison
    delegate(Person p1, Person p2)
{
    return p2.Name.CompareTo(p1.Name);
});
IList<Person> persons = db.Query<Person>(    // Query
    delegate(Person person)
{
    return true;    // Return all Person objects
},personCmp);
```

Searching Data: SODA (Chapter 6)

Basic Query

```
Query query=db.Query();
query.Constrain(typeof(Person));
query.Descend("_age").Constrain(56);    // _age=56
ObjectSet result = query.Execute();    // Always execute the query
```

"And" Query

```
Constraint firstConstr = query.Descend("_age").Constrain(86); // _age=86
query.Descend("_name").Constrain("Mandela").And(firstConstr); // and _name="Mandela"
```

"Greater" Query

```
query.Descend("_age").Constrain(80).Greater();
```

Range Query

```
Constraint firstConstr = query.Descend("_age").Constrain(60).Greater();
query.Descend("_age").Constrain(80).Smaller().And(firstConstr);
```

"Like" Query

```
query.Descend("_name").Constrain("Ma").Like();
```

Sorted Query

```
query.Descend("_name").OrderAscending();
```

Object Activation (Chapter 7)

```
db.Activate(obj, 1);
```

Activates object to the specified depth

```
Db4o.Configure().ActivationDepth(10);
```

Default is 5, which means that objects are activated to a depth of 5 object references.

```
Db4o.Configure().ObjectClass(typeof(Person)).MinimumActivationDepth(10);
```

Configures minimum activation depth for objects of the specified class.

```
Db4o.Configure().ObjectClass(typeof(Manager)).CascadeOnActivate(true);
```

Configures the database to cascade activation for the specified class.

Open a Network Server and Client (Chapter 8)

```
ObjectServer server = Db4o.OpenServer(DATABASEFILE, PORT);
```

Free ports include 4488 and 8732.

```
ObjectContainer client = Db4o.OpenClient(HOST, PORT, USER, PASS);
```

HOST is the IP address or hostname of the computer running the server.

Open an Embedded Server and Client (Chapter 8)

```
ObjectServer server = Db4o.OpenServer(DATABASEFILE, 0);
ObjectContainer client = server.OpenClient();    //need server object reference
```

Transaction Rollback and Commit (Chapter 9)

```
try
{
    // operations
}
catch (Exception e)
{
    db.Rollback();
}
finally
{
    db.Commit();
}
```

Refresh an Object Reference (Chapter 9)

```
db.Ext().Refresh(obj, int.MaxValue);    // specify refresh cascade depth
```

Replaces the local cached copy with a stored object. Useful after a commit or rollback. db.Ext() gives ExtObjectContainer, which extends the capabilities of the ObjectContainer.

Get Persisted Object (Chapter 9)

```
Person persisted = (Person) db.Ext().PeekPersisted(p, int.MaxValue, true);
```

p is the Person object previously returned by a query. Use this to check whether a stored object has been changed since the query.

Create and Release Semaphore (Chapter 9)

```
if (db.Ext().SetSemaphore("MY SEMAPHORE", 1000)
{
    // Critical code section
    ...
    // Release after critical section
    db.Ext().ReleaseSemaphore("MY SEMAPHORE");
}
```

Used to protect critical code sections and to control object locking in the database. The second parameter specifies the time in milliseconds to wait for availability.

Apply Configurations (Chapter 10)

```
Configuration conf = Db4o.Configure();
conf.BlockSize(8);    // one example - see chapter 10 for all options
```

Global—do before opening ObjectContainer.

```
myObjectContainer.Ext().Configure()
myObjectServer.Ext().Configure()
```

Configure an individual ObjectContainer or ObjectServer.

Configure for UUIDs and Version Numbers (Chapters 11 and 12)

Required for replication between databases.

```
Db4o.Configure().GenerateUUIDs(int.MaxValue);
Db4o.Configure().GenerateVersionNumbers(int.MaxValue);
```

All classes.

```
Db4o.Configure().ObjectClass(typeof(Person)).
    GenerateUUIDs(true);
Db4o.Configure().ObjectClass(typeof(Person)).
    GenerateVersionNumbers(true);
```

Specified class only.

Working with Object IDs (Chapter 12)

```
long myID = db.Ext().GetID(object);
```

Gets the ID of an object.

```
db.Ext().Bind(object, anID);
```

Binds an in-memory object to a stored object with a specified ID.

```
Object o = db.Ext().GetByID(anID);
db.Activate(object, depth);  // Don't forget to activate the object
```

Gets the object with a specified ID.

Setting an Index (Chapter 12)

```
Db4o.Configure().ObjectClass(typeof(Person)).ObjectField("name").Indexed(true);
```

Callbacks (Chapter 12)

Object classes can implement these methods to execute code in response to events.

```
bool ObjectCanActivate(ObjectContainer container);
bool ObjectCanDeactivate(ObjectContainer container);
bool ObjectCanDelete(ObjectContainer container);
bool ObjectCanNew(ObjectContainer container);
bool ObjectCanUpdate(ObjectContainer container);
```

Called before the event. Returning false will prevent the action.

```
void ObjectOnActivate(ObjectContainer container);
void ObjectOnDeactivate(ObjectContainer container);
void ObjectOnDelete(ObjectContainer container);
void ObjectOnNew(ObjectContainer container);
void ObjectOnUpdate(ObjectContainer container);
```

Called after the event.

Configure db4o In-Memory Mode (Chapter 12)

```
Db4o.Configure().Io(new MemoryIoAdapter());
ObjectContainer db = Db4o.OpenFile("anyString");
```

Very fast, but don't forget: in-memory data is lost when your program exits.

Encryption (Chapter 12)

```
Db4o.Configure().Encrypt(true);
Db4o.Configure().Password("mypassword");
```

Simple db4o encryption. Configure before creating and accessing the database.

```
Db4o.Configure().Io(new XTeaEncryptionFileAdapter(
    "mypassword", XTEA.ITERATIONS16));
```

Strong encryption. Use XTEA.ITERATIONS8, ~16, ~32, ~64 to control the grade of speed and security.

Java Reference

Open a Database File (Chapter 5)

```
new File("mydata.yap").delete(); // Might want to delete before test run
ObjectContainer db = Db4o.openFile("mydata.yap");
```

db is an ObjectContainer reference throughout this appendix.

Storing Data (Chapter 5)

```
db.set(new Person("Gandhi", 79)); // Store an object
db.set(new Person("Lincoln", 56));
db.commit() // Always remember to commit
```

Person is an ordinary Java class used as an example throughout this appendix.

Searching Data: Query by Example (Chapters 5 and 6)

All Objects of a Specified Class

```
ObjectSet result = db.get(new Person());  // or Person.class
listResult(result);
```

Iterating Through an ObjectSet

```
listResult(ObjectSet result)
{
    while (result.hasNext())
        System.out.println(result.next());
}
```

All Objects That Match a Template Object

```
Person p = new Person();
p.setName("Lincoln");
ObjectSet result = db.get(p);
```

Modifying Data (Chapter 5)

```
ObjectSet result = db.get(new Person("Gandhi"));  // Use QBE to find object
Person p = (Person) result.next();   // First object in ObjectSet
p.setAge(90);     // Modify
db.set(p);        // Store
db.commit();
```

Deleting Data (Chapter 5)

```
Person p = (Person) db.get(new Person("Gandhi")).next();
db.delete(p);
```

Searching Data: Native Queries (Chapter 6)

Search Using Query Expression

```
List<Person> result = db.query(new Predicate<Person>()
{
    public boolean match(Person person)
    {
        return person.getAge() > 60;    // Query expression
    }
});
for(Person person : result)    // List results
{
    System.out.println(person);
}
```

Native Query with Sorting

```
Comparator<Person> personCmp = new Comparator<Person>()    // Comparator
{
    public int compare(Person p1, Person p2)
    {
        return p1.getName().compareTo(p2.getName());
    }
};
```

```
List<Person> result = db.query(new Predicate<Person>()    // Query
{
    public boolean match(Person person)
    {
        return true;    // Return all Person objects
    }
},personCmp);
```

Searching Data: SODA (Chapter 6)

Basic Query

```
Query query=db.query();
query.constrain(Person.class);
query.descend("_age").constrain(56);   // _age=56
ObjectSet result = query.execute();    // Always execute the query
```

"and" Query

```
Constraint firstConstr = query.descend("_age").constrain(86); // _age=86
query.descend("_name").constrain("Mandela").and(firstConstr); // and _name="Mandela"
```

"greater" query

```
query.descend("_age").constrain(80).greater();
```

Range Query

```
Constraint firstConstr = query.descend("_age").constrain(60).greater();
query.descend("_age").constrain(80).smaller().and(firstConstr);
```

"like" Query

```
query.descend("_name").constrain("Ma").like();
```

Sorted Query

```
query.descend("_name").orderAscending();
```

Object Activation (Chapter 7)

```
db.activate(obj, 1);
```

Activates object to the specified depth.

```
Db4o.configure().activationDepth(10);
```

Default is 5, which means that objects are activated to a depth of 5 object references.

```
Db4o.configure().objectClass(Person.class).minimumActivationDepth(10);
```

Configures minimum activation depth for objects of the specified class.

```
Db4o.configure().objectClass(Person.class).cascadeOnActivate(true);
```

Configures the database to cascade activation for the specified class.

Open a Network Server and Client (Chapter 8)

```
ObjectServer server = Db4o.openServer(DATABASEFILE, PORT);
```

Free ports include 4488 and 8732.

```
ObjectContainer client = Db4o.openClient(HOST, PORT, USER, PASS);
```

HOST is the IP address or hostname of the computer running the server.

Open an Embedded Server and Client (Chapter 8)

```
ObjectServer server = Db4o.openServer(DATABASEFILE, 0);
ObjectContainer client = server.openClient();    // need server object reference
```

Transaction Rollback and Commit (Chapter 9)

```
try
{
    // operations
}
catch (Exception e)
{
    db.rollback();
}
finally
{
    db.commit();
}
```

Refresh an Object Reference (Chapter 9)

```
db.ext().refresh(obj, Integer.MAX_VALUE);    // specify refresh cascade depth
```

Replaces local cached copy with stored object. Useful after commit or rollback. `db.ext()` gives `ExtObjectContainer`, which extends the capabilities of the `ObjectContainer`.

Get Persisted Object (Chapter 9)

```
Person persisted = (Person) db.ext().peekPersisted(p, Integer.MAX_VALUE, true);
```

`p` is the `Person` object previously returned by a query. Use this to check whether a stored object has been changed since the query.

Create and Release Semaphore (Chapter 9)

```
if (db.ext().setSemaphore("MY SEMAPHORE", 1000)
{
    // Critical code section
    ...
    // Release after critical section
    db.ext().releaseSemaphore("MY SEMAPHORE");
}
```

Used to protect critical code sections and to control object locking in the database. The second parameter specifies the time in milliseconds to wait for availability.

Apply Configurations (Chapter 10)

```
Configuration conf = Db4o.configure();
conf.blockSize(8);    // one example - see Chapter 10 for all options
```

Global—do before opening `ObjectContainer`.

```
myObjectContainer.ext().configure()
myObjectServer.ext().configure()
```

Configure an individual `ObjectContainer` or `ObjectServer`.

Configure for UUIDs and Version Numbers (Chapters 11 and 12)

Required for replication between databases.

```
Db4o.configure().generateUUIDs(Integer.MAX_VALUE);
Db4o.configure().generateVersionNumbers(Integer.MAX_VALUE);
```

All classes.

```
Db4o.configure().objectClass(Person.class).
    generateUUIDs(true);
Db4o.configure().objectClass(Person.class).
    generateVersionNumbers(true);
```

Specified class only.

Working with Object IDs (Chapter 12)

```
long myID = db.ext().getID(object);
```

Gets the ID of an object.

```
db.ext().bind(object, anID);
```

Binds an in-memory object to a stored object with a specified ID.

```
Object o = db.ext().getByID(id);
db.activate(object, depth);  // Don't forget to activate the object
```

Gets the object with a specified ID.

Setting an Index (Chapter 12)

```
Db4o.configure().objectClass(Person.class).objectField("name").indexed(true);
```

Callbacks (Chapter 12)

Object classes can implement these methods to execute code in response to events.

```
public boolean objectCanActivate(ObjectContainer container);
public boolean objectCanDeactivate(ObjectContainer container);
public boolean objectCanDelete(ObjectContainer container);
public boolean objectCanNew(ObjectContainer container);
public boolean objectCanUpdate(ObjectContainer container);
```

Called before the event. Returning false will prevent the action.

```
public void objectOnActivate(ObjectContainer container);
public void objectOnDeactivate(ObjectContainer container);
public void objectOnDelete(ObjectContainer container);
public void objectOnNew(ObjectContainer container);
public void objectOnUpdate(ObjectContainer container);
```

Called after the event.

Configure db4o In-Memory Mode (Chapter 12)

```
Db4o.configure().io(new MemoryIoAdapter());
ObjectContainer db = Db4o.openFile("anyString");
```

Very fast, but don't forget: in-memory data is lost when your program exits.

Encryption (Chapter 12)

```
Db4o.configure().encrypt(true);
Db4o.configure().password("mypassword");
```

Simple db4o encryption. Configure before creating and accessing the database.

```
Db4o.configure().io(new XTeaEncryptionFileAdapter(
    "mypassword", XTEA.ITERATIONS16));
```

Strong encryption. Use XTEA.ITERATIONS8, ~16, ~32, ~64 to control the grade of speed and security.

APPENDIX C

■■■

Bibliography

Db4o is designed to work alongside some other important technologies. Since it is a native object database, it integrates closely with the .NET Framework, Mono, and Java. Each of these platforms allows you to create, for example, GUI applications, web applications, or mobile applications. In the list that follows, we suggest some books that may be useful to you if you need to work on your C# or Java skills to help you understand the examples in this book, or if you want to explore application areas where you can use your knowledge of db4o.

Java and .NET Titles

Recommended .NET Titles

Pro ASP.NET 2.0 Website Programming, by Damon Armstrong (Apress, 2005)

Beginning C# Objects: From Concepts to Code, by Jacquie Barker and Grant Palmer (Apress, 2004)

Mono: A Developer's Notebook, by Edd Dumbill and Niel M. Bornstein (O'Reilly, 2004)

Programming the .NET Compact Framework, by Wei Meng Lee and Brian Jepson (O'Reilly, 2006)

Pro ASP.NET 2.0 in C# 2005, by Matthew MacDonald and Mario Szpuszta (Apress, 2005)

Practical Mono, by Mark Mamone (Apress, 2005)

Data Binding with Windows Forms 2.0: Programming Smart Client Data Applications with .NET, by Brian Noyes (Addison-Wesley, 2006)

Core C# and .NET: The Complete and Comprehensive Developer's Guide to C# 2.0 and .NET 2.0, by Stephen C. Perry (Prentice Hall PTR, 2005)

Pro C# 2005 and the .NET 2.0 Platform, Third Edition, by Andrew Troelsen (Apress, 2005)

Recommended Java Titles

Beginning Java Objects: From Concepts to Code, by Jacquie Barker (Apress, 2003)

Hibernate in Action, by Christian Bauer and Gavin King (Manning, 2004)

Pro JSP 2, Fourth Edition, by Simon Brown, Sam Dalton, Daniel Jepp, Dave Johnson, Sing Li, and Matt Raible (Apress, 2005)

Beginning J2ME: From Novice to Professional, Third Edition, by Sing Li and Jonathan Knudsen (Apress, 2005)

Pro Hibernate 3, by Jeff Linwood and Dave Minter (Apress, 2005)

Professional Java, JDK 5 Edition, by W. Clay Richardson, Donald Avondolio, Joe Vitale, Scot Schrager, Mark W. Mitchell, and Jeff Scanlon (Wrox, 2005)

Pro Java Programming, Second Edition, by Brett Spell (Apress, 2005)

Java Development on PDAs: Building Applications for Pocket PC and Palm Devices, by Daryl Wilding-McBride (Addison-Wesley, 2003)

Objects and Databases

The titles listed here provide additional reading and key texts on some of the concepts covered in this book, particularly in Part I.

Object-Oriented Design and Patterns

The Object Primer: Agile Model-Driven Development with UML 2.0, Third Edition, by Scott W. Ambler (Cambridge University Press, 2004)

Patterns of Enterprise Application Architecture, by Martin Fowler (Addison-Wesley, 2002)

UML Distilled: A Brief Guide to the Standard Object Modeling Language, Third Edition, by Martin Fowler (Addison-Wesley, 2003)

Design Patterns: Elements of Reusable Object-Oriented Software, by Erich Gamma, Richard Helm, Ralph Johnson, and John Vlissides (Addison-Wesley, 1995)

Foundations of Object-Oriented Programming Using .NET 2.0 Patterns, by Christian Gross (Apress, 2005)

Databases

Agile Database Techniques: Effective Strategies for the Agile Software Developer, by Scott Ambler (Wiley, 2003)

Refactoring Databases: Evolutionary Database Design, by Scott W. Ambler (Addison-Wesley, 2006)

Succeeding with Object Databases: A Practical Look at Today's Implementations with Java and XML, by Akmal B. Chaudhri and Roberto Zicari (Wiley, 2000)

Database Systems: A Practical Approach to Design, Implementation, and Management, Fourth Edition, by Thomas M. Connolly and Carolyn E. Begg (Pearson Education, 2004)

An Introduction to Database Systems, Eighth Edition, by C. J. Date (Addison-Wesley, 2003)

Object-Oriented Database Design Clearly Explained, by Jan L. Harrington (Morgan Kaufmann, 1999)

Java Database Best Practices, by George Reese (O'Reilly, 2003)

Relational Database Principles, Second Edition, by Colin Ritchie (Int. Thomson Business Press, 2002)

The Object Data Standard: ODMG 3.0, by Craig Russell, Olaf Schadow, Torsten Stanienda, Fernando Velez, R. G. Cattell, Douglas K. Barry, Mark Berler, Jeff Eastman, and David Jordan (Morgan Kaufmann, 2000)

Java Persistence for Relational Databases, by Richard Sperko (Apress, 2003)

Object Relational DBMS: Tracking the Next Great Wave, by Michael Stonebraker and Dorothy Moore Paul Brown (Morgan Kaufmann, 1999)

Advanced Database Systems, by Carlo Zaniolo, Stefano Ceri, Christos Faloutsos, Richard T. Snodgrass, V. S. Subrahmanian, and Roberto Zicari (Morgan Kaufmann, 1997)

Index

Find it faster at http://superindex.apress.com

You Need the Companion eBook

Your purchase of this book entitles you to its companion eBook for only $10.

We believe this Apress title will prove so indispensable that you'll want to carry it with you everywhere, which is why we are offering the companion eBook for $10 to customers who purchase this book now. Convenient and fully searchable, the eBook version of any content-rich, page-heavy Apress book makes a valuable addition to your programming library. You can easily find, copy, and apply code—and then perform examples by quickly toggling between instructions and the application. Even simultaneously tackling a donut, diet soda, and complex code becomes simplified with hands-free eBooks!

Once you purchase this book, getting the $10 companion eBook is simple:

❶ Visit **www.apress.com/promo/tendollars/**.

❷ Complete a basic registration form to receive a randomly generated question about this title.

❸ Answer the question correctly in 60 seconds and you will receive a promotional code to redeem for the $10 eBook.

2560 Ninth Street • Suite 219 • Berkeley, CA 94710

eBookshop

THE EXPERT'S VOICE™

Offer valid through 12/06.